JOY IN MUDVILLE
The Big Book of Baseball Humor

JOY
in
Mudville

The Big Book of Baseball Humor

EDITED BY DICK SCHAAP
AND
MORT GERBERG

Doubleday

NEW YORK   LONDON   TORONTO   SYDNEY   AUCKLAND

PUBLISHED BY DOUBLEDAY
a division of Bantam Doubleday Dell Publishing Group, Inc.
666 Fifth Avenue, New York, New York 10103

DOUBLEDAY and the portrayal of an anchor with a dolphin
are trademarks of Doubleday, a division of
Bantam Doubleday Dell Publishing Group, Inc.

Library of Congress Cataloging-in-Publication Data

Joy in Mudville : the big book of baseball humor / edited by Dick
Schaap and Mort Gerberg.—1st ed.
    p.   cm.
    1. Baseball—Humor. I. Schaap, Dick, 1934–   . II. Gerberg,
Mort.
PN6231.B35J69   1992
817'.5080355—dc20   91-42417
                                                        CIP

Book Design by Carol Malcolm-Russo

ISBN 0-385-42151-6

To the memory of our fathers,
Robert Gerberg and Maurice Schaap,
and our uncles,
Al Lavin and Harold Imber.
Boy, they really would have loved this one.

To the memory of our fathers,
Robert Gerberg and Maurice Schaap,
and our uncles,
Al Lavin and Harold Imber.
Boy, they really would have loved this one.

THE AUTHORS WOULD LIKE TO THANK Rebecca Brown, Lisa Siegel, Jeremy Schaap and Jeremy Goldstein for their help in gathering the stories, songs, cartoons and photographs that put the joy in Mudville. We would like to thank Renée Zuckerbrot of Doubleday for baby-sitting both the project and the authors. We would especially like to thank the writers and cartoonists whose work was squeezed out when we discovered, at the last moment, that there were more picks than pages. Wait till next time!

Contents

Introduction

BY DICK SCHAAP

BASEBALL WAS ALWAYS FUN. AS A TEEN-ager, I organized a team that won the New York State Kiwanis championship two years in a row, once at the Polo Grounds, once at Ebbets Field. One of our best players was George Kandiloros, whose immigrant mother spoke very little English.

Every time I called George to tell him when and where our next game would be played, his mother would ask who was calling, and I would say, "Dick Schaap," and she would say, "Big shot?"

Twice a week for two full seasons, I said, "Dick Schaap," and she said, "Big shot?"

George's English, at the time, wasn't much better. The next time I saw him, a decade later, he had changed his name to George Loros and he was working as a Shakespearean actor.

Baseball is a funny game.

♦

When I was in college, Roger Kahn, who would write *The Boys of Summer,* took me out to dinner one night with Jackie Robinson, Jim Gilliam and Joe Black, three of the gods of my childhood.

The three Dodgers took turns telling stories about how dumb a young New York Yankee named Mickey Mantle was supposed to be. When it came to Jackie Robinson's turn, he said, "Hell, we've got plenty of guys that dumb, but nobody that good!"

♦

A few years later, I met Lenny Bruce because of baseball. I was covering the 1960 World Series between Pittsburgh and the Yankees, and Bruce, who had just been labeled the sickest of the so-called sick comics by *Time* magazine, was appearing in a small night club on the outskirts of Pittsburgh.

The night before each of the four games played in Pittsburgh—they actually played all World Series games in daylight then, and that's no

joke—I went to see Lenny Bruce perform. We struck up a friendship that lasted until he died half a dozen years later, mostly of harassment.

Bruce had only one baseball bit in his routine. He broke open a mezuzah, a case holding a small parchment scroll often affixed to the doorpost of Jewish homes, and read not the usual holy prayer, but the Pittsburgh rallying cry that season: "Beat 'em Bucs!"

I took Lenny to the seventh game of the World Series, the one Bill Mazeroski won with a home run in the bottom of the ninth, the only time a home run ever ended a baseball season, and I led him into the locker room afterward to witness the Pirates' celebration. Dick Stuart, the first baseman known as Dr. Strangeglove for sufficient cause, sprayed Lenny with champagne. Lenny loved it. It was his first baseball game, and he never went to another. Any other game would have been anticlimactic.

◆

Baseball helped me strengthen a friendship with another comedian. I didn't actually meet Billy Crystal through baseball—I met Billy through boxing, but that's another story, and another anthology—but not long after I met him, I introduced him to Joe DiMaggio. The Clipper and the Quipper. What an impressive moment!

Only one of the two was impressed. Billy was unknown at the time. He was also considerably shorter than DiMaggio. He is now famous, but he is still shorter than DiMaggio.

Billy is a baseball player himself. He is the funniest shortstop I've ever met (although Larry Bowa, once you get to know him, can really be hilarious).

Billy also plays baseball better than any comedian I've ever met (Pee Wee Herman *must've* been named after Pee Wee Reese and Billy Herman, the 1941 Brooklyn Dodgers infielders, shortstop and second base, who ended up in the Hall of Fame, but I don't think it rubbed off).

Billy Crystal went to college on a baseball scholarship. He's gone through life on a humor scholarship.

I once asked Billy, "Who would you rather be—Charlie Chaplin or Mickey Mantle?"

I figured it was a simple question, but an alliterative one.

Billy thought it over and picked Mantle.

Billy once played catch with Mickey Mantle—at Cooperstown.

Billy once played Charlie Chaplin—in an HBO special shot in the Soviet Union.

Mantle *and* Chaplin.

Crystal must consider himself the luckiest person on the face of the earth.

◆

Besides the home run Bill Mazeroski hit in 1960, I have witnessed other memorable baseball moments, historic and dramatic. As a thirteen-year-old, I saw, faintly, from a seat in the right-field corner of Yankee Stadium, Al Gionfriddo's incredible catch of Joe DiMaggio's bid for a home run to left-center field; I saw Carlton Fisk's game-winning twelfth-inning home run in the sixth game of the 1975 World Series in Boston; I saw Nolan Ryan record his 5,000th strikeout, Pete Rose his 4,192nd hit and Gaylord Perry his 300th victory. But the moments I remember most vividly are the funny not the dramatic ones.

In 1956, I had tickets for the fifth game of the World Series between the Dodgers and the Yankees. I chose to skip the game and search for an apartment. That day Don Larsen pitched the only perfect game in World Series history. To this day, I have never seen a no-hitter. That's funny to almost everyone, except me.

I'll never forget the day in 1978 when Reggie Jackson returned to the Yankees after a five-day absence. Billy Martin had suspended Jackson for disobeying instructions, for bunting when Martin wanted him to swing away. The incident created an uproar. An army of journalists awaited Reggie's return in Chicago.

We surrounded him in the clubhouse before the game, peppered him with questions, wondered who had sent him the dozen roses that lay in his locker. I outlasted everyone else.

No one remained except Reggie, my TV camera crew and me.

"Reggie," I said, "you've had five days to think about what happened. What was the one thought that was uppermost in your mind?"

Reggie considered the question, stared straight into the camera and said, "The magnitude of me."

I wanted to kiss him. You can't make up lines like that.

In the 1980s, when the baseball card business began to boom, I went to Yogi Berra one day and asked him if he had any old baseball cards at home. "Yeah, I got some," Yogi said.

"You have any cards of Mickey when he was a rookie?" I said.

The 1951 Mantle cards were soaring in value.

"Yeah, I think I've got some lying around someplace," Yogi said.

"You really ought to look for them," I said. "They're worth a lot of money."

"Nah," Yogi said. "I prefer to remember Mickey as he is."

I didn't want to kiss Yogi. I have limits.

And in 1991, when the Atlanta Braves were leaping from last place to first in a single year, I asked Steve Avery, the Braves' twenty-one-year-old lefthander, if he could describe the change in the clubhouse atmosphere, and he said, "It's a three-hundred-and-sixty-degree turnaround."

Avery stopped and thought for a moment.

"No, wait," he said. "I mean a one-hundred-and-eighty-degree turnaround."

And when a group of reporters began to laugh, Avery said, "What do you want from me? I only went to high school."

◆

I could tell George Brett stories and Pete Rose stories and Tug McGraw stories, but I've kept you long enough from the essays and articles and anecdotes and cartoons and comic strips and photographs and poems and songs that make this a very big book of baseball humor.

You've got Ring Lardner coming up, and James Thurber and Jimmy Breslin and John Lardner and Charles Addams and Charles Schulz and Garry Trudeau and Jules Feiffer.

That's the funniest lineup I've ever seen.

Introduction

BY MORT GERBERG

I NEVER THOUGHT THERE WAS ANYTHING funny about baseball. I was much too intense a fan, living or dying according to the daily box scores.

I grew up in Brooklyn—you know, *Dodger* country—and my father, innocently starting me off marching through life to the beat of a different drummer, raised me to root, as he did, for the New York Giants. Being jeered at as a Benedict Arnold on my own block because I liked Mel Ott instead of Dixie Walker, and Willie Mays, not Duke Snider, was probably very funny to the rest of the world, but not to me. (Of course, everything is funny as long as it's happening to someone else, as Will Rogers said.) After Bobby Thomson's miracle (oh, be still, my heart!), at least six months had to pass before Aunt Eleanor, the most rabid of all my Dodger-fan aunts and uncles, would even *speak* to my father and me, let alone allow us in her house. Not too many giggles there.

The very act of rooting more often produced a stomach pained from nervousness than sides aching from laughter. When I listened to radio broadcasts of the games or went to the Polo Grounds or Ebbets Field (an act of pure masochism), my entire body would tremble from the first inning to the last. On the day following a Giant loss I avoided newspapers, afraid of accidentally seeing a story about the game, and reliving the hurt I'd experienced.

Of course, it was fun to *play* ball—even though it wasn't exactly a lot of laughs trying to get into a game. While I was a pretty good player, I was always the smallest kid around, which automatically guaranteed that I'd be the last one picked for any softball or stickball game, the closest we city kids got to actual baseball. Sometimes I'd be the designated catcher for both teams. Once I was named as official mascot. Not one of my joys of summer.

I guess that I didn't experience any real humor in baseball until the

New York Mets arrived in 1962. Coincidentally, that's the year I seriously started flirting with the idea of becoming a cartoonist—and began looking for humor in everything. Still, although I mined every other aspect of my life for cartoon ideas, I drew very few, if any, about our national pastime. Drawing cartoons, by definition, means poking fun at something, and obviously, I was still taking the game too seriously to make jokes about it.

But things change. The Giants moved to San Francisco and Willie Mays retired. I became a New York Mets fan and was no longer considered a deviate baseball person by my friends and family. Aunt Eleanor and I now root for the same team. *The New Yorker,* replying to a subscriber's inquiry last summer, identified me as "a fine softball player," referring to my performances on the magazine's free-form employee team.

Now *that* was funny.

Humor is based upon clichés—and baseball is just one big bundle of clichés. Like kids trying to play, or not getting picked to play the game. Women being excluded. Husbands and wives arguing about watching the game on television. The big-business side of baseball. Umpires. Theories about the origins of the game. The fans. The heroics of the players, creating legendary feats, blurring the line between fact and fiction, the Babe dissolving into Casey at the bat.

These familiar themes are presented here through widely varying humorous approaches—by cartoonists, novelists, reporters, columnists, poets, photographers, songwriters, essayists and playwrights—from the classic to the contemporary—offered up with a dazzling array of spins; like curves, sliders, knucklers and sinkers.

You can browse through this collection an inning at a time or devour it like an old-fashioned daylong doubleheader. You may smile. You may laugh.

After all, I think there's a *lot* funny about baseball.

Batter up!

xx

JOY IN MUDVILLE
The Big Book of Baseball Humor

"**C**ASEY AT THE BAT: A BALLAD OF THE RE-public, Sung in the Year 1888" was first published on June 3, 1888, among a group of editorials in the San Francisco Examiner. The author was listed, pseudonymously, as "Phin."

The work attracted little attention until, in August 1889, in front of a New York vaudeville audience that included the Hall of Fame baseball player Cap Anson, an actor named DeWolf Hopper recited "Casey at the Bat." The audience loved it.

By Hopper's own estimation, he recited the poem ten thousand times more during the next forty-five years. It became a piece of Americana treasured by almost everyone except its author, Ernest Lawrence Thayer, who waited a few years to confess that he was "Phin."

Thayer found the poem's success to be "simply unaccountable," and he consistently refused to accept any royalties for the republication of "Casey."

"All I ask is never to be reminded of it again," Thayer said.

Thayer died in 1940. The poem is indestructible.

It has survived thousands of parodies, sequels, analyses and dramatizations.

It inspired the title of this collection, and inspired us to include a few of Casey's offspring: James Wilson offers his view of a rematch in Mudville, a common theme; Phil Bolsta puts a modern player in Casey's spikes, another frequent spinoff; and Mitch Albom of the Detroit Free Press, one of the country's finest sports columnists, does the reverse, puts Casey in modern dress. More ambitiously, Robert Coover, author of a most imaginative baseball novel, The Universal Baseball Association, J. Henry Waugh, Prop., delivers the pitcher's point of view.

Casey at the Bat

BY ERNEST LAWRENCE THAYER

The outlook wasn't brilliant for the Mudville nine that day;
The score stood four to two with but one inning more to play;
And then, when Cooney died at first, and Barrows did the same,
A sickly silence fell upon the patrons of the game.

A straggling few got up to go, in deep despair. The rest
Clung to that hope which "springs eternal in the human breast;"
They thought, If only Casey could but get a whack at that,
We'd put up even money now, with Casey at the bat.

But Flynn preceded Casey, as did also Jimmy Blake,
And the former was a lulu and the latter was a cake;
So, upon that stricken multitude grim melancholy sat,
For there seemed but little chance of Casey's getting to the bat.

But Flynn let drive a single, to the wonderment of all,
And Blake, the much despised, tore the cover off the ball,
And when the dust had lifted and men saw what had occurred,
There was Jimmy safe at second, and Flynn a-huggin' third.

Then from five thousand throats and more there rose a lusty yell,
It rumbled through the valley; it rattled in the dell,
It knocked upon the mountain and recoiled upon the flat,
For Casey, mighty Casey, was advancing to the bat.

There was ease in Casey's manner as he stepped in to his place;
There was pride in Casey's bearing and a smile on Casey's face,
And when, responding to the cheers, he lightly doffed his hat,
No stranger in the crowd could doubt 'twas Casey at the bat.

Ten thousand eyes were on him as he rubbed his hands with dirt;
Five thousand tongues applauded when he wiped them on his shirt.

Then, while the writhing pitcher ground the ball into his hip,
Defiance gleamed in Casey's eye, a sneer curled Casey's lip.

And now the leather-covered sphere came hurtling through the air,
And Casey stood a-watching it in haughty grandeur there,
Close by the sturdy batsman the ball unheeded sped—
"That ain't my style," said Casey. "Strike one," the umpire said.

From the benches, black with people, there went up a muffled roar,
Like the beating of the storm-waves on a stern and distant shore.
"Kill him; kill the umpire!" shouted someone from the stand;—
And it's likely they'd have killed him had not Casey raised his hand.

With a smile of Christian charity great Casey's visage shone;
He stilled the rising tumult; he bade the game go on;
He signaled to the pitcher, and once more the spheroid flew;
But Casey still ignored it, and the umpire said, "Strike two."

"Fraud," cried the maddened thousands, and echo answered "Fraud,"
But one scornful look from Casey, and the multitude was awed.
They saw his face grow stern and cold; they saw his muscles strain,
And they knew that Casey wouldn't let that ball go by again.

The sneer is gone from Casey's lip; his teeth are clenched in hate;
He pounds with cruel violence his bat upon the plate.
And now the pitcher holds the ball, and now he lets it go,
And now the air is shattered by the force of Casey's blow.

Oh! somewhere in this favored land the sun is shining bright;
The band is playing somewhere, and somewhere hearts are light.
And somewhere men are laughing, and somewhere children shout;
But there is no joy in Mudville—mighty Casey has Struck Out.

5

Casey's Revenge

BY JAMES WILSON

There were saddened hearts in Mudville for a week or even more;
There were muttered oaths and curses—every fan in town was sore.
"Just think," said one, "how soft it looked with Casey at the bat!
And then to think he'd go and spring a bush-league trick like that."

All his past fame was forgotten; he was now a hopeless "shine."
They called him "Strike-out Casey" from the mayor down the line,
And as he came to bat each day his bosom heaved a sigh,
While a look of hopeless fury shone in mighty Casey's eye.

The lane is long, someone has said, that never turns again,
And Fate, though fickle, often gives another chance to men.
And Casey smiled—his rugged face no longer wore a frown;
The pitcher who had started all the trouble came to town.

All Mudville had assembled; ten thousand fans had come
To see the twirler who had put big Casey on the bum;
And when he stepped into the box the multitude went wild.
He doffed his cap in proud disdain—but Casey only smiled.

"Play ball!" the umpire's voice rang out, and then the game began;
But in that throng of thousands there was not a single fan
Who thought that Mudville had a chance; and with the setting sun
Their hopes sank low—the rival team was leading "four to one."

The last half of the ninth came round, with no change in the score;
But when the first man up hit safe the crowd began to roar.
The din increased, the echo of ten thousand shouts was heard
When the pitcher hit the second and gave "four balls" to the third.

Three men on base—nobody out—three runs to tie the game!
A triple meant the highest niche in Mudville's hall of fame;

But here the rally ended and the gloom was deep as night
When the fourth one "fouled to catcher" and the fifth "flew out to right."

A dismal groan in chorus came—a scowl was on each face—
When Casey walked up, bat in hand, and slowly took his place;
His bloodshot eyes in fury gleamed; his teeth were clinched in hate;
He gave his cap a vicious hook and pounded on the plate.

But fame is fleeting as the wind, and glory fades away;
There were no wild and woolly cheers, no glad acclaim this day.
They hissed and groaned and hooted as they clamored, "Strike him out!"
But Casey gave no outward sign that he had heard this shout.

The pitcher smiled and cut one loose; across the plate it spread;
Another hiss, another groan. "Strike one!" the umpire said.
Zip! Like a shot, the second curve broke just below his knee—
"Strike two!" the umpire roared aloud; but Casey made no plea.

No roasting for the umpire now—his was an easy lot;
But here the pitcher whirled again—was that a rifle shot?
A whack! a crack! and out through space the leather pellet flew,
A blot against the distant sky, a speck against the blue.

Above the fence in center field, in rapid whirling flight,
The sphere sailed on; the blot grew dim and then was lost to sight.
Ten thousand hats were thrown in air, ten thousand threw a fit,
But no one ever found the ball that mighty Casey hit!

Oh, somewhere in this favored land dark clouds may hide the sun,
And somewhere bands no longer play and children have no fun;
And somewhere over blighted lives there hangs a heavy pall;
But Mudville hearts are happy now—for Casey hit the ball!

Hrbek at the Bat

It looked extremely rocky for the Twins in '89,
When Hrbek hurt his shoulder and Frank began to whine.
And so when losses mounted and far outnumbered wins,
A pallor wreathed the features of the patrons of the Twins.

On the last day of the season, though, the fans were not depressed,
For there's hope that springs eternal within a Twins fan's breast.
And they knew if mighty Hrbek could unleash his mighty swing,
'Twould put a smile on their face and keep them warm till spring.

But it looked as if their wounded pride would not be healed this day,
The score stood four to six with but an inning left to play.
And so when Newman popped it up and Gladden hit it flat,
There seemed but little chance of Hrbek's getting to the bat.

But Kirby bounced a single off the artificial grass,
Hatcher lined a shot to left that struck the plexiglass!
A hush swept through the Metrodome, for fate had surely beckoned,
For there was Puckett safe on third, and Hatcher huggin' second.

And then the gladdened multitude cheered and screamed and squealed,
It rattled off the scoreboard and the canvas in right field.
They cheered till they could cheer no more, for this was worth the wait,
For Hrbek, mighty Hrbek, was advancing to the plate.

There was ease in Hrbek's manner and a twinkle in his eyes,
There was grease on Hrbek's fingers as he polished off some fries.
And when some popcorn spilled out as he lightly doffed his hat,
No stranger in the Dome could doubt 'twas Hrbek at the bat.

Ten thousand eyes were on him as the game ground to a halt,
Five thousand tongues applauded as he drained a chocolate malt.

8

And as the pitcher glared at him, his hands upon his hips,
The mighty Hrbek gestured for a hot dog and some chips.

And then the leather-covered sphere came hurtling through the air,
And Hrbek clutched his stomach as if it struck him there.
The trainer started running out, but Kent just shook his head,
"It's just some gas," burped Hrbek. "Strike one," the Umpire said.

With a smile borne of confidence, he took some practice cuts,
And stepped back in the batter's box while munching on some nuts.
He signaled to the pitcher and again the spheroid flew.
"Got some salt?" asked Hrbek, and the Umpire said, "Strike two!"

The smile is gone from Hrbek's lips. He mutters, "Time out, please,"
And hurries to the dugout for a Whopper, double cheese.
And now the pitcher holds the ball and now he lets it go,
And now the air is shattered by the force of Hrbek's blow.

Oh, somewhere there's a stadium where fans all shout and cheer,
As their team wins its division and the playoffs every year.
But inside the empty Metrodome, all is still and quiet.
But just you wait till next year—mighty Hrbek's on a diet!

Today's Casey Finds No Joy in Mudville

BY MITCH ALBOM

The outlook wasn't brilliant for the Mudville nine today,
The score stood four to three with just one inning left to play.
The fans did groan when Jackson hit a dribbler to the mound,
Then Williams went down swinging, he barely got around.

But suddenly a hush did fall—the crowd began to shake;
Was that the Moody Casey walking toward the plate?
He flexed his arms and shook his chains, he checked his Rolex watch,
He spit, he chewed, he spit again, then grabbed and scratched his crotch.

And when responding to the cheers, he tipped his Nike hat,
No stranger in the crowd could doubt 'twas Casey at the bat.

"When did you sign?" the catcher asked as Casey shook his girth.
"This morning," Casey answered. "Guess what my contract's worth?"
The catcher shrugged; he didn't know, our hero had to grin.
"Forty million for one year, plus an island they threw in."

The catcher said, "Not bad" as Casey stepped into the box,
"You hear about Tex Johnson, who just signed with the Sox?"
"Tex Johnson?" Casey asked as the pitch sailed toward his head.
"Fifty million," said the catcher, "STRIKE ONE!" the umpire said.

Casey burped, then spit again, his cockiness did fade.
Just one pitch into the season and he was underpaid.
"Tex Johnson ain't worth that much dough, you sure you got that right?"
The catcher nodded earnestly and chuckled with delight.

The sneer was gone from Casey's lips, his teeth were clenched in hate.
He pounded with cruel violence his bat upon the plate.

10

He thought about Tex Johnson as in the baseball sailed.
"Fifty million?" he repeated, "STRIKE TWO!" the umpire wailed.

Now the fans began to stir but Casey's eyes were slanted.
How dare his tightwad baseball team start taking him for granted?
He sat down on home plate, untied his Nike pumps,
"I want to renegotiate!" he bellowed to the umps.

His manager came running out and begged he'd reconsider.
His teammates said "Just swing the bat!" lest they be late for dinner.
But with the count at oh and two, he sat there like a crate
And nighttime fell on Mudville, Moody Casey on the plate.

Soon a state of panic descended on the park.
How long would Casey sit there just sulking in the dark?
His agent flew from New York, his CPA came, too.
The owner of the team flew in from a trek in Kathmandu.

The TV news reported live, the headlines clearly stated:
"CASEY WON'T PLAY BASEBALL, SAYS HE'S NOT APPRECIATED."

Now all this time in Mudville the scoreboard stayed the same.
The home team still trailed four to three, two strikes by Casey's name.
While on the field they argued over bonuses and cash,
As Casey sat there happily and patted his moustache.

The fans began to boo and hiss—how long there must they linger?
Casey showed his deep concern by giving them the finger.
"How can I survive," he asked, "on a measly forty mill?
"If I don't get my way I just may join the NFL."
Finally, the businessmen who'd argued this till dawn
Sighed that they were finished; "Play ball," the umpire yawned . . .

Now somewhere in this favored land the sun is shining bright.
The band is playing somewhere, and somewhere hearts are light.
And somewhere men are laughing, but here the money's saved
For justice has hit Mudville—Moody Casey has been waived.

11

McDuff on the Mound

BY ROBERT COOVER

IT WASN'T MUCH, A FEEBLE BLOOPER OVER second, call it luck, but it was enough to shake McDuff. He stepped weakly off the left side of the pitcher's mound, relieved to see his catcher Gus take the job of moving down behind the slow runner to back up the throw in to first. Fat Flynn galloped around the bag toward second, crouched apelike on the basepath, waggled his arms, then bounded back to first as the throw came in from short center. McDuff felt lightheaded. Flynn's soft blooper had provoked a total vision that iced his blood. Because the next batter up now was Blake: oh yes, man, it was all too clear. "Today's my day," McDuff told himself, as though taking on the cares of the world. He tucked his glove in his armpit briefly, wiped the sweat from his brow, resettled his cap, thrust his hand back into his glove.

Gus jogged over to the mound before going back behind the plate, running splaylegged around the catcher's guard that padded his belly. McDuff took the toss from first, over Gus's head, stood staring dismally at Flynn, now edging flatfooted away from the bag, his hands making floppy loosewristed swirls at the cuffs of his Mudville knickers. Gus spat, glanced back over his shoulder at first, then squinted up at McDuff. "Whatsa matter, kid?"

McDuff shrugged, licked his dry lips. "I don't know, Gus. I tried to get him." He watched Flynn taunt, flapping his hands like donkey ears, thumbing his nose. Rubbing it in. Did he know? He must. "I really tried." He remembered this nightmare, running around basepaths, unable to stop.

Gus grinned, though, ignoring the obvious: "Nuts, the bum was lucky. C'mon, kid, ya got this game in ya back pocket!" He punched McDuff lightly in the ribs with his stiff platter of a mitt, spat in encouragement, and joggled away in a widelegged trot toward home plate, head cocked warily toward first, where Flynn bounced insolently and

12

made insulting noises. Settling then into his crouch, and before pulling his mask down, Gus jerked his head at the approaching batter and winked out at McDuff. Turkey Blake. Nothing to it. A joke. Maybe Gus is innocent, McDuff thought. Maybe not.

Now, in truth, McDuff was not, by any standard but his own, in real trouble. Here it was, the bottom of the ninth, two away, one more out and the game was over, and he had a fat two-run lead going for him. A lot of hometown Mudville fans had even given it up for lost and had started shuffling indifferently toward the exits. Or was their shuffle a studied shuffle and itself a cunning taunt? a mocking rite like Flynn's buffoonery at first? Had they shuffled back there in the shadows just to make Flynn's fluke hit sting more? It was more than McDuff could grasp, so he scratched his armpits and tried to get his mind off it. Now, anyway, they were all shuffling back. And did they grin as they shuffled? Too far away to tell. But they probably did, goddamn them. You're making it all up, he said. But he didn't convince himself. And there was Blake. Blake the Turkey. Of course.

Blake was the league clown, the butt. Slopeshouldered, potbellied, broadrumped, bandylegged. And a long goiter-studded neck with a small flat head on top, overlarge cap down around the ears. They called him "Turkey," Blake the Turkey. The fans cheered him with a gobbling noise. And that's just what they did now as he stepped up: gobbled and gobbled. McDuff could hardly believe he had been brought to this end, that it was happening to him, even though he had known that sooner or later it must. Blake had three bats. He gave them a swing and went right off his feet. Gobble gobble gobble. Then he got up, picked out two bats, chose one, tossed the other one away, but, as though by mistake, hung on to it, went sailing with it into the bat racks. Splintering crash. Mess of broken bats. Gobble gobble gobble. McDuff, in desperation, pegged the ball to first, but Flynn was sitting on the bag, holding his quaking paunch, didn't even run when the ball got away from the first baseman, just made gobbling noises.

Vaguely, McDuff had seen it coming, but he'd figured on trouble from Cooney and Burroughs right off. A four-to-two lead, last inning, four batters between him and Casey, two tough ones and two fools, it was all falling into place: get the two tying runs on base, then two outs, and bring Casey up. So he'd worked like a bastard on those two

13

guys, trying to head it off. Should've known better, should've seen that would have been too easy, too pat, too painless. McDuff, a practical man with both feet on the ground, had always tried to figure the odds, and that's where he'd gone wrong. But would things have been different if Cooney and Burroughs had hit him? Not substantially maybe, there'd still be much the same situation and Casey yet to face. But the stage wouldn't have been just right, and maybe, because of that, somehow, he'd have got out of it.

Cooney, tall, lean, one of the best percentage hitters in the business: by all odds, see, it should have been him. That's what McDuff had thought, so when he'd sucked old Cooney into pulling into an inside curve and grounding out, third to first, he was really convinced he'd got himself over the hump. Even if Burroughs should hit him, it was only a matter of getting Flynn and Blake out, and they never gave anybody any trouble. And Burroughs *didn't* hit him! Big barrelchested man with a bat no one else in the league could even lift—some said it weighed half a ton—and he'd wasted all that power on a cheap floater, sent it dribbling out to the mound and McDuff himself had tossed him out. Hot damn! he'd cried. Waiting for fat Flynn to enter the batter's box, he'd even caught himself giggling. And then that unbelievable blooper. And—*bling*—the light.

McDuff glared now at Blake, wincing painfully as though to say: get serious, man! Blake was trying to knock the dirt out of his spikes. But each time he lifted his foot, he lost his balance and toppled over. Gobble gobble gobble. Finally, there on the ground, teetering on his broad rump, he took a healthy swing with the bat at his foot. There was a bang like a firecracker going off, smoke, and the shoe sailed into the stands. Turkey Blake hobbled around in mock pain (or real pain: who could tell and what did it matter? McDuff's pain was real), trying to grasp his stockinged foot, now smoking faintly, but he was too round in the midriff, too short in the arms, to reach it. Gobble gobble gobble. Someone tossed the shoe back and it hit him in the head: bonk! Blake toppled stiffly backwards, his short bandy legs up in the air as though he were dead. Gobble gob—

McDuff, impatient, even embittered, for he felt the injury of it, went into his stretch. Blake leaped up, grabbed a bat from the mad heap,

14

came hopping, waddling, bounding, however the hell it was he moved, up to the plate to take his place. It turned out that the bat he'd picked up was one he'd broken in his earlier act. It was only about six inches long, the rest hanging from it as though by a thread. McDuff felt himself at the edge of tears. The crowd gobbled on, obscenely, delightedly. Blake took a preparatory backswing, and the dangling end of the bat arced round and hit him on the back of the head with a hollow exaggerated clunk. He fell across the plate. Even the umpire now was emitting frantic gobbling sounds and holding his trembling sides. Flynn the fat baserunner called time-out and came huffing and puffing in from first to resuscitate his teammate. McDuff, feeling all the strength go out of him, slumped despairingly off the mound. He picked up the resin bag and played with it, an old nervous habit that now did not relieve him.

His catcher Gus came out. "Gobble gobble," he said.

McDuff winced in hurt. "Gus, for God's sake, cut that out!" he cried. Jesus, they were all against him!

Gus laughed. "Whatsa matter, kid? These guys buggin' ya?" He glanced back toward the plate, where Flynn was practicing artificial respiration on Blake's ass-end, sitting on Blake's small head. "It's all in the game, buddy. Don't forget: gobble and the world gobbles with ya! Yak yak!" McDuff bit his lip. Past happy Gus, he could see Flynn listening to Blake's butt for a breath of life.

"Play baseball and you play with yourself," McDuff said sourly, completing Gus's impromptu aphorism.

"Yeah, you *got* it, kid!" howled Gus, jabbing McDuff in the ribs with his mitt, then rolling onto the grass in front of the mound, holding his sides, giddy tears springing from his eyes, tobacco juice oozing down his chin.

There was a loud moist sound at the plate, like air escaping a toy balloon, and it was greeted by huzzahs and imitative noises from the stands. Flynn jumped up, lifted one of Blake's feet high in the air in triumph, and planted his fallen cap in the clown's crotch, making Blake a parody of Blake, were such a thing absurdly possible. Cheers and courteous gobbling. Blake popped up out of the dust, swung at Flynn, hit the ump instead.

15

"Why don't they knock it off?" McDuff complained.

"Whaddaya mean?" asked Gus, now sober at his side.

"Why don't they just bring on Casey now and let me get it over with? Why do they have to shove my nose in it first?"

"Casey!" Gus laughed loosely. "Never happen, kid. Blake puts on a big show, but he'd never hit you, baby, take it from old Gus. You'll get him and the game's over. Nothin' to it." Gus winked reassuringly, but McDuff didn't believe it. He no longer believed Gus was so goddamn innocent either.

Flynn was bounding now, in his apelike fashion, toward first base, but Blake had a grip on his suspenders. Flynn's short fat legs kept churning away and the dust rose, but he was getting nowhere. Then Blake let go—*whap!*—and Flynn blimped nonstop out to deep right field. Gobble gobble gobble. While Flynn was cavorting back in toward first, Blake, unable to find his own hat, stole the umpire's. It completely covered his small flat head, down to the goiter, and Blake staggered around blind, bumping into things. Gobble. The ump grabbed up Blake's cap from where it had fallen and planted it defiantly on his own head. A couple of gallons of water flooded out and drenched him. Gobble. Blake tripped over home plate and crashed facefirst to the dirt again. The hat fell off. Gobble. The umpire took off his shoes and poured the water out. A fish jumped out of one of them. Gobble. Blake spied his own hat on the umpire's soggy head and went for it. Gobble. The ump relinquished it willingly, in exchange for his own. The ump was wary now, however, and inspected the hat carefully before putting it back on his head. He turned it inside out, thumped it, ran his finger around the lining. Satisfied at last, he put the hat on his head and a couple of gallons of water flooded out on him. Gobble gobble, said the crowd, and the umpire said: "PLAY BALL!"

Flynn was more or less on first, Blake in the box, the broken bat over his shoulder. McDuff glanced over toward the empty batter-up circle, then toward the Mudville dugout. Casey had not come out. Casey's style. And why should he? After all, Blake hadn't had a hit all season. Maybe in all history. He was a joke. McDuff considered walking Blake and getting it over with. Or was there any hope of that: of "getting it over with"? Anyway, maybe that's just what they wanted him to do,

16

maybe it was how they meant to break him. No, he was a man meant to play this game, McDuff was, and play it, by God, he would. He stretched, glanced at first, studied Gus's signal, glared at Turkey Blake. The broken end of the bat hung down Blake's sunken back and tapped his bulbous rump. He twitched as though shooing a fly, finally turned around to see who or what was back there, feigned great surprise at finding no one. Gobble gobble. He resumed his batter's stance. McDuff protested the broken bat on the grounds that it was a distraction and a danger to the other players. The umpire grumbled, consulted his rulebook. Gus showed shock. He came out to the mound and asked: "Why make it any easier for him, kid?"

"I'm not, Gus. I'm making it easier for myself." That seemed true, but McDuff knew Gus wouldn't like it.

"You are nuts, kid. Lemme tell ya. Plain nuts. I don't folla ya at all!" Blake was still trying to find out who or what was behind him. He poised very still, then spun around—the bat swung and cracked his nose: loud honking noise, chirping of birds, as Blake staggered around behind home plate holding his nose and splattering catsup all around. Gobble gobble gobble. Gus watched and grinned.

"I mean, a guy who can't hit with a good bat might get lucky with a broken one," McDuff said. He didn't mean that at all, but he knew Gus would like it better.

"Oh, I getcha." Gus spat pensively. "Yeah, ya right." The old catcher went back to the plate, showed the ump the proper ruling, and the umpire ordered Blake to get a new bat. Gus was effective like that when he wanted to be. Why not all the time then? It made McDuff wonder.

Blake returned to the plate dragging Burroughs's half-ton bat behind him. He tried to get it on his shoulder, grunted, strained, but he couldn't even get the end of it off the ground. He sat down under it, then tried to stand. Steam whistled out his nose and ears and a great wrenching sound was heard, but the bat stayed where it was. While the happy crowd once more lifted its humiliating chorus, Flynn called time-out and came waddling in from first to help. The umpire, too, lent a hand. Together, they got it up about as high as Blake's knees, then had to drop it. Exaggerated thud. Blake yelped, hobbled around grotesquely,

pointing down at the one foot still shoed. The toe of it began to swell. The seams of the shoe split. A red bubble emerged, expanded threateningly: the size of a plum, a crimson baseball, grapefruit, cannonball, a red pumpkin. Everyone held his ears. The umpire crawled down behind Flynn and then Flynn tried to crawl behind the umpire. It stretched, quivered. Strained. Flynn dashed over and, reaching into Blake's behind, seemed to pull something out. Sound of a cork popping from a bottle. The red balloon-like thing collapsed with a sigh. Laughter and relieved gobbling. Blake bent over to inspect his toe. Enormous explosion, blackening Blake's face. Screams and laughter.

Then Burroughs himself came out and lifted the half-ton bat onto Blake's shoulder for him. What shoulder he had collapsed and the bat slid off, upending Blake momentarily, so Burroughs next set it on Blake's head. The head was flat and, though precariously, held it. Burroughs lifted Blake up and set him, bat on head, in the batter's box. Blake under his burden could not turn his head to see McDuff's pitch. He just crossed his eyes and looked up at the bat. Gus crouched and signaled. McDuff, through bitter sweaty tears, saw that Flynn was still not back on first, but he didn't care. He stretched, kicked, pitched. Blake leaned forward. McDuff couldn't tell if he hit the ball with the bat or his head. But hit it he did, as McDuff knew he would. It looked like an easy pop-up to the mound, and McDuff, almost unbelieving, waited for it. But what he caught was only the cover of the ball. The ball itself was out of sight far beyond the mowed grass of left-center field, way back in the high weeds of the neighboring acreage.

McDuff, watching then for Casey to emerge from the Mudville dugout, failed at first to notice the hubbub going on around the plate. It seemed that the ump had called the hit a home run, and Gus was arguing that there were no official limits to the Mudville outfield and thus no automatic homers. "You mean," the umpire cried, "if someone knocked the ball clean to Gehenny, it still wouldn't be considered outa the park? I can't believe that!" Gus and the umpire fought over the rulebook, trying to find the right page. The three outfielders were all out there in the next acreage, nearly out of sight, hunting for the ball in the tall grass. "I can't believe that!" the umpire bellowed, and tore pages from the rulebook in his haste. Flynn

18

and Blake now clowned with chocolate pies and water pistols.

"Listen," said McDuff irritably, "whether it's an automatic home run or not, they still have to run the bases, so why don't they just do that, and then it won't matter."

Gus's head snapped up from his search in the rulebook like he'd been stabbed. He glared fiercely at McDuff, grabbed his arm, pushed him roughly back toward the mound. "Whatsa matter with you?" he growled.

"Lissen! I ain't runnin' off nowheres I ain't got to!" Flynn hollered, sitting down on a three-legged stool which Blake was pulling out from under him. "If it's automanic, I'll by gum walk my last mile at my own dadblamed ease, thank ya, ma'am!" He sprawled.

"Of *course* it ain't automatic," Gus was whispering to McDuff. "You know that as well as I do, Mac. If we can just get that ball in from the outfield while they're screwin' around, we'll tag *both* of 'em for good measure and get outa this friggin' game!"

McDuff knew this was impossible, he even believed that Gus was pulling his leg, yet, goddamn it, he couldn't help but share Gus's hopes. Why not? Anyway, he had to try. He turned to the shortstop and sent him out there with orders: *"Go bring that ball in!"*

The rulebook was shot. Pages everywhere, some tumbling along the ground, others blowing in the wind like confetti. The umpire, on hands and knees, was trying to put it all back together again. Gus held up a page, winked at McDuff, stuffed the page in his back pocket. Flynn and Blake used other pages to light cigars that kept blowing up in their faces. That does it, thought McDuff.

He looked out onto the horizon and saw the shortstop and the outfielders jumping up and down, holding something aloft. And then the shortstop started running in. Yet, so distant was he, he seemed not to be moving.

At home plate, the umpire had somehow discovered the page in Gus's back pocket, and he was saying: "I just can't believe it!" He read it aloud: " 'Mudville's field is open-ended. Nothing is automatic here, in spite of appearances. A ball driven even unto Gehenna is not necessarily a homerun. In short, anything can happen in Mudville, even though most things are highly improbable. Blake, for example, has

never had a hit, nor has Casey yet struck out.' And et cetera!" The crowd dutifully applauded the reading of the rulebook. The umpire shook his head. "All the way to Gehenny!" he muttered.

The baserunners, meanwhile, had taken off, and Turkey Blake was flapping around third on his way home, when he suddenly noticed that fat Flynn, who should be preceding him, was still grunting and groaning down the basepath toward first.

The shortstop was running in from the next acreage with the ball.

Blake galloped around the bases in reverse, meeting Flynn head-on with a resounding thud at first. Dazed, Flynn headed back toward home, but Blake set him aright on the route to second, pushed him on with kicks and swats, threw firecrackers at his feet. The fans chanted: *"Go! Go! Go!"*

The shortstop had reached the mowed edge of the outfield. McDuff hustled back off the mound, moved toward short to receive the throw, excitement grabbing at him in spite of himself.

Flynn fell in front of second, and Blake rolled over him. Blake jumped up and stood on Flynn's head. Honking noise. Flynn somersaulted and kicked Blake in the teeth. Musical chimes.

The shortstop was running in from deep left-center. *"Throw it!"* McDuff screamed, but the shortstop didn't seem to hear him. He ran, holding the ball high like a torch.

Flynn had Blake in a crushing bearhug at second base, while Blake was clipping Flynn's suspenders. Blake stamped on Flynn's feet— sound of wood being crushed to pulp—and Flynn yowled, let go. Blake produced an enormous rocket. Flynn in a funk fled toward third, but his pants fell down, and he tripped.

The shortstop was still running in from the outfield. McDuff was shouting himself hoarse, but the guy wouldn't throw the goddamn ball. McDuff's heart was pounding and he was angry at himself for finding himself so caught up in it all.

Flynn had pulled up his pants and Blake was chasing him with the rocket. They crashed into McDuff. He felt trampled and heard hooting and gobbling sounds. When the dust had cleared, McDuff found himself wearing Flynn's pants, ten sizes too large for him, and Blake's cap, ten sizes too small, and holding a gigantic rocket whose fuse was lit.

20

Flynn, in the confusion, had gone to second and Blake to third. The fuse burned to the end, there was a little pop, the end of the rocket opened, and a little bird flew out.

The shortstop was running in, eyes rolled back, tongue lolling, drenched in sweat, holding the ball aloft.

Flynn and Blake discovered their error, that they'd ended up on the wrong bases, came running toward each other again. McDuff, foreseeing the inevitable, stepped aside to allow them to collide. Instead, they pulled up short and exchanged niceties.

"After *you*," said Blake, bowing deeply.

"No, no, dear fellow," insisted Flynn with an answering bow, "after *you!*"

The shortstop stumbled and fell, crawled ahead.

Flynn and Blake were waltzing around and around, saying things like "Age before beauty!" and "Be my guest!" and "Hope springs eternal in the human breast!", wound up with a chorus of "Take Me Out to the Ballgame!" with all the fans in the stands joining in.

The shortstop staggered to his feet, plunged, gasping, foward.

The umpire came out and made McDuff give Flynn his pants back. He took Blake's cap off McDuff's head, looked at it suspiciously, held it over his own head, and was promptly drenched by a couple of gallons of water that came flooding out.

McDuff felt someone hanging limply on his elbow. It was the short-stop. Feebly, but proudly, he held up the baseball. Blake, of course, was safe on second, and Flynn was hugging third. The trouble is, thought McDuff, you mustn't get taken in. You mustn't think you've got a chance. That's when they really kill you. "All right," he said to Blake and Flynn, his voice choking up and sounding all too much like a turkey's squawk, "screw you guys!" They grinned blankly and there was a last dying ripple of mocking gobbling in the stands. Then: silence. Into it, McDuff dropped Blake's giant rocket. No matter what he might have hoped, it didn't go off. Then he turned to face the Man.

And now, it was true about the holler that came from the maddened thousands, true about how it thundered on the mountaintop and re-coiled upon the flat, and so on. And it was true about Casey's manner, the maddening composure with which he came out to take his turn

at bat. Or was that so, was it true at that? McDuff, mouth dry, mind awhirl, could not pin down his doubt. "Quit!" he said, but he couldn't, he knew, not till the side was out.

And Casey: who *was* Casey? A Hero, to be sure. A Giant. A figure of grace and power, yes, but wasn't he more than that? He was tall and mighty (omnipotent, some claimed, though perhaps, like all fans, they'd got a bit carried away), with a great moustache and a merry knowing twinkle in his eye. Was he, as had been suggested, the One True Thing? McDuff shook to watch him. He was ageless, older than Mudville certainly, though Mudville claimed him as their own. Some believed that "Casey" was a transliteration of the initials "K.C." and stood for King Christ. Others, of a similar but simpler school, opted for King Corn, while another group believed it to be a barbarism for Krishna. Some, rightly observing that "case" meant "event," pursued this reasoning back to its primitive root, "to fall," and thus saw in Casey (for a case was also a container) the whole history and condition of man, a history perhaps as yet incomplete. On the other hand, a case was also an oddity, was it not, and a medical patient, and maybe, said some, mighty Casey was the sickest of them all. Yet a case was an example, cried others, plight, the actual state of things, while a good many thought all such mystification was so much crap, and Casey was simply a good ballplayer. Certainly, it was true, he could belt the hell out of a baseball. All the way to Gehenny, as the umpire liked to put it. Anyway, McDuff knew none of this. He only knew that there he was, that here was Casey, and the stage was set. He didn't need to know the rest. Just that was enough to shake any man.

Gus walked out to talk to McDuff, while the first baseman covered home plate. Gus kept a nervous eye on Flynn and Blake. "How the hell'd you let that bum hit ya, Mac?"

"Listen, I'm gonna walk Casey," McDuff said. Gus looked pained. "First base is open, Gus. It's playing percentages."

"You and ya goddamn percentages!" snorted Gus. "Ya dumb or somethin', kid? Dontcha know this guy's secret?" Gus wasn't innocent, after all. Maybe nobody was.

"Yeah, I know it, Gus." McDuff sighed, swallowed. Knew all along he'd never walk him. Just stalling.

"Well, then, *kill* him, kid! You can do it! It's the only way!" Gus punctuated his peptalk with stiff jabs to McDuff's ribs. At the plate, Casey, responding to the thunderous ovation, lightly doffed his hat. They were tearing the stands down.

"But all these people, Gus—"

"Don't let the noise fool ya. It's the way they want it, kid."

Casey reached down, bat in armpit, picked up a handful of dust, rubbed it on his hands, then wiped his hands on his shirt. Every motion brought on a new burst of enraptured veneration. McDuff licked his dry lips, ground the baseball into his hip. "Do you really think—?"

"Take it from old Gus," said this catcher gently. "They're all leanin' on ya." Gus clapped him on the shoulder, cast a professional glance over toward third, then jogged splaylegged back to the plate, motioning the man there back to first.

Gus crouched, spat, lowered his mask; Casey swung his bat in short choppy cuts to loosen up; the umpire hovered. McDuff stretched, looked back at Blake on second, Flynn on third. Must be getting dark. Couldn't see their faces. They stood on the bags like totems. Okay, thought McDuff, I'll leave it up to Casey. I'm just not gonna sweat it (though in fact he had not stopped sweating, and even now it was cold in his armpits and trickling down his back). What's another ballgame? Let him take it or leave it. And without further wind-up, he served Casey a nice fat pitch gently down the slot, a little outside to give Casey plenty of room to swing.

Casey ignored it, stepped back out of the box, flicked a gnat off his bat. *"Strike one!"* the umpire said.

Bottles and pillows flew and angry voices stirred the troubled air. The masses rose within the shadows of the stands, and maybe they'd have leapt the fences, had not Casey raised his hand. A charitable smile, a tip of the cap, a twirl of the great moustache. For the people, a pacifying gesture with a couple of mighty fingers; for the umpire, an apologetic nod. And for McDuff: a strange sly smile and flick of the bat, as though to say . . . everything. McDuff read whole books into it, and knew he wasn't far from wrong.

This is it, Case, said McDuff to himself. We're here. And he fingered the resin bag and wiped the sweat and pretended he gave a damn

23

about the runners on second and third and stretched and lifted his left leg, then came down on it easily and offered Casey the sweetest, fattest, purest pitch he'd ever shown a man. Not even in batting practice had he ever given a hitter more to swing at.

Casey only smiled. And the umpire said: *"Strike two!"*

The crowd let loose a terrible wrathful roar, and the umpire cowed as gunfire cracked and whined, and a great darkness rose up and all the faces fell in shadows, and even Gus had lost his smile, nor did he wink at McDuff.

But Casey drew himself up with a mighty intake of breath, turned on the crowd as fierce as a tiger, ordered the umpire to stand like a man, and then even, with the sudden hush that fell, the sun came out again. And Casey's muscles rippled as he exercised his bat, and Casey's teeth were clenched as he tugged upon his hat, and Casey's brows darkened as he gazed out on McDuff, and now the fun was done because Casey'd had enough.

McDuff, on the other hand, hadn't felt better all day. Now that the preliminaries were over, now that he'd done all he could and it was on him, now that everybody else had got serious, McDuff finally found it was all just a gas and he couldn't give a damn. You're getting delirious, he cautioned himself, but his caution did no good. He giggled furtively: there's always something richly ludicrous about extremity, he decided. He stepped up on the rubber, went right into his stretch. Didn't bother looking at second and third: irrelevant now. And it was so ironically simple: all he had to do was put it down the middle. With a lot of stuff, of course, but he had the stuff. He nearly laughed out loud. He reared back, kicking high with his left, then hurtled forward, sent the ball humming like a shot right down the middle.

Casey's mighty cut split the air in two—*WHEEEEP!*—and when the vacuum filled, there was a terrible thunderclap, and some saw light, and some screamed, and rain fell on the world.

Casey, in the dirt, stared in openjawed wonderment at his bat.

Gus plucked the ball gingerly out of his mitt, fingered it unbelievingly. Flynn and Blake stood as though forever rooted at third and second, static parts of a final fieldwide tableau.

And forget what Gus said. No one cheered McDuff in Mudville when he struck Casey out.

24

Who's on First?

ANONYMOUS

Whose was it first?
What was whose first?
"Who's on First?"

If those three questions strike a familiar chord, then you are among the millions who have watched, listened to, or read *the* classic baseball comedy sketch "Who's on First?"

Whose was it first?

The routine is generally associated with Bud Abbott and Lou Costello, the comedy team that polished it and performed it in a 1940s movie called *The Naughty Nineties.*

But to say that Abbott and Costello *invented* "Who's on First?" is like saying with certainty that Abner Doubleday invented baseball. But more of *that* controversy later.

"Who's on First?" was born, like so many stock routines, on the stages of vaudeville and burlesque, and countless comics, some of them in baggy pants, pitched their own versions of the sketch.

The sketch is based on misunderstanding compounded by confusion. One man (or woman, for that matter) tells another the peculiar names of the players on his (her) baseball team. "Who" plays first. "What" plays second. "I Don't Know" plays third. "Why" is in left field, "Because" is in center, "Today" is catching, and "Tomorrow" is pitching. The shortstop, of course, is "I Don't Care."

In the Abbott-and-Costello version, Costello asks the name of the first baseman, and Abbott straight-facedly replies, "Who is on first base."

COSTELLO: Well, what are you asking me for?
ABBOTT: I'm not asking you—I'm telling you. Who is on first.
COSTELLO: *I'm* asking *you*—who's on first?
ABBOTT: That's the man's name.
COSTELLO: That's whose name?

25

ABBOTT: Yes.

COSTELLO: Well, go ahead, tell me!

ABBOTT: Who.

COSTELLO: The guy on first.

ABBOTT: Who.

COSTELLO: The first baseman.

ABBOTT: Who is on first.

COSTELLO: Have you got a first baseman on first?

ABBOTT: Certainly.

COSTELLO: Well, all I'm trying to find out is what's the guy's name on first base.

ABBOTT: Oh, no, no, what is on second base.

COSTELLO: I'm not asking you who's on second.

ABBOTT: Who's on first.

COSTELLO: That's what I'm trying to find out.

The complications multiply. When Abbott again states that Who is on first, Costello replies, "I don't know," and is told *he's* on third.

And so on.

Abbott and Costello performed "Who's on First?" thousands of times, often adapting the dialogue to the setting, always sharpening. They are still performing it, on film, in the Baseball Hall of Fame in Cooperstown, N.Y.

"Who's on First?" is not so easy as, say, "Casey at the Bat" to parody, but with a little help from a trio of real baseball players named (Mike) Dunne, (Randy) Ready, and (Jim) Gott, a gifted columnist, Mike Downey of the *Los Angeles Times,* was able to burlesque the burlesque.

Ready or Not, It's Time We Got Started

BY MIKE DOWNEY

YOU THINK PETE ROSE GOT A NATIONAL League umpire angry? You should have seen Larry Bowa and Jim Leyland.

The San Diego Padres came to bat against the Pittsburgh Pirates the other day, with no leadoff man.

The plate umpire went up to Bowa, the Padre manager, and said: "Need a batter here."

Bowa said: "He's still in the clubhouse. Be out in a minute."

The umpire waited a few minutes, then asked impatiently: "Well, where is he?"

Bowa said: "Hold on. He's almost here."

The umpire: C'mon, we ain't got all day. Get whoever it is out here.

Bowa: My first batter's Ready.

The ump: Good.

Bowa: He'll be out in a minute.

The ump: I thought you said he was ready.

Bowa: I did.

The ump: Then let's get started.

Bowa: We can't until my batter gets here.

The ump: You said he was here.

Bowa: Who?

The ump: Your batter.

Bowa: He's still in the clubhouse.

The ump: I don't understand. Is your batter ready or isn't he?

Bowa: Yes.

The ump: Yes, what?

Bowa: He's Ready.

The ump: Then let's play ball.

Bowa: But he's still in the clubhouse.

The ump: Who's still in the clubhouse?

Bowa: My batter.

The ump: I don't understand this at all.

Bowa: Wait, I'll be right back.

The ump: Where do you think you're going?

Bowa: To the clubhouse to get Ready.

The ump: For what?

Bowa: For the game.

The ump: You're going to get ready?

Bowa: Yes.

The ump: In the clubhouse?

Bowa: That's right.

The ump: And what about your batter?

Bowa: That's why I'm going.

The ump: Why?

Bowa: To get my batter.

The ump: Where?

Bowa: In the clubhouse.

The ump: What's in the clubhouse?

Bowa: My batter.

The ump: And so the reason you're going to the clubhouse is . . . ?

Bowa: To get Ready.

The Padre manager disappeared into the tunnel.

The Pirate pitcher, meanwhile, stiffened up waiting for the first batter, so Jim Leyland went to the mound. The manager talked to his pitcher for a very long time, until the umpire finally had to intervene.

The ump: So, what's going on?

Leyland: What do you mean?

The ump: Your pitcher's done?

Leyland: Yes.

The ump: OK. Who are you bringing in?

Leyland: To do what?

The ump: To pitch.

Leyland: Maybe nobody.

28

The ump: I thought you said your pitcher's done.
Leyland: I did.
The ump: Well, is he or isn't he?
Leyland: Yes.
The ump: He is what?
Leyland: He's Dunne.
The ump: Then you're bringing in a relief pitcher?
Leyland: I don't know yet.
The ump: Look, this guy here is done, right?
Leyland: Right.
The ump: So, you've got to bring in a relief pitcher.
Leyland: Not necessarily.
The ump: Sure you do.
Leyland: I'm still thinking about it.
The ump: Look, your starting pitcher is done, right?
Leyland: Right.
The ump: He's out of the game?
Leyland: No, he's standing right here.
The ump: Who's standing right here?
Leyland: My starting pitcher. He's Dunne.
The ump: Then take him out.
Leyland: But I might leave him in.
The ump: Make up your mind!
Leyland: Actually, I was just stalling until I got one of my relief pitchers up.
The ump: You were?
Leyland: Yeah.
The ump: Got one?
Leyland: What?
The ump: Got a relief pitcher?
Leyland: Yes, he is.
The ump: Who is?
Leyland: Gott.
The ump: Got what?
Leyland: He's one of my relief pitchers.
The ump: Let me get this straight. Your starting pitcher's done?

Leyland: Yes.

The ump: And your relief pitcher?

Leyland: Just got up in the bullpen.

The ump: And the one you want?

Leyland: Gott.

The ump: Got the one you want?

Leyland: Yes.

The ump: You want this one here?

Leyland: Who?

The ump: The one standing next to you?

Leyland: No, he's done.

The ump: Who is?

Leyland: This one here.

The ump: Let me try this one more time. You're bringing in a new pitcher?

Leyland: Yes.

The ump: The one you've got up in the bullpen.

Leyland: Yes, I think he's ready.

The ump: I thought he was the batter!

Bowa and Leyland each were suspended for 30 days.

30

*F*rom the macabre world of the late Charles Addams to the kids' world of Charles Schulz, from the prehistoric world of Johnny Hart to the fantasy world of Bill Watterson, baseball finds a comfortable home in cartoons and comic strips.

The Origins of Baseball: Darwin or Doubleday?

BY MORT GERBERG

The following cartoon spread marked the first time that Dick Schaap and Mort Gerberg worked together. We had known each other for a long time. We're cousins, sort of. Mort's Aunt Eleanor, the Dodger fan turned Met fan, is also Dick's Aunt Eleanor, but from a different direction. But enough about us. Almost enough. When we decided to examine the origins of baseball for Sport Magazine, of which Dick was editor, we thought we had an original idea. (When the sportscaster Bill Stern made up the story that Abraham Lincoln's dying words to a young soldier named Doubleday were "Abner, don't let baseball die," that was an original idea.) In gathering material for this collection, we discovered that many other people had the same original idea.

"Not bad—but can he hit?"

"Say . . . who is that kid?"

"Well—all we need now is a ball."

"C'mon, kid—let's see you get a piece of the old apple!"

"A cute idea, but it needs fleshing out!"

"Abner Doubleday would have had a fit."

"Listen—try it the other way."

"I don't understand it, Leonardo, but it certainly
does make me smile. . . ."

38

Evil Umpires? Not in Soviet Baseball

BY JOHN LEO

ergei Shachin, citing cultural historians, insists that baseball descended from an ancient Russian game of bats and balls called lapta, brought by Russian émigrés to what is now California some two centuries before the arrival of the Dodgers and Giants.

Lapta is a folk game in which the batter swats a ball tossed gently in front of him by a teammate. Then he tries to run across a field before an opponent can fetch the ball and hit the runner with it.

"Baseball is the younger brother of lapta," Mr. Sachin explained to the eight million readers of Izvestia. ". . . It's just a shame that we allowed lapta to be undeservedly forgotten, while baseball fans were aggressively promoting it."

—The New York Times, July 20, 1987

Although some Americans seem a bit skeptical about the recent news that Russians invented baseball, or lapta, as it has been known for the last sixty or seventy Soviet pennant races, the matter is old hat to knowledgeable sports fans. As Izvestia recently explained to its readers. Russian émigrés brought the game to what is now California two hundred years ago, with batters striking at a ball with a stick, and fielders throwing the ball (a rock) at opposition players to register outs.

The Russian origin of American baseball is a simple fact and a closed issue, but Soviet Leader Mikhail Gorbachev, jocularly dubbed "Goose Glasnost" by the professional Lapta Writers Association, has graciously allowed speculation on how the game actually got to America. Pravda believes it was stolen by a Marine guard at the U.S. embassy in Moscow who scurrilously wheedled crucial lapta information out of an unwary Russian cook during an evening of illicit and probably drug-induced lovemaking sometime in the eighteen forties.

Another school of thought holds that the game arose in the tenth

century, and was brought to America by one of the earliest people's explorers, Eric the Red, who is said to have founded a team named for himself in what is now Cincinnati. Other equally respected laptologists maintain that the spirited game evolved from the famous sporting rides of the Cossacks. In this view, games occurred spontaneously on the Russian steppes, with peasants hurling stones up at the fabled horsemen in attempts to achieve outs, while the free-swinging Cossacks, many of them boasting nine- or ten-village hitting streaks, were responsible for most of the offense. The amazing success of the Cossacks, who often went undefeated for decades at a time, is sometimes cited by *Izvestia* as proof that polo as well as baseball originated in sports-minded Russia. It also helps explain why so many modern Russians show up for work every Monday morning proudly displaying full-body lapta bruises.

This pro-Cossack school generally aligns itself with the West Coast theory of American baseball. In this opinion, the first American team was not the Cincinnati Reds, but the Los Angeles Engels, named for the wealthy crony who liked to toss the lapta around with Karl Marx, the game's greatest theoretician and the main reason why so many modern lapta stars have been nicknamed "Lefty." Marx and Engels introduced the dialectical theory of lapta: the pitchers are always ahead of the hitters, and vice versa. Marx's classic one-liner about lapta, "Nice right-wing deviationists finish last," ranks with Lenin's famous admonition about the Russian psyche: "Anyone who wishes to understand the Russian soul had better learn lapta."

It was Lenin, in fact, who called for expansion of the Russian national pastime from a stagnant game merely played east of the Urals to one that offered its excitement to a waiting world. The historic postwar expansion brought coveted major-league franchises to such cities as Warsaw, Prague, and Budapest, where local sportsmen, eager to learn the new game, playfully threw a great many welcoming laptas at the arriving Russian players. The game even reached Kabul, where enthusiastic Afghan players dramatically altered traditional notions of defense by using the first heat-seeking laptas during regular season play. Much like the introduction of the corked bat and the designated hitter in the U.S., the Afghan innovation clearly irritated a few hidebound older

fans back in Moscow, who talked constantly of "lowering the mound" in mountainous Afghanistan to bring offense and defense back into classic balance.

Over the centuries, lapta has developed many colorful customs and expressions. For instance, the peasant who had only one lapta in hand, but two cossacks bearing down on him, was said to be confronting a "fielder's choice." Third base has been known as "the hot corner" since the Minsk-Pinsk World Series of 1937, when a Pinsk third-base coach, who happened to double as a political-education instructor, repeatedly harassed the Minsk third baseman with probing theoretical questions. Tragically, this led to the only fatality in big-league lapta. During the seventh game of the Series, after uttering the ill-advised suggestion "Stick it in your ear, comrade coach," the luckless Minsk third baseman was dragged from the Cosmodome by large men in bulky suits, executed, and later brought to trial.

Unlike capitalist versions of the game, lapta does not permit base-stealing, since the bases belong to all the people and cannot be appropriated for individual use. Sacrifices, on the other hand, are encouraged, and often occur even with no runners on base. Instead of a left, center, and right fielder, the typical lapta outfield will feature two left fielders followed around by a fleet fellow traveler, or perhaps yet another British free agent eager to play ball with the Russians.

Diehard lapta fans bitterly resented President Reagan's recent remark about the Soviets' "evil umpires." In truth, umpires are so revered in the Soviet Union that players often call out, "Honor to the umpires!" and managers run out of the dugouts to congratulate the men in blue on successfully making difficult calls. This is because the umpires are scrupulously fair and usually have close relatives on the party's Central Committee.

They are also famous for appreciating a good joke. One was told by the illustrious star Lefty Jabov, who once hit eighty-nine homers in a single year, more than Babe Ruth, Roger Maris, or other inferior Americans weakened by decades of debilitating capitalist exploitation of the toiling masses. After a called third strike, the fun-loving slugger turned to the beloved umpire and quipped, "But, comrade, Marx said that when workers controlled the means of production, there would be no

41

more strikes!" The joke was considered so funny that Jabov was not jailed at all, merely sent down to the Siberian League for a brief attitudinal readjustment.

As it happens, the slugger's seven-foot-tall younger brother, Kareem Jabov, is a famous Soviet sports figure in his own right. Shortly after the Russian invention of soccer, the gangly Kareem picked up a soccer ball and playfully thrust it back over his head into a potato basket hanging from the rafter of a people's barn, thus simultaneously inventing both the in-your-face reverse slam dunk and the entire game of basketball. But that is another story. Watch for it soon in the pages of *Izvestia*.

◆

The True Origins of Baseball

BY WAYNE N. FARR

*E*ditor's note: *When I read the following letter and reviewed the artifacts presented here, I knew immediately that I was privy to the most remarkable baseball discovery since Sidd Finch (thank God he returned to Tibet or my beloved Cardinals might never have defeated the Mets ever again). After all the wrangling between the curators of Cooperstown and the sages at SABR over baseball's genesis, the real beginnings of the National Pastime are revealed at last in these humble pages. What havoc the proof that the Great American Game was invented by an Italian may wreak on our national self-esteem I cannot estimate. I only know that if truth and justice are to be regarded as the American way—or, more importantly, valued as the human way—these facts must be made known to the public regardless of the consequences. So it is with excitement and not a little trepidation that we share with you, O loyal Minneapolis Review of Baseball reader, the startling new evidence that baseball in fact and in fancy predated both Doubleday and rounders. But take heed: you may want to read this article sitting down. The MRB is not responsible for any physical or mental anguish incurred perusing the following revelations.*

Dear Steve and the Exiled One:

Prophets come in pairs—ever notice that? John the Baptist, we are told, lost his head over a dance while echoing Jeremiah's cry in the wilderness. Both had something important to say. Few seemed to be listening. You have to search pretty hard to find a pair of prophets these days. When you do, the premise is usually the most absurd thing you ever heard. M*A*S*H* aficionados like to claim that Hawkeye's cynicism with the ongoing Korean War meets with Radar's eerie precognition of incoming helicopters (I have trouble seeing a set of TV characters as prophets, but, this is the age of domeball and some people are willing to accept the lowest denominator). This is all wet to me. Hawkeye and Radar were working on angst and intuition respectively,

not prophecy. Then again, we may never get the straight dope on John the Baptist or Jeremiah.

Prediction loves any game but it's not the same as prophecy. It rests on the facts, then guesses on such. The Mets taking the N.L. East is a prediction, an educated guess. Prophecy is declaring the Indians to take the World Series, a leap of faith. Prophecy rises from the signs of the times, it's a tremor in the marrow of one's bones. Knowledge and guesswork comprise prediction whereas prophecy is 9/10ths faith. Predictors are born with every turn of the daily sports page. Prophets walk out of the woods and speak when you least expect it.

Two true baseball Prophets have been a part of my life. The "Jeremiah" is the unsung Michael C. Farr, this writer's older brother. Michael C., more than me, was blessed with a pun for a name: Michael, being an archangel (Gabriel was another), matched with the middle initial/verb "C" leading to "far," or transliterated into Lakota, "one who sees the edge of the world." In other words, a prophet by name. It was courtesy in my younger days, as it is out of respect today, to refer to my brother as "Michael C." He saw the future.

When I was a kid there were actually five minutes when I wasn't running at the mouth, which was just enough time for Michael C. to live up to his name. (Two other baseball nuts huddled around the radio with us bore witness that I indeed had my mouth shut that long.) Not a man then or now given to broad generalities (he would never say, as unversed fans too often jabber, "the Twins stink"), Michael C. blurted out in the middle of a Braves-ChiSox game, "Hank Aaron is the greatest hitter of our time. He will beat Babe Ruth's Record." We three sat stunned by his declaration, but, young as we were in 1963, too naive to have written down The Great Prophecy and have it notarized.

I ceased believing in baseball prophets sometime between The Great Prophecy and Aaron Makes History. Hammerin' Hank would claim his fame breaking The Record over the long haul. That much I still believed. I wasn't some backsliding reprobate shunning the Faith of Baseball. It was more Michael C's fallibility which sobered my perspective on prophets. His record on picks for Division, League and Series winners were sterling but not perfect. Prophets, I thought, were perfect in their

44

pronouncements. But, no matter how hard he argued the beauty of the '69 Oriole stats, history would not budge—the Mets beat 'em. Thereafter, I knew Michael C. was no longer a prophet but merely a baseball genius.

Prophecy, however, often comes through the back door. It's the nagging thought that something should have happened but no one has any proof. It's the full score of Beethoven's Tenth Symphony; it's the completed draft of Gogol's *Dead Souls* (he didn't *really* burn the third part—did he?); it's the first lineup card of the Chamberlain Mallards against the Rapid City Chiefs. You hope they may be squirreled away because to think they are irretrievably lost, well, the mind begs to say it just ain't so. Hindsight prophecy is a tougher call to make and even tougher to make it stick. Forgers feed on our innocent expectations. But when the proof *does* show up, it seems more bizarre than John the Baptist's severed head grinning from ear to ear.

One such prophecy of baseball came to light recently and not a season too late. Just when d&d (domes and drugs) aimed to destroy The Game, by the grace of the gods appeared the Second Prophet of Baseball, W. P. Kinsella.

Observe in Kinsella's latest gem, *The Iowa Baseball Confederacy,* a passage describing Leonardo da Vinci's descent onto the playing field in a hot-air balloon. Da Vinci then explains that he is the true inventor of baseball. Oh, it sounds so *perfect,* so *right* to have such a distinguished father, we think. But it's only Kinsella's fiction and the mind quickly nods, distastefully perhaps, back to the tradition of a third-rate Union general.

But what if . . . ?

In 1985, renovation began on the oldest commercial building in Minneapolis: the Upton Block. Built in 1855, the Upton hadn't seen the light of commerce in over half a century. It was the forgotten sister of Pracna-On-Main, famed for food, drink, camaraderie, and booting out bums who slept in the Upton overnight. During reconstruction, workmen found a 3'x4' wooden casket sheltered in a corner of the first floor where Gringolet Books now resides. Having signed on the dotted line for the space before renovation began, Gringolet owner Michael Leimer claimed the casket under Minnesota's Unowsky Rule.

I was directed to take care of the casket and whatever effects it held.

History on the wooden box is skimpy. This much we do know: It was owned by a 19th century art dealer named Vados Carmason who ran an unsuccessful gallery on the city's East Bank, known today as the St. Anthony Main district. It seems odd that Carmason would run an art gallery out of the predominately metalwork and tool district of Minneapolis. But I don't know why cheap art auctions are held at motels either. Carmason left the area soon after the Civil War. His name appears humbly on the pages of history for a final time in March 1887 in the obituary column of the Hannibal, Missouri, newspaper (his occupation was listed as advertising agent). No one knows why he left the wooden box in Minneapolis. The Upton Block, for its part, went into slower obscurity, closing its doors when Ruth was in his prime and Gehrig was just another hot player looking for a pro club.

If what was inside the casket proved authentic it would be The Find of the Century; the evidence irrefutably showed Leonardo da Vinci invented Baseball! Somehow, experts had to be found to test the articles. But where? Then, I remembered a conversation.

My friend Shawn Mahoney once told me about an oddball museum he visited in Milan, Italy during one of his globetrots. The museum, he said, was at the end of a long back alley which no tourist or Milanese citizen in his right mind would walk down. One evening, full of Chianti and rigatoni, probably more of the former, Shawn stumbled on the place and snooped about like any good American tourist. The ramshackle room featured a handful of rare prints and objects supporting the theory that da Vinci created bocci ball. The curator, one Marco Seerup, whose name Shawn found oddly memorable, dropped some questionable remarks about Leonardo also being the father of baseball. Shawn waved off the man's talk to bad translation. I wouldn't have recalled Shawn's story were it not for the aging prints I held in my hands and the urge to quaff a few at the Prince Street Bar where Shawn holds court. It seemed reasonable to assume Signore Seerup was on to something. He was the guy who would know what to make of the evidence.

The articles were insured and shipped to the L'Bocchi Musi in Milan

the next day. Three long weeks later we received a telegram at Gringolet from Signore Seerup who excitedly authenticated the Carmason cache. The provenance of the casket itself, Seerup said, came from the same age and area around Ferrara that the wooden bat model was made. Copies of the evidence were painstakingly made in Milan as payment for his research. The originals I requested to be securely sent back to the States for additional chemical analysis at the Sydd Finch Memorial Museum in Cooperstown, New York.

With the Finch Museum's further confirmation a month later, the only thing remaining was to publicly announce The Great Discovery. On May 1, 1986, in pointed defiance of the Soviet Union's May Day celebration, Gringolet Books formally announced and displayed The Glorious Truth: Leonardo da Vinci, Father of Baseball. Like a cherished clutch hit to break a ninth-inning tie, that very day Mr. Kinsella visited Gringolet to see what his prophecy had wrought.

There are, of course, loose threads to this yarn. Is there a da Vinci–Doubleday–Carmason connection wandering in the murky pages of time? Did Albrecht Dürer have a hand in inventing the game as the evidence seems to suggest? Does this tell us more as to why the Italian people are hot-to-trot about baseball? Did "Slammin' Sammy" Scheidt ever find the ballpark? And just who did win the very first baseball game? These questions I leave to historical detectives to ponder. For my part, association with two Prophets of Baseball is a fan's life fulfilled.

On behalf of the Michael Leimer and the Gringolet Books Gang, it is my pleasure to present The True Relics to *The Minneapolis Review of Baseball*'s responsible hands (pearls before swine came to mind when someone suggested *Sports Illustrated* keep The Relics). No other standard bearer of The Game does more honor to baseball's name.

Sincerely and Thank you,
Wayne N. Farr
Gringolet Books
Minneapolis, Mn.

p.s. When in Italy, visit Milan.

47

THREE BASEBALL CAP DESIGNS

As recorded in "The Last Inning" and "Josquin des Prés Hit by Pitch," Leonardo favored the one in the lefthand corner.

(lead on parchment)

ANALYSIS OF THE PITCHING ARM

48

JOSQUIN DES PRÉS HIT BY PITCH

Josquin was clobbered in practice and missed the first game.
The culprit is unknown.

(charcoal on light vellum)

OUT AT SECOND

Hans Holbein's fielding was so impressive Dürer drew this lead and ink cartoon a few days after the first game. Da Vinci would allow no more than a pencil sketch until Dürer received expressed written consent to complete the drawing.

(lead and ink on vellum)

SIGNALING THE CATCHER

The pitcher portrayed here may be Jack Grimmelshausen, considered the Phil Niekro of his time.

51

VAN EYCK MAKING FINGER PLACEMENT STUDIES

This silverpoint sketch shows Van Eyck, Senior, studiously analyzing finger placements on a large model of a baseball. Scholars who believe the writers won the first game point to this as the main piece of evidence supporting their theory. If the artists had won, the argument goes, Van Eyck would not have sought a new pitch. An opposing view says Van Eyck was mesmerized by the game and spent the rest of his days studying da Vinci's mathemetical wonder.

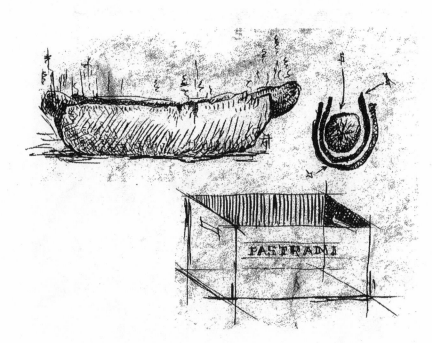

BALLPARK FOOD

The depth of Leonardo's thinking on the game went as far as providing sustenance for the fans. The side view of the "Hot Dog" shows he had a double-wrap of small flat bread in mind for the bun. The inscription 'A.D.' under the right side of the weiner was da Vinci's way of thanking the German artist Albrecht Dürer for the idea.

(silverpoint and charcoal on light vellum napkin)

54

THE LAST INNING

The badly decomposed cartoon of da Vinci's "The Last Inning" with his friend Dürer as the central character.

(silverpoint on parchment)

Once the game was invented, by Russians or cavemen or even Abner Doubleday, baseball had to be refined, rules and rituals polished, clichés coined—all the little things that give the game spice. The editor of The Minneapolis Review of Baseball, in his column, "In the Owner's Box," strikes up the tone for this section.

In the Owner's Box

BY STEPHEN LEHMAN

I'M REMINDED OF THE TALE OF A GERMAN count who was something of an American West aficionado. He determined one day to visit the Lone Star State, selecting as his destination, for its evocative name, the small, south Texas town of Roundup.

The impending visit from European nobility set the townspeople abuzz with plans and preparations. The city council determined to treat the Count to a genuine Texas barbecue. This was to be followed by a symphony concert in order to prove, they hoped, that they weren't entirely devoid of an appreciation of high culture. They selected for this performance the greatest symphony of all time, Beethoven's Ninth.

Plans for the barbecue continued apace; after all, the folks of Roundup well knew how to throw a party. The concert was a different matter, however, and preparations were fraught with challenges. First of all, not only would the budget not allow the hiring of an entire chorale for the final movement, but there was no room on the stage of the high school auditorium for both musicians and vocalists. To solve this problem, it was determined by council vote that only four singers would be hired—two male and two female—and that an intermission would precede the final movement to allow the janitors an opportunity to push the musicians' chairs and music stands in tightly enough to create room on the stage for the vocalists.

As the day of the Count's visit approached, the musicians practiced furiously. All was going well, except with the bass players. Marginally talented in the first place, the bass players also had a taste for the Texas night life, such as it was, and were spending more time honky-tonking than practicing their instruments.

On a blisteringly hot day in mid-July, the Count arrived amid much hoopla and fanfare. He was presented the key to the city, dined on the finest in Tex-Mex cuisine till he could literally not consume another bite, and escorted with appropriate solemnity (in the mayor's '78 Cadillac, with steer horns on the hood) to the high school auditorium for the culminating event. Despite the heat, the auditorium was packed. The tiny, ancient ventilation fans at the windows tried valiantly to circulate the air.

Backstage at the auditorium all was not well. Fifteen minutes before the concert was to begin, the women vocalists arrived stating they had not heard from the male singers all day and had no idea of their whereabouts. Young boys were promptly dispatched to locate them. Five minutes later, the bass players showed up in a state of advanced inebriation. They had apparently had a trifle too much fun at the barbecue and could barely stand up. Finally the concert had to begin without the male singers; they were nowhere to be found.

Under such adverse circumstances, the concert progressed remarkably well until the intermission prior to the final movement. As the musicians enjoyed a much needed respite, the janitors prepared the stage. In the course of moving the chairs, however, one janitor inadvertently knocked over the conductor's stand, scattering the sheet music. Embarrassed and flustered, the janitors gathered up the music, bound it with a string and placed it back on the conductor's stand, telling no one of their misadventure.

The curtain opened for the finale. The two women vocalists stood alone on the stage. The conductor raised his baton, and . . . suddenly an electrical surge caused the ventilation fans at the windows to whine piercingly, the blades spinning faster and still faster, until smoke began to exude from their overwrought motors.

Now picture this situation: It's the last of the Ninth. Two men are out. The basses are loaded. The score is tied, the Count is full, and the fans—ah, the fans!—are going *wild*.

57

Now that you know the roots of the game, you might as well learn the lingo, and there is no better guide than Mr. Arbuthnot, the cliché expert who was created for The New Yorker *by Frank Sullivan. Mr. Arbuthnot knows every cliché in the book. He also knows baseball like the back of his hand.*

The Cliché Expert Testifies on Baseball

BY FRANK SULLIVAN

Q—MR. ARBUTHNOT, YOU STATE THAT your grandmother has passed away and you would like to have the afternoon off to go to her funeral.

A—That is correct.

Q—You are an expert in the clichés of baseball—right?

A—I pride myself on being well versed in the stereotypes of our national pastime.

Q—Well, we'll test you. Who plays baseball?

A—Big-league baseball is customarily played by brilliant outfielders, veteran hurlers, powerful sluggers, knuckle-ball artists, towering first basemen, key moundsmen, fleet base runners, ace southpaws, scrappy little shortstops, sensational war vets, ex-college stars, relief artists, rifle-armed twirlers, dependable mainstays, doughty right-handers, streamlined backstops, power-hitting batsmen, redoubtable infielders, erstwhile Dodgers, veteran sparkplugs, sterling moundsmen, aging twirlers, and rookie sensations.

Q—What other names are rookie sensations known by?

A—They are also known as aspiring rookies, sensational newcomers, promising freshmen, ex-sandlotters, highly touted striplings, and youngsters who will bear watching.

59

Q—What's the manager of a baseball team called?

A—A veteran pilot. Or youthful pilot. But he doesn't manage the team.

Q—No? What does he do?

A—He guides its destinies.

Q—How?

A—By the use of managerial strategy.

Q—Mr. Arbuthnot, please describe the average major-league-baseball athlete.

A—Well, he comes in three sizes, or types. The first type is tall, slim, lean, towering, rangy, huge, husky, big, strapping, sturdy, handsome, powerful, lanky, rawboned, and rugged.

Q—Quite a hunk of athlete.

A—Well, those are the adjectives usage requires for the description of the Type One, or Ted Williams, ballplayer.

Q—What is Type Two like?

A—He is chunky or stocky—that is to say, Yogi Berra.

Q—And the Third?

A—The third type is elongated and does not walk. He is Ol' Satchmo, or Satchel Paige.

Q—What do you mean Satchmo doesn't walk?

A—Not in the sports pages, he doesn't. He ambles.

Q—You mentioned a hurler, Mr. Arbuthnot. What is a hurler?

A—A hurler is a twirler.

Q—Well, what is a twirler?

A—A twirler is a flinger, a tosser. He's a moundsman.

Q—Moundsman?

A—Yes. He officiates on the mound. When the veteran pilot tells a hurler he is to twirl on a given day, that is a mound assignment, and the hurler who has been told to twirl is the mound nominee for that game.

Q—You mean he pitches?

A—That is right. You have cut the Gordian knot.

Q—What's the pitcher for the other team called?

A—He is the mound adversary, or mound opponent, of the mound nominee. That makes them rival hurlers, or twirlers. They face each other and have a mound duel, or pitchers' battle.

Q—Who wins?

A—The mound victor wins, and as a result he is a mound ace, or ace moundsman. He excels on the mound, or stars on it. He and the other moundsmen on his team are the mound corps.

Q—What happens to the mound nominee who loses the mound duel?

A—He is driven off the mound.

Q—What do you mean by that?

A—He's yanked. He's knocked out of the box.

Q—What's the box?

A—The box is the mound.

Q—I see. Why does the losing moundsman lose?

A—Because he issues, grants, yields, allows, or permits too many hits or walks, or both.

Q—A bit on the freehanded side, eh? Where does the mound victor go if he pitches the entire game?

A—He goes all the way.

Q—And how does the mound adversary who has been knocked out of the box explain his being driven off the mound?

A—He says, "I had trouble with my control," or "My curve wasn't working," or "I just didn't have anything today."

◆

Q—Mr. Arbuthnot, how do you, as a cliché expert, refer to first base?

A—First base is the initial sack.

Q—And second base?

A—The keystone sack.

Q—What's third base called?

A—The hot corner. The first inning is the initial frame, and an inning without runs is a scoreless stanza.

Q—What is one run known as?

A—A lone run, but four runs are known as a quartet of tallies.

Q—What is a baseball?

A—The pill, the horsehide, the old apple, or the sphere.

Q—And what's a bat?

A—The bat is the willow, or the wagon tongue, or the piece of lumber. In the hands of a mighty batsman, it is the mighty bludgeon.

Q—What does a mighty batsman do?

A—He amasses runs. He connects with the old apple. He raps 'em out and he pounds 'em out. He belts 'em and he clouts 'em.

Q—Clouts what?

A—Circuit clouts.

Q—What are they?

A—Home runs. Know what the mighty batsman does to the mighty bludgeon?

Q—No. What?

A—He wields it. Know what kind of orgies he fancies?

Q—What kind?

A—Batting orgies. Slugfests. That's why his team pins.

Q—Pins what?

A—All its hopes on him.

Q—Mr. Arbuthnot, what is a runner guilty of when he steals home?

A—A plate theft.

Q—And how many kinds of baseball games are there?

A—Five main classifications: scheduled tussles, crucial contests, pivotal games, drab frays, and arc-light tussles.

Q—And what does the team that wins—

A—Sir, a baseball team never wins. It scores a victory, or gains one, or chalks one up. Or it snatches.

Q—Snatches what?

A—Victory from the jaws of defeat.

Q—How?

A—By a ninth-inning rally.

Q—I see. Well, what do the teams that chalk up victories do to the teams that lose?

A—They nip, top, wallop, trounce, rout, down, subdue, smash, drub, paste, trip, crush, curb, whitewash, erase, bop, slam, batter, check, hammer, pop, wham, clout, and blank the visitors. Or they zero them.

Q—Gracious sakes! Now I know why ballplayers are old at thirty-five.

A—Oh, that isn't the half of it. They do other things to the visitors.

Q—Is it possible?

A—Certainly. They jolt them, or deal them a jolt. They also halt, sock, thump, larrup, vanquish, flatten, scalp, shellac, blast, slaughter, K.O., mow down, topple, whack, pound, rap, sink, baffle, thwart, foil, maul, and nick.

Q—Do the losers do anything at all to the victors?

A—Yes. They bow to the victors. And they taste.

Q—Taste what?

A—Defeat. They trail. They take a drubbing, pasting, or shellacking. They are in the cellar.

Q—What about the victors?

A—They loom as flag contenders. They're in the first division.

◆

Q—Mr. Arbuthnot, what is the first sign of spring?

A—Well, a robin, of course.

Q—Yes, but I'm thinking of our subject here. How about when the ballplayers go south for spring training?

A—Ballplayers don't go south for spring training.

Q—Why, they do!

A—They do *not*. They wend their way southward.

Q—Oh, I see. Well, do all ballplayers wend their way southward?

A—No. One remains at home.

Q—Who is he?

A—The lone holdout.

Q—Why does the lone holdout remain at home?

A—He refuses to ink pact.

Q—What do you mean by that?

A—He won't affix his Hancock to his contract.

Q—Why not?

A—He demands a pay hike, or salary boost.

Q—From whom?

A—From baseball's biggies.

Q—And what do baseball's biggies do to the lone holdout?

A—They attempt to lure him back into the fold.

Q—How?

A—By offering him new contract.

63

Q—What does lone holdout do then?

A—He weighs offer. If he doesn't like it, he balks at terms. If he does like it, he inks pact and gets pay hike.

Q—How much pay hike?

A—An undisclosed amount in excess of.

Q—That makes him what?

A—One of the highest-paid baseball stars in the annals of the game, barring Ruth.

♦

Q—Mr. Arbuthnot, what is the opening game of the season called?

A—Let me see-e-e. It's on the tip of my tongue. Isn't that aggravating? Ah, I have it—the opener! At the opener, fifty-two thousand two hundred and ninety-three fans watch Giants bow to Dodgers.

Q—What do those fifty-two thousand two hundred and ninety-three fans constitute?

A—They constitute fandom.

Q—And how do they get into the ballpark?

A—They click through the turnstiles.

Q—Now, then, Mr. Arbuthnot, the climax of the baseball season is the World Series, is it not?

A—That's right.

Q—And what is the World Series called?

A—It's the fall classic, or crucial contest, also known as the fray, the epic struggle, and the Homeric struggle. It is part of the American scene, like ham and eggs or pumpkin pie. It's a colorful event.

Q—What is it packed with?

A—Thrills. Drama.

Q—What kind of drama?

A—Sheer or tense.

Q—Why does it have to be packed with thrills and drama?

A—Because if it isn't, it becomes drab fray.

Q—Where does the fall classic take place?

A—In a vast municipal stadium or huge ball park.

Q—And the city in which the fall classic is held is what?

A—The city is baseball mad.

Q—And the hotels?

A—The hotels are jammed. Rooms are at a premium.

Q—Tickets, also, I presume.

A—Tickets? If you mean the cards of admission to the fall classic, they are referred to as elusive Series ducats, and they *are* at a premium, though I would prefer to say that they are scarcer than the proverbial hen's teeth.

♦

Q—Now, the team that wins the Series—

A—Again, I'm sorry to correct you, sir. A team does not win a Series. It wraps it up. It clinches it.

Q—Well, then what?

A—Then the newly crowned champions repair to their locker room.

Q—What reigns in that locker room?

A—Pandemonium, bedlam, and joy.

Q—Expressed how?

A—By lifting youthful pilot, or his equivalent, to the shoulders of his teammates.

Q—In the locker room of the losers, what is as thick as a day in— I mean so thick you could cut it with a knife?

A—Gloom. The losers are devoid.

Q—Devoid of what?

A—Animation.

Q—Why?

A—Because they came apart at the seams in the pivotal tussle.

Q—What happens to the newly crowned champions later?

A—They are hailed, acclaimed, and fêted. They receive mighty ovations, boisterous demonstrations, and thunderous welcomes.

♦

Q—Thank you, Mr. Arbuthnot. You have been most helpful. I won't detain you any longer, and I hope your grandmother's funeral this afternoon is a tense drama packed with thrills.

A—Thanks a lot. Good-by now.

Q—Hold on a moment, Mr. Arbuthnot. Just for my own curiosity— couldn't you have said "thanks" and "good-by" and let it go at that, without adding that "lot" and "now" malarkey?

A—I could have, but it would have cost me my title as a cliché expert.

65

The McGreevey brothers, Eddie (batting average .184) and Nate (batting average .377), on the day Eddie decided to wear his pants longer.

Sportswriter Bob Kessler, of the Moonachie Plain Dealer, as he typed the first column to use the word "increment."

Journeyman outfielder Jackie Grimes interrupts a discussion about dames to ask if anybody knows anything about tax-exempt municipals.

66

Shad Finneran, catcher for the Troy (N.Y.) Haymakers in the old National Association, having just been struck in the stomach by a spitball delivered by Howie Schalk, suddenly envisions "Shad's Place," the very first restaurant to be owned and operated by a retired athlete.

Owner Walter T. Moran at the moment he said, "Why don't we sell some sort of food at the park and make a few nickels on the side?"

Mayor Fred F. Beall on the evening of the day when he made the suggestion that some dignitary be invited to throw out the first ball at the World Series. Walter Schmierer, president of the local Kiwanis Club, was asked, and accepted.

Willie Carr, who has always pretended to like the taste of chewing tobacco, becomes the first player to take the field with a wad of bubble gum in his cheek.

Ed Sobeleski, the first highly intelligent and articulate player who did not subsequently go into big business or broadcasting. He returned to his farm.

Baseball's first contract with a no-drinking clause is signed by Wally Plank, as owner Otto Pfeister looks on approvingly. Plank, who did not touch a drop all year, popped up in sixty-three consecutive plate appearances in April, thus establishing an all-time National League record. He finished the season with the Elmsford (N.C.) Bumblebees.

Jack J. Leach, who that morning bet his wife ten dollars that the Phillies would sweep their doubleheader against the Giants, shouts, for the first time anywhere, "Kill the umpire!"

Ollie Nehf in the stance he developed which became standard for major-league photo sessions.

Exhausted after a big night on the town, Artie Schang invents the sacrifice bunt.

Jimmy Tipke gets the first baseball autograph from Ossie Strunk, who in turn collected fifteen cents.

Owner John Dinneen, whose team finished fourth that year, at the moment the thought occurred that teams finishing in second, third, and fourth place should get a share of the World Series receipts.

69

*C*y Young's 511 victories, Joe DiMaggio's 56-game hitting streak, Lou Gehrig's 2,130 consecutive games—those are magic numbers, baseball monuments. So is "Who's on First?" And "Casey at the Bat." And so is "Take Me Out to the Ball Game," the anthem of the sport. The song was written in 1908, and in the original version, the woman asking to be escorted to the park was named Katie Casey. But when Jack Norworth and Albert Von Tilzer polished their work, they changed Katie Casey to Nelly Kelly and modified several lines. Just as well. It would've been too confusing to have "Casey at the Bat" and "Casey at the Ball Game." Here are both versions of the song; the classic chorus did not change.

Take Me Out to the Ball Game

BY JACK NORWORTH AND ALBERT VON TILZER

(original version)

Katie Casey was baseball mad,
Had the fever and had it bad;
Just to root for the hometown crew,
Ev'ry sou, Katie blew.
On a Saturday, her young beau
Called to see if she'd like to go,
To see a show but Miss Kate said, "No,
I'll tell you what you can do":

Take me out to the ball game,
Take me out with the crowd.
Buy me some peanuts and crackerjack,
I don't care if I never get back.
Let me root root root for the home team,
If they don't win it's a shame.
For it's one two three strikes, you're out,
At the old ball game.

Nelly Kelly loved baseball games,
Knew the players, knew all their names,
You could see her there ev'ry day,
Shout "Hurray," when they'd play.
Her boy friend by the name of Joe
Said, "To Coney Isle, dear, let's go,"
Then Nelly started to fret and pout,
And to him I heard her shout.

    Take me out to the ball game,
    Take me out with the crowd,
    Buy me some peanuts and crackerjack,
    I don't care if I never get back.
    Let me root root root for the home team,
    If they don't win it's a shame,
    For it's one two three strikes, you're out,
    At the old ball game.

Nelly Kelly was sure some fan,
She would root just like any man,
Told the umpire he was wrong,
All along, good and strong.
When the score was just two to two,
Nelly Kelly knew what to do,
Just to cheer up the boys she knew,
She made the gang sing this song.

"There it goes, folks, high over center field and still traveling. It looks like—
Yes, sir, it is! It's bye-bye, baby."

♦

72

Nelly Kelly could be called the ultimate fan, gripped by what could be called "The Base Ball Fever," which was the title of a song written in 1867, in the infancy of the game (unless, of course, you subscribe to the Leonardo da Vinci theory of baseball's birth, or the caveman theory). Notice in the chorus the lament for a good reliever, the cry of every manager for a century and a quarter. "The Fever" has struck such accomplished humorists as Russell Baker, who is proud to be a fan, and Calvin Trillin, who used to be a fan. Willie Morris, who was once the "boy genius" editor of Harper's *magazine, caught the fever early; Willie's "Memories of a Short-Wave Prophet" brings to life old-time baseball broadcasts. Jules Feiffer, Garry Trudeau, and Ogden Nash have listened, too.*

The Base Ball Fever

BY H. ANGELO

(1867)

All 'round about we've queer complaints,
Which needs some Doctors patching;
But something there is on the brain,
Which seems to me more catching;
'Tis raging too, both far and near,
Or else I'm a deceiver;
I'll tell you what it is, now, plain,
It is the Base Ball fever.

    Chorus:
    O my, O my, O my, O my,
    We want a safe reliever,
    For ev'rybody old and young,
    Has got the Base Ball fever.

73

Our Merchants have to close their stores,
Their clerks away are staying,
Contractors too can do no work,
Their hands are all out playing;
There's scarce a day that folks don't run,
As true as I'm a liver;
To see a match 'bout to be played,
'Cause they've the Base Ball fever.   (Chorus)

Our little boys as well as big,
All, to the Bat are taking;
And smarter folks are coining cash,
At Bat and Base Ball making:
You cannot walk along the street,
I'll bet my patent lever,
That two boys ain't a-playing *catch*,
'Cause they've the Base Ball fever.   (Chorus)

To be in fashion, ladies too,
In place of Waterfalls, sirs;
Way back behind the ears, they wear,
An awful big Base Ball, sirs;
I shouldn't wonder but 'ere long,
Each Miss, if you'll perceive her,
Will carry Bats all through her hair
'Cause she too has the fever.   (Chorus)

Our papers teem with base ball News,
Four columns good and over;
Our stores now sell more bats and balls
Than would three acres cover;
We've clubs no end, and players sharp,
But I will bet my Beaver;
That I can *catch,* as well as they,
For I have *kotcht* the fever.   (Chorus)

74

A Civilized Pastime

BY RUSSELL BAKER

I'M A BASEBALL FAN. IT IS A GAME YOU don't have to weigh 250 pounds, or stand 7 feet tall, or be South American to play well. Also, it is not played on ice.

I used to think I could grow up and be a major league baseball player, since I knew by age 9 that I would never weigh 250 pounds, grow 7 feet tall, be South American, or learn to keep my balance on ice skates while acting like a saloon brawler.

What changed my mind was inferior baseball gloves. Some men blame their troubles on never having had a dog when they were boys. What I never had when I was a boy was a baseball glove with six inches of padding in the palm.

It is amazing how hard a baseball can be when it is thrown at maximum speed by the biggest kid on the block and has to be stopped by a hand wearing a glove without a nice thick cushion in the palm. I was appalled to realize that this was a game where you could end up with a broken palm.

When it was my turn to bat, memories of how hard the ball felt smacking into a thinly protected hand made me worry about how hard it would feel colliding with a totally unprotected head. It is hard to bat as dynamically as Babe Ruth, or even Willie Tasby, when all you can think about at the plate is getting a hole in the head.

Unfortunately, batting helmets hadn't then been invented, so my name never comes up when the sportswriters talk about which old-timers ought to go into the Baseball Hall of Fame.

As a fan, my team is the Orioles. They are not the worst team to be a fan of. That distinction goes to the Yankees. Living in New York, I once tried to be a Yankees fan. My first visit to the Yankee Stadium I felt lucky to get out alive. The players probably did, too. At the Yankee Stadium they don't have fans, they have assault troops.

I don't go to baseball parks to relive the excitement of Iwo Jima. Among other things, I like reading the newspaper in peace during the long pauses that make baseball the only civilized sport west of the cricket belt.

The trick to being a successful baseball fan is to ignore one of the two major leagues and half of the other. For instance, I ignore the entire National League and the Western Division teams of the American League. This leaves only the American League's seven Eastern teams to worry about.

You can keep track of seven teams. Keeping track of the 19 others, though, is impossible unless you're a sportswriter.

By ignoring all but the Big Seven, I have long spells when I hardly have to think at all about baseball. I enjoy long breathers when the Orioles disappear below the western horizon, as they frequently do, to play teams I have never heard of and wouldn't care about if I did: teams like the Minneapolis Carpenters' Helpers and the Seattle Fogs, or whatever they call themselves.

The only games that count are those involving the Orioles, Red Sox, Yankees, Indians, Blue Jays, Tigers and Brewers. Fandom also means agony, and one agony in being an Orioles fan is that the only seats they'll sell you for games with the Red Sox, Yankees, Indians, Blue Jays, Tigers and Brewers are so high above the field that acrophobia can make you hysterical and so far from home plate that you need a radio to know what's happening in the game.

Some fans say it makes more sense to stay in Hagerstown, sit in your rocker and listen to the Orioles on radio, but these are not real fans. I am a real fan. I drive an hour and a half to the game where parking lot tyrants bury my car so deep that after the game 10,000 other cars will have to leave before I can get out.

In the park I climb up to where the oxygen is thin. Far away I can see some men in Oriole orange and black but can't tell whether they are the great Eddie Murray or just six guys named Juan. I have forgotten my radio but the howling mass of Yankee fans behind me—how can two fans manage to create the sense of a riot in progress?—leave no doubt that the Yankees are in town.

Game starts, Yankees bat for 30 minutes and score five runs. Orioles

bat for three minutes and score nothing. Second inning. Yankees bat for 35 minutes and score five more runs. The Yankee fans behind us, having gloated themselves out and finished the last keg of beer left in the park, depart without violence. Yankee fans have no loyalty. Not like Orioles fans. We don't leave just because it's 10 to 0 in the second inning. No siree. When your car's buried behind 10,000 in the parking lot, you sit there and take it like a fan.

◆

"Just for a change, why don't you scream something <u>supportive</u>!"

My Team

BY CALVIN TRILLIN

ENNO SCHMIDT, JR., THE NEW PRESI-
dent of Yale, has been described in the press as a "re-
nowned constitutional-law scholar who is an expert on the First
Amendment, race relations, and the New York Rangers." The man he
will replace, A. Bartlett Giamatti, has been described as "a professor of
English and comparative literature and an expert on Dante, Spenser,
and the Boston Red Sox." It's no wonder I'm never asked to be the
president of a major educational institution: I don't have a team.

I used to have a team. When I was growing up, the Kansas City
Blues were my team. They were in the American Association, along
with the Minneapolis Millers and the Milwaukee Brewers and the Toledo Mud Hens (the league patsies) and several other teams that
Schmidt and Giamatti don't know the first thing about.

Because I grew up in Kansas City, people assume that the Kansas
City Royals are my team. Not so. My loyalty to the Kansas City Blues
was so pure that their demise ended my interest in the national pastime.
Oh sure, I could have skipped to the Kansas City Athletics and then
to the Royals. I had opportunities. "It's the big leagues," everyone in
Kansas City said when the Athletics came in to replace the Blues.

"Big leaguers don't ditch their pals," I replied.

I could see myself running into one of the old Kansas City Blues
someday—Cliff Mapes, maybe, or Eddie Stewart, or Carl DeRose, the
sore-arm right-hander I once saw pitch a perfect game. Or maybe Odie
Strain, the no-hit shortstop. "I guess you follow the Royals now," Odie
would say, with that same look of resignation he used to wear when
the third strike whisked past him and thwocked into the catcher's mitt.

"No," I'd say. "I don't have a team. My team's gone." A smile would
spread slowly across Odie's face.

Meanwhile, I don't have a team. I can just imagine my appearance
before the presidential search committee of, say, the Harvard trustees.

I'm being interviewed in a private room at the New York Harvard Club by a former secretary of defense, an enormously wealthy investment banker, and an Episcopalian bishop. So far, I feel that things have been going my way. I have analyzed Dante's *Divine Comedy* in constitutional terms, concentrating on whether moaning in purgatory is a First Amendment–protected right. I have transposed the first ten amendments to the Constitution into Spenserian stanzas, although not in a pushy way.

I can see that the committee is impressed. The former secretary of defense, who at first seemed to be concentrating on some doodling that resembled the trajectory of an intercontinental ballistic missile, is now giving the interview his complete attention. The investment banker has slipped me a note that says, "Hold on to Humboldt Bolt & Tube. Sell Worldwide Universal short." The interviewers are exchanging pleased glances and nodding their heads. Finally, as the interview seems to be coming to an end, the investment banker says, "Just one more question. What is your team?"

"Team?" I say.

There is a long silence. Then the bishop in a kindly voice says, "You do have a team, don't you?"

"Well, not exactly," I say.

"No team?" the bishop says.

"I used to have a team," I say, "and I still turn on the tennis now and then, just to hiss McEnroe."

The bishop shakes his head sadly.

I am beginning to get desperate. "I know the University of Missouri fight song by heart," I say.

But they are gathering up their papers, preparing to leave. The former defense secretary is carefully feeding his doodles into a paper shredder.

"But why do I need a team?" I say.

Nobody pays any attention except the bishop, who says, "We need a regular guy. Presidents who aren't regular guys frighten the alumni."

"But I *am* a regular guy," I say. "I owe the Diners Club. I had a dog named Spike."

"Regular guys have teams," the bishop says.

Desperately, I begin to sing: "Every true son so happy hearted, skies

above us are blue. There's a spirit so deep within us. Old Missouri, here's to you—rah, rah. When the band plays the Tiger . . ."

But now they are at the door. Suddenly the investment banker walks back to where I'm sitting, snatches his stock tips off the table, and marches out with the rest of the committee. I sit stunned at the table as a club steward comes in to straighten up the room. He glances down at my résumé, still on the table.

"Kansas City, huh?" he says. "You must be proud of those Royals."

"The Royals are not my team," I say. "I don't have a team. If I had a team, I'd be the president of Harvard."

◆

LIFE'S DARKEST MOMENTS   H. T. Webster

GUMMY MC CABE IS COMING TO BAT. HE'S O FOR 2, HITTING AT 119. THE VETERAN SHORTSTOP USED TO HAVE PLENTY OF STUFF, BUT AGE IS TAKING ITS TOLL. WHEN A MAN GETS TO BE THIRTY YEARS OLD HE DOESN'T MOVE AROUND WITH HIS CUSTOMARY ZIP — HIS REFLEXES SHOW THE RAVAGES OF TIME — BUT — OH, WELL, THAT'S LIFE

A DODDERING OLD GENT OF 45 LISTENS TO A BASE BALL BROADCAST —

© 1940·N·Y TRIBUNE INC.

80

Memoirs of a Short-Wave Prophet

BY WILLIE MORRIS

THE TOWN IN MISSISSIPPI WHERE I GREW up sits tentatively on the edge of the great delta. It is half red hills, half black flatland, and about thirty miles from the river as the crow flies. Once, lounging in front of the Phillips station on the main street, which comes hellbent out of the hills as a U.S. highway, I watched a couple of tourists emerge from a Buick with Illinois plates; the woman of the pair paused for a second to look at the shrivelled vistas and whispered, "My God!" This was in the summer of my thirteenth year, in the late nineteen-forties, and although I knew even then that the town was not the cultural capital of Christendom, I had recently become aware that at least a quiet renaissance was occurring in the place—an intense religiosity, which later developed a finer and more mature edge, on the subject of baseball. Baseball was all-meaning; it was the link with the outside. A place known around town simply as the Store was the principal center of this intellectual ferment. The Store had sawdust on the floor and long shreds of flypaper hanging down from the ceiling. Its most familiar staples were Rexall supplies, oysters on the half shell, legal beer, and illegal whiskey, the latter served up, Mississippi bootleg fashion, by the bottle from a hidden shelf and costing not merely the price of the whiskey but the investment in gas required to go to Louisiana to fetch it. There was a long counter in the back. On one side of it, the Caucasian *petite bourgeoisie* congregated after working hours every afternoon to compare the day's scores and talk batting averages, and on the other side, also talking baseball, were the Negroes, juxtaposed in a face-to-face arrangement with their white brethren. The scores were chalked up on a blackboard hanging on a red and purple wall, and the conversations were carried on in fast, galloping shouts from one end of the room to the other. An intelligent white lad of twelve was even permitted, in that atmosphere of heady freedom before anyone knew the name of Justice Warren, a quasi-public position favoring the Dodgers, who had Jackie Robinson, Roy Campanella, and

Don Newcombe—not to mention, so it was rumored, God knows how many Chinese and mulattoes being groomed in the minor leagues.

There were two firehouses in town, and on hot afternoons the firemen at both establishments sat outdoors in shirtsleeves, with the baseball broadcast turned up as loud as it would go. On his day off work, my father, who was a wholesale grocer, usually started with Firehouse No. 1 for the first few innings and then hit No. 2 before ending up at the Store for the usual post-game conversations. I usually accompanied him, and was thankful for these diversions, because in the summers the town was a bore—ten thousand souls and nothing doing. In the mornings, for instance, three or four of us boys might get together and play stud poker, but only for toothpicks. Once, by telephone, we managed to have six bottles of Kentucky bourbon delivered by the bootlegger himself to an afternoon meeting of the Women's Society of Christian Service. Sometimes we would have picnics in the cemetery, the coolest place in town and in many ways the most sensible, where we lunched on ham sandwiches, moonpies, and Nehi strawberry drink near the resting place of a couple of John Hancock's nephews, who died of some eccentric disease while passing through town many years before. These activities, however, were trivial, and plainly out of the mainstream.

I didn't try out for the American Legion Junior Baseball team that summer. Legion baseball was an important thing for country boys in those parts, but I was too young and skinny, and I had heard that the coach, a dirt farmer named Gentleman Joe, made his protégés lie flat on the infield while he walked on their stomachs; forced them to take three-mile runs down the main boulevards of the town; harangued them about going to church; and persuaded them to give up Coca-Colas. A couple of summers later, when I did go out for the team, I discovered that Gentleman Joe did in fact insist on these soul-strengthening rituals; because of them, we won the Mississippi state championship and a free trip to St. Louis to see the Cardinals play the Phillies. My main concern that earlier summer lay in the more academic aspects of the game, however, and I can now proudly say, with the judgment that almost sixteen years can bring, that I knew more about baseball, its technology and its ethos, than all the firemen and Store experts put

82

together. Having read all its literature, I could give a fair-sized filibuster on the infield-fly rule alone, which only a thin minority of the towns-people knew existed. Gentleman Joe was held in high local esteem for his strategical sense, yet he was the only man I ever knew who could call for a sacrifice bunt with two men out and not have a bad conscience about it. I remember one dismaying moment that came to me while I was watching a country semi-pro game. The home team had runners on first and third, with one out, when the batter hit a ground ball to the first baseman, who stepped on first and then threw to second. The shortstop, covering second, stepped on the base but made no attempt to tag the runner. The man on third had crossed the plate, of course, but the umpire, a dirt farmer unfamiliar with the subtleties of the rules, signalled a double play. Sitting in the grandstand, I knew that it was not a double play at all and that the run had scored, but when I went down, out of my Christian duty, to tell the manager of the local team that he had just been done out of a run, he told me I was crazy. This was the kind of baseball brainpower I was up against.

That summer, the local radio station started a baseball quiz program. A razor-blade company offered free blades and the station chipped in a dollar, all of which went to the first listener to telephone with the correct answer to the day's baseball question. If there was no winner, the next day's pot would go up a dollar. At the end of a month, they had to close down the program because I was winning all the money. It became so monumentally easy, in fact, that I stopped phoning in the answers some afternoons, so that the pot could build up and make my winnings more spectacular. I netted about twenty-five dollars and a ten-year supply of double-edged, smooth-contact razor blades before they gave up. One day, when the jackpot was a mere two dollars, the announcer tried to confuse me. "Babe Ruth," he said, "hit sixty home runs in 1927 to set the major-league record. What man had the next-highest total?" I telephoned and said, "George Herman Ruth. He hit fifty-nine in another season." My adversary, who had developed a particularly avid dislike of me, said that was not the correct answer. He said it should have been *Babe* Ruth. This incident angered me, and I won for the next four days, just for the hell of it.

Every Sunday afternoon, my father and I went to see a game. Some-

times we drove out of town and along winding dirt roads to baseball fields that were little more than parched red clearings, the outfield sloping out of the woods and ending in some tortuous gully full of yellowed paper, old socks, and cow manure. One of the backwoods teams had a fastball pitcher named Eckhardt, who didn't have any teeth, and a fifty-year-old left-handed catcher. Since there were no catcher's mitts made for left-handers, this unfortunate had to wear a mitt on his throwing hand. In his simian posture, he would catch the ball and toss it lightly into the air and then whip his mitt off and catch the ball in his bare left hand before throwing it back. I can still vividly recall those Sunday afternoons—my father and I sitting in the grass behind the chicken-wire backstop with eight or ten dozen farmers, watching the wrong-handed catcher go through his strange gyrations, and listening at the same time to our portable radio, which brought us the rising inflections of a baseball announcer called the Old Scotchman. The sounds of the two games, our own and the one being broadcast from Brooklyn or Chicago, merged and rolled across the bumpy outfield and the gully and into the woods.

The Old Scotchman was a local institution. His real name was Gordon McLendon, and he described the big-league games for the Liberty Broadcasting System, which had outlets mainly in the South and Southwest. He had a rich, deep voice, and I think he was the best rhetorician outside of Nye Bevan and Theodore Bilbo I have ever heard. Under his handling, a baseball game took on a life of its own. His games were rare and remarkable entities, things of beauty. Casual pop flies had the flow of history behind them, double plays resembled the stark, tragic clashes of old armies, and home runs deserved acknowledgment on Grecian urns. Later, when I came across Thomas Wolfe, I felt I had heard him before, from Shibe Park, Crosley Field, and Yankee Stadium. On those summer afternoons, almost every radio in town was turned to the Old Scotchman, and his rhetoric dominated the place; it hovered in the branches of the trees, bounced off the hills, and came out of car exhausts.

◆

One afternoon, I was lounging around my house listening to the Old Scotchman, admiring the sheer vivacity of a man who said he was a contemporary of Connie Mack. (I learned later that McLendon was in his late twenties.) That day, he was doing the Dodgers and Giants from the Polo Grounds. The game, as I recall, was in the fourth inning, and the Giants were ahead by about 4–1. It was a rather boring game, however, and I began experimenting with my father's short-wave radio, an impressive mechanism a couple of feet wide, which had an aerial that almost touched the ceiling and the name of every major world city on its dial. It was by far the best radio I had ever seen; there was not another one like it in town. I switched the dial to short wave and began picking up African drum music, French jazz, and Australian news broadcasts. Then a curious thing happened. I came across a baseball game—the Giants and the Dodgers, from the Polo Grounds. After a couple of minutes, I discovered that the game was in the eighth inning. Thinking that I had not been listening closely enough to the Old Scotchman, I turned back to the local station. But no, the Giants and Dodgers were still in the fourth. I turned again to the short-wave broadcast and listened to the last inning, a humdrum affair that ended with Carl Furillo popping out to short, Gil Hodges grounding out second to first, and Roy Campanella lining out to center. Then I went back to the Old Scotchman and listened to the rest of the game. In the top of the ninth, an hour or so later, a ghostly thing occurred; to my astonishment and titillation, the game ended with Furillo popping out to short, Hodges grounding out second to first, and Campanella lining out to center.

I kept this unusual discovery to myself, and the next day, an hour before the Old Scotchman began his play-by-play of the second game of the series, I dialled the short-wave frequency, and, sure enough, they were doing the Giants and the Dodgers again. I learned that I was listening to the Armed Forces Radio Service, which broadcast games played in New York. As the game progressed, I began jotting down notes on the action. When the first four innings were over, I turned to the local station just in time to get the Old Scotchman for the first batter. The Old Scotchman's account of the game matched the short-wave's almost perfectly. The Scotchman's game, in fact, struck me as

85

being considerably more exciting and poetic than the one I had heard first. But I did not doubt him, since I could hear the roar of the crowd, the crack of the bat, and the Scotchman's precise description of foul balls that fell into the crowd, the gestures of the base coaches, and the expression on the face of a small boy who was eating a popsicle in a box seat behind first base. I decided that the broadcast was being delayed somewhere along the line, perhaps because we were so far from New York.

That was my first thought, but after a close comparison of the two broadcasts for the rest of the game I sensed that something more sinister was taking place. For one thing, the Old Scotchman's description of the count on a batter, though it jibed ninety per cent of the time, did not always. For another, the Scotchman's crowd, compared with the other, kept up an ungodly noise. When Robinson stole second on short wave, he did it without drawing a throw and without sliding, while for Mississippians the feat was performed in a cloud of angry, petulant dust. A foul ball that went over the grandstand and out of the park for short-wave listeners in Alaska and the Argentine produced for the local firemen, bootleggers, farmers, and myself a primitive scramble in an upper-deck aisle that ended with a feeble old lady catching the ball on the first bounce to the roar of the assembled masses. But the most revealing development came after the Scotchman's game was over. After the usual summaries, he mentioned that the game had been "recreated." I had never taken notice of that particular word before, perhaps because I lost interest once a game was over. I went to the dictionary, and under "recreate" I found "To invest with fresh vigor and strength; to refresh, reinvigorate (nature, strength, a person or thing)." The Old Scotchman most assuredly invested a game with fresh vigor and strength, but this told me nothing. My deepest suspicions were confirmed, however, when I found the second definition of the word— "To create anew."

So there it was. I was happy to have fathomed the mystery, as perhaps no one else in the whole town had done. The Old Scotchman, for all his flaming rhetoric, was not only several innings behind every game he described but was no doubt sitting in some air-conditioned studio in the hinterland, where he got the happenings of the game by news

ticker; sound effects accounted for the crack of bat on ball and the accompanying crowd noises. Instead of being disappointed in the Scotchman, I was all the more pleased by his artistry, for he made pristine facts more actual than actuality. I must add, however, that this renewed appreciation did not obscure the realization that I had at my disposal a weapon of unimaginable dimensions.

Next day, I was at the short-wave again, but I learned with much disappointment that the game being broadcast on short wave was not the one the Old Scotchman had chosen to describe. I tried every afternoon after that and discovered that I would have to wait until the Old Scotchman chose to describe a game out of New York before I could match his game with one described live on short wave. Sometimes, I learned later, these coincidences did not occur for days; during an important Dodger or Yankee series, however, his game and that of the Armed Forces Radio Service often coincided for two or three days running. I was happy, therefore, to find, on an afternoon a few days later, that both the short-wave and the Scotchman were carrying the Yanks and the Indians.

I settled myself at the short-wave with notebook and pencil and took down every pitch. This I did for four full innings, and then I turned back to the local station, where the Old Scotchman was just beginning the first inning. I checked the first batter to make sure the accounts jibed. Then, armed with my notebook, I ran down the street to the corner grocery, a sort of minor outpost of baseball intellection, presided over by a young Negro friend of mine named Bozo, who was a knowledgeable student of the game. I found Bozo behind the meat counter, with the Old Scotchman going full blast. I arrived in the interim between the top and bottom of the first inning.

"Who's pitchin' for the Yankees, Bozo?" I asked.

"They pitchin' Allie Reynolds," Bozo said. "Old Scotchman says Reynolds really got the stuff today. He just set 'em down one, two, three."

The Scotchman, meanwhile, was describing the way the flags were flapping in the breeze. Phil Rizzuto, he reported, was stepping to the plate.

"Bozo," I said, trying to sound rather cut-and-dried, "you know what

I think? I think Rizzuto's gonna take a couple of fast called strikes, then foul one down the left-field line, and then line out straight to Boudreau at short."

"Yeah?" Bozo said. He scratched his head and leaned lazily across the counter.

I went up front to buy a Double Cola and then came back. The count worked to nothing and two on Rizzuto—a couple of fast called strikes and a foul down the left side. "This one," I said to Bozo, "he lines straight to Boudreau at short."

The Old Scotchman, pausing dramatically between words, as was his custom, said, "Here's the windup on nothing and two. Here's the pitch on its way— There's a hard line drive! But Lou Boudreau's there at shortstop and he's got it. Phil hit that one on the nose, but Boudreau was right there."

Bozo looked over at me, his eyes widening. "How'd you know that?" he asked.

Ignoring the query, I made my second prediction. "Bozo," I said, "Tommy Henrich's gonna hit the first pitch up against the right-field wall and slide in with a double."

"How come you think so?"

"Because I can predict anything that's gonna happen in baseball for the next ten years," I said. "I can tell you anything."

The Old Scotchman was describing Henrich at the plate. "Here comes the first pitch. Henrich swings, there's a hard smash into right field! . . . This one may be out of here! It's going, going—No! It hits the wall in right center. Henrich's rounding first, on his way to second. Here's the throw from Doby. . . . Henrich slides in safely with a double!" The crowd sent up a devastating roar in the background.

"Say, how'd you know that?" Bozo asked. "How'd you know he was gonna wind up on second?"

"I just can tell. I got extra-vision," I said. On the radio, far in the background, the public-address system announced Yogi Berra. "Like Berra right now. You know what? He's gonna hit a one-one pitch down the right-field line—"

"How you know?" Bozo said angrily.

"Just a second," I said. "I'm gettin' static." I stood dead still, put my

hands up against my temples and opened my eyes wide. "Now it's comin' through clear," I told Bozo. "Yeah, Yogi's gonna hit a one-one pitch down the right-field line, and it's gonna be fair by about three or four feet—I can't say exactly—and Henrich's gonna score from second, but the throw is gonna get Yogi at second by a mile."

This time Bozo remained silent, listening to the Scotchman, who described the ball and the strike, then said, "Henrich takes his lead off second. Benton looks over, stretches, delivers. Yogi swings." (There was a bat crack.) "There's a line drive down the right side! . . . It's barely inside the foul line. It may go for extra bases! Henrich's rounding third and coming in with a run, Berra's moving toward second. Here comes the throw! . . . And they *get* him! They get Yogi easily on the slide at second!"

Before Bozo could say anything else, I reached in my pocket for the notes. "I've just written down here what I think's gonna happen in the first four innings," I said. "Like DiMag. See, he's gonna pop up to Mickey Vernon at first on a one-nothing pitch in just a minute. But don't you worry. He's gonna hit a 380-foot homer in the fourth with nobody on base on a full count. You just follow these notes and you'll see I can predict anything that's gonna happen in the next ten years." I handed him the paper, turned around, and left the store just as DiMaggio, on a one-nothing pitch, popped up to Vernon at first.

Then I went back home and took more notes from the short-wave. The Yanks clobbered the Indians in the late innings and won easily. On the local station, however, the Old Scotchman was in the top of the fifth inning. At this juncture, I went to the telephone and called Firehouse No. 1.

"Hello," a voice answered. It was the fire chief.

"Hello, Chief, could you tell me the score?" I said. Calling the firehouse for baseball information was a common practice in our town.

"The Yanks are ahead, 5–2."

"This is the Phantom you're talkin' with," I said.

"Who?"

"The Phantom. Listen carefully. Reynolds is gonna open this next inning with a popup. Then Rizzuto will single to left on a one-one count. Henrich's gonna force him at second on a two-and-one pitch but make it to first. Berra's gonna double to right on a nothing-and-one pitch, and Henrich's goin' to third. DiMaggio's gonna foul a couple off and then double down the left-field line, and both Henrich and Yogi are gonna score. Brown's gonna pop out to third to end the inning."

"Aw, go to hell," the chief said and hung up.

This was precisely what happened, of course. I phoned No. 1 again after the inning.

"Hello."

"Hi. This is the Phantom again."

"Say, how'd you know that?"

"Stick with me," I said ominously, "and I'll feed you predictions. I can predict anything that's gonna happen anywhere in the next ten years." After a pause, I added, "Beware of fire real soon," for good measure, and hung up.

I left my house and hurried back to the corner grocery. When I got there, the entire meat counter was surrounded by friends of Bozo's, about a dozen of them. They were gathered around my notes, talking very passionately and shouting. Bozo saw me standing beside the bread counter. "There he is! There's the one!" he declared. His colleagues turned and stared at me in undisguised awe. They parted respectfully as I strolled over to the meat counter and ordered a dime's worth of bologna for my dog. A couple of questions were directed at me from the group, but I replied, "I'm sorry for what happened in the fourth. I predicted DiMag was gonna hit a full-count pitch for that homer. It came out he hit it on two-and-two. There was too much static in the air."

"Too much static?" one of them asked.

"Yeah. Sometimes the static confuses my extra-vision. But I'll be back tomorrow if everything's O.K., and I'll try not to make any more big mistakes."

"Big mistakes!" one of them shouted, and the crowd laughed admiringly, parting once more as I turned and left the store.

◆

That day was only the beginning of my brief season of triumph. A schoolmate of mine, Bubber Jay, offered me five dollars, for instance, to tell him how I had known that Johnny Mize was going to hit a two-

run homer to break up one particularly close game for the Giants. One afternoon, on the basis of a one-sided first four innings, I had an older friend sneak into the Store and place a bet, which netted me fourteen-fifty. I felt so bad about it I tithed a dollar forty-five in church the following Sunday. At Bozo's grocery store, I was a full-scale oracle. To the firemen, I remained the Phantom, and when I look back on it I like to think that local firefighting reached a peak of efficiency that month, simply because the firemen knew what was going to happen in many games and did not need to tarry when an alarm came.

One afternoon, my father was at home listening to the Old Scotch-man with a couple of out-of-town salesmen. They were sitting in the front room, and I had already managed to get the first three or four innings of the Cardinals and the Giants on paper before they arrived. The Old Scotchman was in the top of the first when I casually walked in and said hello. The men were talking business and listening to the game with one ear.

"I'm gonna make a prediction," I said. They stopped talking and looked at me. "I predict Musial's gonna take a ball and a strike and then hit a double to right field, scoring Schoendienst from second, but Marty Marion's gonna get tagged out at the plate."

"You're mighty smart," one of the visitors said. He suddenly sat up straight when the Old Scotchman reported, "Here's the windup and the pitch coming in. . . . Musial *swings!*" (Bat crack, crowd roar.) "He drives one into right field! This one's going up against the boards! . . . Schoendienst rounds third. He's coming on in to score! Marion dashes around third, legs churning. His cap falls off, but here he *comes!* Here's the toss to the plate. He's nabbed at home. He is *out* at the plate! Musial holds at second with a run-producing double."

Before I could parry the inevitable questions, my father took my elbow and hustled me into a back room. "How'd you know that?" he asked.

"I was just guessin'," I said nervously. "It was nothin' but luck."

He stopped for a moment, and then a new expression showed on his face. "Have *you* been callin' the firehouse?" he asked.

"Yeah, I guess a few times."

"Now, you tell me how you find out about all that. I mean it."

When I told him about the short-wave radio, I was afraid he might be angry, but on the contrary he laughed uproariously. "Do you remember these next few innings?" he asked a minute or two later, when he had his breath back.

"I got it all written down," I said, and reached in my pocket for the notes. Still laughing to himself, my father took the notes and told me to go off and play somewhere. From the yard, a few minutes later, I heard him predicting the next inning to his visitors.

A couple of days later, I phoned No. 1 again. "This is the Phantom," I said. "With two out, Branca's gonna hit Stanky with a fast ball, and then Alvin Dark's gonna send him home with a triple."

"Yeah, we know it," the fireman on the line said in a bored voice. "We're listenin' to a short-wave set, too. You think you're somethin', don't you?"

I knew everything was up. The next day, as a sort of final gesture, I took some more notes down to the corner grocery in the third or fourth inning. Some of the old crowd was there, but the atmosphere was grim. They looked at me coldly. "Oh, man," Bozo said, "*we* know the Old Scotchman ain't at that game. He's four or five innings behind. He's makin' all that stuff up." The others grumbled and turned away. I slipped quietly out the door.

My days as a seer were over, but I went on listening to the short-wave broadcasts out of New York a few days more. Then, somewhat to my surprise, I went back to the Old Scotchman, and in time I found that the firemen, the bootleggers, and the dirt farmers who had short-wave sets all did the same. From then on, accurate, up-to-the-minute baseball news was disreputable in the town. I believe we all went back to the Scotchman not merely out of loyalty but because he touched our need for a simple and unmitigated eloquence. In Mississippi, I sometimes think now, it was the final flowering of a poetic age.

92

Jules Feiffer

IT STARTED WHEN I WAS A LITTLE KID AND I WAS PLAYING BALL AND I WAS IN A TIGHT SPOT- SO INSIDE MY HEAD I BEGAN **ANNOUNCING** MY WAY THROUGH THE BALL GAME:- "O.K. THE COUNT IS THREE AND TWO. JOEY STEPS OUT OF THE BOX. DIGS A TOE INTO THE DIRT. O.K.-HE'S BACK IN NOW. HE CHECKS THE RUNNERS. HE'S INTO THE WINDUP. AND HERE'S THE PITCH--

FROM THAT POINT ON, INSIDE MY HEAD I WAY THROUGH **EVERYTHING**! SCHOOL. FOR INSTANCE :- "THE OLD SECOND HAND IS TICKING AWAY. THREE MINUTES TO GO IN THIS HISTORY EXAM. JOEY CAN'T SEEM TO COME UP WITH AN ANSWER TO QUESTION 5. HE LOOKS OUT THE WINDOW. HE PICKS AT A NAIL. HE LOOKS OVER AT THE OTHER KIDS— AND, **WAIT A MINUTE —IS HE?** **YES, HE IS! HE PICKS UP HIS PEN!**"

AND EVEN **AFTER** I GOT OUT OF SCHOOL:-"THE SUPERVISOR IS LOOKING OVER JOEY'S SHOULDER. JOEY PRETENDS TO BE BUSY. THE SUPERVISOR HAS FOUND A MISTAKE. JOEY CAN'T SEEM TO LISTEN. THE SUPERVISOR ASKS JOEY IF HE UNDERSTANDS. JOEY SAYS HE DOES. JOEY STARES OUT THE WINDOW. THE SUPERVISOR MOVES ON--"

"JOEY WANTS TO SCREAM."

I EVEN ANNOUNCED MY WAY THROUGH MY MARRIAGE:- "JOEY HAS NOTHING TO SAY. JOEY'S WIFE HAS NOTHING TO SAY. JOEY'S FATHER-IN-LAW SAYS ISN'T IT TIME YOU WERE MAKING SERIOUS PLANS, JOEY? JOEY DIGS A TOE INTO THE CARPET AND STARES OUT THE WINDOW. JOEY'S LITTLE BOY SAYS, FIX IT, DADDY."

AND SO IT GOES. FROM EARLY MORNING TO LATE AT NIGHT. EVEN WHEN I'M IN BED:-"JOEY POUNDS HIS PILLOW. HE CLOSES ONE EYE. HE CLOSES THE OTHER. HE FEELS SLEEP COMING. IT'S COMING---. JOEY'S WIDE AWAKE. JOEY SNEAKS DOWNSTAIRS AND MAKES HIMSELF A DRINK—

4-28

93

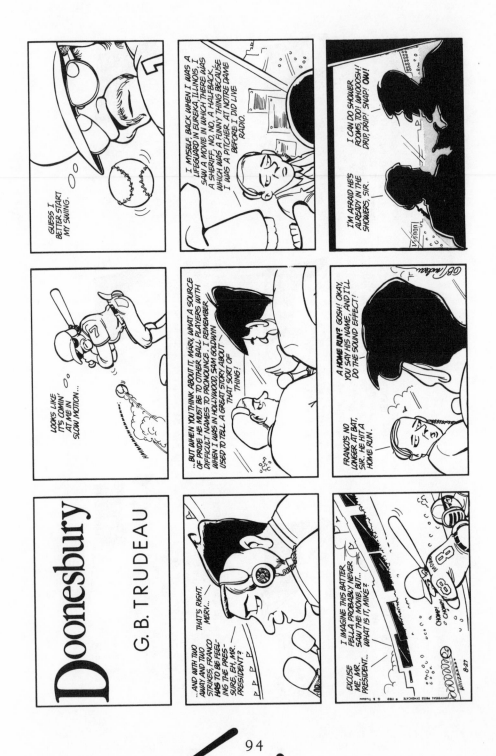

94

Backward, Turn Backward, O Commentator, in Thy Flights

BY OGDEN NASH

There is almost no major-league city in which I have not sat around a hotel
room with time to spare,
And innumerable are the ball games I have listened to on the air.
Innumerable also are the announcers who of ineptness are the quintessence,
Although they have the virtue of recalling to me the vanished and sometimes
golden days of my pre-adolescence.
Their terminology was stale even when the natty fan in moments of ecstasy
stamped on his brown derby hat;
I get the feeling that either Dick Rover or Napoleon Lajoie will be next at bat.
I hear the rattle of tin Lizzies and flivvers
When I am told that the hurler kicks, rocks, and either deals or delivers.
I am again a tan-cheeked boy with no socks
When the gardener first backpedals, then commits a miscue, and allows the
runner to dent the platter as Pale Hose bow to Bosox.
It's a brand-new ball game and I am an openmouthed child
When with two on, two out, and a count of two and two I learn that it's
deuces wild.
I will say for the announcers that in Latin-American pronunciation they are
completely or even too completely versed.
It gives me infinite pleasure to know that Hozay is on third, Hayzoos is on
second, and—shades of Abbott and Costello—Hoolio's on first.

Jeff MacNelly, the creator of "Shoe," is the quintessential "long-suffering" fan. In other words, he roots for the Chicago Cubs, the team that has gone longer than any other (almost half a century) without winning a pennant. (The Chicago columnist Mike Royko once suggested that fathers who teach their sons to be Cub fans should be charged with child abuse.) Still, MacNelly shares the sentiments of "Gee, It's a Wonderful Game," a song most notable because it proves that its co-creators could do other things much better. R. N. Lardner, the lyricist, gained greater fame as Ring Lardner, reporter and author, and G. Harris "Doc" White, the composer, won 197 games pitching for the Chicago White Sox. He is one of the best composers ever to pitch in the major leagues. He doesn't quite measure up, however, to a catcher named Hal Smith, who once wrote a Country-and-Western song called "I Got a Stomach Full of Chitlins, and a Bellyful of You."

SHOE   Jeff MacNelly

SHOE   Jeff MacNelly

Gee! It's a Wonderful Game

BY R. N. LARDNER
AND G. HARRIS (DOC) WHITE

Who discovered the land of the brave and the free?
I don't know, I don't know.
'Twas Christy Columbus is what they tell me;
Maybe so, I don't know.
There's only one Christy that I know at all,
One Christy that I ever saw,
He's the one who discovered the fade away ball,
And he pitches for Muggsy McGraw.

Baseball, Baseball, ain't it a wonderful game?
Old Christy Colum' found this country, by gum,
But the extras don't carry his name.
If old man Columbus had sat in the stand,
Had seen Matty pitching that "fader" so grand,
He'd have said, "Boys, I'm glad I discovered this land."
Gee! it's a wonderful game.

Who lost out in the battle of old Waterloo?
I don't know, I don't know.
They say 'twas Napoleon, maybe it's true;
Maybe so, I don't know.
The pink sheets don't print Mister Bonaparte's face,
No stories about him today,
'Cause he never could hold down that old second base,
Like his namesake, Big Nap Laj'ooway.

Baseball, Baseball, ain't it a dandy old game?
The Gen'ral of France couldn't lead 'em like Chance,
So no wonder his Waterloo came.
If down in his pocket Napoleon had dug,
Had paid his five francs to see Tyrus Cobb slug,
He'd have said, "I give up, I'm a bug, I'm a bug."
Gee! it's a wonderful game.

*T*he Brooklyn Dodgers never went almost half a century without winning a pennant. They did, however, go more than half a century without winning a World Series. But they were the best team in the world at inspiring laughter, and not always for their play. The absolute classic baseball cartoon is George Price's parody of a sign that graced the right-field wall of Ebbets Field, the home of the Dodgers. The real sign said Abe Stark, not Abe Feldman, and Stark the clothier became, in time, the elected president of the borough of Brooklyn; he represented millions of people, but he was always better known for the right-field sign in the ball park that John Lardner, the son of Ring Lardner, and heir to Ring's writing genes, called "the mother temple of daffiness." John Lardner paid homage to the high priest of that temple, Floyd "Babe" Herman.

Babe Herman

BY JOHN LARDNER

FLOYD CAVES HERMAN, KNOWN AS BABE, did not always catch fly balls on the top of his head, but he could do it in a pinch. He never tripled into a triple play, but he once doubled into a double play, which is the next best thing. For seven long years, from 1926 through 1932, he was the spirit of Brooklyn baseball. He spent the best part of his life upholding the mighty tradition that anything can happen at Ebbets Field, the mother temple of daffiness in the national game.

Then he went away from there. He rolled and bounced from town to town and ball club to ball club. Thirteen years went by before he appeared in a Brooklyn uniform again. That was in the wartime summer of 1945, when manpower was so sparse that the desperate Dodger scouts were snatching beardless shortstops from the cradle and dropping their butterfly nets over Spanish War veterans who had played the outfield alongside Willie Keeler. In the course of the great famine Branch Rickey and Leo Durocher lured Babe Herman, then forty-two, from his turkey farm in Glendale, California, to hit a few more for the honor of Flatbush. A fine crowd turned out to watch the ancient hero on the first day of his reincarnation.

"It looks like they haven't forgotten you here, Babe," said one of the players, glancing around the grandstand.

Mr. Herman shook his head. "How could they?" he said with simple dignity.

And he went on to show what he meant. In his first time at bat he was almost thrown out at first base on a single to right field. The Babe rounded the bag at a high, senile prance, fell flat on his face on the baseline, and barely scrambled back to safety ahead of the throw from the outfield. The crowd roared with approval. Fifteen years earlier they would have booed themselves into a state of apoplexy, for that was a

100

civic ritual at Ebbets Field—booing Herman. But this was 1945. You don't boo a legend from out of the past, a man who made history.

Before he went home to California to stay, a few weeks later, the Babe gathered the younger players around his knee and filled them with bloodcurdling stories about his terrible past.

"You know that screen on top of the right-field fence," he said. "They put that there on account of me. I was breaking all the windows on the other side of Bedford Avenue."

Looking around to see if this had sunk in, he added, "There used to be a traffic tower on Bedford Avenue there. Once I hit one over the wall that broke a window in the tower and cut a cop's hand all to pieces. Wasn't my fault," said the Babe philosophically. "When I busted 'em, there was no telling where they'd go."

It's beyond question that Mr. Herman could bust them. He always admitted it. He used to be irritated, though, by the rumor that he was the world's worst outfielder and a constant danger to his own life. He was also sensitive about his base running.

"Don't write fresh cracks about my running," he once told an interviewer, "or I won't give you no story. I'm a great runner."

He proceeded to tell why he stole no bases in 1926, his first year with Brooklyn, until the very end of the season. It seems that the late Uncle Wilbert Robinson, then managing the Dodgers, came up to Mr. Herman one day and said sourly, "What's the matter, can't you steal?"

"Steal?" said the Babe. "Why, hell, you never asked me to."

So then he stole a couple of bases, to prove he could do everything.

One talent for which Babe never gave himself enough public credit was making money. He was one of the highest-salaried players of his time, year after year. He got these salaries by holding out all through the training season. Other players, starving slowly on the ball club's regular bill of fare in Southern hotels, used to go down the street to the restaurants where Herman, the holdout, ate, and press their noses against the window like small boys, watching the Babe cut huge sirloin steaks to ribbons. It wasn't just the food that kept Babe from signing early. Holding out is a common practice with good-hit-no-field men like Herman, Zeke Bonura, and Rudy York in his outfielding days. The reason is obvious. The longer they postpone playing ball in the spring

(for nothing), the less chance there is of getting killed by a fly ball.

Mr. Herman had such ambitious ideas about money that one year, returning his first contract to the Brooklyn office unsigned, he enclosed an unpaid bill from his dentist for treatment during the winter. The ball club ignored the bill. After all, Herman didn't hit with his teeth.

The Babe, as a player, was a gangling fellow with spacious ears who walked with a slouch that made him look less than his true height, six feet four inches. He was born in Buffalo in 1903. Leaving there for the professional baseball wars in 1921, Mr. Herman worked for eighteen different managers before he met up with Uncle Robbie, and for nine more after that. It is said that he broke the hearts of 45 per cent of these gentlemen. The rest avoided cardiac trouble by getting rid of the Babe as fast as they could.

He came up from Edmonton, in the Western Canada League, to Detroit, in the year 1922, and was promptly fired by Ty Cobb, the Tigers' idealistic manager.

"The Detroit club," said the Babe, his feelings wounded, "has undoubtedly made some bad mistakes in its time, but this is the worst they ever made."

He was fired from the Omaha club later in the same year while batting .416. A pop fly hit him on the head one day, and the Omaha owner lost his temper. The owner and the manager began to argue.

"Much as I would like to," said the manager, "I can't send away a man who is hitting four sixteen."

"I don't care if he's hitting four thousand!" yelled the owner. "I am not going to have players who field the ball with their skulls. Fire him!"

The Babe explained later that the incident was greatly exaggerated.

"It was a foul ball," he said, "that started to go into the stands. The minute I turned my back, though, the wind caught the ball and blew it out again, and it conked me. It could happen to anybody."

Just the same, Mr. Herman was fired.

The Babe tried baseball in Boston briefly, when Lee Fohl managed the Red Sox. He never played an inning there. Studying his form on the bench, Mr. Fohl fired him. The Babe was just as well pleased. He said the Boston climate did not suit him. He went to Atlanta, where

Otto Miller, later a Brooklyn coach, managed the team. Every morning for five days in a row Mr. Miller resolved to fire Mr. Herman. Every afternoon of those five days Mr. Herman got a hit that drove in runs and changed Mr. Miller's mind for the night. On the fifth day, playing against Nashville, he had four hits in his first four times at bat. He was robbed of a fifth hit by a sensational catch by Kiki Cuyler. After the game Mr. Miller told the Babe that they might have won the game but for Cuyler's catch. He meant it kindly, but Mr. Herman took it as a personal criticism of himself. He was hurt. He began a loud quarrel with Otto, and was traded to Memphis on one bounce.

The Brooklyn club bought the Babe for $15,000 a couple of years later, while he was causing nervous breakdowns and busting up ball games in Seattle. Then Brooklyn tried to get rid of him for nothing, and failed. This gross insult to the name of Herman occurred as follows: The Dodgers wanted a Minneapolis player, of no subsequent consequence, named Johnny Butler. They traded Herman and eight other men to Minneapolis for Butler. Minneapolis took the eight other men but refused to take Herman. Brooklyn was stuck with the Babe, and history began to be made.

Jacques Fournier, the Dodger first baseman, hurt his leg one day in the summer of 1926. Herman replaced him. He had a good season at bat that year and the Brooklyn fans began to take to the Babe, wide ears, chewing tobacco, and all. Uncle Robbie took to him some days. Other days he gave him pause, like the day famous in ballad and prose when Mr. Herman smote a two-base hit that ended in a double play.

The bases were full of Brooklyns, with one out, when the Babe strode to the plate on that occasion, swinging his bat like a cane in his right hand. Physically, he was a phenomenon, a left-handed hitter with most of his power in his right arm. Scattered around the landscape before him were Hank DeBerry, the Brooklyn catcher, on third base; Dazzy Vance, the Dodger fireball pitcher, on second; and Chick Fewster, an outfielder, on first. Mr. Herman swung ferociously and the ball hit the right-field wall on a line. DeBerry scored. Vance, however, being a man who did not care to use his large dogs unnecessarily, hovered between second and third for a moment on the theory that the ball might be caught. When it rebounded off the wall, he set sail again, lumbered to

third base, and made a tentative turn toward home. Then, deciding he couldn't score, he stepped back to third. This move confounded Fewster, who was hard on Vance's heels. Fewster started back toward second base. At that moment, a new character, with blond hair and flapping ears, came into their lives.

Mr. Herman has described himself as a great runner. What he meant was, he was a hard runner. He forgot to mention that he ran with blinkers on, as they say at the race track. He concentrated on running and ignored the human and animal life around and ahead of him. Passing Fewster like the Limited passing a whistle stop, the Babe slid into third just as Vance returned there from the opposite direction. Herman was automatically out for passing Fewster on the baseline, though nobody realized it at once but the umpire, who made an "out" sign. The third baseman, not knowing who was out, began frantically to tag Herman, who was already dead, and Vance, who stood perfectly safe on third base.

"What a spectacle!" observed Vance nonchalantly to Herman, as the third baseman looked in vain to the umpire for the sign of another out. Fewster, confused, stood a little distance away. His proper move was to go back to second and stay there, but Herman's slide had destroyed his powers of thought. Finally the third baseman caught on. He began to chase Fewster, who ran in a panic and did not even stop at second, where he would have been safe. He was tagged in the outfield for the third out of the inning.

Cheap detractors may say what they like about Herman's merely doubling into a double play. It's obvious that what he really did—the rule book to the contrary—was triple into a double play.

It's also obvious that Vance and Fewster were as much at fault as Herman. That is the old, true spirit of Brooklyn co-operation. But Vance regarded Herman as the star of the act. A few years afterward, when Chicago officials announced that they expected a Chicago pennant in 1933 to make things complete for the Century of Progress exposition, Vance announced his counterplan for that year in Brooklyn. Instead of a Century of Progress, said Dazzy, they would feature "A Calvacade of Chaos; or, the Headless Horsemen of Ebbets Field." Herman was to be the star. Unfortunately, by the time the year 1933 rolled into

104

Brooklyn, Herman had rolled out of there to quieter pastures.

Uncle Robbie's comment on the celebrated double play of 1926 was "————." However, that was Robbie's comment on practically everything, and he meant it in a friendly way. He was tolerant of Herman, for he understood that criticism or scolding drove the Babe crazy. When 30,000 people booed him in unison—and that happened often enough in 1927, when his batting average slipped to .272, and 1929, when he led the league's outfielders in errors—the Babe would sulk for days. It took Robbie a little while, at that, to learn patience with Herman. He asked waivers on him in 1927 but changed his mind and kept the Babe when John McGraw, of the New York Giants, refused to waive.

"If that crafty blank-blank McGraw wants him," reasoned Mr. Robinson, "there must be something in him."

As time went on, the Brooklyn crowds became more sympathetic, too. That's understandable. After 1927, Herman hit for averages of .340, .381, .393, .313, and .326. In 1930 he had 241 hits for a total of 426 bases, including 35 home runs. He scored 143 runs and batted in 130. The fans barbecued him one moment and cheered him the next.

"Not only is that fellow a funny-looking blank-blank-blank," said the manager, "but he is blankety-blank unlucky. Other men, when they're on third base, can sometimes beat the outfielder's catch when they start home on a fly ball. But not this blankety-blank Herman. He always gets called for it."

The wailing and the keening were great in Brooklyn when the Babe, called by Rogers Hornsby "the perfect free-swinger," was traded to Cincinnati in December 1932, in a six-player deal. It was not a bad deal for Brooklyn, in a strictly practical way. Herman never hit in high figures again after that year, while some of the players from Cincinnati helped the Dodgers into the first division. But the fans, in the main, never forgave Max Carey, who had replaced Uncle Robbie as manager, for sending Herman away. They didn't care about being practical. They wanted salt in their stew.

Removed from the choice Brooklyn atmosphere where he had flourished, the Babe began to bounce from place to place again as he had in the days of his youth. Managers resumed the practice of firing him

to save their health. He went from Cincinnati to Chicago to Pittsburgh to Cincinnati to Detroit to Toledo to Syracuse to Jersey City, and finally, with a strong tail wind, clear out to the Pacific Coast. The slower he got as a player, the more money he asked, and the more loudly he asked for it. The Babe, however, did not like the word "holdout." Once, in the early spring of 1934, he denounced the press of Los Angeles, near his home, for using that term to describe him.

"You got the wrong idea entirely," he told the reporters sternly. "I am not holding out. I just don't want to sign this————contract the Cubs have sent me, because the dough ain't big enough."

On his second time around in Cincinnati, in 1936, Mr. Herman came into contact with baseball's leading genius, Leland Stanford MacPhail, who was the Reds' general manager. They were bound to get together sometime, even though the Babe left Brooklyn before MacPhail was ripe for that city. It was also inevitable that MacPhail should some day fine Herman, and some day fire him. They were not made to be soulmates. MacPhail fined him and Paul Derringer, the pitcher, two hundred dollars each, one day in July. It was a true Herman episode. With hostile runners on first and third, Derringer made a balk, the runner on third went home, and the runner on first went to second. Herman, communing with nature in the outfield, missed the play completely. He thought there were still men on first and third. When the next hitter singled to the Babe on one bounce, he studied the stitches on the ball and lobbed it back to the infield. The runner on second scored standing up. MacPhail turned purple and levied his fines on both the pitcher and the Babe.

It's a matter of record that Derringer got his fine canceled by throwing an inkwell at MacPhail, which impressed the great man. Mr. Herman was less direct, and therefore less successful. He waited a few weeks after being fined; then he demanded from MacPhail a cash bonus over and above his salary. It was an ill-timed request.

"A bonus!" yelled the genius. "Why, you're not even good enough to play on the team!" He added that Herman was fired. And he was.

Right to the end of his playing days the Babe retained his fresh young affection for cash money. He was farming turkeys at his home in Glendale by the time he landed with the Hollywood club of the Pacific

106

Coast League in the twilight of his career. One day in 1942—just a short while before that final, nostalgic, wartime bow in Brooklyn—he arranged to have his turkeys advertised on the scorecards in the Hollywood ball park. He then announced that he was holding out. The holdout kept him home in comfort among the turkeys, but not so far away from Hollywood that he couldn't drive over from time to time to negotiate. When he finally got his price and signed up to play ball, the Babe was fat and his reflexes were slow. So he made his season's debut at a disadvantage.

Hollywood was playing a game with Seattle. The score was tied going into the tenth inning. Seattle's young pitcher, a kid named Soriano, had already struck out ten men. Hollywood filled the bases on him, with two out, in the last of the tenth, but the boy was still strong and fast. The manager asked Mr. Herman if he was in shape to go in and pinch hit.

"I may not be sharp," said the Babe, reaching for a bat, "and maybe I can't hit him. But I won't have to. I'll paralyze him."

He walked to the plate. He glowered at the pitcher and held his bat at a menacing angle. He never swung it. Five pitches went by—three of them balls, two of them strikes. Then Mr. Herman pounded the plate, assumed a fearful scowl, and made as though his next move would tear a hole in the outfield wall. The last pitch from the nervous Soriano hit the ground in front of the Babe's feet for ball four. A run was forced in, and the ball game was over.

"That's a boy with an education," said the Babe, as he threw away his bat. "I see he's heard of Herman."

The Dodgers stopped being a baseball joke, on the field, in the 1940s (with occasional lapses, one punctuated by the wartime comeback of the aging Babe Herman) under the leadership of manager Leo Durocher, who knew both baseball and show business. Durocher appeared on Garry Moore's radio show and made fun of his own tendency to scream, yell and kick dirt at umpires. Leo was gone by the time the Dodgers won their first World Series, in 1955, but Willard Mullin, the foremost sports cartoonist of his and all other days, was not. Mullin, whose marvelous masterpieces dominated the sports page of the New York World-Telegram & Sun, *had created his shabby symbol of the Dodgers after a cab driver casually asked him, "How did our bums do today?" Dem Bums did great in '55. Two years later, the Dodgers abandoned Brooklyn, fled to Los Angeles. Playwright Herb Gardner, author of* A Thousand Clowns *and* I'm Not Rappaport, *mourned the Dodgers' departure, saw it as a sign of the decay of Western civilization.*

"Philco Radio Hall of Fame"

WITH LEO DUROCHER
AND GARRY MOORE

MOORE: April the first this year brings spring. It brings Easter, and it brings the training season for America's national sport, baseball. We think that a place on the Radio Hall of Fame has been earned by one of the most colorful figures ever developed in baseball. Ladies and gentlemen, the manager of the Brooklyn Dodgers, Leo "Lippy" Durocher.

[APPLAUSE & MUSIC]

Leo, as manager of the Brooklyn Dodgers, maybe we can get some firsthand information. Now in your opinion, how are the teams going to end up in the pennant race?

DUROCHER: Well, Garry, it looks like it's going to be very close.

MOORE: It does?

DUROCHER: Yes. I don't know whether it's the Giants or the Cards for second place. [LAUGHTER]

MOORE: And for first place?

DUROCHER: Who else?

MOORE: Pardon me.

DUROCHER: Not at all. [*LAUGHTER*] Let me ask you, Garry, speaking objectively.

MOORE: Objectively?

DUROCHER: Oh, it's a word I picked up while trying out for the Boston Braves. [*LAUGHTER*] Speaking objectively, how do you think the Dodgers will come out this year?

MOORE: Huh? Wha? I didn't hear you. What were you saying?

DUROCHER: Uh, how do you think the Dodgers will come out this year?

MOORE: From what I hear, in wheelchairs. [*LAUGHTER*]

DUROCHER: Well, uh, we have been hit pretty bad by the manpower shortage.

MOORE: Yeah, I imagine it must be tough.

DUROCHER: Sure. You find a good man. You sign him up. He's all ready to start the season with you. And bing! He gets that letter from the government.

MOORE: His draft notice?

DUROCHER: No. His old age pension. [*LAUGHTER*]

MOORE: Oh, that makes it tough. Then you gotta break in a new man.

DUROCHER: Yeah, but with my system it's easy.

MOORE: Oh, you've got a system?

DUROCHER: Yeah. I'll give you a for instance.

MOORE: Uh-huh.

DUROCHER: I need a right fielder.

MOORE: Yeah?

DUROCHER: That's all. If he can get there, he's got the job. [*LAUGHTER*]

MOORE: And if he can't quite make it out to right field under his own power?

DUROCHER: He plays first base. [*LAUGHTER*]

MOORE: He plays first base if he makes it. And I suppose if he can't budge at all you prop him up behind home plate, put on an oxygen tent over him, and he's the catcher?

DUROCHER: Unless he's too old and can't even see. Then he automatically becomes the umpire. [*LAUGHTER*] By the way, Garry, what ever became of Magerkurth?

MOORE: I, I don't know, Leo, but I hope you'll send me a ticket to the opening game. I certainly want to be there when you slug the first umpire.

DUROCHER: Wait a minute, Garry. You've got me all wrong. You're looking at the new Durocher.

MOORE: Frankly, Leo, I don't see much improvement. [*LAUGHTER*]

DUROCHER: Well, you remember how it used to be out at Ebbets field. My

110

pitcher would throw a ball right across the plate. Waist high. So naturally the umpire says . . .

UMPIRE: Baaaaall one!

DUROCHER: What? That one was right in the groove!

UMPIRE: I said ball one!

DUROCHER: Don't you know a strike when you see one, you blind fathead?

UMPIRE: That'll cost you a twenty-five-dollah fine!

DUROCHER: Why, you cement-head!

UMPIRE: That'll cost ya fifty dollahs!

DUROCHER: Why you—you—! I could tell you what you really are, but I can't afford it! [LAUGHTER]

MOORE: Er, yeah, that sounds like the old Durocher all right, Leo.

DUROCHER: Oh, but now you're looking at the new Durocher, Garry. High-class, cultured all over! This season I'm going to be polite or bust!

MOORE: Uh-huh. Polite or bust. Would you mind standing back out of the way so you won't splash anybody? [LAUGHTER]

DUROCHER: Oh, Garry, the whole club is high-class now. You know how a ball player grips his bat?

MOORE: Yeah?

DUROCHER: Well, on our team we do it with the pinky sticking out. [LAUGHTER]

MOORE: Things are going to look awfully strange at Ebbets field this year!

DUROCHER: Well, for instance, the same pitcher throws the same kind of a ball, straight down the center. So the umpire says . . .

UMPIRE: Baaall one!

DUROCHER: Oh, you must be mistaken! [LAUGHTER]

UMPIRE: I said ball one!

DUROCHER: Well, you know best!

UMPIRE: And I don't want no arguments either!

DUROCHER: Oh, I'm sorry. I guess I lost my head. Pardon me, I must confer with my pitcher. Oh, Mr. Moore! Oh, Mr. Moore!

MOORE: Coming, Mr. DuRochay! [LAUGHTER] By the way, do you think I should throw a slow curve to this gentleman at bat? [LAUGHTER]

DUROCHER: Would you mind a suggestion, Mr. Moore?

MOORE: Perish the thought, Mr. DuRochay! [LAUGHTER]

DUROCHER: I would suggest a fast ball. We don't want to be late for tea. [LAUGHTER]

MOORE: Quite, quite so. And, Leopold? [LAUGHTER]

DUROCHER: Yes. Garrison? [LAUGHTER]

MOORE: Leopold, you remember the chap to whom I pitched four balls thereby allowing him to reach first base?

DUROCHER: Yes?

MOORE: Well, don't look now, but he's scampering like mad towards second. [LAUGHTER]

DUROCHER: Well, Garry, if he's the type of fellow who would steal second base, let's pay no attention to him. He'll just *hate* himself in the morning. [LAUGHTER]

UMPIRE: Ah, play ball!

DUROCHER: Hey, that's that ruffian from the St. Louis team, Butterball Whiteman. [LAUGHTER]

MOORE: Butterball Whiteman? Now I'll have to throw a curve, otherwise I'll hit him! [LAUGHTER]

UMPIRE: Okay, let's go! Batter up!

[BALL HIT, OOHS AND AAHS FROM CROWD]

DUROCHER: Oh! Mr. Whiteman hit the ball a dandy clout! It is now rolling toward the pitcher's box. Oh, Mr. Moore?

MOORE: Yes, Mr. DuRochay?

DUROCHER: Have you retrieved the ball?

MOORE: Why, bless your little catcher's mitt! Of course, of course I have. [LAUGHTER]

DUROCHER: Well, Mr. Whiteman is running towards first base. You'd better throw it.

MOORE: Oh no, no. You throw it. I'm not on speaking terms with our first baseman. [LAUGHTER]

DUROCHER: Well, I'm not either.

MOORE: Oh heavens! We'd better think of something. We must think of something, Mr. Whiteman is fast approaching first base. [LAUGHTER]

DUROCHER: Well, I have it! Let's both walk over there with it.

MOORE: That would be dandy! Well, here we are at first base. What time is Mr. Whiteman due? [LAUGHTER]

DUROCHER: Here comes Butterball now.

WHITEMAN: (panting) Ho, ho, ho . . .

MOORE: There. I tagged him.

UMPIRE: Saaafe at first.

DUROCHER: Safe? Who said that?

UMPIRE: I said that. And I'm the umpire, that's who!

DUROCHER: You mean that's whom. [LAUGHTER]

MOORE: Yes, you see, old man, we frown on bad grammar here at Ebbets
Field.

UMPIRE: I said that's who, and I mean that's who!

DUROCHER: You don't understand! When you use the objective case—

UMPIRE: Watch your language!

DUROCHER: But you are erroneous!

UMPIRE: I'm a what? That'll cost ya twenny-fi' dollahs! [*LAUGHTER*]

DUROCHER: But you've misconstrued the—

UMPIRE: FIF-ty dollars! [*LAUGHTER*] What've you got to say now?

DUROCHER: Well, for the amount of money it's costing me, I can tell you what
I really think of you. You flat-headed, featherbrained, nearsighted . . .

MOORE: Leopold! Leopold!!

DUROCHER: Wall-eyed, biddy-eyed . . .

◆

THE TIMID SOUL   H.T. Webster

MR. MILQUETOAST KNOWS
BETTER THAN TO TALK TO
STRANGERS ON VITAL TOPICS

© 1941 N Y TRIBUNE INC

113

Herb Gardner writes good, and Herb Gardner writes long, sometimes too long for his own good. This speech was written for a play called The Goodbye People, *which was, in early drafts, a bit long. So this speech disappeared, then resurfaced a few years later, in modified form, in one of a trio of one-act plays called* Life and/or Death.

What follows is the original version. The Goodbye People *is about leavers: slow leavers, fast leavers, some for whom it's an art form, and one Max Silverman, who refuses to go. Max, at seventy-two, has come from the hospital, where he's "just recovered from a serious and delicate operation on my only heart." Before he dies, and mostly so he won't, he wants to reopen Max's Hawaiian Ecstasies, an old, boarded-up frankfurter stand under the boardwalk at Coney Island which has been closed for eighteen years. Unfortunately, it's mid-February and the beach is deserted, but Max is now, as he describes it, "buddies with the angel of death and operating on a very tight schedule." It is before dawn on the beach at Coney Island.*

"I'm Witcha, Duke, I'm Witcha"

BY HERB GARDNER

MAX: (*He enters from under the boardwalk; he wears an antique overcoat, a baseball cap with "Dodgers '55" printed on it and an unlit cigar that appears to be part of his face. He speaks in a rich, full-bodied, tasty, Jewish-Hungarian accent.*) Yessir, I'll tell you the truth about God; I got that boy's number. He's a joker, a fooler, a whimsical fellah and a rascal altogether. From all eternity, what moment does he pluck for Max? A whole bunch eras I would be a happy man: in the Age of Pericles—a winner; in the Renaissance—I fit like a glove; so where does that dopey God put me? In the Pepsi Generation! Max in the Burger Circus! The Vanishing Hungarian in Marlboro Country! A careful cobbler does custom work in the Thom McAnn factory,

114

making by hand beautiful sandals—around me they're puttin' out a million sneakers a day! You see the cap? Dodgers of '55. I do them honor. You ask me why an old cap? I'll tell you why. You don't throw Mozart away for Rodgers and Hammerstein. Dodgers, '55; you know who came to take their place? I'll tell you who. Nobody! They took Ebbetts Field away. You take the Pyramids away from Egypt all you got is sand and rotten weather. Walter O'Malley, he sells them like shoes without even discussing with me. What's left? Banks! You don't got teams now, you got Irving Trust plays Chemical Corn Exchange! They went, and the city went with them. The heart went with them and the city started to die. Look what you got now, look what you got without no heart. What's to root for? Without what to root the voice goes away. Duke Snider! He went away! How many years in the stands hollering? A life time in the afternoon hollering "I'm witcha, Duke, I'm witcha;" never dreaming for a moment that he wasn't with *me!* Edwin Donald Snider, six feet tall, 180 pounds, lefthanded batter, righthanded thrower, a person you *knew,* goes to California which doesn't even *exist!* They all went. Names. The names, just to say the names, you could sing them, Sandy Amoros, Jim Gilliam, Hodges, Newcombe, Campanella, Erskine, Furillo, Podres, gone, gone . . . even the sound is gone . . . to California, a wonderful place to die. They took them to California, they threw the lions to the Christians. What's left? A cap, I got a cap, Dodgers, '55, and sometimes on the wind I hear a gull, and Red Barber's voice. . . .

115

When the Dodgers left New York, all the laughter turned to sorrow—
till the Mets arrived. The Mets were born in 1962, lovable, laughable
losers. They were managed by Casey Stengel, who, almost 40 years earlier,
was labeled "old" by Damon Runyan; Runyan's reportage, abridged here,
is a fine example of work on a deadline, as impressive in its way as his
"Guys and Dolls" short stories. Stengel went on to manage the Yankees and,
as you can see in the excerpt from The Congressional Record, confound
the country before moving in with the Mets and Marv Throneberry. Columnist Stan Isaacs may have been the first to see the humor in Throneberry.
Pulitzer Prize winner Jimmy Breslin, a latter-day Runyan, captured the
comedy of the team in "Can't Anybody Here Play This Game?" from which
we have lifted a chapter, the one with the marvelous comparison of Throneberry the first baseman to Willie Sutton the bank robber. The Mets remained
futile, the stuff of comedy, for several reasons, as Dick Schaap's reports
from the 1965 season indicate. But, in 1969, something weird happened.
The Mets started to win. A book called The Year the Mets Lost Last Place
followed the team, minute-by-minute, through the first critical week of its
existence, and one of those dramatic days is reprinted here. By the end of
the season, the Mets were in, of all places, the playoffs, and Mort Gerberg
teamed up with a Life photographer for a report blending fact and fantasy,
a perfect reflection of the Mets' magic year. In his mind, Mort spied Richard
Nixon and Charlie Brown watching the Mets, all of them survivors of losing
streaks. The novelist Avery Corman offered a wholly different view of the
Mets phenomenon.

New York Giants 5, New York Yankees 4

BY DAMON RUNYON

THIS IS THE WAY OLD CASEY STENGEL RAN yesterday afternoon, running his home run home.

This is the way old Casey Stengel ran, running his home run home to a Giant victory by a score of 5 to 4 in the first game of the World Series of 1923.

This is the way old Casey Stengel ran, running his home run home, when two were out in the ninth inning and the score was tied and the ball was still bounding inside the Yankee yard.

This is the way—

His mouth wide open.

His warped old legs bending beneath him at every stride.

His arms flying back and forth like those of a man swimming with a crawl stroke.

His flanks heaving, his breath whistling, his head far back.

Yankee infielders, passed by old Casey Stengel as he was running his home run home, say Casey was muttering to himself, adjuring himself to greater speed as a jockey mutters to his horse in a race, that he was saying: "Go on, Casey! Go on!"

People generally laugh when they see old Casey Stengel run, but they were not laughing while he was running his home run home yesterday afternoon. People—60,000 of 'em, men and women—were standing in the Yankee stands and bleachers up there in the Bronx roaring sympathetically, whether they were for or against the Giants.

"Come on, Casey!"

The warped old legs, twisted and bent by many a year of baseball campaigning, just barely held out under Casey Stengel until he reached the plate, running his home run home.

117

Then they collapsed.

They gave out just as old Casey slid over the plate in his awkward fashion as Wally Schang made futile efforts to capture the ball which eluded him and rolled toward the dugout. Billy Evans, the American League umpire, poised over him in a set pose, arms spread to indicate that old Casey was safe.

Half a dozen Giants rushed forward to help Casey to his feet, to hammer him on the back, to bawl congratulations in his ears as he limped unsteadily, still panting furiously, to the bench where John J. McGraw, chief of the Giants, relaxed his stern features in a smile for the man who had won the game.

Casey Stengel's warped old legs, one of them broken not so long ago, wouldn't carry him out for the last half of the inning, when the Yankees made a dying effort to undo the damage done by Casey. His place in center field was taken by young Bill Cunningham, whose legs are still unwarped, and Casey sat on the bench with John J. McGraw.

No one expected much of Casey Stengel when he appeared at the plate in the Giants' side of the ninth inning, the score a tie at 4 to 4.

Ross Young and Irish Meusel, stout, dependable hitters, had been quickly disposed of by the superb pitching of Bullet Joe Bush.

No one expected Stengel to accomplish anything where they had failed. Bush, pitching as only Bush can pitch in an emergency, soon had two strikes and three balls on Casey.

He was at the plate so long that many of the fans were fidgeting nervously, wondering why he didn't hurry up and get put out, so the game could go on. Casey Stengel is not an imposing figure at bat, not an imposing figure under any circumstances. Those warped old legs have something to do with it. A man with warped legs cannot look very imposing.

People like to laugh at Casey—Casey likes to make people laugh.

A wayfarer of the big leagues—Brooklyn, Pittsburgh, Philadelphia, and finally New York—he has always been regarded by the fans as a great comedian, a funny fellow, a sort of clown.

The baseball land teems with tales of the strange didoes cut by Casey Stengel, whose parents started him out as Charles, with his sayings.

Who knows but that "Bullet Joe" may have been thinking of Casey

Stengel more as a comedian than as a dangerous hitter when he delivered that final pitch yesterday afternoon? Pitchers sometimes let their wits go wool-gathering.

"Bap"—Stengel's bat connected with the last pitch, connected surely, solidly. The ball sailed out over left field, moving high, moving far.

Long Bob Meusel and Whitey Witt, the Yankee outfielders, raced toward each other as they marked the probable point where the ball would alight, and in the meantime Casey Stengel was well advanced on his journey, running his home run home.

As the ball landed between Meusel and Witt it bounded as if possessed toward the left center-field fence. Everybody could see it would be a home run inside the yard, if Casey Stengel's warped old legs could carry him around the bases.

Witt got the ball about the time Stengel hit third, and about that time Stengel was laboring, "all out." Witt threw the ball in to Bob Meusel who had dropped back and let Witt go on. Meusel wheeled and fired for the plate, putting all his strength behind the throw. Few men have ever lived who can throw a baseball as well as Bob Meusel.

Stengel was almost home when Meusel's throw was launched, and sensing the throw Casey called on all that was left in those warped old legs, called no doubt on all the baseball gods to help him—and they helped.

It is something to win a World Series with a home run, and that home run inside the yard.

John J. McGraw perhaps feels that his judgment in taking Stengel on at a time when Casey was a general big-league outcast has been vindicated.

◆

If you are curious to know the origin of the nickname "Casey," it might be explained that Stengel's home town is Kansas City. . . .

Stengel is around thirty-three, if you are seeking more information about the first hero of the World Series of 1923. They call that old in baseball. He has been with the Giants since 1921, from the Philadelphia club. He is all right, Casey Stengel is, and you can prove it by John J. McGraw. . . .

From The Congressional Record

CASEY STENGEL

SENATOR KEFAUVER: MR. STENGEL, YOU ARE THE manager of the New York Yankees. Will you give us very briefly your background and your views about this legislation?

MR. STENGEL: Well, I started in professional ball in 1910. I have been in professional ball, I would say, for forty-eight years. I have been employed by numerous ball clubs in the majors and in the minor leagues.

I started in the minor leagues with Kansas City. I played as low as Class D ball, which was at Shelbyville, Kentucky, and also Class C ball and Class A ball, and I have advanced in baseball as a ballplayer.

I had many years that I was not so successful as a ballplayer, as it is a game of skill. And then I was no doubt discharged by baseball in which I had to go back to the minor leagues as a manager, and after being in the minor leagues as a manager, I became a major-league manager in several cities and was discharged, we call it discharged because there was no question I had to leave.

And I returned to the minor leagues at Milwaukee, Kansas City and Oakland, California, and then returned to the major leagues.

In the last ten years, naturally, in major-league baseball with the New York Yankees; the New York Yankees have had tremendous success, and while I am not a ballplayer who does the work, I have no doubt worked for a ball club that is very capable in the office.

I have been up and down the ladder. I know there are some things in baseball thirty-five to fifty years ago that are better now than they were in those days. In those days, my goodness, you could not transfer a ball club in the minor leagues, Class D, Class C ball, Class A ball.

How could you transfer a ball club when you did not have a highway? How could you transfer a ball club when the railroad then would take you to a town, you got off and then you had to wait and sit up five hours to go to another ball club?

120

How could you run baseball then without night ball?

You had to have night ball to improve the proceeds, to pay larger salaries, and I went to work, the first year I received $135 a month.

I thought that was amazing. I had to put away enough money to go to dental college. I found out it was not better in dentistry. I stayed in baseball. Any other question you would like to ask me?

SENATOR KEFAUVER: Mr. Stengel, are you prepared to answer particularly why baseball wants this bill passed?

MR. STENGEL: Well, I would have to say at the present time, I think that baseball has advanced in this respect for the player help. That is an amazing statement for me to make, because you can retire with an annuity at fifty and what organization in America allows you to retire at fifty and receive money?

I want to further state that I am not a ballplayer, that is, put into that pension fund committee. At my age, and I have been in baseball, well, I will say I am possibly the oldest man who is working in baseball. I would say that when they start an annuity for the ballplayers to better their conditions, it should have been done, and I think it has been done.

I think it should be the way they have done it, which is a very good thing.

The reason they possibly did not take the managers in at that time was because radio and television or the income to ball clubs was not large enough that you could have put in a pension plan.

Now I am not a member of the pension plan. You have young men here who are, who represent the ball clubs.

They represent the players and since I am not a member and don't receive pension from a fund which you think, my goodness, he ought to be declared in that, too, but I would say that is a great thing for the ballplayers.

That is one thing I will say for the ballplayers, they have an advanced pension fund. I should think it was gained by radio and television or you could not have enough money to pay anything of that type.

Now the second thing about baseball that I think is very interesting to the public or to all of us that it is the owner's own fault if he does not improve his club, along with the officials in the ball club and the players.

121

Now what causes that?

If I am going to go on the road and we are a traveling ball club and you know the cost of transportation now—we travel sometimes with three Pullman coaches, the New York Yankees and remember I am just a salaried man, and do not own stock in the New York Yankees, I found out that in traveling with the New York Yankees on the road and all, that it is the best, and we have broken records in Washington this year, we have broken them in every city but New York and we have lost two clubs that have gone out of the city of New York.

Of course, we have had some bad weather, I would say that they are mad at us in Chicago, we fill the parks.

They have come out to see good material. I will say they are mad at us in Kansas City, but we broke their attendance record.

Now on the road we only get possibly 27 cents. I am not positive of these figures, as I am not an official.

If you go back fifteen years or so if I owned stock in the club, I would give them to you.

SENATOR KEFAUVER: Mr. Stengel, I am not sure that I made my question clear.

MR. STENGEL: Yes, sir. Well, that is all right. I am not sure I am going to answer yours perfectly, either.

SENATOR O'MAHONEY: How many minor leagues were there in baseball when you began?

MR. STENGEL: Well, there were not so many at that time because of this fact: Anybody to go into baseball at that time with the educational schools that we had were small, while you were probably thoroughly educated at school, you had to be—we only had small cities that you could put a team in and they would go defunct.

Why, I remember the first year I was at Kankakee, Illinois, and a bank offered me $550 if I would let them have a little notice. I left there and took a uniform because they owed me two weeks' pay. But I either had to quit but I did not have enough money to go to dental college so I had to go with the manager down to Kentucky.

What happened there was if you got by July, that was the big date. You did not play night ball and you did not play Sundays in half of the cities on account of a Sunday observance, so in those days when

122

things were tough, and all of it was, I mean to say, why they just closed up July 4 and there you were sitting there in the depot.

You could go to work someplace else, but that was it.

SENATOR CARROLL: The question Senator Kefauver asked you was what, in your honest opinion, with your forty-eight years of experience, is the need for this legislation in view of the fact that baseball has not been subject to antitrust laws?

MR. STENGEL: No.

SENATOR LANGER: Mr. Chairman, my final question. This is the Anti-monopoly Committee that is sitting here.

MR. STENGEL: Yes, sir.

SENATOR LANGER: I want to know whether you intend to keep on monopolizing the world's championship in New York City.

MR. STENGEL: Well, I will tell you. I got a little concern yesterday in the first three innings when I saw the three players I had gotten rid of, and I said when I lost nine what am I going to do and when I had a couple of my players. I thought so great of that did not do so good up to the sixth inning I was more confused but I finally had to go and call on a young man in Baltimore that we don't own and the Yankees don't own him, and he is doing pretty good, and I would actually have to tell you that I think we are more the Greta Garbo type now from success.

We are being hated, I mean, from the ownership and all, we are being hated. Every sport that gets too great or one individual—but if we made 27 cents and it pays to have a winner at home, why would not you have a good winner in your own park if you were an owner?

SENATOR KEFAUVER: Thank you very much, Mr. Stengel. We appreciate your presence here. Mr. Mickey Mantle, will you come around? . . . Mr. Mantle, do you have any observations with reference to the application of the antitrust laws to baseball?

MR. MANTLE: My views are just about the same as Casey's.

"Last week five former baseball greats were indicted into the Hall of Fame."

—From a high school composition

Marvelous Marv

BY STAN ISAACS

HAT'S A LOVE AFFAIR FLOWERING BE-
tween the Met fans and Marv Throneberry. It's not quite
apparent right now because Throneberry is the only Met player the
fans at the Polo Grounds boo regularly. The perceptive mind, however,
can read beyond mere outward appearances. Just as love and hate are
the opposite sides of the same coin, so is this passion for Throneberry
building up among Met rooters. At the rate he was booed on the last
home stand, he may turn out to be one of the most popular athletes
New York ever had.

Right now, the love affair is in the stage where the lovers snap at
each other. They already suspect they might be liking each other and
that intensifies the bickering—until the whole thing flowers into true
love. I have already moved to be one of the first on the bandwagon
by forming a press-box chapter of the "I Love Marv Throneberry Club."
I am not disturbed that only one other has agreed to join—as mem-
bership secretary, because there would be no work. I can see other
potential members whose expressions of exasperation with Marv's work
indicate that they are potentially fervent club members.

A prime recruit would be the reporter who used the name, "Marvelous Marv," by which Throneberry is known in the press box, as a
form of scorn throughout a story about a game in which Throneberry
figured prominently: Marv forgot to touch third base on a triple and
he made a costly interference error.

Met clubhouse man Herb Norman took that as a cue and substituted
the sobriquet, "Marvelous Marv," for "Throneberry" on the namecard
above Throneberry's locker. "Other players might not go for that,"
Norman said. "But I can do it with Marv, because he has a good sense
of humor."

Marv appreciated the gag. He even pointed the sign out to the man

who wrote the story and told him before a doubleheader: "Hey, I've got good news for you—I'm playing in only one of the games today."

Marv is too big a man to be upset by bad writeups. "You once wrote something bad about me," he said to the president of his fan club, "but I never said anything, did I?" He didn't. The piece, which the president is sorry for because it kicked a man when he was down, knocked Throneberry for his seeming lack of spirited movement.

It is that lack of outward hustle and bustle that makes Throneberry a target for boos. Of course, his fielding and hitting failures have helped, but other Mets err and hit badly without becoming such a target. "These are my natural movements," Throneberry said. "If I were to start dashing about like little Elio Chacon just to look as if I were hustling, it would be phony."

Marv says, "They're not going to run me out of New York the way they did Norm Siebern." He points out that Mickey Mantle used to be booed. He is also able to comfort himself that some of the boos are directed at him because he plays instead of the No. 1 Met love, Gil Hodges.

The other day he even twitted Casey Stengel for going out to the mound to take out pitchers. "Every time you go out there, they start booing you. Are you trying to take away my fans?" Marv promises that one of these days, when the time is right, "I'm going to surprise them; I'm going to doff my cap to them in a big way, the way Stengel does."

If he does it at the right time, he should wow them. There have been some hints already of what will happen when the love affair does turn into the mad thing it is destined to be. The other day Throneberry ran a long way for a foul pop, then caught it with a deft stab just as he almost hit the field boxes. An ovation followed, and it seemed then that the time was ripe for Marv. All he had to do was make another good play or two, hit a few homers, and he would have them eating out of his glove.

Alas, he missed that chance. Shortly afterward, he not only fumbled a grounder, but then, as the pitcher came to take his toss, he threw an underhanded lob that went over the pitcher's head. "Gene Conley (a six-foot, eight-inch pitcher) would have had it," was the remark of one potential member of the fan club. This was the same chap who

refused to admit that Marv made a good play on the foul pop-up, saying he had overrun the ball. Which just goes to show how much this bloke is going to love Throneberry when the time comes.

People react negatively to Marv because they regard him as the prototype of the "losing ballplayer." Marv has been with the Yankees, Athletics, and Orioles so far and hasn't realized his slugging potential. Aware of the rap against him, Marv says: "So far I have never had a real chance. Wherever I have been, I have played behind an established first baseman. I feel that this is the first time I'm getting a full chance.

"I think I wasn't nearly ready to play when I first came to the Mets. I had not played in so long, I was defensive at the plate and not sharp in the field. I'm beginning to feel like an offensive hitter now. And I think my fielding will get better as I play more."

Those of us whose eyes are ready to see the glory of the coming of Marv Throneberry are aware that the marriage of Marvelous Marv and the Met fans was made a long time ago; the initials of Marvin Eugene Throneberry read M-E-T.

◆

Casey Stengel, who had an eye for talent, once said of an unpromising prospect, "He's nineteen years old, and in ten years, he's got a chance to be twenty-nine."

"Just Like the WPA"

BY JIMMY BRESLIN

The Mets is a very good thing.
They give everybody a job.
Just like the WPA.
—Billy Loes, the only pitcher in the history of baseball to be defeated in a World Series game
because he lost a ground ball in the sun

THE JOB PROGRESS SHEET IN THE OFFICE says the weather is clear, with a high for the day of 54 and a low of 40, which is fine to keep work moving along on this $19,100,000 stadium New York City is having built alongside its World's Fair grounds.

Outside, a pale sun washes what is now a latticework of steel, but which will be, hopefully by summer, a horseshoe-shaped ballpark seating 55,000 people. And crawling over the steel beams on this day is the flower of New York's construction trades, a group of 483 tin-hatted workers.

As you watch, you are struck with the immenseness of a construction job such as this one. Take that guy way up on the top, the one moving along a solitary white-painted beam that seems to be held up by nothing. His name is Tommy McLaughlin, and he has a wife and six kids at home. He is over five hundred feet in the air, without even a rope to hold onto. One strong gust of wind or one slippery spot on the beam, and that will do it. You'd be surprised how many times this happens on a construction job. But here he is, walking like a guy going over to play the jukebox in the neighborhood saloon. And all around the place there are workers just as high up and taking just as many chances. It makes you nervous to look at them.

It also would frighten hell out of you to pay them. McLaughlin is on the clock as an iron worker. At $5.25 an hour. There are steamfitters up there, too, and they come in at $5.37 an hour. Then there are electricians ($7.63), laborers ($4.94), wire lathers ($5.72), and operating engineers ($5.43). The payroll for this one day is going to run $15,585.72 by quitting time.

This is only part of the story. The planning and political wrangling that went on earlier were incredible. Why, once they argued for two days about how many toilets the new stadium should have. Plans called for 329, but somebody insisted that he would not be associated with a stadium that did not have at least 600 johns. Finally a Parks Commissioner named Newbold Morris put his foot down when he found an architect busily penciling in a spot to hook up Unit No. 526 of American Sanitary's best.

"What are we building, a ballpark or a place to go to the toilet?" Morris said.

You think of all these things as you stand and watch this big job. And then just for a minute, everything changes. The ground, piled with dirt and covered with empty beer cans and crushed coffee containers, turns into cropped Merion blue. The turf surrounds an infield that doesn't have a pebble on it. The bare steel beams turn into gleaming stands, and they are filled. You can hear the crowd making noise.

And now it hits you. Now you realize, for the first time, what this is all about. All of it, all of the workers risking their lives, and all of the huge payrolls and all of the political wrangling. There is a reason for it all:

They are building a brand-new stadium for Marv Throneberry.

Marvin Throneberry, who is known as Marvelous Marv to his admirers, plays first base for the New York Mets, the team which is going to play its home games in this new stadium. In fact, Marvelous Marv does more than just play first base for the Mets. He *is* the Mets.

The New York Mets are a team that was formed at the start of last season. They lost 120 games, which made them, on paper, the poorest team in modern baseball history. On the field they were even worse. The Mets did not lose games merely because they played badly. Never. The Mets lost because they played a brand of baseball which has not been seen in the Big Leagues in over twenty-five years. And in doing this they warmed the hearts of baseball fans everywhere. They became, in their first year of existence, almost a national symbol. Name one loyal American who can say that he does not love a team which loses 120 games in one season.

As far as all of sport is concerned, the Mets are the most delightful occurrence in a long time. For this is the era of the businessman in sports, and it has become as dry and agonizing a time as you would want to see. In golf, for example, all they talk about is how much money Arnold Palmer makes and how he uses top corporation thoroughness in running his career. This is fine for Palmer, but who ever wanted a sports guy to be like a business executive? Once the big thing in that sport was whether the bartender would close up in time for Walter Hagen to get out to the first tee on schedule. Things have gone like this every place else in sports too. And it is even worse in baseball. Today you hear of pension funds and endorsements, and the players all seem to know what to say and what not to say, and after a while, as you go around, everything seems to come down to this kind of conversation:

REPORTER: Did you know it was going to be a home run?

PLAYER: Sure.

REPORTER: How could you tell?

PLAYER: Because I seen it go into the stands.

The Mets have changed all this. In one season they stepped out and gave sports, and the people who like sports, the first team worthy of being a legend in several decades. And they are a true legend. This is rare. You see, most of the stories which have been handed down over the years about ballplayers or teams are either vastly embellished or simply not true at all. The stories dealing with Babe Herman of the old Brooklyn Dodgers are a good example. He was the worst outfielder ever to live, they tell you, and fly balls fell on his head and nearly killed him as a matter of course. Well, two or three guys we know who watched the old Dodgers for twenty years or more never saw Herman get hit any place by a baseball. And one of them, the respected Tommy Holmes of the *New York Herald-Tribune,* will go so far as to tell you that Herman was a good fielder. He had good hands and could move, Tommy insists. Once in a while he would misjudge a fly badly. But only once in a while. Day in and day out, he was as good as they ever came, Tommy says.

In fact, in eighteen years of being able to look at things and remember what I have seen, the only sports legend I ever saw who completely lived up to advance billing was Babe Ruth.

It was a hot summer afternoon, and the Babe, sweat dripping from his jowls and his shirt stuck to him, came off the eighteenth green at the old Bayside Golf Club in the borough of Queens and stormed into the huge barroom of the club.

"Gimme one of them heavens to Betsy drinks you always make for me," the Babe said in his gravelly voice.

The bartender put a couple of fistfuls of ice chunks into a big, thick mixing glass and then proceeded to make a Tom Collins that had so much gin in it that the other people at the bar started to laugh. He served the drink to the Babe just as it was made, right in the mixing glass.

Ruth said something about how heavens to Betsy hot he was, and then he picked up the glass and opened his mouth, and there went everything. In one shot he swallowed the drink, the orange slice and the rest of the garbage, and the ice chunks too. He stopped for nothing. There is not a single man I have ever seen in a saloon who does not bring his teeth together a little bit and stop those ice chunks from going in. A man has to have a pipe the size of a trombone to take ice in one shot. But I saw Ruth do it, and whenever somebody tells me about how the Babe used to drink and eat when he was playing ball, I believe every word of it.

Otherwise, most legends should be regarded with suspicion. Although, if one is to have any fun out of life, one should proceed with the understanding that reminiscences are to be enjoyed, not authenticated. But with the Mets you do not need any of this. They made it on their own and required no help from imaginative bystanders. This team was, simply, a great, colorful spectacle, and they are held here in the highest affection. The way they played baseball made them the sports story of our time. This was not another group of methodical athletes making a living at baseball. Not the Mets. They did things.

Which brings us back to Marvelous Marvin Throneberry. On a hot Sunday last summer at old Busch Stadium in St. Louis. The Mets were in the field. Marvelous Marv was holding down first base. This is like saying Willie Sutton works at your bank.

It was the eighth inning of the first game of a doubleheader, and

the Cardinals had Ken Boyer on first and Stanley Musial at third. Two were out. Boyer took a lead, then broke for second on the pitch. The throw to second from the Mets' catcher was, by some sort of miracle, perfect. It had Boyer beat a mile, and the Cardinal runner, only halfway down, turned and tried to go back to first. The Mets' second baseman, Rod Kanehl, threw to Throneberry. Boyer was trapped.

Standard operating procedure in a situation of this kind is for the man with the ball to chase the runner, but with one eye firmly fixed on the man on third. If he breaks for home, you're supposed to go after him and forget the other guy.

So Boyer turned and started to run away from Throneberry. This seemed to incense Marv. Nobody runs away from Marvin Throneberry. He took after Boyer with purpose. He did not even wink at Musial. Marvelous Marv lowered his head a little and produced wonderful running action with his legs. This amazed the old manager, Casey Stengel, who was standing on the top step of the Mets' dugout. It also amazed Mr. Musial, who was relaxing on third. Stanley's mouth opened. Then he broke for the plate and ran across it and into the dugout with the run that cost the Mets the game. Out on the basepaths, Throneberry, despite all his intentions and heroic efforts, never did get Boyer. He finally had to flip to his shortstop, Charley Neal, who made the tag near second.

It was an incredible play. But a man does not become an institution on one play.

Therefore. There was a doubleheader against the Chicago Cubs at the Polo Grounds, the Mets' home until their new park is ready. In the first inning of the first game Don Landrum of Chicago was caught in a rundown between first and second. Rundowns are not Throneberry's strong point. In the middle of the posse of Mets chasing the runner, Throneberry found himself face to face with Landrum. The only trouble was that Marvin did not have the ball. Now during a rundown the cardinal rule is to get out of the way if you do not have the ball. If you stand around, the runner will deliberately bang into you and claim interference, and the umpire will call it for him, too.

Which is exactly what happened. Landrum jumped into Throneberry's arms, and the umpire waved him safely to first. So, instead of

an out, the Cubs still had a runner at first—and the Mets were so upset the Cubs jumped them for a four-run rally.

When the Mets came to bat, Throneberry strode to the plate, intent on making up for the whole thing. With two runners on, Marv drove a long shot to the bullpen in right center field. It went between the outfielders and was a certain triple. As usual, Marv had that wonderful running action. He lowered his head and flew past first. Well past it. He didn't come within two steps of touching the bag. Then he raced to second, turned the corner grandly, and careened toward third. The stands roared for Marvin Throneberry.

While all this violent action and excitement were going on, Ernie Banks, the Cubs' first baseman, casually strolled over to Umpire Dusty Boggess.

"Didn't touch the bag, you know, Dusty," Banks said. Boggess nodded. Banks then called for the ball. The relay came, and he stepped on first base. Across the infield Throneberry was standing on third. He was taking a deep breath and was proudly hitching up his belt, the roar of the crowd in his ears, when he saw the umpire calling him out at first.

"Things just sort of keep on happening to me," Marvin observed at one point during the season.

Which they did. All season long. And at the end, here was this balding twenty-eight-year-old from Collierville, Tennessee, standing at home plate with a big smile on his face as he proudly accepted a boat which he had won as a result of a clothing-store contest. Throneberry was not too certain what he would do with the boat. The most water he had seen in several years was a filled-up bathtub on Saturday night back in Collierville. The nearest lake to his house is 150 miles away, and 150 miles as the coon dog runs, Marv cautioned. "Take the road, it's a little further," he said.

But this was all right. If he had been living in Johnstown, they would have given him a well pump. Things just go like this for Throneberry. It was all right with him. It was, that is, until two days later, when Marvin found out just how rough the season really was.

The whole incredible thing started in the agile brain of a Madison Avenue public-relations man whose accounts included a large chain

134

clothing company. He also represents a book publisher, but the clothing store does not hold that against him. The clothes client had made a ticket sales tie-in with the Mets. Just before the season started, the P.R. man barged into the clothing company's offices with an idea that was so hot he was dizzy from it.

"We'll put up a sign on the outfield fence," he said. "The player who hits it the most over the season gets a boat. Where do we get the boat? We work a tie-in with another client of mine who makes them. It'll be terrific."

The first sign certainly was. Out on the left-field fence, it spelled out the client's name, and inside a circle was a picture of the boat. Anybody who hit the circle on the fly got five points. Anybody who hit any other part of the sign on the fly received three points. If the ball hit it on the bounce it was worth two points. Whoever had the most points at the end of the season was to win the boat. An official point-keeper was assigned to watch every Met game and keep a tally on the points. Before half the season was over, the scorer wanted to go to the needle trades union over the matter.

The sign was a beauty. It also was remindful of the famous *New Yorker* cartoon which showed the outfield wall of a ballpark and a sign on it stating, "Hit the sign and Abe Feldman will give you a suit absolutely *free*." In front of the sign, hands on knees, was the outfielder, waiting for the next pitch. And right behind him, at the ready, was Abe Feldman. Abe was bald and he wore a vest. He had a catcher's mitt on his right hand and a first baseman's mitt on the other.

The clothing sign disturbed Casey Stengel, however. Upon seeing it for the first time, Casey squawked.

"We get to the end of the season, and I might need a couple of games to finish higher [optimism was rampant at this time] and what am I going to get? Everybody will be standing up there and going, whoom! Just trying to win theirselves a nice boat while I'm sittin' here hopin' they'll butcher boy the ball onto the ground and get me a run or two. I don't like it at all."

George Weiss, the Mets' general manager, moved quickly to satisfy Stengel. In a lifetime of baseball, Weiss has learned many things, one of which is that when a man like Stengel has a complaint of this

type, it is to be acted upon promptly. The sign, Weiss decreed, had to go.

He was telling this to the wrong guy. This P.R. man leaves in the middle of a job for only one reason: the client isn't coming up with the money.

"Casey is worried about his left-handed hitters *deliberately* trying to hit the left-field fence?" the P.R. man inquired in wonderment. Told that this was the case, he had an antidote. "My client is buying the same sign on the right-field fence," he announced. This cost the client another chunk of dough. So the contest was still on.

Over the year, Throneberry hit the sign in right field exactly four times. But twice his line drive landed inside the circle for five points, and on the last day of the home season at the Polo Grounds he found himself the proud owner of a $6000 luxury cabin cruiser.

The clothing company awarded another boat on the same day. It went to the Met who was named the team's most valuable player in a poll of sports writers. Richie Ashburn was the winner. Ashburn is from Nebraska.

"We'll both sail our boats all over the bathtub," Throneberry told the boat people. Marvelous Marv was in high humor.

A day later, Judge Robert Cannon, who handles legal matters for the Major League Baseball Players Association, told Marvelous Marv something about the boat. Humor fled as the judge spoke.

"Just don't forget to declare the full value," Cannon said.

"Declare it? Who to, the Coast Guard?" Throneberry asked.

"Taxes," Cannon said. "Ashburn's boat was a gift. He was voted it. Yours came the hard way. You hit the sign. You *earned* it. The boat is *earnings*. You pay income tax on it."

Last winter, at a very late date in the tax year, Throneberry sat in his living room in Collierville and he still was not quite over his conversation with Cannon.

"In my whole life I never believed they'd be as rough a year as there was last season," he said. "And here I am, I'm still not out of it. I got a boat in a warehouse someplace and the man tells me I got to pay taxes on it and all we got around here is, like I say, filled-up bathtubs and maybe a crick or two. I think maybe I'll be able to sell it off

136

someplace. I think you could say prospects is all right. But I still don't know what to do about that tax thing."

The whole season went this way for the Mets. Take any day, any town, any inning. With the Mets nothing changed, only the pages on the calendar. It was all one wonderful mistake.

There was the Fourth of July, which certainly has some significance, and the Mets were at Candlestick Park in San Francisco. Jim Davenport, the Giants' third baseman, swung at a pitch and lifted it high into the air. Rod Kanehl, the Met stationed at shortstop this time around, turned and raced into left field. Sunglasses flipping, glove up in the air, feet moving, Kanehl went for the ball.

The Mets' third baseman, Felix Mantilla, came in and made the catch right at the pitcher's mound.

There was even something about this team before it ever played a game. Go to the summer of 1961, before it was even formed, and you find that, at this time, the club hired the fabled Rogers Hornsby to prepare a scouting report on every player in the major leagues. The Mets of 1962 were to be formed with baseball players given to them by the other teams. As we are going to see, this little matter is, by itself, a saga of American charity rivaling that of United States Steel. Hornsby operated out of his home city of Chicago. He watched National League teams at Wrigley Field, which he did not like so much because only day games are played there and this interfered badly with his attendance at the horse races. He watched American League teams at Comiskey Park, which was a bit better because most of the games were played at night—although not so much, because he still had to look at baseball players.

"They say we're going to get players out of a grab bag," Hornsby said one afternoon at Wrigley Field. "From what I see, it's going to be a garbage bag. Ain't nobody got fat off eating out of the garbage, and that's just what the Mets is going to have to be doing. This is terrible. I mean, this is really going to be bad."

Rogers did not take his job lightly. On this day, for example, he slipped his hand into a pocket of his checked sports jacket and came out with a pair of contact lenses which he put on so he could study closely what was on the field, in front of him. And what was on the

137

field gagged the Rajah. In his time, Hornsby was an unbelievable hitter who three times finished with an average of over .400, reaching .424 in 1924, a record still standing. This background has not made him exactly tolerant of the ability of baseball players. To illustrate, we reprint herewith the most glowing report on an individual which Hornsby handed in all season:

LOOKS LIKE A MAJOR-LEAGUE PLAYER

The name at the top of the sheet said the report was about Mickey Mantle.

It did not take long for the Mets to have an adverse effect on Hornsby's luck. There was one day, when he had no game to attend, that Rajah got into his yellow Cadillac at a little before ten o'clock and headed for Arlington Heights, Illinois, a suburb of Chicago where Arlington Park Race Track happens to be located. En route to the track, Hornsby stopped for gas, or to have the windshield wiped, or just to stop, period, and each time he would jam himself into a phone booth and make phone calls dealing with situations at such places as Rockingham Park and Aqueduct.

He arrived at Arlington Park at 11:15. Post time for the first race was 2:30. This gave Rogers just enough time to get a seat in the grandstand—he feels the clubhouse is a place for suckers—and begin the tedious job of handicapping a nine-race card. He also had invested in two fifty-cent tout cards sold at the track entrance. One of them, in which Rogers placed great stock, had a horse named Frisky Phil, 15–1 in the morning line, on top in the sixth race.

Frisky Phil was trained by a Kentucky gentleman named Henry Forrest, and the Rajah caught up with Forrest before the race.

"This is a horse that's been out with leg trouble for seven months now," Forrest said. "As a rule now, only one horse in a hundred that's been away for six months or more can win first time out. The price should be 50–1 to begin with. Here you're takin' 15–1 on a horse that just don't seem to figure at all. Don't bet."

"Well, then you pick me a winner here in the race," Rajah said.

138

"I don't do that," Forrest said. "Every time I give out a horse, it loses, and a man don't make many friends like that."

"Never mind that, you just give me the horse you like in this race," Hornsby insisted.

Forrest relented and mentioned a horse, the name of which is forgotten. Hornsby bet $200 on him. The name of the horse is forgotten because of what happened in the race. Frisky Phil got out of the gate on top, and his legs folded and unfolded beautifully, and he never took a bad step. They are still trying to get him. He paid $33.60.

Hornsby went home. He did not forget.

Last season, as things got rougher and rougher with the Mets, Rogers Hornsby could be found at the Polo Grounds, or in Chicago and on his way to a scouting trip in Decatur, and he summed up his feelings in one bitter quote:

"You can't trust them Kentucky bastard trainers."

The Mets' run of luck held to the end. They finished their first season on September 30, a dull afternoon in Chicago. They were at Wrigley field, playing the Cubs. Losing, 5–1, in the eighth inning, the Mets went to work on Bob Buhl. Solly Drake opened with a single, then Richie Ashburn singled. Nobody out, runners on first and second, and Joe Pignatano, the catcher, up. Buhl gave him a fast ball, and Pignatano, a right-hander swinging late, hit a looper into right field. Drake, on second, thought the ball would drop in. He took off for third. Ashburn, on first, was certain the ball would drop in. He went for second.

Ken Hubbs, the Chicago second baseman, was absolutely positive he could catch the ball. He went out into right field and proved he was correct. Then he threw to Ernie Banks at first base. Ashburn was all the way to second. This made it a double play. It also gave Solly Drake, who was somewhere around third base, the idea that he was in trouble. He was. Banks threw to Andre Rodgers, who covered second, and it was a triple play.

It was things like this which made it a memorable summer for the manager of the team, Casey Stengel. But the season was no more memorable than Stengel was. At seventy-three, and coming from a run of ten pennants and eight world championships in twelve years of managing the New York Yankees, Stengel last year gave what must be

the finest performance of his life. He came to the Mets expecting it to be tough. He never expected it to be as tough as it turned out to be. But it made no difference. He gave one of the finest performances under bad circumstances that can be seen in any walk of life.

Casey Stengel last season was simply *the* stand-up guy. He went through 120 losses with a smile, a try, and a few badly needed drinks. He tried to teach his players. They simply could not learn. When he realized this, he would sit back and smile and take the heat off the poor player.

"I can't change a man's life," Stengel would say softly. When he put it that way, nobody was going to go out and make a point of how bad the player in question was.

Now there is supposed to be nothing new anybody can tell you about Casey Stengel. In his twelve years with the Yankees he was the most written-of and spoken-about figure in sports. When he was fired from the Yankees, he was given a huge check by *The Saturday Evening Post* to tell of his life in baseball. For free, Casey Stengel talks for hours. For the big check he sat down and wrecked tape recorders, and by now he is supposed to be an old story.

But if you had seen Stengel manage the New York Mets last season, you would know that he was anything but an old story.

You see, the notion here is that Stengel never quite was what he always was purported to be in the newspapers. The double-talk, for example. The man is not a double-talker. As colorful a conversationalist as we've ever had, yes. But a mysterious double-talker, never. Except when he was putting on a show. The newspaper sports writers, as a rule fairly horrible at writing quotes even from a plain talker, went overboard on Casey's double-talk gag. In doing so, they succeeded in losing much of his humor. And they also gave the reader the impression that Stengel was a man only Communists did not truly love.

Well, Stengel is a human being. And with the Yankees he had his human habits. One of which was to be awfully rough and impatient with young ballplayers at times. Once he called an outfielder named Norman Siebern into his office and gave him a going-over that was so rough there are baseball people today who insist it was the thing that ruined Siebern, who once was a tremendous prospect. And players like

140

Clete Boyer and Bobby Richardson, both the real goods, were anything but relaxed under Stengel. Richardson came this close to quitting baseball—and this is a fellow who acts, not talks—over Stengel's gruffness.

But last season Stengel was everything they ever wrote or said about him. He came with humor, compassion, and, above all, class. He also came onto some awfully tough days and nights, and, no matter how nice he was about it, you knew he really wasn't used to it.

There was one afternoon in training at St. Petersburg, Florida, when the exact quality of this ball club started to show itself to Casey. When he came into the clubhouse he did not seem to be completely filled with confidence.

And that night old Rogers Hornsby sat in his double-breasted suit in a chair a few strides from the bar of the Colonial Inn and expounded in the subtle, couched tones that have cost Rogers fifty jobs in baseball.

"Casey come back today like a ghost," he said. "I mean, those players out there frighten him. Like a ghost, I tell you. Don't you know, that man is used to good teams. These fellas here, I tell you they frighten you."

Throughout the year Stengel insisted he never was frightened. "Shocked" was the word he kept using. Back in the old days, as manager of the Brooklyn Dodgers and Boston Braves, he had had some bad players under him. But this was so long ago it was hard to recall. The problems Stengel were used to when he came to the Mets consisted mainly of nagging Mickey Mantle to chop down at a high pitch so that, in between his five-hundred-foot home runs, Mickey would not hit a fly ball or two that would be caught. With the Mets, Stengel was confronted with some rather strange things. His third baseman of record, Felix Mantilla, had a funny habit. If a ball was hit to the shortstop side of third, Mantilla broke toward the foul line. If the ball was hit down the foul line, Mantilla threw himself toward short. It was surprising how often balls went right past Mantilla because of this.

One memorable night in St. Louis, on the occasion of his seventy-third birthday, although he produced a doctored Kansas City certificate to show he was only seventy-two, Casey came into a private party room at the Chase Hotel with his gray hair slicked down, and he sat in a leather arm chair in front of a small cocktail table, accepted a Manhattan, and talked about his team.

"I've seen these do a lot of things to people," he said of the Manhattan. Then he began to puff on cigarettes and talk. He went from Brooklyn to Oakland to Kansas City and then to the Yankees and the old Newark Bears of the International League, and then he leaned forward and came to the Mets.

"We're going into Los Angeles the first time," he was saying, "and, well, I don't want to go in there to that big new ballpark in front of all them people and have to see the other fellas running around those bases the way they figured to on my pitchers and my catchers, too. Wills [Maury] and those fellows, they start running in circles and they don't stop and so forth and it could be embarrassing, which I don't want to be.

"Well, we have this Canzoneri [catcher Chris Cannizzaro] at Syracuse, and he catches good and throws real good and he should be able to stop them. I don't want to be embarrassed. So we bring him and he is going to throw out these runners."

Stengel took a big drag on the cigarette. Then he leaned forward and shook his head.

"We come in there and you never seen anything like it in your life. I find I got a defensive catcher, only who can't catch the ball. The pitcher throws. Wild pitch. Throws again. Passed ball. Throws again. Oops! The ball drops out of the glove. And all the time I am dizzy on account of these runners running around in circles on me and so forth.

"Makes a man think. You look up and down the bench and you have to say to yourself, 'Can't anybody here play this game?'"

Later, long after midnight and well after the birthday celebration was over, the bartender was falling asleep and the only sound in the hotel was the whine of a vacuum cleaner in the lobby. Stengel banged his empty glass on the red-tiled bar top and then walked out of the room.

In the lobby, the guy working the vacuum cleaner was on his big job, the rug leading into a ballroom, when Mr. Stengel stopped to light a cigarette and reflect on life.

"I'm shell-shocked," Casey addressed the cleaner. "I'm not used to gettin' any of these shocks at all, and now they come every three innings. How do you like that?" The cleaner had no answer. "This is a disaster," Stengel continued. "Do you know who my player of the year is? My player of the year is Choo Choo Coleman, and I have him for only two days. He runs very good."

142

Casey then went to bed.

This, then, is the way the first year of the New York Mets went. It was a team that featured three twenty-game losers, an opening day outfield that held the all-time major-league record for fathering children (nineteen), a defensive catcher who couldn't catch, and an over-all collection of strange players who performed strange feats. Yet it was absolutely wonderful. People loved it. The Mets gathered about them a breed of baseball fans who quite possibly will make you forget the characters who once made Brooklyn's Ebbets Field a part of this country's folklore. The Mets' fans are made of the same things. Brooklyn fans, observed Garry Schumacher, once a great baseball writer and now part of the San Francisco Giants management, never would have appreciated Joe DiMaggio on their club.

"Too perfect," Garry said.

It is that way with those who follow the Mets.

"They are without a doubt the worst team in the history of baseball," Bill Veeck was saying one day last summer. "I speak with authority. I had the St. Louis Browns. I also speak with longing. I'd love to spend the rest of the summer around the team. If you couldn't have any fun with the Mets, you couldn't have any fun any place."

◆

"This is Ken Michaels. Ken very nearly caught a foul ball at the Mets game last night."

End of the Season

BY DICK SCHAAP

AUGUST 11, 1965

THE METS LAUNCHED THEIR FINAL 1965 VIS-
it to the West Coast on a positive note last night. They showed
up. There is some question as to whether they can keep up that pace
for the rest of the eight-game road trip.

The Mets brought along an eight-game losing streak. They also
brought with them an inferiority complex, which is a tribute to their
intelligence. When the jet taxied up the runway at Los Angeles Airport
early Monday evening, the pretty blonde stewardess brightly announced: "Welcome to Los Angeles. All of us at United Air Lines wish
the New York Mets the best of luck tomorrow and Wednesday night."

"We'll need it," shouted one of the Mets. "Koufax is pitching to-
morrow."

The stewardess didn't have to remind the Mets. She could have said
something pleasant, like, "Fasten your seat belts."

A few minutes later, the Met players were gliding along a moving
ramp through the terminal. "Don't anybody walk," someone suggested.
"Save all your strength for Koufax." The Mets, if they are nothing else,
are realists.

Sandy Koufax opened the first-place Dodgers' two-game series
against New York last night with a 1965 record of 19 victories and
four defeats.

During the four-year life of the Mets, they have never defeated
Koufax, which is a tribute to their consistency. He has beaten them 12
times, including three this year. Since 13 is considered an unlucky
number, superstition was the best thing the Mets had going for them
last night.

They also had the winningest pitcher in their history on the mound,
Al Jackson, the lefthanded suit salesman. Of course, Jackson is also the

144.

losingest pitcher in Met history, but you can't have everything. The last pitcher remaining from the original Mets, Jackson has a record of 37 Met victories and 68 Met defeats. He has beaten the Dodgers once this year, which is a record for him. He shut them out in Los Angeles in June. He has lost to them eight times in four years.

Jackson's over-all record this season was 5–15, entering the game. Last year he did not lose his 16th game until Sept. 25. He is also running ahead of his personal record pace of 1962, when he achieved 20 defeats.

Koufax, like Jackson, is moving toward personal records for the season. He is not moving in the same direction. In 1963, when he won 25 games and the Cy Young Award, Koufax did not record his 20th victory until Aug 29. Last year he was 19–5 on Aug. 16, when his bad elbow forced him out of action. He still has a bad elbow, but it is hard to notice. He has struck out 253 batters in 222 innings and has an earned-run average of 2.18.

Neither team had a .300 hitter in the regular line-up. The Mets, as a matter of fact, did not have a .270 hitter. The Dodgers' leading hitters are Ron Fairly, at .295, and Maury Wills, at .291.

Wills is nursing a swollen right knee, which is not much encouragement for the Met catchers. They would have preferred something more serious. In the Dodgers' first 113 games, Wills had stolen 75 bases. In 1963, when Wills set the modern major-league record of 104 stolen bases, he did not steal his 75th base until his 137th game.

The arrival of the Mets is the nicest thing, psychologically, that could have happened to the Dodgers. Their grip on first place had dwindled to one game over San Francisco and two over Cincinnati and Milwaukee. They are 12–3 against the Mets, which made them glad to be hosts last night.

There was one happy note for Mets fans. The road trip is only eight games long, two here, three in Houston, and three in San Francisco. If the Mets are going to break their all-time losing record of 17 games, established in 1962, they will do it at home, where it will be appreciated.

There is something about the Mets that strikes strength into the hearts of opposing pitchers. Probably it is their batting averages.

Don Drysdale had a choice of pitching against the Mets last night, with two days of rest, or against the Pittsburgh Pirates tomorrow night, with four days of rest. "We were planning to use Osteen in the second game," Los Angeles manager Walt Alston said before the two-game Dodger–Met series opened here Tuesday night, "but if Drysdale feels strong, he'll pitch."

Drysdale felt strong. Faster than you could say Clemente, Clendenon and Stargell, he told the manager he was ready to face the Mets. And then late Tuesday night, after Sandy Koufax had stopped the Mets, 4–3, for his 20th victory of the season, Drysdale stood outside the Dodger lockerroom and said, with a straight face, that he did not feel any more confident than usual pitching against the Mets.

"They're a much improved ball club," the 6-foot-6 righthander explained, earnestly. "They can give you a lot of trouble. No team's easy in this game. You have to bear down all the time."

"You still have to go out there and throw one pitch at a time," somebody suggested.

Drysdale nodded.

Drysdale insists he takes no special pleasure in pitching against the Mets. His insistence is not convincing. Going into last night's game, he had a lifetime record against the Mets of 16 victories and two defeats, which sounds like a perfect definition of pleasure.

In 1965, Drysdale had a 3–1 record against the Mets, an overall record of 15–10, with an earned run average of 2.87. Between them, Koufax and Drysdale had won one more game than the entire Met team, a good indication of why the Dodgers were clinging to first place and the Mets were embracing last.

This brief series must already be considered a success for the Mets. They gave Koufax a very hard time Tuesday night. They didn't do anything ridiculous, like beating him, but they made him work.

As a matter of fact, the Mets did do something ridiculous. They did it in the third inning, and it provided the margin Koufax needed for his 13th consecutive victory over the Mets. They have never beaten him.

In the bottom of the third inning, the Mets were still even, 0–0, with one out. Maury Wills, whose swollen right knee has slowed him to a gazelle's pace, sliced a ground-rule double on one bounce into the rightfield seats. Then Jim Gilliam lined a single up the middle, which gave the Mets an opportunity to show off.

Johnny Lewis, in centerfield, charged the ball smartly as Wills rounded third and whipped toward home. Lewis scooped the ball and, in one fluid motion, threw hard and fast, but not straight. The throw was up the third-base line. It sailed past the cut-off man, first baseman Jim Hickman. It sailed past the catcher, Chris Cannizzaro. It sailed past the pitcher, Al Jackson, backing up. Jackson retrieved the ball and, unfortunately, spotted Gilliam heading for third. Jackson tried for him, and threw the ball into leftfield. Gilliam, who is, at 36, too old for this sort of thing, continued home. Lewis had an error, Jackson had an error and the Dodgers had a 2–0 lead. Six innings later, Jackson, who pitched well, had his 16th defeat. He has won five games. And the Mets had extended their current losing streak to nine games.

AUGUST 13, 1965

The Mets have reached the crucial stage of their current Western road trip. If they can get through Houston without suffering a victory, they stand a good chance to come home next week possessing a 16-game losing streak.

This would put them within one game of their all-time losing streak, of 17 games, which was one of the most exciting accomplishments of their maiden 1962 season.

It is not going to be easy. Houston can, at times, be awfully tough to lose to. Yet the Mets seem to have the knack. They have managed to lose nine of 10 games to the ninth-place Astros so far this season, including six straight under the Houston dome.

The Astros are refusing to make it simple for the Mets to keep their streak alive. Houston has nominated Don Nottebart, the righthander

who used to be with Milwaukee, to open the three-game series tonight. Nottebart has a record this season of two victories and 10 defeats. It is a real challenge to lose to him.

For the Mets, who had an open day yesterday to reflect upon their 10 consecutive defeats, Jack Fisher will pitch the first game of the series. Fisher has a 7–14 record. He leads the Mets starters in innings pitched, complete games, victories and earned-run average. He is the closest thing to a stopper the Mets have.

"Lose 10 in a row," said interim manager Wes Westrum, as he sat in front of his locker after the 1–0 defeat Wednesday night, "and, with a few breaks, we could have won six of them. What can you say? We just didn't hit."

Westrum scraped his foot along the floor. He is a nice man who has played on good teams, and he takes defeat hard. "Doesn't everyone?" he said.

Westrum was a coach during the Mets' two 10-game losing streaks earlier this season. Now he has demonstrated that Casey Stengel is not the only man who can guide the Mets to consistent defeat. "Definitely, it hurts more when you're the manager," he said. "But it always hurts."

From the standpoint of the manager, the two-game trip to Los Angeles was a total loss. But from the standpoint of a Met fan, the trip was a resounding success.

Actually, how much do two more defeats hurt the Mets? They can't fall out of 10th place. And the defeat served one positive purpose. The losing streak is the last element of drama that Mets can conjure up this season. Beating Sandy Koufax and Don Drysdale would have been dramatic, too, of course, but these are the Mets and you must maintain a reasonable frame of reference.

And, in defeat, the Mets looked good. True, there were a few instances of mental and physical clumsiness in the field, but, again, consider the frame of reference. It is no disgrace to lose to Koufax, 4–3, or to Drysdale, 1–0. Better teams than the Mets have been doing that all season. The Mets made Koufax sweat for his 20th victory; they made Drysdale sweat for his 16th. Cynics might say that Koufax and Drysdale sweated because the humidity in Los Angeles has been uncommonly high, but the Mets contributed something.

148

Each of the Met pitchers who worked in Los Angeles was reasonably effective. The Dodger lineup, admittedly, is not exactly frightening. It seems a bit strange for the National League's first-place team to have a .230-hitting infielder, Jim Lefebvre, batting third, and not a single .300 hitter in the regular lineup.

Ron Hunt returns to the Met lineup tonight. They can always use a major leaguer. Ed Kranepool, who collected three singles Wednesday, will stay at first base and Jim Stephenson will catch to give the Mets additional lefthanded strength against the righthanded Nottebart. You can't say the Mets aren't trying to break their losing streak. They have too much class to want to back into a record.

AUGUST 14, 1965

The airplane carrying the Mets from Los Angeles to Houston was showing a new Marlon Brando film, "Morituri," a World War II story. The Mets identified with the Germans. They had a losing streak going, too.

The Germans kept their streak alive in World War II. The Mets attempted to keep theirs alive under the Houston dome last night. The New Yorkers were looking for their 11th straight defeat, which would be a team record for 1965.

Jack Fisher was the starting pitcher for interim manager Wes Westrum. Fisher was seeking his 15th defeat of the season. He had won seven times. He had an 0–2 record against the Houston Astros this year, a 2–4 record lifetime.

The Mets had never won a game under the dome, which made them unique among National League teams. Unique is the nicest thing the Mets can be called. Houston had defeated the Mets six straight times here, and three out of four in New York. Don Nottebart started for Houston. He had a 2–10 record, but when anyone plays the Mets, you can throw records out the window. Nottebart is a righthander, which didn't make any difference to the Mets. They are skilled at losing to any kind of pitcher.

149

The Mets have a vacancy on their roster, created by the departure of Gary Kroll, optioned to Buffalo, presumably because his 6–6 pitching record made the rest of the staff look bad. There is no place on the Mets for .500 ball players.

The vacancy probably will be filled by a pitcher, to be obtained from Milwaukee, as part of a deal which sent outfielder Billy Cowan from the Mets' Buffalo farm to Milwaukee the other day. The acquisition of a capable new pitcher could spell the difference for the Mets between disaster and holocaust.

For the statistically-minded, the Mets did snap their losing streak, in Houston, after it reached a relatively modest 11 games.

The First Crucial Game in Met History

BY PAUL D. ZIMMERMAN AND
DICK SCHAAP

JULY 8, 1969
8:00 A.M.

FOR FIFTEEN YEARS, JOSEPH IGNAC OF Elizabeth, New Jersey, has not had a winner. In 1954, he cheered the New York Giants to the world championship, but in 1958, when the Giants and Willie Mays fled to San Francisco, Ignac became a man without a team.

He turned, like thousands of National League fans, to Yankee Stadium, the other league, and he pulled for the Chicago White Sox, the Boston Red Sox, the Cleveland Indians, even the Kansas City Athletics, whichever club happened to be facing the New York Yankees. From 1958 through 1961, as the Yankees won three pennants and two World Series, Ignac discovered that Yankee-hating was an exercise in futility.

Logically, when the New York Mets were born in 1962, Joseph Ignac became a follower of futility.

Ignac is not going to work today. The maintenance crew at the Elizabeth courthouse will have to get along without him, but the Mets will not. A white-haired, sixty-five-year-old bachelor, Ignac is going to Shea Stadium. He slips into a plain brown sports shirt and a pair of drab slacks. His socks peek through rips in the stitching of his battered brown shoes.

Fully six hours before game time, he leaves his home to start the two-hour trip to Shea Stadium, first by bus to Manhattan, then by subway to Flushing Meadow. He is leaving so early to make certain he gets a decent seat for a mid-week afternoon game against the Chicago Cubs. As he heads for the park, Ignac is looking forward for the first time to watching his team fight to become a pennant contender.

152

Jerry Koosman awakens after a restless night. The twenty-five-year-old left-handed pitcher had tried to get to sleep early, after watching the eleven o'clock news, but the opening game of the Chicago series had kept him awake. Koosman, who has an earned run average of 1.67, the best in the National League, is scheduled to start the first game of the series against Chicago's top pitcher, a strapping black Canadian with the unlikely name of Ferguson Jenkins.

With or without Jenkins, the Chicago lineup is enough to ruin any pitcher's sleep. The first three men—shortstop Don Kessinger, second baseman Glenn Beckert and left fielder Billy Williams—are all hitting around .300. After Williams comes Ron Santo, talkative and talented third baseman who leads the league in runs batted in. Then comes Ernie Banks, the first baseman, even more talkative and, at thirty-eight, almost equally talented, still a wise, dangerous power hitter. Behind Banks comes the catcher, Randy Hundley, also a capable power hitter. Even the pitcher is a threat; early in the year, Jenkins blasted a home run off Tom Seaver, the Mets' best pitcher. There are only two visible soft spots. The center fielder, Don Young, is basically a defensive player, and the right fielder, Jim Hickman, doesn't figure to hurt the Mets with his bat. Hickman has already hurt the Mets enough with his bat; he was one of the original Mets and, in 1962 and 1963, he led the team in its strongest batting department—striking out. In 1965, however, Jim Hickman became the first and, so far, only Met to hit three home runs in one game; after one more season, naturally, the Mets traded him away.

Koosman gets up, walks into his kitchen and stares out the back door of his rented two-family home near LaGuardia Airport, some ten minutes by car from Shea Stadium. He is checking to see which way the wind is blowing. "Left field to right," he says. Koosman is pleased. The wind, at least, is on his side, blowing against the power of Chicago's predominantly righthanded lineup.

9:45 A.M.

Donn Clendenon breakfasts at a luncheonette not far from his sixteenth-floor apartment on West 58th Street in Manhattan. A lean, rangy, powerful first baseman, Clendenon came to the Mets a few weeks ago from Montreal in exchange for a handful of young players. In their formative years, the Mets picked up older players, like Duke Snider and Warren Spahn and Ken Boyer, mostly in the hope of luring people to Shea Stadium to watch the past perform. But the trade for the thirty-three-year-old Clendenon was different. He could actually help a club that might have a shot at winning its division. And, in his short stay with the Mets, Clendenon has already made the trade look good. Two days ago, his home run over the right-field screen in Pittsburgh's Forbes Field helped the Mets overcome a four-run Pirate lead and win their fifth straight game.

Nobody recognizes Clendenon or bothers him for autographs as he eats his breakfast. He is still new to New York. He has no complaints about his anonymity. "When people start knowing me here," he says "I'll find another place to eat. I don't want people asking for autographs. I want to keep my mind on the pitcher."

9:50 A.M.

The Mets' twenty-three-year-old second baseman, Ken Boswell, puts the finishing touches on a steak he is cooking for himself and his roommate, pitcher Danny Frisella, who has just rejoined the team from its Tidewater, Virginia, farm club. Boswell insists he is relaxed. "Nobody feels pressure here," he says. "We're all too young. It's like fighting for the high school championship."

The steak is ready. Boswell, a Texan, takes it to the table, carves it and serves it for himself and Frisella on paper plates. "When we have company," Boswell says, "we use dishes."

Jerry Koosman, wearing black slacks and a blue sports shirt, walks into his back yard. "It's a beautiful day for a ball game," he says, "just the way I like it—not too hot, not too cool." In his last start, in 90-degree weather in St. Louis, he lost fifteen pounds in eight innings of pitching. In the eighth inning, he also lost his control, a 4–0 lead and a chance to win his sixth game of the season. He walked the bases loaded and his relief pitcher, Ron Taylor, gave up a game-tying home run a few moments later. "After a game like that," says Koosman, as he comes back into his house for a breakfast of eggs and sausage, "I can get a cramp in any part of my body. Even if I just lift up my arm, I feel like I can get a cramp."

For Koosman, most of the early part of the 1969 season was spent in pain. He enjoyed a brilliant rookie year in 1968, winning nineteen games, the most ever won by a Met pitcher, but in 1969, his left arm, his pitching arm, began bothering him during spring training in Florida. In his first start of the season, he was hit hard by the St. Louis Cardinals. In his second start, he was hit hard by the Pittsburgh Pirates. He lost that game, 11–2, and afterward, when reporters asked him what was wrong, he told them wryly, "My trouble is that I'm not getting anyone out."

The trouble, actually, was in a muscle behind the shoulder, and, after winning only one game in April, Koosman did not pitch at all for four weeks. He returned late in May, his shoulder ailment cured, and, immediately, he was effective.

Now, coming into the Cub series, he has permitted only nine earned runs in his last seventy-four innings, an incredibly stingy record. Yet, during that stretch, he has won only four games and lost three, mostly because the Mets have not been scoring runs for him. Koosman is not particularly annoyed by the lack of support. The Mets do not score many runs for anyone. They have only one .300-hitting regular, Cleon Jones, and one .300-hitting part-time outfielder, Art Shamsky.

10:05 A.M.

Joseph Ignac of Elizabeth, New Jersey, walks down the subway steps at Shea Stadium, catching a glimpse of the empty green outfield, and heads toward a general admission gate, where tickets go on sale, for $1.30 each, in two hours. Ignac does not worry about finding a decent seat. He is the first man on line at gate E-4.

11:20 A.M.

Jerry Koosman is ready to leave for Shea Stadium. His wife, Lavonne, herds their twenty-one-month-old son, Michael, and two of the neighbors' children—Lavonne baby-sits each morning—into the Koosmans' Pontiac Bonneville. Koosman has worked out a system so that his wife always fills the tank of their car; the key to the system is a limited amount of driving—mostly to the stadium and back—while the pitcher is at home. "My wife waits till we go on the road," Koosman says. "It makes sense, doesn't it, to have a girl buy the gas? They get better service than a man. For a woman, they wash the windshield and check the battery and everything."

Koosman is a farm boy in New York. He grew up in Appleton, Minnesota, where he learned to play baseball in local beer leagues because his high school wasn't big enough to have a team. He played the outfield, and his brother, Orville, usually pitched. But one day the two brothers collided in the outfield; Orville came up with a broken leg, and Jerry moved into the pitching rotation. He was ready. "I'd been practicing in the top of my father's hay barn," he says.

Red Murff, a Met scout who pitched briefly in the big leagues himself, spotted Koosman in 1964 when the young farmer was pitching for Fort Bliss, Texas, and averaging eighteen strikeouts a game. Murff originally offered Koosman a $1,600 bonus to sign, but when the lefthander held out for more money—some of his army teammates told him he ought to get at least $20,000—Murff kept reducing his offer. Koosman signed, finally, for $1,200. He was a bargain. "I figured," says Koosman, "I'd better sign before I owed them money."

156

On the way to Shea Stadium, young Michael Koosman climbs all over the car, tugging on his father's right arm, the expendable one. Koosman remains calm, undisturbed by his son's antics. But, as the stadium comes into view, Koosman says quietly, "I've never been so nervous about a game in my life."

12:25 P.M.

Shea Stadium has started to fill with the kids who always come out early to watch batting practice and collect autographs. The batting cage has been wheeled out by the ground crew. Coach Joe Pignatano is hitting grounders to the infield. A second- and third-string catcher with the Dodgers in Brooklyn and Los Angeles, Pignatano spent the twilight of a mediocre career as an extra catcher with the original Mets in 1962. Sal Marchiano, a young sportscaster with CBS, is setting up his camera crew to take pictures of batting practice. Pignatano has not forgotten the early days of the Mets. Worried that a wild throw may kill someone, he persuades Marchiano to move his crew.

The area behind the batting cage is crawling with writers and photographers. "There are more writers here than at Cape Kennedy," says one reporter. Nine hundred miles south, at Cape Kennedy, the Apollo 11 astronauts are one week from blastoff.

"It looks like the World Series," another writer agrees. "Everyone's here."

12:35 P.M.

Ken Boswell stands in the batting cage. He hits several shots that clear the 396-foot mark in right-center field.

"Beautiful," says Jerry Koosman, waiting for his turn to bat. "Hit two or three of those today." Boswell has hit two home runs all season.

157

Jerry Koosman is taking his final turn in the batting cage. The rest of the Mets turn their eyes away, afraid that Koosman's swing may be catching. He has one hit and nineteen strikeouts in thirty-three official times at bat, but he thinks he is beginning to find his groove. "I've been hitting better," Koosman insists. "Well, actually, better in the last game. The first time up I lined out to the second baseman. The second time I flied out to right field and the third time I flied out to center. That's unusual for me, because I usually strike out." In 1968, Koosman set a major league record for strikeouts by a pitcher.

Satisfied with his batting practice, Koosman walks slowly off the field and through the tunnel leading from the Met dugout to the clubhouse. He stands in front of his locker and removes his soaked sweatshirt—"I perspire more than the normal guy"—and puts on a dry one. Joe Deer, the assistant Met trainer, walks up to him.

"Any time you're ready, Jerry," he says.

Koosman takes his pants off and heads for the trainer's room. The ritual is always the same. Sitting on the trainer's table, he extends his left foot. Deer applies a straight razor to a few hairs on the pitcher's instep. He dips a Q-tip into a bottle of tincture of benzoin and smears it around the instep to protect the skin from the adhesive Deer will wrap there. But, before he puts on the adhesive, Deer applies a square patch of moleskin, a soft rabbit fur, to the side of Koosman's big toe.

"I drag my left foot across the mound when I pitch," says Koosman. "If I don't have all this stuff on it, it gets raw."

Deer wraps a strip of elastic tape around the moleskin patch to fix it in place. Koosman is finished and walks back into the locker room.

Matt Winick, the assistant director of Met public relations, hands Koosman a sheet that carries all of the Chicago statistics for that day. Koosman immediately searches for the figures on Ferguson Jenkins, looking for an edge.

"Three wild pitches for him," says Koosman. "I think I've only got two."

12:52 P.M.

The Mets finish batting practice. One by one, they start drifting into the clubhouse. Jerry Koosman sits near his locker. "It was so hot on the last trip," he says, "St. Louis . . . Pittsburgh. This is such a nice day. It would be a damn shame if we didn't win." He gets up, moves across the clubhouse and finally sprawls out on the green clubhouse rug in front of pitcher Don Cardwell's locker. Koosman lies there for forty-five minutes.

1:15 P.M.

Ron Santo, the Cub third baseman, spots the Mets' starting line-up posted in the Chicago dugout. He walks over to it, looks it over carefully, then shakes his head.

"I know Los Angeles won with pitching," Santo says. "But this is ridiculous."

1:20 P.M.

Outside the Cub dugout, Ernie Banks is humming the Met theme song, "Meet the Mets," occasionally singing his own lyrics. "Beat the Mets, beat the Mets," Bank sings. "Come on out and beat the Mets . . ."

Banks is Mr. Sunshine, smiling as usual. Reporters crowd around him, enjoying his performance. After seventeen years in the big leagues, Banks still loves the pre-game whirl of photographers, reporters, kids pleading for autographs.

"What a beautiful day for baseball," he says, as he does before virtually every game. "New York. The melting pot. The Great White Way. What's going on?"

"The Mets," someone tells him.

"What about 'Oh Calcutta?'" Banks asks, referring to the off-Broadway Kenneth Tynan nudity pageant. "Twenty-five dollars a ticket and you can't get a hold of them."

"Don't tell us that beneath that sunshine smile beats the heart of a dirty old man," says one reporter.

"No, no," answers Banks, smiling. "You can't say that. What will all these kids think?"

Finally, someone asks him about the Mets.

"People used to laugh and laugh at the Mets," says Banks. "But not any more. Now they have a good team. They have good pitching and they play together. People laughed a few years ago, but the Mets play together now."

Banks stops and listens to "The Queen of Melody of Shea Stadium," playing a medley on the Thomas Organ.

"That's Jane Jarvis," says Banks, running his hands over an imaginary keyboard. "I remember her when she played at County Stadium in Milwaukee." He smiles broadly.

A reporter asks him what keeps him so exuberant after seventeen seasons with the Cubs, seventeen years without winning a pennant.

"You have to be happy," says Banks, "and sports does it. What kind of world would this be without sports, without baseball?" He raises his bat like a bayonet. "Why, you'd have people at each other all the time."

1:55 P.M.

Leo Durocher slouches in the Chicago dugout, leaning on an outstretched hand, awaiting the start of the game. Durocher spans the history of post-1925, pre-Met baseball in New York. At twenty-two, he was the regular shortstop for the Yankees, a teammate of Babe Ruth; at thirty-five, he managed the Brooklyn Dodgers to a pennant; at forty-five, he managed the New York Giants to a pennant. Blunt, opinionated, excitable, friend of Frank Sinatra and George Raft, baiter of umpires and creator of Willie Mays, Durocher is now, on the brink of his sixty-third birthday, the enemy in New York, the manager of the Cubs.

When Durocher took over the Cubs in 1966, ten years after his last managerial job in the major leagues, he faced a difficult chore. He had a reputation for being able to manage only a winner, and the Cubs

were losers. They had finished eighth the previous season. Durocher looked over his material and announced, "This is not an eighth-place ball club."

He was right. By his own definition, Durocher was a nice guy in 1966. The Cubs finished dead last, tenth in the National League. They were the first team in the history of baseball to finish behind the Mets.

But Durocher did not quit, and he guided the Cubs out of the cellar and into third place in both 1967 and 1968. Now, as his Cubs bid for the team's first pennant in a quarter of a century, Durocher is no longer Mr. Nice Guy. He flatly refuses to talk to any reporters before the game.

1:58 P.M.

Jack Lightcap, the Met announcer, delivers the starting lineups over the public address system. The crowd greets every Met name with wild cheers, every name except that of the starting first baseman, Ed Kranepool.

Kranepool is the only current Met who has been with the team since its maiden season. He was brought up at the end of 1962, only seventeen years old, fresh from James Monroe High School in the Bronx, where he had broken the school's homerun record set by Hank Greenberg.

Kranepool was the heart of what Casey Stengel, the first Met manager, once called "The Youth of America," the mythical Met club that would one day win a pennant. But Kranepool was young only in chronology, not in manner. He ran like an eighty-year-old man catching a commuter train. His modest ability to hit became even more modest with men on base. In 1963, when he was only eighteen, teammates considered him "a young fogey," and a banner at the ballpark asked: IS ED KRANE-POOL OVER THE HILL?

But, every now and then, Kranepool showed flashes of the brilliance that had been expected of him. For a few weeks, usually at the start of the season, he would hit over .300, and Met fans, starved for a hero, would rally to him. But then Kranepool would start slipping toward his own level—his own level, according to his career batting average,

161

is .248—and the fans would abandon him. Rumors persisted that Kranepool's attitude was not ideal, that he could have worked harder to break his slumps. The harsher fans called him lazy.

This season, although he has already driven in thirty-one runs, ten more than he did in all of 1968, the Mets still are not in love with him. He is too easy a target for all the frustrations of what Kranepool himself calls "a seven-year losing streak."

Kranepool's name, floating over the P.A. system in the middle of the lineup, the sixth spot in the order, inspires a chorus of boos.

2:03 P.M.

Jerry Koosman walks to the dugout from the bullpen. He has finished warming up. He is sweating, but his blue Met jacket is buttoned all the way up to the neck. "One thing a shoulder injury does for you," he says. "It teaches you to protect your arm at all times."

2:05 P.M.

Above the field, behind home plate, Bob Murphy, one of the Mets' radio and television announcers, is telling everyone who stayed home from work to watch the telecast that he did the right thing: This is a very important baseball game. Murphy's voice is picked up in New York, New Jersey, Connecticut and, for the first time, in Maine. The Met network has been extended to Maine temporarily so that the president of the ball club, Joan Whitney Payson, vacationing at the Elizabeth Arden health farm, can watch the very important game. All three Cub games, in fact, will be beamed to Elizabeth Arden's at Mrs. Payson's expense. She can afford it.

Mrs. Payson, the wife of financier Charles Payson and sister of John Hay Whitney, formerly the United States Ambassador to the Court of St. James, does not like to miss her Mets. At the start of their first season in 1962, when she traveled to Greece with her daughter and son-in-law, she had the scores cabled to her. After a while, the news

grew so depressing that she fired back a cable: PLEASE TELL US ONLY WHEN METS WIN.

"That was the last word I heard from America," she later reported.

2:07 P.M.

Don Kessinger, the first Cub batter, dumps a perfect bunt toward second base. It bounds past Jerry Koosman. Wayne Garrett, a rookie second baseman, sweeps the ball up barehanded perfectly and, in the same motion, throws to first. Kessinger beats the throw.

Glenn Beckert, an excellent bunter, sacrifices Kessinger to second and, quickly, the Cubs have a runner in scoring position. Kessinger, standing on second base, turns to one of the Met infielders. "Our three and four hitters haven't done anything for us in weeks," he says.

The three and four hitters, Billy Williams and Ron Santo, do nothing now. Jerry Koosman strikes out the lean, graceful Williams with a good fast ball at the knees, then, working carefully to Santo, walks him.

Ernie Banks steps up, first in the National League in good humor and third in runs batted in. The crowd, which has swelled to 55,096, the brink of capacity, grows quiet. But seated behind home plate, a fan in his late twenties, dressed in a white polka-dot shirt and sandals, screams, "Strike him out, strike him out."

Koosman gets ahead of Banks, one ball, two strikes. The fan is standing now, pleading, "Strike him out, Jerry, strike him out."

Koosman fires a fast ball on the outside corner, and Banks swings.

The man in the polka-dot shirt jumps up and down, announcing the result, "See, he did it! He did it!"

Koosman has struck out Banks.

2:16 P.M.

Ferguson Jenkins, his fast ball blazing, his curve breaking sharply, dismisses the first three Met batters on ten pitches. He strikes out two, gets the other man on a harmless infield grounder.

163

When Jerry Koosman gets a full count, three balls, two strikes, on Randy Hundley, the Cubs' leadoff batter in the second inning, umpire Shag Crawford walks out to the mound to examine Koosman's glove and hands, searching for illegal traces of pine tar. Koosman is clean. "I don't know why he checked me so early in the game," Koosman says later. "That's when I was having so much trouble getting anything on the ball. He should have checked me in the middle innings, when I was pitching better."

Koosman walks Hundley, and, in the stands, Richie Parsons, a Met fanatic from Long Island, drains a beer and begins a private monologue. "Ah, damn, he gave up a walk to Hundley. C'mon, Koos, Hickman's up, let's get a double play . . ."

Hickman slams a hard ground ball toward third. "There's the double-play ball," says Parsons, starting a fresh beer.

The ground ball bounces off the chest of Bobby Pfeil, the forty-first man in eight years to play third base for the Mets. Both runners are safe, and Hickman is credited with a single.

"Aw, c'mon, Pfeil, don't mess up chances like that. I'd like a triple play, but it's not damn likely . . ."

Two thirteen-year-old Met fans from Brooklyn unfurl a banner and begin a march through the grandstand. The banner reads: TODAY THE METS GRADUATE; TOMORROW THEY SHALL REIGN.

Koosman's first pitch to Don Young is called a ball. "The umps know they're on TV today," says Parsons, finishing his second beer of the inning. "Boy, are they bad!"

Koosman strikes out Young on the next three pitches.

"Got him . . . got him . . . got him. All right. C'mon, sit down in front. C'mon, Koos, get a double play. Jenkins can't hit. Bear down, Koos! C'mon, you can do it. Strike one! All right! C'mon, Jerry, pitch to him. There's a grounder to short. Let's get two . . ."

But Ferguson Jenkins' ground ball to deep shortstop goes for another infield hit. The bases are loaded with one out.

"Please bear down, Jerry, please. Let's get out of the inning." Parsons gulps deep into his third beer of the inning, and Koosman strikes out Kessinger.

164

"One more, baby, one more, Koos, don't let me down."

Beckert flies deep to right, and Art Shamsky, the best Jewish out-fielder in New York since the Dodgers' Cal Abrams—and the first, and the slowest—ambles back to the screen in front of the Met bullpen, reaches up and makes the catch. The inning is over.

In section twelve, behind third base, Joe Delberti, a Met fan since their first season, waves his banner: UNBELIEVABLE.

"Yahoo!" shouts Richie Parson, polishing off the third beer. "Yahoo! That's the way to go, Jerry. Yahoo!"

3:12 P.M.

It is the last of the fifth inning, a scoreless game, and Ferguson Jenkins has not yet surrendered a single hit. Jenkins strikes out Wayne Garrett, and Ed Kranepool moves to the plate, preceded, as always, by boos. With one strike, Ferguson throws a slider, and Kranepool lofts the ball high to right field. Jim Hickman, the ex-Met, moves back, looks up, moves back a little farther, looks up again and watches the ball sail over the wall. The crowd roars, the Mets lead, 1–0, and Kranepool trots around the bases as easily as if this were the sort of thing he did every day.

3:13 P.M.

As the last of the first-year Mets circles the bases, the first of the original Mets, Hobie Landrith, a catcher who was plucked from the San Francisco Giants at the start of the expansion draft, is perched on the roof of his home outside San Francisco. Landrith, who endured only one season as a Met, is out of baseball now, an automobile dealer. He is painting his roof white and charcoal gray. He reaches for a brush and, accidentally, drops a can of paint. Eluding Landrith's grasp, the can splashes to the ground. "That's one of the reasons the Mets let me go," he says later.

165

3:17 P.M.

The Mets' 1–0 lead is less than half an inning old, and Ernie Banks picks out a fast ball and drives it over the left-field wall, tying the score. At the end of the inning, as he trots out toward his position at first base, Banks passes Cleon Jones, the Met outfielder. "Boy," says Banks, smiling, "can we hit!"

3:29 P.M.

Jerry Koosman, who has thrown a lot of pitches, is having trouble with his control. He walks Ferguson Jenkins, the opposing pitcher, to start the seventh inning. Don Kessinger sacrifices Jenkins to second, and Glenn Beckert singles to left, scoring Jenkins. The Cubs lead, 2–1.

3:36 P.M.

As Ferguson Jenkins, pitching smoothly, crisply, efficiently, disposes of the heart of the Met batting order, two young brunettes parade through the lower stands with a banner asking a simple, pointed question: WHAT EVER HAPPENED TO MARV THRONEBERRY?

3:37 P.M.

As the banner waves in Shea Stadium, stirring strong memories, if not quite golden ones, Marv E. Throneberry, whose initials and charmingly graceless ineptitude both spelled MET in 1962, is at work in Memphis, Tennessee. Still only thirty-five years old, out of baseball since 1963, Throneberry is calling upon potential new customers for Carl Carson Car and Truck Rentals, not even aware that the Mets are playing an afternoon game against the Cubs. "I just don't get interested in baseball any more," says Throneberry, a sales and public relations specialist, "not till World Series time, anyway." Some of the crueler

166

critics used to say Marv felt the same way when he played for the Mets.

To each new customer he sees, Throneberry hands his business card. Inside the card are the three main telephone numbers of Carl Carson Car and Truck Rentals. The outside of the card has a hole cut in the middle, and through the hole stares a head-and-shoulders portrait of Marv Throneberry in his old Met uniform. The face of the card reads, modestly: EIGHT MILLION NEW YORKERS CALLED HIM MARVELOUS MARV.

3:45 P.M.

With two men out in the top of the eighth, Jim Hickman comes to bat against Jerry Koosman, the old breed Met against the new. Hickman is greeted, familarly, with boos. He played for the Mets under a strange curse; someone once suggested he had "potential." If he did, he kept it well hidden.

Hickman added nothing to the comedy at Shea Stadium—he didn't drop fly balls; he simply didn't get to them—and little to the drama. Under pressure, in the mini-crises of the past, Hickman always seemed to harm the Mets.

He does it again now in a major crisis. He hits Koosman's first pitch deep into the Chicago bullpen in left field. Hickman trots around the bases, and the Cubs lead, 3–1.

3:52 P.M.

With two out and no one on base in the bottom of the eighth, shortstop Al Weis comes to the plate. If Weis can get a hit—something no Met has managed since Ed Kranepool's home run—manager Gil Hodges will send up a pinch-hitter for the next batter, Jerry Koosman. Koosman, moving up to the on-deck circle, silently hopes that Ferguson Jenkins will retire Weis. Koosman wants to pitch the ninth inning. "I felt bad and I wanted to make up for some of the pitches I'd thrown," Koosman says later.

● 167

Weis grounds out to shortstop, pleasing Koosman, disappointing Barbara Weis, a petite brunette who is seated in the lower stands. "You just wait," Barbara Weis tells her in-laws, Al's parents, who are sitting with her. "The Mets will do it . . . somehow."

At the same moment, Yogi Berra, coaching at first base, calls to Ernie Banks, trotting off the field, "We're gonna get three in the ninth and beat you." Banks does not even turn his head.

3:58 P.M.

Jerry Koosman, still pitching, retires the Cubs in order in the ninth inning, and the Mets move in for their final chance. The odds against them seem infinite: Ferguson Jenkins is pitching magnificently, and of the batters coming up for the Mets—a pinch-hitter, Tommie Agee and Bobby Pfeil—only Agee is a proven threat. Yet few fans leave the park; in recent weeks, the Mets have been rallying dramatically. In seasons past, half the crowd would be fleeing to the parking lot, with logic and history on their side.

4:00 P.M.

Frank Graddock is settled comfortably before the TV set at his home in the Ridgewood section of Queens, not far from Shea Stadium. He is watching the Mets, and, according to later police reports, he has been drinking during the telecast. His wife, Margaret, walks over to the set and switches the channel away from the Met game. It is time for one of her favorite daytime serials, "Dark Shadows," and today she will find out whether Quentin, who carries the curse of the werewolf, will be able to keep the mummy's hand he has pursued through the last few episodes. Frank Graddock doesn't care about Quentin, his curse or the mummy's hand. He wants to see the ninth inning of the ball game, and he and his wife begin to argue over the Mets and the monsters.

168

4:01 P.M.

To start the last of the ninth inning, Gil Hodges sends up a pinch-hitter for Jerry Koosman—Ken Boswell, the regular second baseman who has been sitting out the game with a bruised hand. Boswell, a pull-hitter, is hitting .245, normal by Met standards. Yet Boswell has some power to right-center field, so the Cub outfield plays him deep. Ferguson Jenkins works the count on Boswell to two balls, two strikes. The Mets, newly conditioned to expect the impossible, crowd the front steps of their dugout.

Boswell hits Jenkins' next pitch high into short right-center field. Don Young, the Cub center fielder who plays mainly on the strength of his fielding, hesitates for a moment, waiting for the ball to come out of the haze and background of white shirts in the crowd. He hesitates too long. As he charges in and Don Kessinger and Glenn Beckert pedal back, the ball falls to the ground. Second base is left uncovered, and Boswell alertly stretches his pop fly into a double. The Cubs have committed a combination mental-and-physical error straight out of Met tradition.

4:04 P.M.

On "Dark Shadows," Quentin is faced with an agonizing decision: Should he keep the mummy's paw or return it in exchange for advice from Angelique, a witch, on how to shake the werewolf's curse? Margaret Graddock wants to find out, but her husband insists upon watching a baseball game. She switches the channel; he switches back to Shea Stadium.

4:05 P.M.

With Ken Boswell at second base and the huge crowd chanting for a rally, Tommie Agee, the strong, powerful Met outfielder, slashes a ball past third base, just foul. Ferguson Jenkins misses the plate with his

169

next two pitches, and catcher Randy Hundley goes to the mound to settle him down. In the Cub dugout, Leo Durocher, outwardly unworried, sits with his legs crossed. Agee hits Jenkins's next pitch straight up, and Ernie Banks drifts over by the Met dugout and makes the catch for the first out. Cleon Jones watches from the dugout steps. His mind drifts back to a game earlier in the season, when the Mets came from behind and beat the Atlanta Braves.

4:07 P.M.

Gil Hodges pulls out Bobby Pfeil and sends up Donn Clendenon to pinch-hit. A restaurateur in Atlanta in the off-season, Clendenon has, he confesses, "a propensity for striking out." He holds the National League record with 163 strikeouts in a single season. But he also has a propensity for hitting a baseball great distances.

Clendenon moves his hands up on the bat. While a home run would tie the game, Clendenon is hoping mainly to keep the mild rally alive, trying to get the bat on the ball, looking for a single or a double. He drives Ferguson Jenkins's first pitch foul down the right-field line. The next pitch, a curve ball, misses the inside corner.

Jenkins takes a deep breath and throws. Clendenon swings and lines the ball deep toward the left-field wall. The drive sinks, falling short of a home run, and Don Young, the Chicago center fielder, racing full speed, reaches out and snares the ball before it can hit the wall. But Young, the ball resting tentatively in the webbing of his glove, cannot brake. He slams into the fence. The ball pops loose.

Boswell, forced to wait at second to see if the ball will be caught, moves only to third. Clendenon reaches second. The tying runs are in scoring position, and the fans at Shea Stadium are screaming.

4:08 P.M.

Margaret Graddock is screaming, too. She wants to see "Dark Shadows." On the show, Angelique, the witch, is explaining how she was once bitten by a vampire.

170

Frank Graddock screams back at his wife and starts hitting her, too, the police say later. Reportedly, Frank Graddock punches his wife in the head and body. Angelique, the witch, is about to strangle a man to death. Cleon Jones is about to come to bat.

4:09 P.M.

Cleon Jones moves from the on-deck circle to the plate. He has been hitless all day, still looking for his 100th base hit of the season; he started the day leading the National League in batting, but his average has slipped a few points. "You gotta get a hit now," Jones tells himself. "If you don't, you'll kick yourself all the way home in the car. It's time to do your thing."

Donn Clendenon leads off second base. "Don't get picked off," he tells himself. "If I ever get picked off in front of all these people, I'll kill myself."

Jones watches the first pitch. It is low. Then Ferguson Jenkins throws a curve, which failing to break, hangs over the plate. Jones cracks the ball on a line over third base and into the left-field corner. Before Billy Williams, in left field, can chase the ball down, Ken Boswell and Clendenon have scored, tying the game, and Jones is standing on second base.

The Met players, pouring out of their dugout, devour the two runners, pounding their backs, shaking their fists defiantly at the Cub dugout.

Leo Durocher emerges, walks to the mound, and talks to Jenkins. He leaves his ace in the game.

4:11 P.M.

Leo Durocher, after consulting with Ferguson Jenkins, orders the Mets' clean-up hitter, Art Shamsky, deliberately walked, setting up a possible double-play situation. But the next batter, Wayne Garrett, grounds softly to second base, and Glenn Beckert has to make the play at first, allowing the runners to move up to second and third.

171

The next batter is Ed Kranepool, greeted by cheers, partly redeemed by his home run.

"C'mon, Everitt," shouts Jack Wakefield, a professional comedian who is sitting behind home plate, a dedicated fan who often treats Met pitchers to dinner after winning performances. "C'mon, Everitt."

Wakefield turns to the people around him. "He hates the name Everitt," says Wakefield. "I call him that to get him mad enough to get a hit."

Kranepool may have regained stature in the eyes of Met fans by his home run, but he has not convinced the Cubs. Rather than walk him and face J. C. Martin, the Met catcher, Durocher and Jenkins decide to pitch to Kranepool.

4:13 P.M.

Frank Graddock is watching the Mets on his television set. His wife, Margaret, is lying in bed, nursing the injuries she allegedly suffered trying to get to see "Dark Shadows." Her husband concentrates upon the game, unaware that his wife is fatally hurt, unaware that he will be charged the following day, with first-degree murder.

4:14 P.M.

Ed Kranepool lugs a 36-ounce bat to the plate, several ounces heavier than the one he customarily uses. A heavier bat has helped the hitting of both Cleon Jones and Donn Clendenon. "You can't argue with success," Kranepool says later.

Ferguson Jenkins' first pitch is high. Kranepool watches the next one for a strike and misses the third.

The crowd is on its feet. Kranepool digs in. He notices that shortstop Don Kessinger is playing him towards second base, leaving lots of room through the left side to the infield. Kranepool is expecting an outside pitch—but not the one Jenkins throws him. It is outside and low, and Kranepool fooled, practically throws his bat at the ball. The bat con-

nects. The ball bloops out toward left field, over the head of Kessinger.

Cleon Jones dances down the line, jumping every few feet, as he scores the winning run. Jerry Koosman, suddenly the winning pitcher, is the first to greet Jones, hugging him, lifting him off the ground. Mets hug each other all over the field. In the record books, it will read simply as a 4–3 victory over the Chicago Cubs on a July afternoon. But, for the Mets, it is, for an instant, the seventh game of an imaginary world series.

Upstairs, in the television booth, announcer Lindsey Nelson is screaming. "It's absolute bedlam. You could not believe it. It's absolute bedlam."

In the stands, Barbara Weis points her finger at her in-laws. "See," she says. "I told you they'd do it . . . somehow."

Near Barbara Weis, in a beige-and-brown sleeveless dress, Lavonne Koosman sits, tears streaming down her face and smearing her make-up.

4:20 P.M.

Joseph Ignac of Elizabeth, New Jersey, heads out of Shea Stadium, starting his two-hour trip home. Never once, in his eight seasons of cheering for the Mets, has he felt so good. For the first time, he doesn't miss Willie Mays quite so much.

4:23 P.M.

In the Chicago clubhouse, Don Young the outfielder, is dressing as fast as he possibly can. "If I value my life," he tells himself, "I'll get the hell out of here."

Several of the Cub players, like friends paying a condolence call, drift over to Young's locker and tell him to forget about the two mistakes he made, not to worry about them. A few suggest that he get himself a drink quickly.

Back in the manager's room, Leo Durocher is opening up to re-

porters. "That kid in center field," he says to the Chicago writers. "Two little fly balls. He just stands there watching one, and he gives up on the other." Durocher flavors his remarks with his choicest obscenities, and Durocher is a master of the idiom.

"If a man can't catch a fly ball," Durocher says, "you don't deserve to win."

The manager glances toward Ferguson Jenkins, who is slumped in front of his locker. "Look at him," Durocher says. "He threw his heart out. You won't see a better-pitched game. And that kid in center field gives it away on him. It's a disgrace."

4:29 P.M.

Ron Santo, the Cub third baseman, is no more charitable than his manager. "He was just thinking about himself, not the team," says Santo, angrily, referring to Don Young. "He had a bad day at the bat, so he's got his head down. He's worrying about his batting average and not the team. All right, he can keep his head down, and he can keep right on going, out of sight for all I care. We don't need that kind of thing."

Santo slams his spikes against the floor. "I don't know who Leo has in mind to play center field," he says, "but I hope I can sell him on Hickman. Any ball Jim reaches, you can bet your money he'll hold onto."

4:35 P.M.

Cleon Jones has returned from Ralph Kiner's post-game show and now, in response to questions, he is reliving the ninth inning. "The Cubs went out there patting their pockets when they took the field in the ninth," says Jones. "They were already started to count that twenty-five grand." He smiles, thinking himself of the potential share for each championship player in the upcoming intra-league championship series and the World Series.

"Banks, he talks to you all the time," Jones says. "He kept saying to me over and over, 'That Jenkins, he can really pitch.' I didn't give up. Nobody gave up. This is a young club and it believes it can win. We've got the momentum now."

Jones looks toward Tom Seaver, who is scheduled to pitch for the Mets tomorrow. "We beat their big man," says Jones. "Now we've got our big man. We're in command now. We can relax."

"Hey, don't save the fireworks until the ninth inning for me," says Seaver. "I'll take a 9–0 lead in the first inning any time. I'll finesse it the rest of the way."

4:37 P.M.

Ron Santo is still fuming in the Chicago locker room. "It's ridiculous," he says. "There's no way the Mets can beat us. Just no way. It's a shame losing to an infield like that. Why, I wouldn't let that infield play in Tacoma."

4:43 P.M.

Ferguson Jenkins has no abuse for Don Young. "With all those people here on a bright day," the pitcher says, "the center fielder is in a constant battle with the sun. I thought Young recovered quickly. After all, he had to find it before he could chase it." Young doesn't hear the words in his defense. He has fled from the clubhouse.

5:10 P.M.

At Camp Drum in Watertown, New York, Sergeant Derrel McKinley Harrelson is getting ready to umpire a softball game between two teams of Army reservists. When he isn't putting in his two weeks of summer training, Sergeant Harrelson is Bud Harrelson, the regular shortstop for the New York Mets.

175

Sergeant Harrelson is umpiring because he fears that, if he played softball, he might lose his batting groove. It is not one of the greatest grooves of baseball—Harrelson, an accomplished fielder, is a confirmed .220 to .240 hitter—but it is the only one he has.

"Your club scored three runs in the ninth and won," somebody says.

Harrelson laughs. He is used to being kidded in his outfit. The previous week, when the Mets won six out of nine games from St. Louis and Pittsburgh without him, his army buddies teased him about his indispensability. Harrelson is a pleasant young man, and he takes jokes well.

"Sure, we got three in the ninth," he says. He had heard earlier that the Mets were losing, 3–1, going into the ninth.

"Hey, sarge," someone else yells from the barracks. "You won, 4–3."

Suddenly, Harrelson realizes he is not being kidded. He breaks into a big grin and, in fatigues, begins umpiring a meaningless softball game.

6:00 P.M.

Ed Kranepool walks into the bar at Tavern on the Green, a restaurant in Central Park. He is accompanied by Howard Cosell, the sportscaster, who is going to interview him on ABC-TV's 6:30 news.

As the two men enter, the bartenders begin to applaud.

Cosell nods gently, presuming, as he always does, that the cheers are for him and his syntax.

"Champagne, Mr. Kranepool?" says one of the bartenders.

"No," says Kranepool. "Just straight Beefeaters on the rocks, with just a touch of vermouth."

Kranepool will save the champagne for the World Series.

The first edition of the *New York Times* goes on sale on the streets of the city. The story of the Mets' rally is on the front page of the newspaper. The Mets have been on the front page before, but only once for winning a ball game, way back in 1962, when, after nine consecutive defeats, they scored the first victory of their existence.

◆

BIG-LEAGUE HUMOR LINEUP

STARTING BATTERIES:	Jim ABBOTT (P) and John COSTELLO (C) or LARRY Douglas (P) or CURLY Brown (P) and MOE Berg (C)
RELIEF PITCHER:	BUSTER KEETON
INFIELD:	3B: JACK GLEASON SS: BILL MURRAY 2B: Henry YOUNGMAN 1B: PAT COOPER
OUTFIELD:	GEORGE BURNS DANNY THOMAS EDDIE MURPHY
RESERVES:	MARTIN & LEWIS, BERGEN & MCCARTHY, PRYOR & GREGORY; HOPE & CARSON; TOMLIN & ALLEN
COACHES:	JESTER, JOLLY & WITT

177

Mets Magic in Atlanta

TEXT AND DRAWINGS BY MORT GERBERG
PHOTOGRAPHS BY JOHN OLSON

BASEBALL HAD A PARTICULARLY EX-
citing year in 1969, due in large part to the Miracle Mets,
whose comeback appeal reached far beyond New York City.

The team that once was only a joke finished first in the East and
went to Atlanta to meet the Braves for the National League championship.

As usual, all eyes—*all* eyes—were turned on the Mets.

"What's the score?"

178

In Atlanta, there was a distinct difference in styles among the spectators. The Atlanta fans were loud enough but, by Met standards, not very demonstrative. They did not fill the ball park. They did not wave at the television cameras. To be fair, the Atlanta fans may have withheld their total love and devotion until they were convinced the franchise-shifting Braves would stay around town this time.

At times, the Atlanta fans were visibly strained by the manners displayed by the hordes of Met fans who had followed their team.

Rivaling the Statue of Liberty as a symbol of hope to the downtrodden everywhere, the Mets hold a special place in the hearts of all losers, great and small.

The Mets beat the Braves convincingly, then went on to win the World Series. Confounded, even the pros were unable to find a natural explanation.

The novel is called Oh, God!
The Title Character is talking to the narrator.

From <u>Oh, God!</u>

BY AVERY CORMAN

"IT'S BETTER THAT I SHOULDN'T MEDDLE. What am I going to do—get into favorites? So I come up with the concepts, the big ideas—the details can take care of themselves."

"Then the way things happen on earth . . ."

"They happen. Don't look at me."

"And there's no plan, no scheme that controls our destinies?"

"A lot of it is luck. Luck and who you know."

I was staggered. He just went zipping along.

"Looking back, of course I made a few mistakes. Giraffes. It was a good thought, but it really didn't work out. Avocados—on that I made the pit too big. Then there are things that worked pretty good. Photosynthesis is a big favorite of mine. Spring is nice. Tomatoes are cute. Also raccoons."

"But what about *Man?*" I was trying to rise to the responsibility. "What about his future? The future of the planet?"

"It's a good question."

"And?"

"I couldn't tell you."

"Don't you know?"

"Well, like I say, I don't get into that. Of course I hope you make it. I mean, I'm a real fan. But it's like in a ball game. If you're in the stands, you can root, but that's about all."

"You're God. You can protect our future, alleviate suffering, work miracles!"

"I don't do miracles. They're too flashy and they upset the natural

182.

balance. Oh, maybe I'll do a miracle now and then, just for fun—if it's not too important. The last miracle I did was the 1969 Mets and before that the 1914 Boston Braves and before that I think you have to go back to the Red Sea."

◆

*T*he New York Yankees never quite measured up to the Dodgers or the Mets—as far as humor is concerned. They were, for most of their existence, too good to be funny. They have gotten funnier in recent years.

Yet even when they were great, there was some humor, most of it supplied by Casey Stengel and his disciple, Yogi Berra. Mickey Mantle offered humor, too, predominantly scatological. Mickey used to read Henry Miller's Tropic of Cancer out loud on the team bus. The same page of Tropic of Cancer. Day after day after day.

Despite his impact on the Yankees, Henry Miller is not represented in this collection. Yogi Berra is. So is Neil Simon, the indefatigable playwright (that has nothing to do with his weight, Yogi), who has been credited with almost as many funny lines as Berra. Simon says that if he could have played center field for the Yankees, he gladly would have abandoned writing. DiMaggio hit in fifty-six straight games; Simon had fifty-six straight hits, or something like that; the similarities end there.

An excerpt from Simon's Brighton Beach Memoirs brightens these pages, along with samples of the prose of a pair of New York Times columnists, Ira Berkow, who always works the sports beat, and Russell Baker, who sometimes does.

"Yogi Berra says it's over."

Yogi Berra is supposed to have once said, "I really didn't say everything I said," and he was probably right. Many of Yogi's best lines may have come out of someone else's typewriter, not out of Yogi's mouth.

Still, whether he said them or not, everyone has a favorite Yogiism. For instance, the pizza line, attributed to Yogi when he was hungry after a night game, phoned a pizza delivery service and ordered a pie to be delivered to his room.

"Do you want it cut into four slices or into eight?" Berra was asked.

"Cut it into four," Yogi decided. "I don't think I can eat eight."

The following are some of Yogi's other gems.

Reflections

BY YOGI BERRA

ON DECLINING ATTENDANCE IN KANSAS city: "If people don't want to come to the ball park, how are you gonna stop them?"

Why the Yankees lost the 1960 World Series to the Pittsburgh Pirates: "We made too many wrong mistakes."

Why he thought he would be a good manager: "You observe a lot by watching."

On becoming a good defensive catcher: "Bill Dickey is learning me all his experience."

His theory on baseball, a thinking man's game: "Ninety percent of the game is half mental."

Explaining his variety of sweaters in assorted colors: "The only color I don't have is navy brown."

When Billy Martin locked his keys in his car: "You gotta call a blacksmith."

To his wife Carmen, about the movie, *The Magnificent Seven*, starring Steve McQueen: "He made that picture before he died."

To a sportswriter complaining that the hotel coffee shop charged $8.95 for a breakfast of orange juice, coffee, and an English muffin: "That's because they have to import those English muffins."

About a popular Minneapolis restaurant: "Nobody goes there any more, it's too crowded."

On the shadows in left field at Yankee Stadium in the fall: "It gets late early out there."

When he was honored at "Yogi Berra Night" in Sportsman's Park in St. Louis: "I want to thank all those who made this night necessary."

After his roommate closed his medical school text with a thud just as Berra finished his comic book: "How did yours come out?"

To Carmen when she said she had taken their son Tim to see *Dr. Zhivago*: "What the hell is wrong with him now?"

Asked by a player for the correct time: "Do you mean now?"

When Cardinals' broadcaster Jack Buck presented him with a check made out payable to "Bearer," after Yogi appeared on a pregame show: "You known me all that time and you still don't know how to spell my name."

Why he approved of Little League: "It keeps the kids out of the house."

Describing his new house in Montclair: "Wotta house. Nothin' but rooms!"

Why he refused to buy new luggage: "You only use it for traveling."

Arguing with an umpire that a drive to the outfield hit the concrete and should have been a home run instead of a double: "Anybody who can't hear the difference between a ball hitting wood and a ball hitting concrete must be blind."

When an elderly woman said to him that he looked very cool in his slacks and polo shirt: "Thank you, ma'am. You don't look so hot yourself."

When asked what he does on the afternoon of a night game: "I usually sleep for two hours, from one o'clock to four."

From *Brighton Beach Memoirs*

BY NEIL SIMON

OUTSIDE ON THE GRASS IS Eugene Jerome, almost but not quite fifteen. He is wearing knickers, a shirt and tie, a faded and torn sweater, Keds sneakers and a blue baseball cap. He has a beaten and worn baseball glove on his left hand and in his right hand he holds a ball that is so old and battered, it is ready to fall apart.

On an imaginary pitcher's mound, facing stage left, he looks back over his shoulder to an imaginary runner on second, then back over to the "batter." Then he winds up and pitches, hitting an offstage wall.

EUGENE. One out, a man on second, bottom of the seventh, two balls, no strikes . . . Ruffing checks the runner on second, gets the sign from Dickey, Ruffing stretches, Ruffing pitches—(*He throws the ball.*) Caught the inside corner, steerike one! Atta baby! No hitter up there. (*He retrieves the ball.*) One out, a man on second, bottom of the seventh, two balls one strike . . . Ruffing checks the runner on second, gets the sign from Dickey, Ruffing stretches, Ruffing pitches—(*He throws the ball.*) Low and outside, ball three. Come on, Red! Make him a hitter! No batter up there. In there all the time, Red.

BLANCHE. (*stops sewing*) Kate, please. My head is splitting.

KATE. I told that boy a hundred and nine times. (*She yells out.*) Eugene! Stop banging the wall!

EUGENE. (*Calls out*) In a minute, Ma! This is for the World Series! (*back to his game*) One out, a man on second, bottom of the seventh, three balls, one strike . . . Ruffing stretches, Ruffing pitches—(*He throws the ball.*) Oh no! High and outside, JoJo Moore walks! First and second and Mel Ott lopes up to the plate . . .

BLANCHE. (*stops again*) Can't he do that someplace else?

KATE. I'll break his arm, that's where he'll do it. (*She calls out*) Eugene, I'm not going to tell you again. Do you hear me?

EUGENE. It's the last batter, Mom. Mel Ott is up. It's a crucial moment in World Series history.

KATE. Your Aunt Blanche has a splitting headache.

BLANCHE. I don't want him to stop playing. It's just the banging.

LAURIE. (*Looks up from her book*) He always does it when I'm studying. I have a big test in history tomorrow.

EUGENE. One pitch, Mom? I think I can get him to pop up. I have my stuff today.

KATE. Your father will give you plenty of stuff when he comes home! You hear?

EUGENE. Alright! Alright!

KATE. I want you inside *now!* Put out the water glasses.

BLANCHE. I can do that.

KATE. Why? Is his arm broken? (*She yells out again*) And I don't want any back talk, you hear? (*She goes back to kitchen*)

EUGENE. (*Slams ball into his glove angrily. Then he cups his hand, making a megaphone out of it and announces to the grandstands*) . . . "Attention, ladeees and gentlemen! Today's game will be delayed because of my Aunt Blanche's headache . . ."

◆

Babe Ruth's roommate, Ping Bodie, was supposedly the first to say, "I didn't room with him, I roomed with his suitcase." The remark was subsequently attributed to most of Ruth's roommates.

◆

Why do the New York Yankees wear their famous pinstripes? Because Jacob Ruppert, the onetime owner of the team, thought the vertical stripes might make Babe Ruth look slimmer.

A Student of Attila the Hun

BY IRA BERKOW

GEORGE STEINBRENNER WAS MAKING A point about running the Yankees, that fifth-place enterprise in the Bronx, and about businesses in general, and the people who comprise them.

"You're the leader; you're the boss," the principal owner of the Yankees was saying Thursday afternoon to a visitor in his office at the Stadium, "and you can't blame others. You must give direction.

"I've been busy recently with my shipbuilding company, I've been involved with our Olympic team, and I was named the president of the Florida Thoroughbred Breeders Association. All of that takes time. But I'm going to have to be more directly involved with the Yankees.

"I used to be very hands-on, but lately I've been more hands-off, and I plan to become more hands-on and less hands-off and hope that hands-on will be better than hands-off, the way hands-on used to be."

Many Yankee followers, however, are convinced that there has never been a hands-off period with the principal owner; it's just that when things go poorly, he leaves no fingerprints, or thinks he doesn't.

◆

He admitted to mistakes even in his hands-on period, like calling Dave Winfield Mr. May, "which I did once, and that was regrettable"; and he let Reggie Jackson go too soon, and there was that display when he went bananas over a decision by his third-base coach in a playoff game. "But I was hot. I wanted to win. But even my mother scolded me for it. She said, 'George, I don't ever want to say what I saw you say on television.' "

He returned to the doctrine of hands-on. "You've got to be around, you've got to take an interest in the troops," he said. "Attila the Hun said it best. He said—"

"Attila the Hun?" interrupted the visitor. "The guy who pillaged and plundered?"

"Well, he wasn't perfect, but he did have some good things to say."

"Like what?"

"Here," Steinbrenner said, "I'll show you."

Seated at his desk he opened a drawer and pulled out a small book. It was: "Leadership Secrets of Attila the Hun," published last year by Warner Books.

"It's an excellent book. I've read this over and over," he said, plucking his reading glasses from his monogrammed shirt pocket. "My copy in my office in Florida is all marked up."

He flipped through the pages. "Look at this," he said, and read: " 'Chieftains must inspect their Huns frequently in order to see that what is accomplished meets with what is expected.' That's what I was saying. Pretty good, huh?"

He found a red pencil on his desk, and made a check mark beside that maxim. "Here's one," he said: " 'Chieftains must work hard to establish discipline and morale, then to maintain them within the tribe.' "

He read again: " 'It is the custom of all Huns to hold strong to personal and national honor. This is a cardinal virtue. One's word must prevail over all other considerations, including political expediency.' "

A lot of thoughts went through a visitor's brain on that one, including the many times Steinbrenner assured a manager he was there for the season and fired him shortly after.

"But George," said the visitor, "you don't follow all this advice."

"What I'm saying," he said, "is that we can all learn from this.

"People have said to me 'You're like Attila the Hun,' and I get, 'You're Patton,' and, look, on every office wall I've always had that up there." He pointed to a framed document, titled "Duty as Seen by Lincoln."

But it was Attila the Hun he was quoting now, and not the Great Emancipator.

"Here's another," he said, buried in the book. " 'You must recognize and accept that your greatness will be made possible through the extremes of personality, the very extremes that sometimes make for campfire satire and legendary stories.' "

190

He looked up over the reading glasses. "I read that one a lot," he said, with a little smile.

There was more in the book: "For Huns, conflict is a natural state." And, "Huns learn much faster when faced with adversity;" and, "If it were easy to be a chieftain, everyone would be one."

"You know," he said, "I wondered if this was Attila the Hun for real, or comical. But I think it's real, or close to it."

Attila, of course, was actual, but these "Attilaisms" are simply metaphors of leadership constructed by the author Wess Roberts, though based on historical research of that paragon of barbarity.

" 'Chieftains should never misuse power,' " Steinbrenner was reading. " 'Such action causes friction and leads to rebellion in the tribe or nation.' Hmm," he said, reaching for his red pencil, "I hadn't seen that one."

◆

When George Steinbrenner, the owner of the New York Yankees, was indicted for making illegal contributions to the Committee to Re-Elect President Nixon, his attorney, Edward Bennett Williams, who did not want to say that his client had lied, instead conceded to the court that some of George's recollections "were not in conformity with objective reality."

191

Love Me, Love My Bear

BY RUSSELL BAKER

I HAVE NEVER BEEN ABLE TO FIRE ANYBODY and, as a result, promotions have always passed me by. This is why I sought out George Steinbrenner, the owner of the New York Yankees and probably the most successful firer in the annals of unemployment.

Naturally, I had expected to meet an ogre, and, so, was delighted by the charm with which he received my proposal. I began by confessing that it was unusual. "Mr. Steinbrenner," I explained, "I want to study firing and I want to study under the best man in the field. Will you help me learn?"

Instead of the tirade I anticipated, these words produced a strange silence during which his eyes moistened and he struggled to hold back emotion. At length he said, "The best. . . . Nobody's ever said anything like that about me before."

"Oh, you have a good heart, Mr. Steinbrenner. I can see that. I know you'll help me, sir." He dabbed at his eyes with a handkerchief.

"I haven't been all torn up inside like this since the time they took away my teddy bear," he said, picking up the phone and asking his receptionist to step in.

"Yes, Mr. Steinbrenner?" said the receptionist.

"You're fired," he said.

"May I ask why?"

"For letting in people who remind me of the time they took my teddy bear away. I can't run a baseball team while I'm wondering whatever happened to that dear old teddy bear of mine."

When the receptionist had gone, I expressed admiration for the ease and rapidity with which he had conducted the firing. "Why, the receptionist didn't even call you a brute or an ingrate," I said.

"She didn't dare," said Mr. Steinbrenner. "If she had, she would have blown her chances of managing the Yankees."

193

I couldn't believe that, after firing her from a receptionist's job, he would hire her back to manage the team.

"Why not?" he asked. "At the rate I fire managers, I can't afford to be picky. Which reminds me—"

He dialed the phone. "I'm calling a sportswriter pal," he whispered. Then: "This is George, Sol. . . . Yeah, terrible about that last road trip. I've got it from the horse's mouth the Yankees are looking for a new manager. . . . Don't quote me."

He hung up. I felt radiant with hero worship. Mr. Steinbrenner was not only going to fire the manager; he was letting me know how he did it. "That will be headlines in the paper tomorrow," I said.

"You bet your sweet patootie," he said. "It'll put the Yankees back on page one, stir up the fans, get the old turnstiles clicking faster. When you fire somebody, son, fire with a purpose. It's good for the box office."

"You're the greatest, Mr. Steinbrenner."

"Now don't go getting me all choked up again," he said.

I saw this was the moment to push my case. "If it's not asking too much," I said, "could I come in some day and fire somebody for you while you watched me to make sure I'm doing it right?"

He rose from his desk and embraced me. "I like you, kid. You could be good, really good," he said. "I'm putting you on the payroll as junior assistant in charge of minor firings. Be in here tomorrow morning early and I'll let you fire a couple of peanut vendors."

I was too overcome to trust my voice, so I merely nodded, sniffled, and moved to the door.

"Before you go," he said.

"Yes."

"About the manager I've got to fire—do you know who's managing the Yankees this week?"

Not wanting to blow my big chance by revealing that I didn't follow baseball, I gave him the name of the only baseball manager I could remember. "It's Earl Weaver," I said.

As I left, he had Weaver on the telephone. "Earl, baby," he was saying "you're through. Drop by the cashier's window and pick up your paycheck. . . ."

194

I reported early next morning to fire peanut vendors. Mr. Steinbrenner led in the first, then stood behind me to observe my technique. The peanut vendor was a small, cuddly fellow with plump, round cheeks and a great deal of hair.

"Vendor," I snarled, and then paused.

"Yes sir. Bag of peanuts, sir?"

"What are you waiting for?" asked Mr. Steinbrenner. "Give him the ax."

"I can't," I said.

"Can't! Why not?"

"He reminds me of my dear old teddy bear," I said.

I heard Mr. Steinbrenner snuffle and suppress a sob behind me. Then: "Nobody can talk about teddy bears around me and get away with it," he said in a voice hoarse with sorrow. "You're fired."

I was leaving the Stadium when a guard said Mr. Steinbrenner wanted me on the phone. "Give me your phone number, kid," he said. "I'm going to need some new managers next spring."

◆

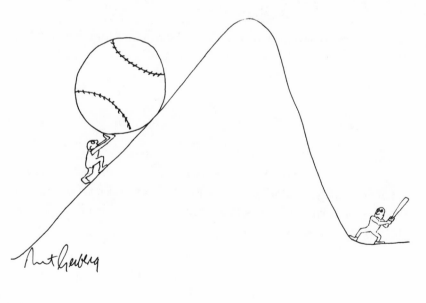

*B*aseball has triggered its share of the skirmishes in the war between the sexes, but only occasionally has the war been waged on the playing field.

"I wish someone would take him out to the ballgame and leave him there."

◆

A Baseball Annie, a camp follower, once sent a love letter to Kirby Higbe of the Brooklyn Dodgers at his home address, and when his wife opened the letter and confronted him with it, Higbe pleaded innocent by saying, "It must've been another Kirby Higbe."

"You will meet a tall, dark handsome man who will take you out to the ballgame, take you out with the crowd."

♦

BIG-LEAGUE BABES

First base—Jewel Ens
Second base—Lena Blackbourne
Shortstop—Dot Fulghum
Third base—Toots Coyne
Outfield—Buttercup Dickerson
Outfield—Bunny Brief
Outfield—Minnie Minoso
Catcher—Bubbles Hargrave
Pitcher—Daisy Davis

Manager—Babe Ruth

"Mind if I put on the game?"

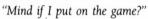

Who's on First?

BY J. M. FLAGLER

THE FUSS IN THE NEWSPAPERS RECENTLY about the thwarted attempt to introduce a girl player from Harrisburg, Pennsylvania, into organized baseball stirred me to recollections of Cassie Brambler. Cassie was the first woman I know of to break into the sport.

The event took place almost twenty years ago, when Cassie played in the championship game of the Shore Line League, a loose federation of four teams that operated during the summer in a resort section along the east side of Lake Michigan. One of the teams was the Macatawa Icemen, so named by Cassie's brother Cal, the playing manager, who ran a small icehouse near Macatawa Lake and supplied the team's uniforms. Macatawa is a short arm of Lake Michigan, and my family rented a cottage there the summer I was sixteen.

When Cal suggested, one day early in the season, that I take over in right field, as the team was shorthanded, I felt very flattered. Most of the players were older than I; Cal was a heavy, squint-eyed man of thirty. He supported our belief that we were a bonafide segment of organized baseball by asserting that he had once had a tryout with the Cincinnati Reds and, until benched for astigmatism, had done a hitch with Moline in the Three-I League. Every summer, along with the first cottagers and resort-hotel guests, Cal arrived out of the brush country behind the dune lands and, wearing a big leather apron with a diagonal shoulder strap, began sawing ice.

With Cal each year came Cassie. She was a muscular girl in her late teens, built squatly, along the lines of Yogi Berra, the Yankee catcher. She had long, stringy curls and a fierce, florid countenance, like an outraged beet. She often *was* outraged, because in our male vanity we refused to let her play in any of our games, despite the fact that she could outhit and outrun nearly everyone on the team. She insisted on practicing with us in the dusty patch of meadow we used for a home

199

diamond, and I must say she was the best natural woman athlete I've ever seen. For one thing, she let her arm go all the way back when she wound up to throw a ball, instead of pulling it about halfway back and then sort of springing the ball forward, as most women do. She ran like a man, too.

At practice, when Cassie wasn't in the field surpassing us, she was on the sidelines belaboring us. Standing with her arms akimbo, she would glower and comment contemptuously on our ballplaying. True, we were a fairly unprofessional group. Besides Cal and me, the hard core was composed of a graduate divinity student, who waited on table at a resort hotel; a summering University of Michigan poet; a slow-witted but incredibly long-armed local man, who played first base; the Pryzewski twins, whose father ran a successful coal business in Ham-tramck, Michigan; and a rich and indolent young eccentric from St. Louis, who spurned the company of his economic peers and was always talking about someday marrying a pure-blooded Cherokee girl. But even so, Cassie was unduly severe, we thought.

"Couldn't hit the broad side of a barn!" she'd yell as someone missed an easy pitch, or, upon noting a bobbled grounder, she'd advise, "Go get a handle for it." Cassie's badinage was not exactly cutting, but through repetition and a certain rasp in her voice, she succeeded in getting on our nerves. At intervals, knowing what her trouble was, we'd try reasoning with her.

"But think how it'd look, Cassie," one of us would say. "A *girl* playing baseball. They'd laugh us out of the league."

Her answer to that would be to point to me and observe, "Got a infant kid playing for you, ain't you? Can't say I ain't as good as him." Or she'd glance at the slow-witted first baseman or the poet. "Oh, you got some darbs playing for you," she'd say.

We'd reach an impasse when one of the men declared that if she played, the rest wouldn't. Then Cal, who generally remained in the background during these tiffs, would have the final say. "Ain't no use niff-nawin' about it, Sis. Comes down to not having a team nor a game, you're just going to have to set."

Cassie would glower some more and then walk angrily away. During games, she'd sit at one end of the bench, looking utterly disgusted, and moan loudly at every misplay.

200

"She's about as inspiring as the Medusa," the poet once remarked, "and just as attractive."

The Icemen were a pretty ragtag assemblage, compared to the other teams in the league. The Meteors consisted of young vacationers from a prosperous resort community a couple of miles down the lake shore. They were mostly from Northwestern or Cornell or Princeton, gymnasia highly regarded by well-to-do young Midwesterners of the period, and they usually showed up to play in a swirl of convertibles and suntanned young women. The Meteors defaulted frequently, because of prior commitments for tennis or tea dances. Then, there were the Amsterdams, a group of wealthy lads from the old Dutch communities of Holland and Grand Rapids. They were mostly named Ten Eyck or de Boom and were taciturn and slow-footed, but, as the sportswriters say, they hit the long ball. The fourth team was made up mainly of permanent residents of the area, good-natured countrymen who showed their scorn for the summer crowd by occasionally spearing our line drives with their bare hands. This team, known as the Silos, was the favorite that year, and everyone was surprised when the Icemen, under the goad of Cassie Brambler, finished the season tied with them for first place.

◆

The playoff game was scheduled for a Sunday late in August on our home diamond. That morning, we had trouble. The divinity student, who had always been reluctant to play on the Sabbath, this time refused outright, because he learned there was a large keg of beer, symbolic of the league pennant, at stake, and the rich young man disappeared, presumably having got a lead on a marriageable Cherokee girl. When we rode out to the grounds, an hour or so early, for a workout, we had eight men, Cassie, and a slim hope that, as sometimes happened, an extra player would show up at the field.

Cassie wasn't talking, for a change, but she looked especially peppery as she went about shagging flies and taking her turn at bat. The rest of us were quiet, too, and a little tense. No extra man appeared, and not long before the other team arrived, Cal called us all together and tossed the problem squarely in our laps.

"Well, Cassie going to play or ain't she?" he asked.

No one spoke for a few moments. Only the chirping of a cricket in

201

the crab grass broke the stillness of the sunny day. Then one of the Pryzewski twins said softly that it was all right with him, he supposed, but that he still thought it would look funny to have a girl playing on the team.

Cassie sucked her breath in sharply. "You just wait," she said, and started toward a nearby shed, where we had our lockers. "Just you wait there a minute." She disappeared inside.

A while later, instead of the Cassie we knew, a short, rotund player in an Iceman uniform emerged from the shed. A baseball cap hid the stringy curls, and some kind of stuffing had disguised the lines of her bosom. "Now do I look funny?" she asked.

"Suits me," said the Pryzewski twin. His brother nodded, and the rest of us did, too, not daring to laugh.

Cal decided she could play second base under an assumed name and nobody would be likely to know the difference if she kept her cap on and her mouth shut. "In that rig," said Cal, "I couldn't tell you was a female, let alone my own baby sister."

A nonpartisan and largely indifferent crowd of perhaps a hundred turned out for the game, including a scattering of Amsterdams, and even several Meteors in white duck trousers. A Pryzewski twin pitched for us, and he was in excellent form. So was the Silo hurler. As a result, we found ourselves in a 2–2 tie when we came to bat in the last half of the ninth inning. There was the prospect of an upset, and the crowd, rather torpid up to then, began clapping for a hit.

Our first man up responded by striking out. I was next, and managed to work the pitcher for a base on balls. That brought Cassie to bat. Cal figured the Silos would be expecting us to try to hit the ball as far as we could, and so, using big-league strategy, he had instructed Cassie to lay down a bunt. She was a first-rate bunter, and, being fast, could probably beat the throw to first base, and in any event I'd presumably get to second and be in a good position to score. Cassie had really played a man's game that day, particularly in the field and as a base runner, and now she bunted perfectly down the third-base line. I made it to second with ease, and, sure enough, Cassie reached first safely, her legs driving hard. The crowd applauded.

Cal was the next batter. As he stepped up to the plate, Cassie led

202

off first base a few yards, and I noticed that while her stuffing was still in place, one curl had slipped down from beneath her cap. The Silo first baseman glanced at her curiously. Cal, whose astigmatic eyes were unpredictable and who had hit once and struck out twice, couldn't seem to get the proper focus, and the Silo pitcher shortly had a two-strike, no-ball count on him. The pitcher's next throw was way wide, however, and the first baseman walked over to him and, after huddling with him for a second, slapped him encouragingly on the shoulder, and then trotted back to his position behind Cassie.

The pitcher stood peering at the catcher, as if to get the signal, and that was as far as he went. The next thing I knew, the first baseman was yelling at the first-base umpire and holding his glove on Cassie's arm and claiming she was out. The umpire looked in the glove and made a thumb-over-the-shoulder gesture.

"Runner's out!" he shouted.

The Silos started hooting. Cassie stood next to the base, stunned and openmouthed. It took several seconds for her to realize they had pulled off about the oldest subterfuge in baseball—the hidden-ball trick. Then she did what any red-blooded American girl betrayed by male perfidy would do. She burst into tears.

The amazed Silos gathered silently around her. Cassie just stood there and wept. Presently, the first baseman walked over and jerked her cap off, and the stringy hair fell around her ears. A yell went up from the Silos. "Hoo gawd!" cried one. "She's a girrul!"

They began laughing and throwing their gloves on the ground. I edged toward third base and then walked on home, past the Silos' catcher and the plate umpire, who were standing just in front of home plate, gawking at the first-base scene. Stepping on the plate, I turned and touched the umpire on the back.

"I'm the winning run," I said.

The umpire wheeled around and goggled. "You're on second," he said.

"No, I'm not," I said, tapping one foot on the plate. "I'm home with the winning run. I stole third and now I've stolen home."

Cal and the other Icemen came running over to us from the bench, and the Silos closed in, and there was a big squabble that made everyone

forget Cassie. The plate umpire wasn't sure at first, but Cal proved to him that the ball was still in play and that I stole the bases fair and square. What was more, he had the spectators, who were laughing and clapping, altogether on his side.

◆

Afterward, going over to a local tavern to pick up the keg of beer, I rode in the front seat of Cal's old Hupmobile, along with him and Cassie. The rest of the team was piled in the back, which Cal had gutted to accommodate ice. Cassie was disconsolate, and there was a respectful silence most of the way. Cal broke the ice, so to speak.

"Well, Sis," he said, "the way I score it, you get credit for batting in the winning run, come right down to it."

She glared at him for a second, as though ready to excoriate him, but she only said, "Oh, bother." Then, for almost the first time, I saw her smile.

◆

Jules Feiffer

What Did We Do Wrong?

BY GARRISON KEILLOR

THE FIRST WOMAN TO REACH THE BIG leagues said she wanted to be treated like any other rookie, but she didn't have to worry about that. The Sparrows nicknamed her Chesty and then Big Numbers the first week of spring training, and loaded her bed at the Ramada with butterscotch pudding. Only the writers made a big thing about her being the First Woman. The Sparrows treated her like dirt.

Annie Szemanski arrived in camp fresh from the Federales League of Bolivia, the fourth second baseman on the Sparrows roster, and when Drayton stepped in a hole and broke his ankle Hemmie put her in the lineup, hoping she would break hers. "This was the front office's bright idea," he told the writers. "Off the record, I think it stinks." But when she got in she looked so good that by the third week of March she was a foregone conclusion. Even Hemmie had to admit it. A .346 average tells no lies. He disliked her purely because she was a woman— there was nothing personal about it. Because she was a woman, she was given the manager's dressing room, and Hemmie had to dress with the team. He was sixty-one, a heavyweight, and he had a possum tattooed on his belly alongside the name "Georgene," so he was shy about taking his shirt off in front of people. He hated her for making it necessary. Other than that, he thought she was a tremendous addition to the team.

Asked how she felt being the first woman to make a major-league team, she said, "Like a pig in mud," or words to that effect, and then turned and released a squirt of tobacco juice from the wad of rum-soaked plug in her right cheek. She chewed a rare brand of plug called Stuff It, which she learned to chew when she was playing Nicaraguan summer ball. She told the writers, "They were so mean to me down there you couldn't write it in your newspaper. I took a gun everywhere

I went, even to bed. *Especially* to bed. Guys were after me like you can't believe. That's when I started chewing tobacco—because no matter how bad anybody treats you, it's not as bad as this. This is the worst chew in the world. After this, everything else is peaches and cream." The writers elected Gentleman Jim, the Sparrows' P.R. guy, to bite off a chunk and tell them how it tasted, and as he sat and chewed it tears ran down his old sunburnt cheeks and he couldn't talk for a while. Then he whispered, "You've been chewing this for two years? God, I had no idea it was so hard to be a woman."

When thirty-two thousand fans came to Cold Spring Stadium on April 4th for Opening Day and saw the scrappy little freckle-faced woman with tousled black hair who they'd been reading about for almost two months, they were dizzy with devotion. They chanted her name and waved Annie flags and Annie caps ($8.95 and $4.95) and held up handpainted bedsheets ("EVERY DAY IS LADIES' DAY," "A WOMAN'S PLACE—AT SECOND BASE," "E.R.A. & R.B.I." "THE GAME AIN'T OVER TILL THE BIG LADY BATS"), but when they saw No. 18 trot out to second with a load of chew as big as if she had the mumps it was a surprise. Then, bottom of the second, when she leaned over in the on-deck circle and dropped a stream of brown juice in the sod, the stadium experienced a moment of thoughtful silence.

One man in Section 31 said, "Hey, what's the beef? She can chew if she wants to. This is 1987. Grow up."

"I guess you're right," his next-seat neighbor said. "My first reaction was nausea, but I think you're right."

"Absolutely. She's a woman, but, more than that, she's a *person.*"

Other folks said, "I'm with you on that. A woman can carry a quarter pound of chew in her cheek and spit in public, same as any man—why should there be any difference?"

And yet. Nobody wanted to say this, but the plain truth was that No. 18 was not handling her chew well at all. Juice ran down her chin and dripped onto her shirt. She's bit off more than she can chew, some people thought to themselves, but they didn't want to say that.

Arnie (the Old Gardener) Brixius mentioned it ever so gently in his "Hot Box" column the next day:

It's only this scribe's opinion, but isn't it about time baseball cleaned up its act and left the tobacco in the locker? Surely big leaguers can go two hours without nicotine. Many a fan has turned away in disgust at the sight of grown men (and now a member of the fair sex) with a faceful, spitting gobs of the stuff in full view of paying customers. Would Frank Sinatra do this onstage? Or Anne Murray? Nuff said.

♦

End of April, Annie was batting .278, with twelve R.B.I.s, which for the miserable Sparrows was stupendous, and at second base she was surprising a number of people, including base runners who thought she'd be a pushover on the double play. A runner heading for second quickly found out that Annie had knees like ballpeen hammers and if he tried to eliminate her from the play she might eliminate him from the rest of the week. One night, up at bat against the Orioles, she took a step toward the mound after an inside pitch and yelled some things, and when the dugouts emptied she was in the thick of it with men who had never been walloped by a woman before. The home-plate ump hauled her off a guy she was pounding the cookies out of, and a moment later he threw her out of the game for saying things to him, he said, that he had never heard in his nineteen years of umpiring. ("Like what, for example?" writers asked. "Just tell us one thing." But he couldn't; he was too upset.)

The next week, the United Baseball Office Workers local passed a resolution in support of Annie, as did the League of Women Voters and the Women's Softball Caucus, which stated, "Szemanski is a model for all women who are made to suffer guilt for their aggressiveness, and we declare our solidarity with her heads-up approach to the game. While we feel she is holding the bat too high and should bring her hips into her swing more, we're behind her one hundred per cent."

Then, May 4th, at home against Oakland—seventh inning, two outs, bases loaded—she dropped an easy pop-up and three runs came across home plate. The fans sent a few light boos her way to let her know they were paying attention, nothing serious or overtly political, just some folks grumbling, but she took a few steps toward the box seats and yelled something at them that sounded like—well, like something

she shouldn't have said, and after the game she said some more things to the writers that Gentleman Jim pleaded with them not to print. One of them was Monica Lamarr, of the *Press,* who just laughed. She said, "Look. I spent two years in the Lifestyles section writing about motherhood vs. career and the biolgical clock. Sports is my way out of the gynecology ghetto, so don't ask me to eat this story. It's a hanging curve and I'm going for it. I'm never going to write about day care again." And she wrote it:

SZEMANSKI RAPS FANS
AS "SMALL PEOPLE"
AFTER DUMB ERROR GIVES
GAME TO A'S

FIRST WOMAN ATTRIBUTES BOOS
TO SEXUAL INADEQUACY IN STANDS

Jim made some phone calls and the story was yanked and only one truckload of papers went out with it, but word got around, and the next night, though Annie went three for four, the crowd was depressed, and even when she did great the rest of the home stand, and became the first woman to hit a major-league triple, the atmosphere at the ballpark was one of moodiness and deep hurt. Jim went to the men's room one night and found guys standing in line there, looking thoughtful and sad. One of them said, "She's a helluva ballplayer," and other guys murmured that yes, she was, and they wouldn't take anything away from her, she was great and it was wonderful that she had opened up baseball to women, and then they changed the subject to gardening, books, music, aesthetics, anything but baseball. They looked like men who had been stood up.

Gentleman Jim knocked on her door that night. She wore a blue chenille bathrobe flecked with brown tobacco-juice stains, and her black hair hung down in wet strands over her face. She spat into a Dixie cup she was carrying. "Hey! How the Fritos are you? I haven't seen your Big Mac for a while," she said, sort of. He told her she was a great person and a great ballplayer and that he loved her and wanted only the best for her, and he begged her to apologize to the fans. "Make a gesture—*anything*. They *want* to like you. Give them a chance to like you."

208

She blew her nose into a towel. She said that she wasn't there to be liked, she was there to play ball.

♦

It was a good road trip. The Sparrows won five out of ten, lifting their heads off the canvas, and Annie raised her average to .291 and hit the first major-league home run ever by a woman, up into the left-field screen at Fenway. Sox fans stood and cheered for fifteen minutes. They whistled, they stamped, they pleaded, the Sparrows pleaded, umpires pleaded, but she refused to come out and tip her hat until the public-address announcer said, "No. 18, please come out of the dugout and take a bow. No. 18, the applause is for you and is not intended as patronizing in any way," and then she stuck her head out for 1.5 seconds and did not tip but only touched the brim. Later, she told the writers that just because people had expectations didn't mean she had to fulfill them—she used other words to explain this, but her general drift was that she didn't care very much about living up to anyone else's image of her, and if anyone thought she should, they could go watch wrist wrestling.

The forty thousand who packed Cold Spring Stadium June 6th to see the Sparrows play the Yankees didn't come for a look at Ron Guidry. Banners hung from the second deck: "WHAT DID WE DO WRONG?" and "ANNIE COME HOME" and "WE LOVE YOU, WHY DO YOU TREAT US THIS WAY?" and "IF YOU WOULD LIKE TO DISCUSS THIS IN A NON-CONFRONTATIONAL, MUTUALLY RESPECTFUL WAY, MEET US AFTER THE GAME AT GATE C." It was Snapshot Day, and all the Sparrows appeared on the field for photos with the fans except you know who. Hemmie begged her to go. "You owe it to them," he said.

"Owe?" she said. *"Owe?"*

"Sorry, wrong word," he said. "What if I put it this way: it's a sort of tradition."

"Tradition?" she said. "I'm supposed to worry about *tradition?"*

That day, she became the first woman to hit .300. A double in the fifth inning. The scoreboard flashed the message, and the crowd gave her a nice hand. A few people stood and cheered, but the fans around them told them to sit down. "She's not that kind of person," they said. "Cool it. Back off." The fans were trying to give her plenty of space. After the game, Guidry said, "I really have to respect her. She's got

209

that small strike zone and she protects it well, so she makes you pitch to her." She said, "Guidry? Was that his name? I didn't know. Anyway, he didn't show me much. He throws funny, don't you think? He reminded me a little bit of a southpaw I saw down in Nicaragua, except she threw inside more."

All the writers were there, kneeling around her. One of them asked if Guidry had thrown her a lot of sliders.

She gave him a long, baleful look. "Jeez, you guys are out of shape," she said. "You're wheezing and panting and sucking air, and you just took the elevator *down* from the press box. You guys want to write about sports you ought to go into training. And then you ought to learn how to recognize a slider. Jeez, if you were writing about agriculture, would you have to ask someone if those were Holsteins?"

Tears came to the writer's eyes. "I'm trying to help," he said. "Can't you see that? Don't you know how much we care about you? Sometimes I think you put up this tough exterior to hide your own insecurity."

She laughed and brushed the wet hair back from her forehead. "It's no exterior," she said as she unbuttoned her jersey. "It's who I am." She peeled off her socks and stepped out of her cubicle a moment later, sweaty and stark naked. The towel hung from her hand. She walked slowly around them. "You guys learned all you know about women thirty years ago. That wasn't me back then, that was my mother." The writers bent over their notepads, writing down every word she said and punctuating carefully. Gentleman Jim took off his glasses. "My mother was a nice lady, but she couldn't hit the curve to save her Creamettes," she went on. "And now, gentlemen, if you'll excuse me, I'm going to take a shower." They pored over their notes until she was gone, and then they piled out into the hallway and hurried back to the press elevator.

Arnie stopped at the Shortstop for a load of Martinis before he went to the office to write the "Hot Box," which turned out to be about love:

> Baseball is a game but it's more than a game, baseball is people, dammit, and if you are around people you can't help but get involved in their lives and care about them and then you don't know how to talk to them or tell them how much you care and

210

how come we know so much about pitching and we don't know squat about how to communicate? I guess that is the question.

◆

The next afternoon, Arnie leaned against the batting cage before the game, hung over, and watched her hit line drives, fifteen straight, and each one made his head hurt. As she left the cage, he called over to her. "Later," she said. She also declined a pregame interview with Joe Garagiola, who had just told his NBC "Game of the Week" television audience, "This is a city in love with a little girl named Annie Szemanski," when he saw her in the dugout doing deep knee bends. "Annie! Annie!" he yelled over the air. "Let's see if we can't get her up here," he told the home audience. "Annie! Joe Garagiola!" She turned her back to him and went down into the dugout.

That afternoon, she became the first woman to steal two bases in one inning. She reached first on a base on balls, stole second, went to third on a sacrifice fly, and headed for home on the next pitch. The catcher came out to make the tag, she caught him with her elbow under the chin, and when the dust cleared she was grinning at the ump, the catcher was sprawled in the grass trying to inhale, and the ball was halfway to the backstop.

The TV camera zoomed in on her, head down, trotting toward the dugout steps, when suddenly she looked up. Some out-of-town fan had yelled at her from the box seats. ("A profanity which also refers to a female dog," the News said.) She smiled and, just before she stepped out of view beneath the dugout roof, millions observed her right hand uplifted in a familiar gesture. In bars around the country, men looked at each other and said, "Did she do what I think I saw her do? She didn't do that, did she?" In the booth, Joe Garagiola was observing that it was a clean play, that the runner has a right to the base path, but when her hand appeared on the screen he stopped. At home, it sounded as if he had been hit in the chest by a rock. The screen went blank, then went to a beer commercial. When the show resumed, it was the middle of the next inning.

On Monday, for "actions detrimental to the best interests of baseball," Annie was fined a thousand dollars by the Commissioner and suspended for two games. He deeply regretted the decision, etc. "I count

myself among her most ardent fans. She is good for baseball, good for the cause of equal rights, good for America." He said he would be happy to suspend the suspension if she would make a public apology, which would make him the happiest man in America.

Gentleman Jim went to the bank Monday afternoon and got the money, a thousand dollars, in a cashier's check. All afternoon, he called Annie's number over and over, waiting thirty and forty rings, then trying again. He called from a pay phone at the Stop 'N' Shop, next door to the Cityview Apartments, where she lived, and between calls he sat in his car and watched the entrance, waiting for her to come out. Other men were parked there, too, in front, and some in back—men with Sparrows bumper stickers. After midnight, about eleven of them were left. "Care to share some onion chips and clam dip?" one guy said to another guy. Pretty soon all of them were standing around the trunk of the clam-dip guy's car, where he also had a case of beer.

"Here, let me pay you something for this beer," said a guy who had brought a giant box of pretzels.

"Hey, no. Really. It's just good to have other guys to talk to tonight," said the clam-dip owner.

"She changed a lot of very basic things about the whole way that I look at myself as a man," the pretzel guy said quietly.

"I'm in public relations," said Jim, "but even I don't understand all that she has meant to people."

"How can she do this to us?" said a potato-chip man. "All the love of the fans, how can she throw it away? Why can't she just play ball?"

Annie didn't look at it that way. "Pall Mall! I'm not going to crawl just because some Tootsie Roll says crawl, and if they don't like it, then Ritz, they can go Pepsi their Hostess Twinkies," she told the writers as she cleaned out her locker on Tuesday morning. They had never seen the inside of her locker before. It was stuffed with dirty socks, half unwrapped gifts from admiring fans, a set of ankle weights, and a small silver-plated pistol. "No way I'm going to pay a thousand dollars, and if they expect an apology—well, they better send out for lunch, because it's going to be a long wait. Gentlemen, goodbye and hang on to your valuable coupons." And she smiled her most winning smile and sprinted up the stairs to collect her paycheck. They waited for her outside the Sparrows office, twenty-six men, and then followed her

212

down the ramp and out of Gate C. She broke into a run and disappeared into the lunchtime crowd on West Providence Avenue, and that was the last they saw of her—the woman of their dreams, the love of their lives, carrying a red gym bag, running easily away from them.

◆

"Martha, do you have anything you want to say before the baseball season starts?"

Foreword from *The Baseball Fan's Guide to Spring Training (1989 Season)*

BY JIM BOUTON

"Many are called, but few are chosen."
Seattle Pilots Manager Joe Schultz,
Tempe, Arizona, 1969
(also Jesus Christ, Jerusalem, 33)

AVE YOU EVER SEEN THOSE NATURE films on public television where the camera zooms in close on a field of flowers? What appears to be a beautiful meadow is, in reality, a life-and-death struggle for survival—an ambush bug is sucking the life juices out of an unsuspecting honey bee. That's what Spring Training is like. Lovely blue skies and acres of green grass while guys are fighting and dying all over the place.

You've got aging veterans struggling to hang on, hotshot rookies looking to break in, guys coming off injuries or operations, non-roster players getting their last chance, and a few stars who have it made. Fifty or more players are battling for only twenty-five jobs. It's a jungle down there.

The country boys call it "nut-cutting time." On the Yankees, getting cut from the team was actually called "dying." Pitcher Fritz Peterson would walk around the locker room asking, "Who died today?" Players having a bad spring were said to be "very sick." And if a utility infielder was 0 for 15 with half a dozen errors, he was "terminally ill."

In Spring Training, death can come at any time. If a coach whispers in your ear that the manager wants to see you in his office, you might as well lie down and pull a sheet up over your head. And sometimes

214

it's not so private. In the spring of '69, Seattle Pilots coach Ron Plaza hollered across the field to pitcher Roland Sheldon that Joe Shultz wanted to see him in his office. "I was so embarrassed," said Sheldon, "I was tempted to holler back, 'Ask him what he wants!' " But he knew.

Even the clubhouse man can be the bearer of bad tidings. One spring with the Yankees, we came in after a workout and all players going north with the team had their equipment bags packed in front of their lockers. And those without bags? Rest in peace.

Some players laugh until they die. Minor league outfielder Don Lock could never crack the Yankee outfield of Mantle, Maris, and Tresh. But he never went down without a fight. One spring, Lock switched the nameplate over his locker with Mickey Mantle's. Then he barricaded himself in his locker behind a camouflage of sweatshirts and jockstraps. Using his bat as a rifle, he'd take potshots at any suspicious coach who might wander near. That was always good for a few laughs . . . until the final curtain.

Teams can be very creative about telling a player that he's history. In a variation of the good news/bad news joke, Detroit Tiger manager Mayo Smith once told outfielder Wayne Comer that he was going to hit .300 that year—but he was going to do it in Montgomery, Alabama. To keep options open, the final cuts are made at the last possible moment. One year, Yankee pitcher Joe Verbanic was told that he'd made the team and he could drive his family north in their car. Halfway up the Florida Turnpike, a toll collector, instructed to be on the lookout for a packed blue station wagon, gave Joe the bad news. He still had to pay the $1.50 toll—twice.

And then there are the uninvited kids who, every spring, pack up their glove and bat and come down to camp hoping for a tryout. They never even get on the field, though John Pappas came close in 1962. Pappas had read in the papers that the Mets were desperate for pitching their first year. So he left his Long Island City home and paid his own way down to the Mets' training camp, where he announced that he could make the club. He had worked out all winter long throwing a ball underneath the Queensboro Bridge. The Mets said "No way" but a few New York sportswriters shamed them into giving the 21-year-old kid a chance. Begrudgingly, Farm Director Johnny Murphy took

Pappas and a catcher to a remote sandlot to see what he had. Scouting report: Couldn't make a high school team.

Most fans are unaware of all this heartbreak. As far as they're concerned, it just looks like this kid, Henderson #94, is now working out over on Diamond Seven across the road. The minor league complex, while only a few yards away, is actually many miles and often years away from the Major Leagues. The moment a player has been cut, he becomes a non-person in the clubhouse. Teammates come by to offer a "Hang in there," but mostly they're just glad it wasn't them. It's the same for injured players. In sports, winning is everything, and if a player cannot contribute to that cause, there is no reason for his existence. So if you happen to stroll by Diamond Seven, remember to give a friendly wave to Henderson.

◆

Spring Training is relaxing only for the few regulars who've got it made, but it's a lot of fun for the occasional rookie invited down to help out. In 1962 the Yankees asked me to pitch batting practice and shag balls in the outfield until the big guys got in shape. I knew I had no chance to make the team because of the uniform number they gave me: 87.

Then one day the Yankees needed a pitcher in the tenth inning of a tie ballgame against the Cardinals. Manager Ralph Houk said, "Get me the kid who pitched batting practice," and suddenly I was in the game. I got the Cardinals out 1-2-3, and we didn't score, so I had to pitch the eleventh. Nobody scored, so I pitched the twelfth, and the thirteenth. In the middle of the fourteenth inning I suddenly realized I led the team in innings pitched and strikeouts.

I was thrilled. My teammates weren't so happy. Catcher John Blanchard was actually angry.

"Hey, Meat! [John called all the rookies Meat.] Throw the damn ball over and let 'em hit it."

"Why?" I asked.

"Because I got a golf date and Yogi's got dinner plans. Besides, it's hot out here."

"But John," I said, "I'm trying to make the ballclub."

"You're not gonna make the team," said John. "You're only pitching

'cause we don't have anybody else." And then he went behind home plate and started telling the hitters what was coming.

Whenever a rookie surprises the coaches in Spring Training, they give him another chance to prove he doesn't belong. It's called getting enough rope to hang yourself. But I kept pitching well, and by the end of Spring Training they had no choice but to give me a Yankee contract. And a new uniform number: 56.

It was "great to be young and a Yankee," as someone once said. I walked around all spring with a silly grin on my face, not quite believing I was actually playing on the same field with Mickey, Whitey, Yogi, and the guys. Of course, the fans were there to remind me who I was: Nobody. People would come up to me with autograph books and ask, "Are you anybody good?" One father sent his son over to get an autograph from a famous Yankee. "It's only Jim Bouton, Dad," said the kid. Whereupon the father replied, "Well, get it anyway."

Spring Training is where I learned about the social habits of Major League ballplayers. In 1962 the Yanks had just moved their training camp from sleepy old St. Petersburg to the "Fun Coast" of Fort Lauderdale. It didn't take the players long to get acclimated to their new surroundings. Players who didn't have their families with them stayed at the Yankee Clipper Motel on the beach. I roomed with Bill Stafford's luggage. Bill Stafford himself was attending late night team meetings at Fazio's restaurant bar or the Bahia Mar cocktail lounge. With the exception of Bobby Richardson, who belonged to the Fellowship of Christian Athletes, none of the Yankees observed curfew, possibly because it was never enforced.

Some players use Spring Training to start getting in trouble for the regular season. Pitcher Don Larsen wrapped his car around a lamppost and spent the night in a St. Petersburg jail before getting bailed out by Casey Stengel. Third baseman Clete Boyer punched a male model in the mouth at a Fort Lauderdale bar. And relief pitcher Marshall Bridges showed up at training camp with a bullet in his leg.

However, there are probably fewer hijinks in Spring Training than during the regular season, for several reasons. Managers and coaches are a lot more mellow (after all, they're not getting cut). Nobody has lost any real ballgames yet, and until opening day every team is still

217

tied for first place. But the biggest deterrence to trouble is the presence of so many players' wives, who insist on leaving a cold climate to come down and sit by the pool while the players work out. In the 1950s, local police caught pitcher Mickey McDermott making love to a woman on a St. Petersburg beach. "It's OK, Officer," said McDermott. "This is my wife." And it was.

As I said, for players who have the team made, Spring Training is a ball. I remember the annual Mickey Mantle fishing tournament in the Everglades. Two players per boat, each guy would kick in twenty bucks before leaving the dock in the morning. At noon everybody came back, and Mickey and Whitey would win all the money for the biggest fish and the most fish caught.

One spring, my roommate Phil Linz and I made our best catch while driving to the fishing site. Along the highway we stopped at a fish store and bought a twenty-pound beauty, which we hid in our beer cooler. That baby was frozen rock-solid and it took all morning to thaw out, but it was worth it. At weigh-in time our fish looked like it could have eaten all the other fish for breakfast and still had room for lunch. The $100 "biggest fish" prize more than offset the $10 purchase price. Everyone was so stunned (it was the only fish we had "caught") that no one questioned how we managed to catch a sea bass in the Everglades. Years later Mantle would begin to wonder why our fish was grey and motionless while all the other fish were green and flopping around.

Personally, I loved Spring Training. Maybe that's because I made the team in nine out of ten springs with the Yankees, Pilots, Astros, and Braves. Since I'm not competing for a job anymore, I can now reveal my secrets of success, accumulated over the years from a variety of experts:

Rule #1, The Whitey Ford Suntan Trick: Go down a week early and lie in the sun. "Makes you look ten years younger," says Whitey.

Rule #2, The Jim Coates Batting Practice Philosophy: Try to strike out every hitter in batting practice, no matter how much the hitters bitch and moan. The coaches will visualize players on opposing teams striking out and swearing a lot.

Rule #3, Here Comes the Rabbit: Like the mechanical bunny at the dog track, you should always lead the pack during the mile run around

the complex every morning. Even if you have to nap in the trainer's room later, everyone will think you're in great shape.

Rule #4, The Roland Sheldon Military Posture Principle: Never stand around in the outfield during batting practice with your arms folded and your legs crossed. Sheldon says baseball is like the army, where you always have to look like you're doing something important. Jog everywhere, especially to the water cooler.

Rule #5, The Moose Skowron Flattop Haircut Theory: Short hair makes coaches feel comfortable. Don't ask me why.

Rule #6, When It's Over, It's Over: When your fastball drops below 65 mph or your knuckleball isn't knuckling, don't go down to Spring Training. What goes down does not necessarily come up. Spring Training, up close and personal, is no picnic.

◆

SPRING FANCY

"The kid's got plenty of stuff, all right, but his control leaves something to be desired."

Who was the best pitcher who ever lived? Was it Satchel Paige, whose color kept him out of the big leagues until he was in his 40s and whose skill kept him in the big leagues until he was in his 50s? Here, a quick taste of Richard Donovan's profile, plus Paige offers his rules for staying young. George Plimpton makes a pitch for the wise Sidd Finch, whose career never got started. And Ring Lardner laments the early "passing" of a pitching genius, Christy Mathewson. Remarkably, Lardner's tongue-in-cheek elegy has been quoted frequently as a solemn eulogy. A whole staff of cartoonists add their artful comments on the art of throwing a baseball.

The Fabulous Satchel Paige

BY RICHARD DONOVAN

MR. SATCHEL PAIGE, THE LANK AND LANguid patriarch, raconteur and relief pitching star of the St. Louis Browns, fairly vibrated with dignity and satisfaction as he strolled around the St. Louis railroad station one recent evening. To begin with, his physical tone was splendid—no stomach gas, store teeth resting easy, plenty of whip in his pitching arm. More important, he was in a powerful moral position.

Because of an error in reading his watch, Mr. Paige had arrived almost an hour early for the train that was to take the Browns to Chicago for a series of games with the White Sox. Never before in nearly thirty years of baseball had Paige, called by many of history's greatest pitchers the greatest pitcher who ever lived, been early for a train or anything else. It gave him an uneasy, but exceedingly righteous, feeling.

As he strolled past the baggage stand, a police officer tapped his shoulder. "What's your name?" he asked, dispensing with preliminaries.

"Leroy Paige," said Paige, surprised.

"How old are you?"

Satchel pondered; it was a question he had heard many times before.

• 221

"Well, now," he said guardedly, "people says different things. I'd judge between thirty and seventy."

"Is that so?" said the policeman, his eyes narrowing. "Just get into town?"

"Oh, I'm in and out, in and out."

"What're you out of lately?" asked the officer.

"California," said Paige, referring to his recent participation in the Browns' spring training.

"And what were you doing in California?"

"Playing," sighed Paige.

The officer was reaching for his handcuffs when Browns catcher Les Moss arrived on the scene. "What's he done?" asked Moss.

"We're looking for a murder suspect," the officer replied triumphantly, "and I think we've got him."

"How old is this suspect?"

"Twenty-two," said the cop

Moss grinned, and Paige swelled visibly. "Twenty-two!" the pitcher exulted. "You hear that?"

◆

HOW TO STAY YOUNG

1. Avoid fried meats which angry up the blood.
2. If your stomach disputes you, lie down and pacify it with cool thoughts.
3. Keep the juices flowing by jangling around gently as you move.
4. Go very light on the vices, such as carrying on in society. The social ramble ain't restful.
5. Avoid running at all times.
6. Don't look back. Something might be gaining on you.

(Signed) LEROY SATCHEL PAIGE

Tug McGraw, who was a screwball pitcher in both senses of the word, was once asked whether he preferred grass or artificial turf, and he replied, "I don't know. I never smoked artificial turf."

◆

Bill Lee, who confirmed the theory that lefthanded pitchers are crazy, was once asked who his favorite poets were, and he replied, "T. S. Eliot—and Ogden Nash."

"I'm here primarily because I gave up just too many home runs with the winning runs on base."

The Curious Case of Sidd Finch

BY GEORGE PLIMPTON

THE SECRET CANNOT BE KEPT MUCH longer. Questions are being asked, and sooner rather than later the New York Mets management will have to produce a statement. It may have started unraveling in St. Petersburg, Fla. two weeks ago, on March 14, to be exact, when Mel Stottlemyre, the Met pitching coach, walked over to the 40-odd Met players doing their morning calisthenics at the Payson Field Complex not far from the Gulf of Mexico, a solitary figure among the pulsation of jumping jacks, and motioned three Mets to step out of the exercise. The three, all good prospects, were John Christensen, a 24-year-old outfielder; Dave Cochrane, a spare but muscular switch-hitting third baseman; and Lenny Dykstra, a swift centerfielder who may be the Mets' leadoff man of the future.

Ordering the three to collect their bats and batting helmets, Stottlemyre led the players to the north end of the complex where a large canvas enclosure had been constructed two weeks before. The rumor was that some irrigation machinery was being installed in an underground pit.

Standing outside the enclosure, Stottlemyre explained what he wanted. "First of all," the coach said, "the club's got kind of a delicate situation here, and it would help if you kept reasonably quiet about it, O.K.?" The three nodded. Stottlemyre said, "We've got a young pitcher we're looking at. We want to see what he'll do with a batter standing in the box. We'll do this alphabetically. John, go on in there, stand at the plate and give the pitcher a target. That's all you have to do."

"Do you want me to take a cut?" Christensen asked.

Stottlemyre produced a dry chuckle. "You can do anything you want."

Christensen pulled aside a canvas flap and found himself inside a

225

rectangular area about 90 feet long and 30 feet wide, open to the sky, with a home plate set in the ground just in front of him, and down at the far end a pitcher's mound, with a small group of Met front-office personnel standing behind it, facing home plate. Christensen recognized Nelson Doubleday, the owner of the Mets, and Frank Cashen, wearing a long-billed fishing cap. He had never seen Doubleday at the training facility before.

Christensen bats righthanded. As he stepped around the plate he nodded to Ronn Reynolds, the stocky reserve catcher who has been with the Met organization since 1980. Reynolds whispered up to him from his crouch, "Kid, you won't believe what you're about to see."

A second flap down by the pitcher's end was drawn open, and a tall, gawky player walked in and stepped up onto the pitcher's mound. He was wearing a small, black fielder's glove on his left hand and was holding a baseball in his right. Christensen had never seen him before. He had blue eyes, Christensen remembers, and a pale, youthful face, with facial muscles that were motionless, like a mask. "You notice it," Christensen explained later, "when a pitcher's jaw *isn't* working on a chaw or a piece of gum." Then to Christensen's astonishment he saw that the pitcher, pawing at the dirt of the mound to get it smoothed out properly and to his liking, was wearing a heavy hiking boot on his right foot.

Christensen has since been persuaded to describe that first confrontation:

"I'm standing in there to give this guy a target, just waving the bat once or twice out over the plate. He starts his windup. He sways way back, like Juan Marichal, this hiking boot comes clomping over—I thought maybe he was wearing it for balance or something—and he suddenly rears upright like a catapult. The ball is launched from an arm completely straight up and *stiff*. Before you can blink, the ball is in the catcher's mitt. You hear it *crack,* and then there's this little bleat from Reynolds."

Christensen said the motion reminded him of the extraordinary contortions that he remembered of Goofy's pitching in one of Walt Disney's cartoon classics.

"I never dreamed a baseball could be thrown that fast. The wrist

226

must have a lot to do with it, and all that leverage. You can hardly see the blur of it as it goes by. As for hitting the thing, frankly, I just don't think it's humanly possible. You could send a blind man up there, and maybe he'd do better hitting at the *sound* of the thing."

Christensen's opinion was echoed by both Cochrane and Dykstra, who followed him into the enclosure. When each had done his stint, he emerged startled and awestruck.

Especially Dykstra. Offering a comparison for SI, he reported that out of curiosity he had once turned up the dials that control the motors of the pitching machine to maximum velocity, thus producing a pitch that went approximately 106 miles per hour. "What I looked at in there," he said, motioning toward the enclosure, "was whistling by another third as fast, I swear."

The phenomenon the three young batters faced, and about whom only Reynolds, Stottlemyre and a few members of the Mets' front office know, is a 28-year-old, somewhat eccentric mystic named Hayden (Sidd) Finch. He may well change the course of baseball history. On St. Patrick's Day, to make sure they were not all victims of a crazy hallucination, the Mets brought in a radar gun to measure the speed of Finch's fastball. The model used was a JUGS Supergun II. It looks like a black space gun with a big snout, weighs about five pounds and is usually pointed at the pitcher from behind the catcher. A glass plate in the back of the gun shows the pitch's velocity—accurate, so the manufacturer claims, to within plus or minus 1 mph. The figure at the top of the gauge is 200 mph. The fastest projectile ever measured by the JUGS (which is named after the oldtimer's descriptive—the "jug-handled" curveball) was a Roscoe Tanner serve that registered 153 mph. The highest number that the JUGS had ever turned for a baseball was 103 mph, which it did, curiously, twice on one day, July 11, at the 1978 All-Star game when both Goose Gossage and Nolan Ryan threw the ball at that speed. On March 17, the gun was handled by Stottlemyre. He heard the pop of the ball in Reynold's mitt and the little squeak of pain from the catcher. Then the astonishing figure 168 appeared on the glass plate. Stottlemyre remembers whistling in amazement, and then he heard Reynolds say, "Don't tell me, Mel, I don't want to know. . . ."

227

The Met front office is reluctant to talk about Finch. The fact is, they know very little about him. He has had no baseball career. Most of his life has been spent abroad, except for a short period at Harvard University.

The registrar's office at Harvard will release no information about Finch except that in the spring of 1976 he withdrew from the college in midterm. The alumni records in Harvard's Holyoke Center indicate slightly more. Finch spent his early childhood in an orphanage in Leicester, England and was adopted by a foster parent, the eminent archaeologist Francis Whyte-Finch, who was killed in an airplane crash while on an expedition in the Dhaulagiri mountain area of Nepal. At the time of the tragedy, Finch was in his last year at the Stowe School in Buckingham, England, from which he had been accepted into Harvard. Apparently, though, the boy decided to spend a year in the general area of the plane crash in the Himalayas (the plane was never actually found) before he returned to the West and entered Harvard in 1975, dropping for unknown reasons the "Whyte" from his name. Hayden Finch's picture is not in the freshman yearbook. Nor, of course, did he play baseball at Harvard, having departed before the start of the spring season.

His assigned roommate was Henry W. Peterson, class of 1979, now a stockbroker in New York with Dean Witter, who saw very little of Finch. "He was almost never there," Peterson told SI. "I'd wake up morning after morning and look across at his bed, which had a woven native carpet of some sort on it—I have an idea he told me it was made of yak fur—and never had the sense it had been slept in. Maybe he slept on the floor. Actually, my assumption was that he had a girl in Somerville or something, and stayed out there. He had almost no belongings. A knapsack. A bowl he kept in the corner on the floor. A couple of wool shirts, always very clean, and maybe a pair or so of blue jeans. One pair of hiking boots. I always had the feeling that he was very bright. He had a French horn in an old case. I don't know much about French-horn music but he played beautifully. Sometimes he'd play it in the bath. He knew any number of languages. He was so adept at them that he'd be talking in English, which he spoke in this distinctive singsong way, quite Oriental, and he'd use a phrase like

228

'pied-á-terre' and without knowing it he'd sail along in French for a while until he'd drop in a German word like 'angst' and he'd shift to that language. For any kind of sustained conversation you had to hope he wasn't going to use a foreign buzz word—especially out of the Eastern languages he knew, like Sanskrit—because that was the end of it as far as I was concerned."

When Peterson was asked why he felt Finch had left Harvard, he shrugged his shoulders. "I came back one afternoon, and everything was gone—the little rug, the horn, the staff. . . . Did I tell you that he had this long kind of shepherd's crook standing in the corner? Actually, there was so little stuff to begin with that it was hard to tell he wasn't there anymore. He left a curious note on the floor. It turned out to be a Zen koan, which is one of those puzzles which cannot be solved by the intellect. It's the famous one about the live goose in the bottle. How do you get the goose out of the bottle without hurting it or breaking the glass? The answer is, 'There, it's out!' I heard from him once, from Egypt. He sent pictures. He was on his way to Tibet to study."

◆

Finch's entry into the world of baseball occurred last July in Old Orchard Beach, Maine, where the Mets' AAA farm club, the Tidewater Tides, was in town playing the Guides. After the first game of the series, Bob Schaefer, the Tides' manager, was strolling back to the hotel. He has very distinct memories of his first meeting with Finch: "I was walking by a park when suddenly this guy—nice-looking kid, clean-shaven, blue jeans, big boots—appears alongside. At first, I think maybe he wants an autograph or to chat about the game, but no, he scrabbles around in a kind of knapsack, gets out a scuffed-up baseball and a small, black leather fielder's mitt that looks like it came out of the back of some Little League kid's closet. This guy says to me, 'I have learned the art of the pitch. . . .' Some odd phrase like that delivered in a singsong voice, like a chant, kind of what you hear in a Chinese restaurant if there are some Chinese in there.

"I am about to hurry on to the hotel when this kid points out a soda bottle on top of a fence post about the same distance home plate is from the pitcher's rubber. He rears way back, comes around and

pops the ball at it. Out there on that fence post the soda bottle *explodes.* It disintegrates like a rifle bullet hit it—just little specks of vaporized glass in a *puff.* Beyond the post I could see the ball bouncing across the grass of the park until it stopped about as far away as I can hit a three-wood on a good day.

"I said, very calm, 'Son, would you mind showing me that again?'

"And he did. He disappeared across the park to find the ball—it had gone so far, he was after it for what seemed 15 minutes. In the meantime I found a tin can from a trash container and set it up for him. He did it again—just kicked that can off the fence like it was hit with a baseball bat. It wasn't the accuracy of the pitch so much that got to me but the *speed.* It was like the tin can got belted as soon as the ball left the guy's fingertips. Instantaneous. I thought to myself, "My god, that kid's thrown the ball about 150 mph. Nolan Ryan's fastball is a change-up compared to what this kid just threw."

"Well, what happens next is that we sit and talk, this kid and I, out there on the grass of the park. He sits with the big boots tucked under his legs, like one of those yoga guys, and he tells me he's not sure he wants to play big league baseball, but he'd like to give it a try. He's never played before, but he knows the rules, even the infield-fly rule, he tells me with a smile, and he knows he can throw a ball with complete accuracy and enormous velocity. He won't tell me how he's done this except that he 'learned it in the mountains, in a place called Po, in Tibet.' That is where he said he had learned to pitch . . . up in the mountains, flinging rocks and meditating. He told me his name was Hayden Finch, but he wanted to be called Sidd Finch. I said that most of the Sids we had in baseball came from Brooklyn. Or the Bronx. He said his Sidd came from 'Siddhartha,' which means 'Aim Attained' or 'The Perfect Pitch.' That's what he had learned, how to throw the perfect pitch. O.K. by me, I told him, and that's what I put on the scouting report, 'Sidd Finch.' And I mailed it in to the front office."

The reaction in New York once the report arrived was one of complete disbelief. The assumption was that Schaefer was either playing a joke on his superiors or was sending in the figment of a very powerful wish-fulfillment dream. But Schaefer is one of the most respected men in the Met organization. Over the past seven years, the clubs he has

230

managed have won six championships. Dave Johnson, the Met manager, phoned him. Schaefer verified what he had seen in Old Orchard Beach. He told Johnson that sometimes he, too, thought he'd had a dream, but he hoped the Mets would send Finch an invitation so that, at the very least, his *own* mind would be put at rest.

When a rookie is invited to training camp, he gets a packet of instructions in late January. The Mets sent off the usual literature to Finch at the address Schaefer had supplied them. To their surprise, Finch wrote back with a number of stipulations. He insisted he would report to the Mets camp in St. Petersburg only with the understanding that: 1) there were no contractual commitments; 2) during off-hours he be allowed to keep completely to himself; 3) he did not wish to be involved in any of the team drills or activities; 4) he would show the Mets his pitching prowess in privacy; 5) the whole operation in St. Petersburg was to be kept as secret as possible, with no press or photographs.

The reason for these requirements—he stated in a letter written (according to a source in the Met front office) in slightly stilted, formal and very polite terminology—was that he had not decided whether he actually wanted to play baseball. He wrote apologetically that there were mental adjustments to be made. He did not want to raise the Mets' expectations, much less those of the fans, and then dash them. Therefore it was best if everything were carried on in secret or, as he put it in his letter, "in camera."

At first, the inclination of the Met front office was to disregard this nonsense out of hand and tell Finch either to apply, himself, through normal procedures or forget it. But the extraordinary statistics in the scouting report and Schaefer's verification of them were too intriguing to ignore. On Feb. 2, Finch's terms were agreed to by letter. Mick McFadyen, the Mets' groundskeeper in St. Petersburg, was ordered to build the canvas enclosure in a far corner of the Payson complex, complete with a pitcher's mound and plate. Reynolds's ordeal was about to start.

Reynolds is a sturdy, hardworking catcher (he has been described as looking like a high school football tackle). He has tried to be close-lipped about Finch, but his experiences inside the canvas enclosure

231

have made it difficult for him to resist answering a few questions. He first heard about Finch from the Mets' general manager. "Mr. Cashen called me into his office one day in early March," Reynolds disclosed. "I was nervous because I thought I'd been traded. He was wearing a blue bow tie. He leaned across the desk and whispered to me that it was very likely I was going to be a part of baseball history. Big doings! The Mets had this rookie coming to camp and I was going to be his special catcher. All very hush-hush.

"Well, I hope nothing like that guy ever comes down the pike again. The first time I see him is inside the canvas coop, out there on the pitcher's mound, a thin kid getting ready to throw, and I'm thinking he'll want to toss a couple of warmup pitches. So I'm standing behind the plate without a mask, chest protector, pads or anything, holding my glove up, sort of half-assed, to give him a target to throw at . . . and suddenly I see this windup like a pretzel gone loony, and the next thing, I've been blown two or three feet back, and I'm sitting on the ground with the ball in my glove. My catching hand feels like it's been hit with a sledgehammer."

He was asked: "Does he throw a curveball? A slider? Or a sinker?"

Reynolds grinned and shook his head, "Good questions! Don't ask me."

"Does it make a sound?"

"Yeah, a little *pft, pft-boom!*"

Stottlemyre has been in direct charge of Finch's pitching regimen. His own playing career ended in the spring of 1975 with a rotator-cuff injury, which makes him especially sensitive to the strain that a pitching motion can put on the arm. Although as close-lipped as the rest of the staff, Stottlemyre does admit that Finch has developed a completely revolutionary pitching style. He told SI: "I don't understand the mechanics of it. Anyone who tries to throw the ball that way should fall flat on his back. But I've seen it. I've seen it a hundred times. It's the most awesome thing that has ever happened in baseball."

Asked what influences might have contributed to Finch's style and speed, Stottlemyre said, "Well, *cricket* may have something to do with it. Finch has taken the power and speed of the running throw of the cricket bowler and has somehow harnessed all that energy to the pitch-

232

ing rubber. The wrist snap off that stiff arm is incredible. I haven't talked to him but once or twice. I asked him if he ever thought of snapping the *arm*, like baseball pitchers, rather than the wrist: It would increase the velocity.

"He replied, very polite, you know, with a little bob of the head: 'I undertake as a rule of training to refrain from injury to living things.'

"He's right, of course. It's Ronn Reynolds I feel sorry for. Every time that ball comes in, first you hear this *smack* sound of the ball driving into the pocket of the mitt, and then you hear this little gasp, this *ai yee!*—the catcher, poor guy, his whole body shakin' like an angina's hit it. It's the most piteous thing I've ever heard, short of a trapped rabbit."

Hayden (Sidd) Finch arrived in St. Petersburg on Feb. 7. Most of the rookies and minor-leaguers stay at the Edgewater Beach Inn. Assuming that Finch would check in with the rest of the early arrivals, the Mets were surprised when he telephoned and announced that he had leased a room in a small boardinghouse just off Florida Avenue near a body of water on the bay side called Big Bayou. Because his private pitching compound had been constructed across the city and Finch does not drive, the Mets assigned him a driver, a young Tampa Bay resident, Eliot Posner, who picks him up in the morning and returns him to Florida Avenue or, more often, to a beach on the Gulf where, Posner reports, Finch, still in his baseball outfit and carrying his decrepit glove, walks down to the water's edge and, motionless, stares out at the windsurfers. Inevitably, he dismisses Posner and gets back to his boardinghouse on his own.

The Met management has found out very little about his life in St. Petersburg. Mrs. Roy Butterfield, his landlady, reports (as one might expect) that "he lives very simply. Sometimes he comes in the front door, sometimes the back. Sometimes I'm not even sure he spends the night. I think he sleeps on the floor—his bed is always neat as a pin. He has his own rug, a small little thing. I never have had a boarder who brought his own rug. He has a soup bowl. Not *much*, is what I say. Of course, he plays the French horn. He plays it very beautifully and, thank goodness, softly. The notes fill the house. Sometimes I think the notes are coming out of my television set."

233

Probably the member of the Met staff who has gotten the closest to Finch is Posner. When Posner returns to the Payson complex, inevitably someone rushes out from the Mets' offices asking, "Did he say anything? What did he say?"

Posner takes out a notebook.

"Today he said, 'When your mind is empty like a canyon you will know the power of the Way.' "

"Anything else?"

"No."

While somewhat taxed by Finch's obvious eccentricities, and with the exception of the obvious burden on the catchers, the Mets, it seems, have an extraordinary property in their camp. But the problem is that no one is sure if Finch really wants to play. He has yet to make up his mind; his only appearances are in the canvas enclosure. Reynolds moans in despair when he is told Finch has arrived. Sometimes his ordeal is short-lived. After Finch nods politely at Reynolds and calls down *"Namas-te!"* (which means "greetings" in Sanskrit), he throws only four or five of the terrifying pitches before, with a gentle smile, he announces *"Namas-te!"* (it also means "farewell") and gets into the car to be driven away.

One curious manifestation of Finch's reluctance to commit himself entirely to baseball has been his refusal to wear a complete baseball uniform. Because he changes in his rooming house, no one is quite sure what he will be wearing when he steps through the canvas flap into the enclosure. One afternoon he turned up sporting a tie hanging down over the logo on his jersey, and occasionally—as Christensen noticed— he wears a hiking boot on his right foot. Always, he wears his baseball cap back to front—the conjecture among the Met officials is that this sartorial behavior is an indication of his ambivalence about baseball.

In hopes of understanding more about him, in early March the Mets called in a specialist in Eastern religions, Dr. Timothy Burns, the author of, among other treatises, *Satori, or Four Years in a Tibetan Lamasery.* Not allowed to speak personally with Finch for fear of "spooking him," Burns was able only to speculate about the Mets' newest player.

According to sources from within the Met organization, Burns told a meeting of the club's top brass that the strange ballplayer in their midst was very likely a *trapas,* or aspirant monk.

234

A groan is said to have gone up from Nelson Doubleday. Burns said that Finch was almost surely a disciple of Tibet's great poet-saint Lama Milaraspa, who was born in the 11th century and died in the shadow of Mount Everest. Burns told them that Milaraspa was a great yogi who could manifest an astonishing phenomenon: He could produce "internal heat," which allowed him to survive snowstorms and intense cold, wearing only a thin robe of white cotton. Finch does something similar—an apparent deflection of the huge forces of the universe into throwing a baseball with bewildering accuracy and speed through the process of *siddhi,* namely the yogic mastery of mind-body. He mentioned that *The Book of Changes,* the *I Ching,* suggests that all acts (even throwing a baseball) are connected with the highest spiritual yearnings. Utilizing the Tantric principle of body and mind, Finch has decided to pitch baseballs—at least for a while.

The Mets pressed Burns. Was there any chance that Finch would come to his senses and *commit* himself to baseball?

"There's a chance," Burns told them. "You will remember that the Buddha himself, after what is called the Great Renunciation, finally realized that even in the most severe austerities—though he conquered lust and fear and acquired a great deal of self-knowledge—truth itself could not necessarily be found. So after fasting for six years he decided to eat again."

Reached by SI at the University of Maryland, where he was lecturing last week, Burns was less sanguine. "The biggest problem Finch has with baseball," he said over the phone, "is that *nirvana,* which is the state all Buddhists wish to reach, means literally 'the blowing out'—specifically the purifying of oneself of greed, hatred and delusion. Baseball," Burns went on, "is symbolized to a remarkable degree by those very three aspects: *greed* (huge money contracts, stealing second base, robbing a guy of a base hit, charging for a seat behind an iron pillar, etc.), *hatred* (players despising management, pitchers hating hitters, the Cubs detesting the Mets, etc.) and *delusion* (the slider, the pitchout, the hidden-ball trick and so forth). So you can see why it is not easy for Finch to give himself up to a way of life so opposite to what he has been led to cherish."

Burns is more puzzled by Finch's absorption with the French horn. He suspects that in Tibet Finch may have learned to play the *rkang-*

235

gling, a Tibetan horn made of human thighbones, or perhaps even the Tibetan long trumpet, the *dung-chen,* whose sonorous bellowing in those vast Himalayan defiles is somewhat echoed in the lower registers of the French horn.

The Met inner circle believes that Finch's problem may be that he cannot decide between baseball and a career as a horn player. In early March the club contacted Bob Johnson, who plays the horn and is the artistic director of the distinguished New York Philomusica ensemble, and asked him to come to St. Petersburg. Johnson was asked to make a clandestine assessment of Finch's ability as a horn player and, even more important, to make contact with him. The idea was that, while praising him for the quality of his horn playing, Johnson should try to persuade him that the lot of a French-horn player (even a very fine one) was not an especially gainful one. Perhaps *that* would tip the scales in favor of baseball.

Johnson came down to St. Petersburg and hung around Florida Avenue for a week. He reported later to SI: "I was being paid for it, so it wasn't bad. I spent a lot of time looking up, so I'd get a nice suntan. Every once in a while I saw Finch coming in and out of the rooming house, dressed to play baseball and carrying a funny-looking black glove. Then one night I heard the French horn. He was playing it in his room. I have heard many great horn players in my career—Bruno Jaenicke, who played for Toscanini; Dennis Brain, the great British virtuoso; Anton Horner of the Philadelphia Orchestra—and I would say Finch was on a par with them. He was playing Benjamin Britten's *Serenade,* for tenor horn and strings—a haunting, tender piece that provides great space for the player—when suddenly he produced a big, evocative *bwong* sound that seemed to shiver the leaves of the trees. Then he shifted to the rondo theme from the trio for violin, piano and horn by Brahms—just sensational. It may have had something to do with the Florida evening and a mild wind coming in over Big Bayou and tree frogs, but it was *remarkable.* I told this to the Mets, and they immediately sent me home—presuming, I guess, that I was going to hire the guy. That's not so far-fetched. He can play for the Philomusica anytime."

Meanwhile, the Mets are trying other ways to get Finch into a more

positive frame of mind about baseball. Inquiries among American lamaseries (there are more than 100 Buddhist societies in the U.S.) have been quietly initiated in the hope of finding monks or priests who are serious baseball fans and who might persuade Finch that the two religions (Buddhism and baseball) are compatible. One plan is to get him into a movie theater to see *The Natural,* the mystical film about baseball, starring Robert Redford. Another film suggested is the baseball classic *It Happens Every Spring,* starring Ray Milland as a chemist who, by chance, discovers a compound that avoids wood; when applied to a baseball in the film, it makes Milland as effective a pitcher as Finch is in real life.

Conversations with Finch himself have apparently been exercises in futility. All conventional inducements—huge contracts, advertising tie-ins, the banquet circuit, ticker-tape parades, having his picture on a Topps bubble-gum card, chatting on *Kiner's Korner* (the Mets' postgame TV show) and so forth—mean little to him. As do the perks ("You are very kind to offer me a Suzuki motorcycle, but I cannot drive"). He has very politely declined whatever overtures the Mets have offered. The struggle is an absolutely internal one. He will resolve it. Last week he announced that he would let the management know what he was going to do on or around April 1.

Met manager Davey Johnson has seen Finch throw about half a dozen pitches. He was impressed ("If he didn't have this great control, he'd be like the Terminator out there. Hell, that fastball, if off-target on the inside, would carry a batter's kneecap back into the catcher's mitt"), but he is leaving the situation to the front office. "I can handle the pitching rotation; let them handle the monk." He has had one meeting with Finch. "I was going to ask him if we could at least give him a decent fielder's mitt. I asked him why he was so attached to the piece of rag he was using. 'It is,' the guy told me, 'the only one I have.' Actually, I don't see why he needs a better one. All he will ever need it for is to catch the ball for the next pitch. So then I said to him, 'There's only one thing I can offer you, Finch, and that's a fair shake.' "

According to Jay Horwitz, the Mets' public-relations man, Finch smiled at the offer of the fair shake and nodded his head politely—perhaps because it was the only nonmaterial offer made. It did not

encroach on Finch's ideas about the renunciation of worldly goods. It was an ingenious, if perhaps unintentional, move on the manager's part.

Nelson Doubleday is especially hopeful about Finch's ultimate decision. "I think we'll bring him around," he said a few days ago. "After all, the guy's not a nut, he's a Harvard man."

In the meantime, the Mets can only wait. Finch periodically turns up at the enclosure. Reynolds summoned. There are no drills. Sometimes Finch throws for five minutes, instantly at top speed, often for half an hour. Then he leaves. Security around the enclosure has been tight. Since Finch has not signed with the Mets, he is technically a free agent and a potential find for another club. The curious, even Met players, are politely shooed away from the Payson Field enclosure. So far Finch's only association with Met players (other than Reynolds) has been the brief confrontation with Christensen, Cochrane and Dykstra when the front office nervously decided to test his control with a batter standing in the box. If he decides to play baseball, he will leave his private world of the canvas enclosure and join manager Johnson and the rest of the squad. For the first time Gary Carter, the Mets' regular catcher, will face the smoke of the Finch pitch, and the other pitchers will stand around and gawk. The press will have a field day ("How do you spell Siddhartha? How do you grip the ball? How do you keep your balance on the mound?"). The Mets will try to protect him from the glare and help him through the most traumatic of culture shocks, praying that in the process he will not revert and one day disappear.

Actually, the presence of Hayden (Sidd) Finch in the Mets' training camp raises a number of interesting questions. Suppose the Mets (and Finch himself) can assuage and resolve his mental reservations about playing baseball; suppose he is signed to a contract (one wonders what an ascetic whose major possessions are a bowl, a small rug, a long stick and a French horn might demand); and suppose he comes to New York's Shea Stadium to open the season against the St. Louis Cardinals on April 9. It does not matter that he has never taken a fielding drill with his teammates. Presumably he will mow down the opposition in a perfect game. Perhaps Willie McGee will get a foul tip. Suppose Johnson discovers that the extraordinary symbiotic relation-

238

ship of mind and matter is indefatigable—that Finch can pitch day after day at this blinding, unhittable speed. What will happen to Dwight Gooden? Will Carter and the backup catchers last the season? What will it do to major league baseball as it is known today?

Peter Ueberroth, baseball's new commissioner, was contacted by SI in his New York office. He was asked if he had heard anything about the Mets' new phenomenon.

No, he had not. He had heard some *rumors* about the Mets' camp this spring, but nothing specific.

Did the name Hayden (Sidd) Finch mean anything to him?

Nope.

The commissioner was told that the Mets had a kid who could throw the ball over 150 mph. Unhittable.

Ueberroth took a minute before he asked, "Roll that by me again?"

He was told in as much detail as could be provided about what was going on within the canvas enclosure of the Payson compound. It was possible that an absolute superpitcher was coming into baseball—so remarkable that the delicate balance between pitcher and batter could be turned into disarray. What was baseball going to do about it?

"Well, before any decisions, I'll tell you something," the commissioner finally said, echoing what may very well be a nationwide sentiment this coming season, "I'll have to see it to believe it!"

*C*riticized for his abuse of the English language, pitcher-turned-broad-caster Dizzy Dean defended himself by saying, "A lot of folks that ain't saying 'ain't' ain't eatin'."

◆

*A*sked by an umpire why he was disputing a "strike" call on a Bob Feller fastball, Mike Kreevich of the Chicago White Sox explained, "It sounded a little high."

◆

B.C.   Johnny Hart

B.C.   Johnny Hart

"Batter is agent of evil secret organization plotting to rule world. Stick me in his ear."

Obituary

BY RING LARDNER

THE BASEBALL WORLD WAS SHOCKED YES-terday by the news that Christy Mathewson, one of the game's greatest exponents, had signed to manage the Cincinnati Reds at the age of thirty-seven years, the very prime of life. Mathewson is the seventh prominent baseballist to succumb to this disease in a space of twelve years.

It is the opinion of prominent physicians that "Matty," as he was fondly known, hastened his own end by taking up golf, which undermines the intellect and, thereby, the general health. Those who were closest to him say that he has never been the same since he first sliced off the tee.

There is no argument for prohibition in the case of the deceased. He was always abstemious. He took the best possible care of himself. Before being bitten by the golf bacillus, his favorite amusements were chess, checkers, poker, and auction bridge, at all of which athletic sports he excelled. He smoked, but never to excess. He usually retired before midnight and was careful as to his victuals.

Christopher Mathewson was born in New York State or somewhere, in or about 1879. He received a common school education and then entered Bucknell College, where he took a P.P.D. degree, Doctor of Pitching and Punting. He pitched more or less professional ball down in Virginia for a time and his work attracted the attention of major-league scouts and a scout from Cincinnati. Cincinnati acquired him and, the directors of the club taking a hand, traded him to New York for Amos Rusie, which was a regular Cincinnati trade, as Rusie was through.

One of Matty's first managers at New York was Horace Fogel, who

saw at a glance that he could never be a successful pitcher and tried to make a first baseman out of him. Unfortunately for many a National League batsman, Horace's career as manager was brief, brevity being the soul of wit. The next manager of the Giants got a crazy notion in his head that Matty might be able, with careful handling, to become an average pitcher. This manager's judgment was proven pretty fair, for Matty, with the aid of great support, pitched his team to victory in quite a few games for a matter of sixteen years. Perhaps his greatest achievement was his three shutout victories over the Athletics in the World Series of 1905. If he had been pitching against this year's Athletics he could have done it left-handed, but it was some trick in those days.

Mathewson had been spending recent winters in California and the climate may have gone to his head.

He leaves a wife and one son, Christopher, Jr.

My eyes are very misty
As I pen these lines to Christy;
   O, my heart is full of heaviness today.
May the flowers ne'er wither, Matty,
On your grave at Cincinnati,
   Which you've chosen for your final fade-away.

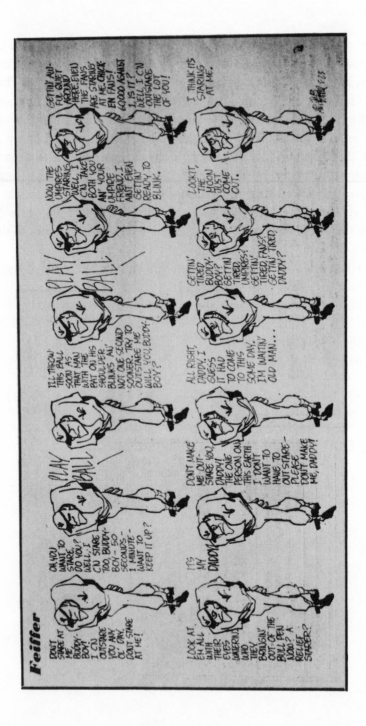

*O*ne day in 1976, when Mark "The Bird" Fidrych of the Detroit Tigers was too briefly the best pitcher in baseball, the actor Walter Matthau took Fidrych to lunch at the Beverly Hills Tennis Club. They happened to sit at a table next to a court on which Hank Greenberg, the Hall of Fame slugger, was playing a match.

"Do you know who that is?" Matthau asked Fidrych.

"No," Fidrych said. "Who's that?"

"That's Hank Greenberg," Matthau said.

"Who's Hank Greenberg?" Fidrych said.

"He used to play for the same team you play for, and he once hit fifty-eight home runs in one season, and he's in the Hall of Fame," Matthau said.

"No kidding," Fidrych said.

Fidrych watched Greenberg play tennis for a few minutes, then stood up and yelled to Greenberg's opponent, "Serve him inside. He'll never hit it."

Greenberg was six-foot-three and sixty-five years old.

Fidrych was six-foot-three and twenty-two years old.

Greenberg threw down his racquet and walked off the court, straight to Fidrych.

"Young man," Greenberg said, "if you pitched me inside, I'd hit a home run, or if you pitched me outside, I'd hit a home run, and don't you forget it."

Then Greenberg turned around and went back on the court and finished his match.

As he walked off the court, Matthau ran up to him and said, "Hank, Hank, I'm sorry, I didn't mean to get you upset."

And Greenberg pointed at Fidrych, one third his age, and said, "Pitchers, they're all the same, you can't let them intimidate you."

*P*itchers, as Hank Greenberg made clear, have natural enemies, who are called hitters. The following stories are about hitters, real and imaginary. A couple of them are certified classics, written by giants, Ring Lardner's "Alibi Ike" and James Thurber's "You Could Look It Up."

"You Could Look It Up" introduces a fictional midget, and then Bill Veeck, who owned the Browns and the Indians and the White Sox, introduces a real midget, who wound up with a line in The Baseball Encyclopedia.

Midgets in the majors? That's nothing. Wilbur Schramm came up with a horse named Jones who played third base for the Dodgers.

♦

Dorlan's Home-Walk

BY ARTHUR GUITERMAN

The ninth; last half; the score was tied,
  The Hour was big with Fate,
For Neal had fanned and Kling had flied
  When Dorlan toed the plate.

And every rooter drew a breath
  And rose from where he sat,
For Weal or Woe, or Life or Death
  Now hung on Dorlan's bat.

The Pitcher scowled; the Pitcher flung
  An inshoot, swift and queer;
But Dorlan whirled his wagon-tongue
  And smote the leathern sphere.

He smote the ball with might and main,
  He drove it long and low,
And firstward like a railway train
  He sped to beat the throw.

He reached first base with time to spare
  (The throw went high and wide),
But what a tumult rent the air
  When "Safe!" the Umpire cried.

"What!" shrieked the Pitcher, lean and tall,
  "What!" roared the Catcher stout,
"What-at!" yelled the Basemen one and all,
  "Ye're off! the man is out!"

The Shortstop swore, the Catcher pled,
    They waved their arms around.
The Umpire shook his bullet-head
    And sternly held his ground,

Though in the wild-eyed Fielders ran
    To tear him limb from limb
Or else to tell that erring man
    Just what they thought of *him*.

The Basemen left the bases clear
    And came to urge their case;—
So Dorlan yawned and scratched his ear
    And strolled to second base.

"Safe? Safe?" the Pitcher hissed, "Ye're blind!"
    And breathed a Naughty Word;
While Dorlan hitched his belt behind
    And rambled on to third.

And throats were hoarse and words ran high
    And lips were flecked with foam,
As Dorlan scanned the azure sky
    And ambled on toward home.

And still he heard in dreamy bliss,
    As down the line he came,
The Umpire growl, "Enough o' this!
    He's safe. Now play the game!"

"All right. Come, boys," the Pitcher bawled;
    "Two out; now make it three!"
When Dorlan touched the plate and drawled,
    "Hey! score that run fer me!"

What wrath was there, what bitter talk,
    What joy and wild acclaim!
For Dorlan's peaceful homeward walk
    Had won the doubtful game.

248

"The TV camera is still on you, kid. Kick the water cooler in disgust."

Gandhi at the Bat

BY CHET WILLIAMSON

HISTORY BOOKS AND AVAILABLE NEWSPAPER FILES HOLD *no record of the visit to America in 1933 made by Mohandas K. Gandhi. For reasons of a sensitive political nature that have not yet come to light, all contemporary accounts of the visit were suppressed at the request of President Roosevelt. Although Gandhi repeatedly appeared in public during his three-month stay, the cloak of journalistic silence was seamless, and all that remains of the great man's celebrated tour is this long-secreted glimpse of one of the Mahatma's unexpected nonpolitical appearances, written by an anonymous press-box denizen of the day.*

Yankee Stadium is used to roaring crowds. But never did a crowd roar louder than on yesterday afternoon, when a little brown man in a loincloth and wire-rimmed specs put some wood on a Lefty Grove fastball and completely bamboozled Connie Mack's A's.

It all started when Mayor John J. O'Brien invited M. K. ("Mahatma") Gandhi to see the Yanks play Philadelphia up at "The House That Ruth Built." Gandhi, whose ballplaying experience was limited to a few wallops with a cricket bat, jumped at the chance, and 12 noon saw the Mayor's party in the Yankee locker room, where the Mahatma met the Bronx Bombers. A zippy exchange occurred when the Mayor introduced the Lord of the Loincloth to the Bambino. "Mr. Gandhi," Hizzoner said, "I want you to meet Babe Ruth, the Sultan of Swat."

Gandhi's eyes sparkled behind his Moxie-bottle lenses, and he chuckled. "Swat," quoth he, "is a sultanate of which I am not aware. Is it by any chance near Maharashtra?"

"Say," laughed the Babe, laying a meaty hand on the frail brown shoulder, "you're all right, kiddo. I'll hit one out of the park for you today."

"No hitting, please," the Mahatma quipped.

250

In the Mayor's front-row private box, the little Indian turned down the offer of a hot dog and requested a box of Cracker Jack instead. The prize inside was a tin whistle, which he blew gleefully whenever the Bambino waddled up to bat.

The grinning guru enjoyed the game immensely—far more than the A's, who were down 3–1 by the fifth. Ruth, as promised, did smash a homer in the seventh, to Gandhi's delight. "Hey, Gunga Din!" Ruth cried jovially on his way to the Yankee dugout. "Know why my battin' reminds folks of India? 'Cause I can really Bangalore!"

"That is a very good one, Mr. Ruth!" cried the economy-size Asian.

By the top of the ninth, the Yanks had scored two more runs. After Mickey Cochrane whiffed on a Red Ruffing fastball, Gandhi remarked how difficult it must be to hit such a swiftly thrown missile and said, "I should like to try it very much."

"Are you serious?" Mayor O'Brien asked.

"If it would not be too much trouble. Perhaps after the exhibition is over," his visitor suggested.

There was no time to lose. O'Brien, displaying a panache that would have done credit to his predecessor, Jimmy Walker, leaped up and shouted to the umpire, who called a time-out. Managers McCarthy and Mack were beckoned to the Mayor's side, along with Bill Dinneen, the home-plate umpire, and soon all of Yankee Stadium heard an unprecedented announcement:

"Ladies and gentlemen, regardless of the score, the Yankees will come to bat to finish the ninth inning."

The excited crowd soon learned that the reason for such a breach of tradition was a little brown pinchhitter shorter than his bat. When the pin-striped Bronx Bombers returned to their dugout after the last Philadelphia batter had been retired in the ninth, the Nabob of Nonviolence received a hasty batting lesson from Babe Ruth under the stands.

Lazzeri led off the bottom of the stanza, hitting a short chop to Bishop, who rifled to Foxx for the out. Then, after Crosetti fouled out to Cochrane, the stadium became hushed as the announcer intoned, "Pinch-hitting for Ruffing, Mohandas K. Gandhi."

The crowd erupted as the white-robed holy man, a fungo bat

251

propped jauntily on his shoulder, strode to the plate, where he remarked to the crouching Mickey Cochrane, "It is a very big field, and
a very small ball."

"C'mon, Moe!" Ruth called loudly to the dead-game bantam batter.
"Show 'em the old pepper!"

"I will try, Mr. Baby!" Gandhi called back, and went into a batting
stance unique in the annals of the great game—his sheet-draped pos-
terior facing the catcher, and his bat held high over his head, as if to
clobber the ball into submission. While Joe McCarthy called time, the
Babe trotted out and politely corrected the little Indian's position in
the box.

The time-out over, Grove threw a screaming fastball right over the
plate. The bat stayed on Gandhi's shoulder. "Oh, my," he said as he
turned and observed the ball firmly ensconced in Cochrane's glove.
"That *was* speedy."

The second pitch was another dead-center fastball. The Mahatma
swung, but found that the ball had been in the Mick's glove for a good
three seconds before his swipe was completed. "Stee-rike two!" Dinneen
barked.

The next pitch was high and outside, and the ump called it a ball
before the petite pundit made a tentative swing at it. "Must I sit down
now?" he asked.

"Nah, it's a ball," Dinneen replied. "I called it before you took your
cut."

"Yes. I *know* that is a ball, and I did swing at it and did miss."

"No, no, a ball. Like a free pitch."

"Oh, I see."

"Wasn't in the strike zone."

"Yes, I see."

"So you get another swing."

"Yes."

"And if you miss you sit down."

"I just *did* miss."

"Play ball, Mister."

The next pitch was in the dirt. Gandhi did not swing. "Ball," Dinneen
called.

252

"Yes, it is," the Mahatma agreed.

"Two and two."

"That is four."

"Two balls, two strikes."

"Is there not but one ball?"

"Two balls."

"Yes, I see."

"And two strikes."

"And if I miss I sit down."

Ruth's voice came booming from the Yankee dugout: "Swing early, Gandy baby!"

"When is early?"

"When I tell ya! I'll shout 'Now!'"

Grove started his windup. Just as his leg kicked up, the Bambino's cry of *"Now!"* filled the park.

The timing was perfect. Gandhi's molasses-in-January swing met the Grove fastball right over the plate. The ball shot downward, hit the turf, and arced gracefully into the air toward Grove. "*Run,* Peewee, *run!*" yelled Ruth, as the crowd went wild.

"Yes, yes!" cried Gandhi, who started down the first-base line in what can only be described as a dancing skip, using his bat as a walking stick. An astonished Grove booted the high bouncer, then scooped up the ball and flung it to Jimmie Foxx at first.

But Foxx, mesmerized by the sight of a sixty-three-year-old Indian in white robes advancing merrily before him and blowing mightily on a tin whistle, failed to descry the stitched orb, which struck the bill of his cap, knocking it off his head, and, slowed by its deed of dishabille, rolled to a stop by the fence.

Gandhi paused only long enough to touch first and to pick up Jimmie's cap and return it to him. By the time the still gawking Foxx had perched it once more on his head, the vital vegetarian was halfway to second.

Right fielder Coleman retrieved Foxx's missed ball and now relayed it to Max Bishop at second, but too late. The instant Bishop tossed the ball back to the embarrassed Grove, Gandhi was off again. Grove, panicking, overthrew third base, and by the time left fielder Bob John-

son picked up the ball, deep in foul territory, the Tiny Terror of Tealand had rounded the hot corner and was scooting for home. Johnson hurled the ball on a true course to a stunned Cochrane. The ball hit the pocket of Cochrane's mitt and popped out like a muffin from a toaster.

Gandhi jumped on home plate with both sandalled feet, and the crowd exploded as Joe McCarthy, the entire Yankee squad, and even a beaming Connie Mack surged onto the field.

"I ran home," giggled Gandhi. "Does that mean that I hit a run home?"

"A home run, Gandy," said Ruth. "Ya sure did."

"Well, technically," said Umpire Dinneen, "it was a single and an overthrow and then—"

"*Shaddup,*" growled a dozen voices at once.

"Looked like a homer to me, too," the ump corrected, but few heard him, for by that time the crowd was on the field, lifting to their shoulders a joyous Gandhi, whose tin whistle provided a thrilling trilling over the mob's acclaim.

Inside the locker room, Manager McCarthy offered Gandhi a permanent position on the team, but the Mahatma graciously refused, stating that he could only consider a diamond career with a different junior-circuit club.

"Which club would that be, kid?" said the puzzled Bambino.

"The Cleveland Indians, of course," twinkled the Mahatma.

An offer from the Cleveland front office arrived the next day, but India's top pinch-hitter was already on a train headed for points west— and the history books.

Alibi Ike

BY RING LARDNER

HIS RIGHT NAME WAS FRANK X. FARRELL, and I guess the X stood for "Excuse me." Because he never pulled a play, good or bad, on or off the field, without apologizin' for it.

"Alibi Ike" was the name Carey wished on him the first day he reported down South. O' course we all cut out the "Alibi" part of it right away for the fear he would overhear it and bust somebody. But we called him "Ike" right to his face and the rest of it was understood by everybody on the club except Ike himself.

He ast me one time, he says:

"What do you all call me Ike for? I ain't no Yid."

"Carey give you the name," I says. "It's his nickname for everybody he takes a likin' to."

"He mustn't have only a few friends then," says Ike. "I never heard him say 'Ike' to nobody else."

But I was goin' to tell you about Carey namin' him. We'd been workin' out two weeks and the pitchers was showin' somethin' when this bird joined us. His first day out he stood up there so good and took such a reef at the old pill that he had everyone lookin'. Then him and Carey was together in left field, catchin' fungoes, and it was after we was through for the day that Carey told me about him.

"What do you think of Alibi Ike?" ast Carey.

"Who's that?" I says.

"This here Farrell in the outfield," says Carey.

"He looks like he could hit," I says.

"Yes," says Carey, "but he can't hit near as good as he can apologize."

Then Carey went on to tell me what Ike had been pullin' out there. He'd dropped the first fly ball that was hit to him and told Carey his glove wasn't broke in good yet, and Carey says the glove could easy of been Kid Gleason's gran'father. He made a whale of a catch out o'

the next one and Carey says "Nice work!" or somethin' like that, but Ike says he could of caught the ball with his back turned only he slipped when he started after it, and besides that, the air currents fooled him.

"I thought you done well to get to the ball," says Carey.

"I ought to been settin' under it," says Ike.

"What did you hit last year?" Carey ast him.

"I had malaria most o' the season," says Ike. "I wound up with .356."

"Where would I have to go to get malaria?" says Carey, but Ike didn't wise up.

I and Carey and him set at the same table together for supper. It took him half an hour longer'n us to eat because he had to excuse himself every time he lifted his fork.

"Doctor told me I needed starch," he'd say, and then toss a shovelful o' potatoes into him. Or, "They ain't much meat on one o' these chops," he'd tell us, and grab another one. Or he'd say: "Nothin' like onions for a cold," and then he'd dip into the perfumery.

"Better try that apple sauce," says Carey. "It'll help your malaria."

"Whose malaria?" says Ike. He'd forgot already why he didn't only hit .356 last year.

I and Carey begin to lead him on.

"Whereabouts did you say your home was?" I ast him.

"I live with my folks," he says. "We live in Kansas City—not right down in the business part—outside a ways."

"How's that come?" says Carey. "I should think you'd get rooms in the post office."

But Ike was too busy curin' his cold to get that one.

"Are you married?" I ast him.

"No," he says. "I never run round much with girls, except to shows onct in a wile and parties and dances and roller skatin'."

"Never take 'em to the prize fights, eh?" says Carey.

"We don't have no real good bouts," says Ike. "Just bush stuff. And I never figured a boxin' match was a place for the ladies."

Well, after supper he pulled a cigar out and lit it. I was just goin' to ask him what he done it for, but he beat me to it.

"Kind o' rests a man to smoke after a good workout," he says. "Kind o' settles a man's supper, too."

256

"Looks like a pretty good cigar," says Carey.

"Yes," says Ike. "A friend o' mine give it to me—a fella in Kansas City that runs a billiard room."

"Do you play billiards?" I ast him.

"I used to play a fair game," he says. "I'm all out o' practice now—can't hardly make a shot."

We coaxed him into a four-handed battle, him and Carey against Jack Mack and I. Say, he couldn't play billiards as good as Willie Hoppe; not quite. But to hear him tell it, he didn't make a good shot all evenin'. I'd leave him an awful-lookin' layout and he'd gather 'em up in one try and then run a couple o' hundred, and between every carom he'd say he put too much stuff on the ball, or the English didn't take, or the table wasn't true, or his stick was crooked, or somethin'. And all the time he had the balls actin' like they was Dutch soldiers and him Kaiser William. We started out to play fifty points, but we had to make it a thousand so as I and Jack and Carey could try the table.

The four of us set round the lobby a wile after we was through playin', and when it got along toward bedtime Carey whispered to me and says:

"Ike'd like to go to bed, but he can't think up no excuse."

Carey hadn't hardly finished whisperin' when Ike got up and pulled it.

"Well, good night, boys," he says. "I ain't sleepy, but I got some gravel in my shoes and it's killin' my feet."

We knowed he hadn't never left the hotel since we'd came in from the grounds and changed our clo'es. So Carey says:

"I should think they'd take them gravel pits out o' the billiard room."

But Ike was already on his way to the elevator, limpin'.

"He's got the world beat," says Carey to Jack and I. "I've knew lots o' guys that had an alibi for every mistake they made; I've heard pitchers say that the ball slipped when somebody cracked one off'n 'em; I've heard infielders complain of a sore arm after heavin' one into the stand, and I've saw outfielders tooken sick with a dizzy spell when they've misjudged a fly ball. But this baby can't even go to bed without apologizin', and I bet he excuses himself to the razor when he gets ready to shave."

"And at that," says Jack, "he's goin' to make us a good man."

"Yes," says Carey, "unless rheumatism keeps his battin' average down to .400."

Well, sir, Ike kept whalin' away at the ball all through the trip till everybody knowed he'd won a job. Cap had him in there regular the last few exhibition games and told the newspaper boys a week before the season opened that he was goin' to start him in Kane's place.

"You're there, kid," says Carey to Ike, the night Cap made the 'nnouncement. "They ain't many boys that wins a big league berth their third year out."

"I'd of been up here a year ago," says Ike, "only I was bent over all season with lumbago."

◆ 2 ◆

It rained down in Cincinnati one day and somebody organized a little game o' cards. They was shy two men to make six and ast I and Carey to play.

"I'm with you if you get Ike and make it seven-handed," says Carey.

So they got a hold of Ike and we went up to Smitty's room.

"I pretty near forgot how many you deal," says Ike. "It's been a long wile since I played"

I and Carey give each other the wink, and sure enough, he was just as ig'orant about poker as billiards. About the second hand, the pot was opened two or three ahead of him, and they was three in when it come his turn. It cost a buck, and he throwed in two.

"It's raised, boys," somebody says.

"Gosh, that's right, I did raise it," says Ike.

"Take out a buck if you didn't mean to tilt her," says Carey.

"No," says Ike, "I'll leave it go."

Well, it was raised back at him, and then he made another mistake and raised again. They was only three left in when the draw come. Smitty'd opened with a pair o' kings and he didn't help 'em. Ike stood pat. The guy that'd raised him back was flushin' and he didn't fill. So Smitty checked and Ike bet and didn't get no call. He tossed his hand away, but I grabbed it and give it a look. He had king, queen, jack and two tens. Alibi Ike he must have seen me peekin', for he leaned over and whispered to me.

"I overlooked my hand," he says. "I thought all the wile it was a straight."

"Yes," I says, "that's why you raised twice by mistake."

They was another pot that he come into with tens and fours. It was tilted a couple o' times and two o' the strong fellas drawed ahead of Ike. They each drawed one. So Ike threw away his little pair and come out with four tens. And they was four treys against him. Carey'd looked at Ike's discards and then he says:

"This lucky bum busted two pair."

"No, no, I didn't," says Ike.

"Yes, yes, you did," says Carey, and showed us the two fours.

"What do you know about that?" says Ike. "I'd of swore one was a five spot."

Well, we hadn't had no pay day yet, and after a wile everybody except Ike was goin' shy. I could see him gettin' restless and I was wonderin' how he'd make the get-away. He tried two or three times. "I got to buy some collars before supper," he says.

"No hurry," says Smitty. "The stores here keeps open all night in April."

After a minute he opened up again.

"My uncle out in Nebraska ain't expected to live," he says. "I ought to send a telegram."

"Would that save him?" says Carey.

"No, it sure wouldn't," says Ike, "but I ought to leave my old man know where I'm at."

"When did you hear about your uncle?" says Carey.

"Just this mornin'," says Ike.

"Who told you?" ast Carey.

"I got a wire from my old man," says Ike.

"Well," says Carey, "your old man knows you're still here yet this afternoon if you was here this mornin'. Trains leavin' Cincinnati in the middle o' the day don't carry no ball clubs."

"Yes," says Ike, "that's true. But he don't know where I'm goin' to be next week."

"Ain't he got no schedule?" ast Carey.

"I sent him one openin' day," says Ike, "but it takes mail a long time to get to Idaho."

"I thought your old man lived in Kansas City," says Carey.

"He does when he's home," says Ike.

"But now," says Carey, "I s'pose he's went to Idaho so as he can be near your sick uncle in Nebraska."

"He's visitin' my other uncle in Idaho."

"Then how does he keep posted about your sick uncle?" ast Carey.

"He don't," says Ike. "He don't even know my other uncle's sick. That's why I ought to wire and tell him."

"Good night!" says Carey.

"What town in Idaho is your old man at?" I says.

Ike thought it over.

"No town at all," he says. "But he's near a town."

"Near what town?" I says.

"Yuma," says Ike.

Well, by this time he'd lost two or three pots and he was desperate. We was playin' just as fast as we could, because we seen we couldn't hold him much longer. But he was tryin' so hard to frame an escape that he couldn't pay no attention to the cards, and it looked like we'd get his whole pile away from him if we could make him stick.

The telephone saved him. The minute it begun to ring, five of us jumped for it. But Ike was there first.

"Yes," he says, answerin' it. "This is him. I'll come right down."

And he slammed up the receiver and beat it out o' the door without even sayin' good-by.

"Smitty'd ought to locked the door," says Carey.

"What did he win?" ast Carey.

We figured it up—sixty-odd bucks.

"And the next time we ask him to play," says Carey, "his fingers will be so stiff he can't hold the cards."

Well, we set round a wile talkin' it over, and pretty soon the telephone rung again. Smitty answered it. It was a friend of his'n from Hamilton and he wanted to know why Smitty didn't hurry down. He was the one that had called before and Ike had told him he was Smitty.

"Ike'd ought to split with Smitty's friend," says Carey.

"No," I says, "he'll need all he won. It costs money to buy collars and to send telegrams from Cincinnati to your old man in Texas and keep him posted on the health o' your uncle in Cedar Rapids, D.C."

And you ought to heard him out there on that field! They wasn't a day when he didn't pull six or seven, and it didn't make no difference whether he was goin' good or bad. If he popped up in the pinch he should of made a base hit and the reason he didn't was so-and-so. And if he cracked one for three bases he ought to had a home run, only the ball wasn't lively, or the wind brought it back, or he tripped on a lump o' dirt, roudin' first base.

They was one afternoon in New York when he beat all records. Big Marquard was workin' against us and he was good.

In the first innin' Ike hit one clear over that right field stand, but it was a few feet foul. Then he got another foul and then the count come to two and two. Then Rube slipped one acrost on him and he was called out.

"What do you know about that!" he says afterward on the bench. "I lost count. I thought it was three and one, and I took a strike."

"You took a strike all right," says Carey. "Even the umps knowed it was a strike."

"Yes," says Ike, "but you can bet I wouldn't of took it if I'd knew it was the third one. The scoreboard had it wrong."

"That scoreboard ain't for you to look at," says Cap. "It's for you to hit that old pill against."

"Well," says Ike, "I could of hit that one over the scoreboard if I'd knew it was the third."

"Was it a good ball?" I says.

"Well, no, it wasn't," says Ike. "It was inside."

"How far inside?" says Carey.

"Oh, two or three inches or half a foot," says Ike.

"I guess you wouldn't of threatened the scoreboard with it then," says Cap.

"I'd of pulled it down the right foul line if I hadn't thought he'd call it a ball," says Ike.

Well, in New York's part o' the innin' Doyle cracked one and Ike run back a mile and a half and caught it with one hand. We was all sayin' what a whale of a play it was, but he had to apologize just the same as for gettin' struck out.

"That stand's so high," he says, "that a man don't never see a ball till it's right on top o' you."

"Didn't you see that one?" ast Cap.

"Not at first," says Ike; "not till it raised up above the roof o' the stand."

"Then why did you start back as soon as the ball was hit?" says Cap.

"I knowed by the sound that he'd got a good hold of it," says Ike.

"Yes," says Cap, "but how'd you know what direction to run in?"

"Doyle usually hits 'em that way, the way I run," says Ike.

"Why don't you play blindfolded?" says Carey.

"Might as well, with that big high stand to bother a man," says Ike. "If I could of saw the ball all the time I'd of got it in my hip pocket."

Along in the fifth we was one run to the bad and Ike got on with one out. On the first ball throwed to Smitty, Ike went down. The ball was outside and Meyers throwed Ike out by ten feet.

You could see Ike's lips movin' all the way to the bench and when he got there he had his piece learned.

"Why didn't he swing?" he says.

"Why didn't you wait for his sign?" says Cap.

"He give me his sign," says Ike.

"What's his sign with you?" says Cap.

"Pickin' up some dirt with his right hand," says Ike.

"Well, I didn't see him do it," Cap says.

"He done it all right," says Ike.

Well, Smitty went out and they wasn't no more argument till they come in for the next innin'. Then Cap opened it up.

"You fellas better get your signs straight," he says.

"Do you mean me?" says Smitty.

"Yes," Cap says. "What's your sign with Ike?"

"Slidin' my left hand up to the end o' the bat and back," says Smitty.

"Do you hear that, Ike?" ast Cap.

"What of it?" says Ike.

"You says his sign was pickin' up dirt and he says it's slidin' his hand. Which is right?"

"I'm right," says Smitty. "But if you're arguin' about him goin' last innin', I didn't give him no sign."

"You pulled your cap down with your right hand, didn't you?" ast Ike.

"Well, s'pose I did," says Smitty. "That don't mean nothin'. I never told you to take that for a sign, did I?"

"I thought maybe you meant to tell me and forgot," says Ike.

They couldn't none of us answer that and they wouldn't of been no more said if Ike had of shut up. But wile we was settin' there Carey got on with two out and stole second clean.

"There!" says Ike. "That's what I was tryin' to do and I'd of got away with it if Smitty'd swang and bothered the Indian."

"Oh!" says Smitty. "You was tryin' to steal then, was you? I thought you claimed I give you the hit and run."

"I didn't claim no such a thing," says Ike. "I thought maybe you might of gave me a sign, but I was goin' anyway because I thought I had a good start."

Cap prob'ly would of hit him with a bat, only just about that time Doyle booted one on Hayes and Carey come acrost with the run that tied.

Well, we go into the ninth finally, one and one, and Marquard walks McDonald with nobody out.

"Lay it down," says Cap to Ike.

And Ike goes up there with orders to bunt and cracks the first ball into that right-field stand! It was fair this time, and we're two ahead, but I didn't think about that at the time. I was too busy watchin' Cap's face. First he turned pale and then he got red as fire and then he got blue and purple, and finally he just laid back and busted out laughin'. So we wasn't afraid to laugh ourselfs when we seen him doin' it, and when Ike come in everybody on the bench was in hysterics.

But instead o' takin' advantage, Ike had to try and excuse himself. His play was to shut up and he didn't know how to make it.

"Well," he says, "if I hadn't hit quite so quick at that one I bet it'd of cleared the center-field fence."

Cap stopped laughin'.

"It'll cost you plain fifty," he says.

"What for?" says Ike.

"When I say 'bunt' I mean 'bunt,'" says Cap.

"You didn't say 'bunt,' " says Ike.

"I says 'Lay it down,' " says Cap. "If that don't mean 'bunt,' what does it mean?"

" 'Lay it down' means 'bunt' all right," says Ike, "but I understood you to say 'Lay on it.' "

"All right," says Cap, "and the little misunderstandin' will cost you fifty."

Ike didn't say nothin' for a few minutes. Then he had another bright idear.

"I was just kiddin' about misunderstandin' you," he says. "I knowed you wanted me to bunt."

"Well, then, why didn't you bunt?" ast Cap.

"I was goin' to on the next ball," says Ike. "But I thought if I took a good wallop I'd have 'em all fooled. So I walloped at the first one to fool 'em, and I didn't have no intention 'o hittin' it."

"You tried to miss it, did you?" says Cap.

"Yes," says Ike.

"How'd you happen to hit it?" ast Cap.

"Well," Ike says, "I was lookin' for him to throw me a fast one and I was goin' to swing under it. But he come with a hook and I met it right square where I was swingin' to go under the fast one."

"Great!" says Cap. "Boys," he says, "Ike's learned how to hit Marquard's curve. Pretend a fast one's comin' and then try to miss it. It's a good thing to know and Ike'd ought to be willin' to pay for the lesson. So I'm goin' to make it a hundred instead o' fifty."

The game wound up 3 to 1. The fine didn't go, because Ike hit like a wild man all through that trip and we made pretty near a clean-up. The night we went to Philly I got him cornered in the car and I says to him:

"Forget them alibis for a wile and tell me somethin'. What'd you do that for, swing that time against Marquard when you was told to bunt?"

"I'll tell you," he says. "That ball he throwed me looked just like the one I struck out on in the first innin' and I wanted to show Cap what I could of done to that other one if I'd knew it was the third strike."

"But," I says, "the one you struck out on in the first innin' was a fast ball."

"So was the one I cracked in the ninth," says Ike.

♦ 4 ♦

You've saw Cap's wife, o' course. Well, her sister's about twict as good-lookin' as her, and that's goin' some.

Cap took his missus down to St. Louis the second trip and the other one come down from St. Joe to visit her. Her name is Dolly, and some doll is right.

Well, Cap was goin' to take the two sisters to a show and he wanted a beau for Dolly. He left it to her and she picked Ike. He'd hit three on the nose that afternoon—of'n Sallee, too.

They fell for each other that first evenin'. Cap told us how it come off. She begin flatterin' Ike for the star game he'd played and o' course he begin excusin' himself for not doin' better. So she thought he was modest and it went strong with her. And she believed everything he said and that made her solid with him—that and her make-up. They was together every mornin' and evenin' for the five days we was there. In the afternoons Ike played the grandest ball you ever see, hittin' and runnin' the bases like a fool and catchin' everything that stayed in the park.

I told Cap, I says: "You'd ought to keep the doll with us and he'd make Cobb's figures look sick."

But Dolly had to go back to St. Joe and we come home for a long serious.

Well, for the next three weeks Ike had a letter to read every day and he'd set in the clubhouse readin' it till mornin' practice was half over. Cap didn't say nothin' to him, because he was goin' so good. But I and Carey wasted a lot of our time tryin' to get him to own up who the letters was from. Fine chanct!

"What are you readin'?" Carey'd say. "A bill?"

"No," Ike'd say, "not exactly a bill. It's a letter from a fella I used to go to school with."

"High school or college?" I'd ask him.

"College," he'd say.

"What college?" I'd say.

Then he'd stall a wile and then he'd say:

"I didn't go to the college myself, but my friend went there."

"How did it happen you didn't go?" Carey'd ask him.

"Well," he'd say, "they wasn't no colleges near where I lived."

"Didn't you live in Kansas City?" I'd say to him.

One time he'd say he did and another time he didn't. One time he says he lived in Michigan.

"Where at?" says Carey.

"Near Detroit," he says.

"Well," I says, "Detroit's near Ann Arbor and that's where they got the university."

"Yes," says Ike, "they got it there now, but they didn't have it there then."

"I come pretty near goin' to Syracuse," I says, "only they wasn't no railroads runnin' through there in them days."

"Where'd this friend o' yours go to college?" says Carey.

"I forget now," says Ike.

"Was it Carlisle?" ast Carey.

"No," says Ike, "his folks wasn't very well off."

"That's what barred me from Smith," I says.

"I was goin' to tackle Cornell's," says Carey, "but the doctor told me I'd have hay fever if I didn't stay up North."

"Your friend writes long letters," I says.

"Yes," says Ike; "he's tellin' me about a ballplayer."

"Where does he play?" ast Carey.

"Down in the Texas League—Fort Wayne," says Ike.

"It looks like a girl's writin'," Carey says.

"A girl wrote it," says Ike. "That's my friend's sister, writin' for him."

"Didn't they teach writin' at this here college where he went?" says Carey.

"Sure," Ike says, "they taught writin', but he got his hand cut off in a railroad wreck."

"How long ago?" I says.

"Right after he got out o' college," says Ike.

"Well," I says, "I should think he'd of learned to write with his left hand by this time."

266

"It's his left hand that was cut off," says Ike; "and he was left-handed."

"You get a letter every day," says Carey. "They're all the same writin'. Is he tellin' you about a different ballplayer every time he writes?"

"No," Ike says. "It's the same ballplayer. He just tells me what he does every day."

"From the size o' the letters, they don't play nothin' but double-headers down there," says Carey.

We figured that Ike spent most of his evenins answerin' the letters from his "friend's sister," so we kept tryin' to date him up for shows and parties to see how he'd duck out of 'em. He was bugs over spaghetti, so we told him one day that they was goin' to be a big feed of it over to Joe's that night and he was invited.

"How long'll it last?" he says.

"Well," we says, "we're goin' right over there after the game and stay till they close up."

"I can't go," he says, "unless they leave me come home at eight bells."

"Nothin' doin,' " says Carey. "Joe'd get sore."

"I can't go then," says Ike.

"Why not?" I ast him.

"Well," he says, "my landlady locks up the house at eight and I left my key home."

"You can come and stay with me," says Carey.

"No," he says, "I can't sleep in a strange bed."

"How do you get along when we're on the road?" says I.

"I don't never sleep the first night anywheres," he says. "After that I'm all right."

"You'll have time to chase home and get your key right after the game," I told him.

"The key ain't home," says Ike. "I lent it to one o' the other fellas and he's went out o' town and took it with him."

"Couldn't you borry another key off'n the landlady?" Carey ast him.

"No," he says, "that's the only one they is."

Well, the day before we started East again, Ike come into the club-house all smiles.

"Your birthday?" I ast him.

"No," he says.

"What do you feel so good about?" I says.

"Got a letter from my old man," he says. "My uncle's goin' to get well."

"Is that the one in Nebraska?" says I.

"Not right in Nebraska," says Ike. "Near there."

But afterwards we got the right dope from Cap. Dolly'd blew in from Missouri and was going to make the trip with her sister.

♦ 5 ♦

Well, I want to alibi Carey and I for what come off in Boston. If we'd of had any idear what we was doin', we'd never did it. They wasn't nobody outside o' maybe Ike and the dame that felt worse over it than I and Carey.

The first two days we didn't see nothin' of Ike and her except out to the park. The rest o' the time they was sight-seein' over to Cambridge and down to Revere and out to Brook-a-line and all the other places where the rubes go.

But when we come into the beanery after the third game Cap's wife called us over.

"If you want to see somethin' pretty," she says, "look at the third finger on Sis's left hand."

Well, o' course we knowed before we looked that it wasn't goin' to be no hangnail. Nobody was su'prised when Dolly blew into the dinin' room with it—a rock that Ike'd bought off'n Diamond Joe the first trip to New York. Only o' course it'd been set into a lady's-size ring instead o' the automobile tire he'd been wearin'.

Cap and his missus and Ike and Dolly ett supper together, only Ike didn't eat nothin', but just set there blushin' and spillin' things on the tablecloth. I heard him excusin' himself for not havin' no appetite. He says he couldn't never eat when he was clost to the ocean. He'd forgot about them sixty-five oysters he destroyed the first night o' the trip before.

He was goin' to take her to a show, so after supper he went upstairs

to change his collar. She had to doll up, too, and o' course Ike was through long before her.

If you remember the hotel in Boston, they's a little parlor where the piano's at and then they's another little parlor openin' off o' that. Well, when Ike come down Smitty was playin' a few chords and I and Carey was harmonizin'. We seen Ike go up to the desk to leave his key and we called him in. He tried to duck away, but we wouldn't stand for it.

We ast him what he was all duded up for and he says he was goin' to the theayter.

"Goin' alone?" says Carey.

"No," he says, "a friend o' mine's goin' with me."

"What do you say if we go along?" says Carey.

"I ain't only got two tickets," he says.

"Well," says Carey, "we can go down there with you and buy our own seats; maybe we can all get together."

"No," says Ike. "They ain't no more seats. They're all sold out."

"We can buy some off'n the scalpers," says Carey.

"I wouldn't if I was you," says Ike. "They say the show's rotten."

"What are you goin' for, then?" I ast.

"I didn't hear about it bein' rotten till I got the tickets," he says.

"Well," I says, "if you don't want to go I'll buy the tickets from you."

"No," says Ike, "I wouldn't want to cheat you. I'm stung and I'll just have to stand for it."

"What are you goin' to do with the girl, leave her here at the hotel?" I says.

"What girl?" says Ike.

"The girl you ett supper with," I says.

"Oh," he says, "we just happened to go into the dinin' room together, that's all. Cap wanted I should set down with 'em."

"I noticed," says Carey, "that she happened to be wearin' that rock you bought off'n Diamond Joe."

"Yes," says Ike. "I lent it to her for a wile."

"Did you lend her the new ring that goes with it?" I says.

"She had that already," says Ike. "She lost the set out of it."

"I wouldn't trust no strange girl with a rock o' mine," says Carey.

"Oh, I guess she's all right," Ike says. "Besides, I was tired o' the stone. When a girl asks you for somethin', what are you goin' to do?"

He started out toward the desk, but we flagged him.

"Wait a minute!" Carey says. "I got a bet with Sam here, and it's up to you to settle it."

"Well," says Ike, "make it snappy. My friend'll be here any minute."

"I bet," says Carey, "that you and that girl was engaged to be married."

"Nothin' to it," says Ike.

"Now look here," says Carey, "this is goin' to cost me real money if I lose. Cut out the alibi stuff and give it to us straight. Cap's wife just as good as told us you was roped."

Ike blushed like a kid.

"Well, boys," he says, "I may as well own up. You win, Carey."

"Yatta boy!" says Carey. "Congratulations!"

"You got a swell girl, Ike," I says.

"She's a peach," says Smitty.

"Well, I guess she's O.K.," says Ike. "I don't know much about girls."

"Didn't you never run round with 'em?" I says.

"Oh, yes, plenty of 'em," says Ike. "But I never seen none I'd fall for."

"That is, till you seen this one," says Carey.

"Well," says Ike, "this one's O.K., but I wasn't thinkin' about gettin' married yet a wile."

"Who done the askin', her?" says Carey.

"Oh, no," says Ike, "but sometimes a man don't know what he's gettin' into. Take a good-lookin' girl, and a man gen'ally almost always does about what she wants him to."

"They couldn't no girl lasso me unless I wanted to be lassoed," says Smitty.

"Oh, I don't know," says Ike. "When a fella gets to feelin' sorry for one of 'em it's all off."

Well, we left him go after shakin' hands all round. But he didn't take Dolly to no show that night. Some time wile we was talkin' she'd came into that other parlor and she'd stood there and heard us. I don't know how much she heard. But it was enough. Dolly and Cap's missus

270

took the midnight train for New York. And from there Cap's wife sent her on her way back to Missouri.

She'd left the ring and note for Ike with the clerk. But we didn't ask Ike if the note was from his friend in Fort Wayne, Texas.

♦ 6 ♦

When we'd came to Boston Ike was hittin' plain .397. When we got back home he'd fell off to pretty near nothin'. He hadn't drove one out o' the infield in any o' them other Eastern parks, and he didn't even give no excuse for it.

To show you how bad he was, he struck out three times in Brooklyn one day and never opened his trap when Cap ast him what was the matter. Before, if he'd whiffed oncet in a game he'd of wrote a book tellin' why.

Well, we dropped from first place to fifth in four weeks and we was still goin' down. I and Carey was about the only ones in the club that spoke to each other, and all as we did was to remind ourself o' what a boner we'd pulled.

"It's goin' to beat us out o' the big money," says Carey.

"Yes," I says. "I don't want to knock my own ball club, but it looks like a one-man team, and when that one man's dauber's down we couldn't trim our whiskers."

"We ought to knew better," says Carey.

"Yes," I says, "but why should a man pull an alibi for bein' engaged to such a bearcat as she was?"

"He shouldn't," says Carey. "But I and you knowed he would or we'd never started talkin' to him about it. He wasn't no more ashamed o' the girl than I am of a regular base hit. But he just can't come clean on no subjec'."

Cap had the whole story, and I and Carey was as pop'lar with him as an umpire.

"What do you want me to do, Cap?" Carey'd say to him before goin' up to hit.

"Use your own judgment," Cap'd tell him. "We want to lose another game."

But finally, one night in Pittsburgh, Cap had a letter from his missus and he come to us with it.

"You fellas," he says, "is the ones that put us on the bum, and if you're sorry I think they's a chancet for you to make good. The old lady's out to St. Joe and she's been tryin' her hardest to fix things up. She's explained that Ike don't mean nothin' with his talk; I've wrote and explained that to Dolly, too. But the old lady says that Dolly says that she can't believe it. But Dolly's still stuck on this baby, and she's pinin' away just the same as Ike. And the old lady says she thinks if you two fellas would write to the girl and explain how you was always kiddin' with Ike and leadin' him on, and how the ball club was all shot to pieces since Ike quit hittin', and how he acted like he was goin' to kill himself, and this and that, she'd fall for it and maybe soften down. Dolly, the old lady says, would believe you before she'd believe I and the old lady, because she thinks it's her we're sorry for, and not him."

Well, I and Carey was only too glad to try and see what we could do. But it wasn't no snap. We wrote about eight letters before we got one that looked good. Then we give it to the stenographer and had it wrote out on a typewriter and both of us signed it.

It was Carey's idear that made the letter good. He stuck in somethin' about the world's serious money that our wives wasn't goin' to spend unless she took pity on a "boy who was so shy and modest that he was afraid to come right out and say that he had asked such a beautiful and handsome girl to become his bride."

That's prob'ly what got her, or maybe she couldn't of held out much longer anyway. It was four days after we sent the letter that Cap heard from his missus again. We was in Cincinnati.

"We've won," he says to us. "The old lady says that Dolly says she'll give him another chance. But the old lady says it won't do no good for Ike to write a letter. He'll have to go out there."

"Send him tonight," says Carey.

"I'll pay half his fare," I says.

"I'll pay the other half," says Carey.

"No," says Cap, "the club'll pay his expenses. I'll send him scoutin'."

"Are you goin' to send him tonight?"

"Sure," says Cap. "But I'm goin' to break the news to him right now. It's time we win a ball game."

So in the clubhouse, just before the game, Cap told him. And I certainly felt sorry for Rube Benton and Red Ames that afternoon! I and Carey was standin' in front o' the hotel that night when Ike come out with his suitcase.

"Sent home?" I says to him.

"No," he says, "I'm goin' scoutin'."

"Where to?" I says. "Fort Wayne?"

"No, not exactly," he says.

"Well," says Carey, "have a good time."

"I ain't lookin' for no good time," says Ike. "I says I was goin' scoutin'."

"Well, then," says Carey, "I hope you see somebody you like."

"And you better have a drink before you go," I says.

"Well," says Ike, "they claim it helps a cold."

♦

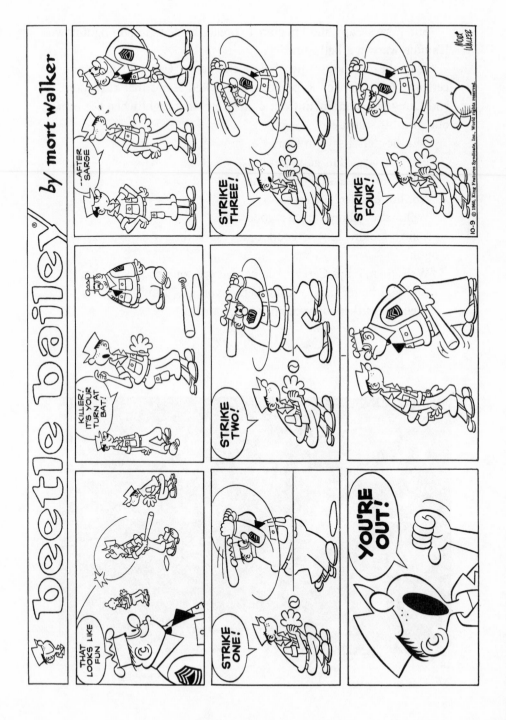

274

Leroy Jeffcoat

BY WILLIAM PRICE FOX

ON LEROY JEFFCOAT'S FORTY-FIRST BIRTH-
day he fell off a scaffold while painting a big stucco rooming
house over on Sycamore Street. Leroy was in shock for about twenty
minutes but when the doctor brought him around he seemed all right.

Leroy went home and rolled up his trousers and shoes into a bundle
with his Sherwin-Williams Company cap and jacket. He tied the bundle
with string to keep the dogs from dragging it off and put it in the
gutter in front of his house. He poured gasoline over the bundle and
set it on fire. That was the last day Leroy Jeffcoat painted a house.

He went uptown to the Sports Center on Kenilworth Street and
bought two white baseball uniforms with green edging, two pairs of
baseball shoes, a Spalding second baseman's glove, eight baseballs and
two bats. Leroy had been painting houses at union scale since he got
out of high school, and since he never gambled nor married he had a
pretty good savings account at the South Carolina National Bank.

We had a bush-league team that year called the Columbia Green
Wave. The name must have come from the fact that most of us got
drunk on Friday nights and the games were always played on Saturdays.
Anyhow the season was half over when Leroy came down and wanted
to try out for second base.

Leroy looked more like a ballplayer than any man I've ever known.
He had that little ass-pinched strut when he was mincing around second
base. He also had a beautiful squint into or out of the sun, could chew
through a whole plug of Brown Mule tobacco in four innings, and
could worry a pitcher to death with his chatter. On and on and
on . . . we would be ahead ten runs in the ninth and Leroy wouldn't
let up.

But Leroy couldn't play. He looked fine. At times he looked great.
But he knew too much to play well. He'd read every baseball book
and guide and every Topp's Chewing Gum Baseball Card ever printed.

275

He could show you how Stan Musial batted, how Williams swung, how DiMaggio dug in. He went to all the movies and copied all the stances and mannerisms. You could say, "Let's see how Rizzuto digs one out, Leroy." He'd toss you a ball and lope out about forty feet.

"All right, throw it at my feet, right in the dirt." And you would and then you'd see the "Old Scooter" movement—low and quick with the big wrist over to first.

Leroy could copy anybody. He was great until he got in an actual game. Then he got too nervous. He'd try to bat like Williams, Musial, and DiMaggio all at once and by the time he'd make up his mind he'd have looked at three strikes. And at second base it was the same story. He fidgeted too much and never got himself set in time.

Leroy played his best ball from the bench. He liked it there. He'd pound his ball into his glove and chatter and grumble and cuss and spit tobacco juice. He'd be the first one to congratulate the home-run hitters and the first one up and screaming on a close play.

We got him into the Leesboro game for four innings and against Gaffney for three. He played the entire game at second base against the State Insane Asylum . . . but that's another story.

When the games ended, Leroy showered, dried, used plenty of talcum powder and then spent about twenty minutes in front of the mirror combing his flat black hair straight back.

Most of the team had maybe a cap and a jacket with a number on it and a pair of shoes. Leroy had two complete uniform changes. After every game he'd change his dirty one for a clean one and then take the dirty one to the one-day dry cleaner. That way Leroy was never out of uniform. Morning, noon, and night Leroy was ready. On rainy days, on days it sleeted, and even during the hurricane season, Leroy was ready. For his was the long season. Seven days a week, three hundred and sixty-five days a year, Leroy was in uniform. Bat in hand, glove fastened to belt, balls in back pocket, and cut plug going. And he never took off his spikes. He would wear a set out every two weeks. You could see him coming two blocks away in his clean white uniform. And at night when you couldn't see him you could hear the spikes and see the sparks on the sidewalk.

The Green Wave worked out on Tuesday and Thursday in the

277

evening and we played on Saturday. Leroy worked out every day and every night. He'd come up to Doc Daniels' drugstore with his bat and ball and talk someone into hitting him fly balls out over the telegraph wires on Mulberry Avenue. It could be noon in August and the sun wouldn't be any higher than a high foul ball, but it wouldn't worry Leroy Jeffcoat. He'd catch the balls or run them down in the gutter until the batter tired.

Then Leroy would buy himself and the batter a couple of Atlantic ales. Doc Daniels had wooden floors and Leroy wouldn't take his baseball shoes off, so he had to drink the ale outside.

Doc would shout out, "Leroy, damn your hide anyway. If you come in here with those spikes on I'm going to work you over with this ice-cream scoop. Now you hear?"

Leroy would spin the ball into the glove, fold it and put it in his back pocket.

"Okay, Doc."

"Why can't you take those damn spikes off and sit down in a booth and rest? You're getting too old to be out in that sun all day."

Leroy was in great shape. As a rule, house painters have good arms and hands and bad feet.

He would laugh and take his Atlantic ale outside in the sun or maybe sit down in the little bit of shade from the mailbox.

Later on, he would find someone to throw him grounders.

"Come on, toss me a few. Don't spare the steam."

He'd crowd in on you and wouldn't be any more than thirty feet out there.

"Come on, skin it along the ground."

You'd be scared to throw it hard but he'd insist.

"Come on, now, a little of the old pepper. In the dirt."

Next thing you'd be really winging them in there and he'd be picking them off like cherries or digging them out of the dust and whipping them back to you. He'd wear you out and burn your hands up in ten minutes. Then he'd find somebody else.

Leroy would go home for supper and then he'd be back. After dark he'd go out to the streetlamp and throw the ball up near the light and catch it. The June bugs, flying ants and bats would be flitting around

278

everywhere but he'd keep on. The June bugs and flying ants would be all over his head and shoulders and even in his glove. He might stop for a while for another Atlantic ale, and if the crowd was talking baseball he'd join it. If it wasn't and the bugs were too bad, he'd stand out in the dark and pound his ball in his glove or work out in the mirror of Doc Daniels' front window. In front of the window he became a pitcher. He worked a little like Preacher Roe but he had more class. He did a lot of rubbing the resin bag and checking signs from the catcher and shaking them off. When he'd agree with a sign he'd nod his head slow . . . exactly like Roe. Then he'd get in position, toss the resin aside, and glare in mean and hard at the batter. He took a big reach and stopped and then the slow and perhaps the most classic look toward second base I've ever seen—absolutely Alexandrian. Then he'd stretch, wind, and whip it through. He put his hands on his knees . . . wait. It had to be a strike. It was. And he'd smile.

And read a sports page? Nobody this side of Cooperstown ever read a page the way Leroy Jeffcoat did. He would crouch down over that sheet for two hours running. He'd read every word and every figure. He went at it like he was following the puzzle maze in *Grit* trying to find the pony or the seventeen rabbits. He had a pencil about as long as your little finger and he'd make notes along the margin. When he finished he'd transfer the notes to a little black book he carried in his back pocket. Leroy would even check the earned run average and the batting and fielding average. I don't mean just *look* at them . . . he'd *study* them. And if he didn't like them he'd divide and do the multiplication and check them over. And if they were wrong he'd be on the telephone to the *Columbia Record* or else he'd write a letter.

Leroy was always writing letters to the sportswriters. Like he'd read an article about how Joe DiMaggio was getting old and slipping and he'd get mad. He'd take off his shoes and go inside Doc Daniels', buy a tablet and an envelope, get in the back booth and write. Like: "What do you mean Joe DiMaggio is too old and he's through. Why you rotten son of a bitch, you just wait and watch him tomorrow."

Next day old Joe would pick up two for four and Leroy would take off his spikes and get back in that back booth again. "What did I tell you. Next time, you watch out who you're saying is through. Also, you

279

print an apology this week or I am going to personally come up there and kick your fat ass. (Signed) Leroy Jeffcoat, taxpayer and second baseman, Doc Daniels' Drugstore, Columbia, S. C."

♦

This would be a much better story if I could tell you that Leroy's game improved and he went on and played and became famous throughout the Sally League. But he didn't.

He got a little better and then he leveled off. But we kept him around because we liked him (number one), that white uniform edged in green looked good (number two), and then, too, we used him as an auxiliary man. A lot of the boys couldn't make it through some of those August games. When you start fanning yourself with a catcher's mitt, it's hot. All that beer and corn whiskey would start coming out and in most games we would wind up with Leroy playing.

One game, Kirk Turner, our right fielder, passed out right in his position in the short weeds. We had to drag him into the shade and Leroy ran out to right field and began chirping. He caught a couple and dropped a couple. At bat he decided he was Ted Williams and kept waiting for that perfect ball that Ted described in *The Saturday Evening Post*. The perfect ball never came and Leroy struck out twice. In the seventh he walked. It was his first time on base in weeks and he began dancing and giving the pitcher so much lip the umpire had to settle him down.

Our last game of the year and the game we hated to play was with the South Carolina State Penitentiary down the hill.

First of all, *no one* beats "The Pen." Oh, you might give them a bad time for a couple of innings but that's about all. It's not that they're a rough bunch so much as it's that they play to win. And I mean they really play to win.

Anyhow we went down and the game started at one-thirty. The high walls kept the breeze out and it was like playing in a furnace. Sweat was dripping off my fingertips and running down my nose.

Billy Joe Jasper pitched the first inning and they hit him for seven runs before Kirk Turner caught two long ones out by the center-field wall.

We came to bat and Al Curry, our catcher, led off. Their pitcher's

name was Strunk and he was in jail for murder. The first pitch was right at Al's head. He hit the dirt. The crowd cheered. The next pitch the same thing; Al Curry was as white as a sheet. The next pitch went for his head but broke out and over the inside of the plate. Al was too scared to swing and they called him out on the next two pitches.

Jeff Harper struck out next in the same manner. When he complained to the umpire, who was a trusty, he went out and talked to Strunk. It didn't do any good.

I batted third. It was terrifying. Strunk glared at me and mouthed dirty words. He was so tall and his arms were so long I thought he was going to grab me by the throat before he turned the ball loose. I kept getting out of the box and checking to see if he was pitching from the mound. He seemed to be awfully close.

I got back in the box. I didn't dig in too deep. I wanted to be ready to duck. He reached up about nine feet and it came right at my left eye. I hit the dirt.

"Ball one."

From the ground: "How about that dusting?"

"You entering a complaint?"

"Yes."

"I'll speak to him."

The umpire went out to see Strunk and the catcher followed. They talked a while and every few seconds one of them would look back at me. They began laughing.

Back on the mound. One more beanball and once more in the dirt. And then three in a row that looked like beaners that broke over the plate. Three up. Three down.

At the end of five innings we didn't have a scratch hit. The Pen had fourteen runs and the pitcher Strunk had three doubles and a home run.

We didn't care what the score was. All we wanted to do was get the game over and get out of that prison yard. The crowd cheered everything their ball team did and every move we made brought only boos and catcalls.

At the end of seven we were still without a hit.

Leroy kept watching Strunk. "Listen, I can hit that son of a bitch."

281

I said, "No, Leroy, he's too dangerous."

"The hell he is. Let me at him."

Kirk Turner said, "Leroy, that bastard will kill you. Let's just ride him out and get out of here. This crowd makes me nervous."

But Leroy kept insisting. Finally George Haggard said, "Okay, Leroy. Take my place." So Leroy replaced George at first.

Strunk came to bat in the eighth and Leroy started shouting. "Let him hit! Let him hit, Billy Joe! I want to see that son of a bitch over here."

He pounded his fist in George's first baseman's glove and started jumping up and down like a chimpanzee.

"Send that bastard down here. I want him. I'll fix his ass."

The crowd cheered Leroy and he tipped his hat like Stan Musial.

The crowd cheered again.

Strunk bellowed, "Shut that nut up, ump."

The umpire raised his hands, "All right, over there, simmer down or I'll throw you out."

The crowd booed the umpire.

Leroy wouldn't stop. "Don't let him hit, Billy! Walk him. Walk that beanball bastard. He might get a double; I want him over here."

Billy Joe looked at Al Curry. Al gave him the walk sign.

Two balls . . . three balls . . .

"You getting scared, you bastard? Won't be long now."

The crowd laughed and cheered.

Again the Musial touch with his cap.

Strunk shouted, "Listen, you runt, you keep quiet while I'm hitting or I'll shove that glove down your throat."

Leroy laughed, "Sure you will. Come on down. I'll help you."

Four balls. . . .

Strunk laid the bat down carefully and slowly walked toward first. Strunk got close. The crowd was silent. Leroy stepped off the bag and Strunk stepped on. Leroy backed up. Strunk followed. Everybody watched. No noise. Leroy stopped and took his glove off. He handed it to Strunk. Strunk took the glove in both hands.

Leroy hit him with the fastest right I've ever seen.

Strunk was stunned but he was big. He lashed the glove into Leroy's face and swung at him.

Leroy took it on the top of his head and crowded in so fast Strunk didn't know what to do. Leroy got him off balance and kept him that way while he pumped in four lefts and six rights.

Strunk went down with Leroy on top banging away. Two of us grabbed Leroy and three got a hold of Strunk. They led Strunk back to the dugout bleeding. He turned to say something and spat out two teeth. "I ain't through with you yet."

The crowd went wild.

Someone shouted, "What's his name? What's his name?"

"Jeffcoat . . . Leroy Jeffcoat."

They cheered again. And shouted, "Leroy Jeffcoat is our boy." And then, "Leroy Jeffcoat is red-hot."

Leroy tipped his hat Musial-style, picked up George Haggard's glove and said, "Okay, let's play ball."

Another cheer and the game started.

The Pen scored two more times that inning before we got them out. We came to bat in the ninth 21 to 0. Strunk fanned me and then hit Coley Simms on the shoulder. He found out that Leroy was batting fifth so he walked the next two, loading the bases so he could get a shot at him.

So Leroy came up with the bases loaded and the prison crowd shouting "Leroy Jeffcoat is our boy."

He pulled his cap down like Musial and dug into the box like DiMaggio. The crowd cheered and he got out of the box and tipped his cap.

Strunk was getting madder and madder and he flung the resin down and kicked the rubber. "Let's go, in there."

Leroy got in the box, whipped the bat through like Ted Williams and hollered, "Okay, Strunk, let's have it."

Zip. Right at his head.

Leroy flicked his head back like a snake but didn't move his feet.

The crowd booed Strunk and the umpire went out to the mound. We could hear the argument. As the umpire turned away, Strunk told him to go to hell.

The second pitch was the same as the first. Leroy didn't move and the ball hit his cap bill.

The umpire wanted to put him on base.

Leroy shouted, "No, he didn't hit me. He's yellow. Let him pitch."

The crowd cheered Leroy again. Strunk delivered another duster and the ball went between Leroy's cap bill and his eyes. This time he didn't even flick his head.

Three balls . . . no strikes.

Two convicts dropped out of the stands and trotted across the infield to the mound. They meant business. When they talked, Strunk listened and nodded his head. A signal passed around the infield.

The fourth pitch was right across Leroy's chest. It was Williams' ideal ball and it was the ball Leroy had been waiting for all season. He hit it clean and finished the Williams swing.

It was a clean single but the right fielder bobbled it and Leroy made the wide turn toward second. The throw into second was blocked and bobbled again and Leroy kept going. He ran in spurts, each spurt faster than the last. The throw to third got past the baseman and Leroy streaked for home, shouting.

He began sliding from twenty feet out. He slid so long he stopped short. He had to get up and lunge for home plate with his hand. He made it as the ball whacked into the catcher's mitt and the crowd started coming out of the stands.

The guards tried to hold the crowd back and a warning siren sounded. But the convicts got to him and paraded around the field with Leroy on their backs. The game was called at this point and the reserve guards and trusties came out with billy clubs.

Later Coley and I learned from the Pen's manager that the committee had told Strunk they wanted Leroy to hit a home run. We never told the rest of the team or anybody else about that.

After we showered at The Pen we all went back to Doc Daniels' drugstore. Everyone told everyone about it and when Doc Daniels heard it he came outside and personally led Leroy into the store with his spikes on.

"Leroy, from now on I want you to feel free to walk right in here anytime you feel like it."

Leroy smiled, and put his bat and his uniform bag up on the soda fountain. Doc bought Atlantic ales for everyone. Later, I bought a round and Coley bought a round.

284

And just as we were settling down in the booths with sandwiches, potato chips, and the jukebox going, Leroy picked up his glove and started spinning his ball off the ends of his fingers and said, "I'm getting a little stiff. Anyone feel like throwing me a few fast ones?"

♦

"Pop! Pop! Everybody's Pop! What this team needs is a complete new set of nicknames."

You Could Look It Up

BY JAMES THURBER

IT ALL BEGUN WHEN WE DROPPED DOWN to C'lumbus, Ohio, from Pittsburgh to play a exhibition game on our way out to St. Louis. It was gettin' on into September, and though we'd been leadin' the league by six, seven games most of the season, we was now in first place by a margin you could 'a' got it into the eye of a thimble, bein' only a half a game ahead of St. Louis. Our slump had given the boys the leapin' jumps, and they was like a bunch a old ladies at a lawn fete with a thunderstorm comin' up, runnin' around snarlin' at each other, eatin' bad and sleepin' worse, and battin' for a team average of maybe .186. Half the time nobody'd speak to nobody else, without it was to bawl 'em out.

Squawks Magrew was managin' the boys at the time, and he was darn near crazy. They called him "Squawks" 'cause when things was goin' bad he lost his voice, or perty near lost it, and squealed at you like a little girl you stepped on her doll or somethin'. He yelled at everybody and wouldn't listen to nobody, without maybe it was me. I'd been trainin' the boys for ten year, and he'd take more lip from me than from anybody else. He knowed I was smarter'n him, anyways, like you're goin' to hear.

This was thirty, thirty-one year ago; you could look it up, 'cause it was the same year C'lumbus decided to call itself the Arch City, on account of a lot of iron arches with electric-light bulbs into 'em which stretched across High Street. Thomas Albert Edison sent 'em a telegram, and they was speeches and maybe even President Taft opened the celebration by pushin' a button. It was a great week for the Buckeye capital, which was why they got us out there for this exhibition game.

Well, we just lost a double-header to Pittsburgh, 11 to 5 and 7 to 3, so we snarled all the way to C'lumbus, where we put up at the Chittaden Hotel, still snarlin'. Everybody was tetchy, and when Billy Klinger took a sock at Whitey Cott at breakfast, Whitey threwed marmalade all over his face.

286

"Blind each other, whatta I care?" says Magrew. "You can't see nothin' anyways."

C'lumbus win the exhibition game, 3 to 2, whilst Magrew set in the dugout, mutterin' and cursin' like a fourteen-year-old Scotty. He bad-mouthed everybody on the ball club and he bad-mouthed everybody on the ball club and he bad-mouthed everybody offa the ball club, includin' the Wright brothers, who, he claimed, had yet to build a airship big enough for any of our boys to hit it with a ball bat.

"I wisht I was dead," he says to me. "I wisht I was in heaven with the angels."

I told him to pull hisself together, 'cause he was drivin' the boys crazy, the way he was goin' on, sulkin' and bad-mouthin' and whinin'. I was older'n he was and smarter'n he was, and he knowed it. I was ten times smarter'n he was about this Pearl du Monville, first time I ever laid eyes on the little guy, which was one of the saddest days of my life.

Now, most people name of Pearl is girls, but this Pearl du Monville was a man, if you could call a fella a man who was only thirty-four, thirty-five inches high. Pearl du Monville was a midget. He was part French and part Hungarian, and maybe even part Bulgarian or somethin'. I can see him now, a sneer on his little pushed-in pan, swingin' a bamboo cane and smokin' a big cigar. He had a gray suit with a big black check into it, and he had a gray felt hat with one of them rainbow-colored hatbands onto it, like the young fellas wore in them days. He talked like he was talkin' into a tin can, but he didn't have no foreign accent. He might 'a' been fifteen or he might 'a' been a hundred, you couldn't tell. Pearl du Monville.

After the game with C'lumbus, Magrew headed straight for the Chittaden bar—the train for St. Louis wasn't goin' for three, four hours—and there he set, drinkin' rye and talkin' to this bartender.

"How I pity me, brother," Magrew was tellin' this bartender. "How I pity me." That was alwuz his favorite tune. So he was settin' there, tellin' this bartender how heartbreakin' it was to be manager of a bunch a blindfolded circus clowns, when up pops this Pearl du Monville outa nowheres.

It give Magrew the leapin' jumps. He thought at first maybe the D.T.'s had come back on him; he claimed he'd had 'em once, and little

287

guys had popped up all around him, wearin' red, white and blue hats.

"Go on, now!" Magrew yells. "Get away from me!"

But the midget clumb up on a chair acrost the table from Magrew and says, "I seen that game today, Junior, and you ain't got no ball club. What you got there, Junior," he says, "is a side show."

"Whatta ya mean, 'Junior'?" says Magrew, touchin' the little guy to satisfy hisself he was real.

"Don't pay him no attention, mister," says the bartender. "Pearl calls everybody 'Junior,' 'cause it alwuz turns out he's a year older'n anybody else."

"Yeh?" says Magrew. "How old is he?"

"How old are you, Junior?" says the midget.

"Who, me? I'm fifty-three," says Magrew.

"Well, I'm fifty-four," says the midget.

Magrew grins and asts him what he'll have, and that was the beginnin' of their beautiful friendship, if you don't care what you say.

Pearl du Monville stood up on his chair and waved his cane around and pretended like he was ballyhooin' for a circus. "Right this way, folks!" he yells. "Come on in and see the greatest collection of freaks in the world! See the armless pitchers, see the eyeless batters, see the infielders with five thumbs!" and on and on like that, feedin' Magrew gall and handin' him a laugh at the same time, you might say.

You could hear him and Pearl du Monville hootin' and hollerin' and singin' way up to the fourth floor of the Chittaden, where the boys was packin' up. When it come time to go to the station, you can imagine how disgusted we was when we crowded into the doorway of that bar and seen them two singin' and goin' on.

"Well, well, well," says Magrew, lookin' up and spottin' us. "Look who's here. . . . Clowns, this is Pearl du Monville, a monseer of the old, old school. . . . Don't shake hands with 'em, Pearl, 'cause their fingers is made of chalk and would bust right off in your paws," he says, and he starts guffawin' and Pearl starts titterin' and we stand there givin' 'em the iron eye, it bein' the lowest ebb a ball-club manager'd got hisself down to since the national pastime was started.

288

Then the midget begun givin' us the bally-hoo. "Come on in!" he says, wavin' his cane. "See the legless base runners, see the outfielders with the butter fingers, see the southpaw with the arm of a little chee-ild!"

Then him and Magrew begun to hoop and holler and nudge each other till you'd of thought this little guy was the funniest guy than even Charlie Chaplin. The fellas filed outa the bar without a word and went on up to the Union Depot, leavin' me to handle Magrew and his new-found crony.

Well, I got 'em outa there finely. I had to take the little guy along, 'cause Magrew had a holt onto him like a vise and I couldn't pry him loose.

"He's comin' along as masket," says Magrew, holdin' the midget in the crouch of his arm like a football. And come along he did, hollerin' and protestin' and beatin' at Magrew with his little fists.

"Cut it out, will ya, Junior?" the little guy kept whinin'. "Come on, leave a man loose, will ya, Junior?"

But Junior kept a holt onto him and begun yellin', "See the guys with the glass arm, see the guys with the cast-iron brains, see the fielders with the feet on their wrists!"

So it goes, right through the whole Union Depot, with people starin' and catcallin', and he don't put the midget down till he gets him through the gates.

"How'm I goin' to go along without no toothbrush?" the midget asts. "What'm I goin' to do without no other suit?" he says.

"Doc here," says Magrew, meanin' me—"doc here will look after you like you was his own son, won't you, doc?"

I give him the iron eye, and he finely got on the train and prob'ly went to sleep with his clothes on.

This left me alone with the midget. "Lookit," I says to him. "Why don't you go on home now? Come mornin', Magrew'll forget all about you. He'll prob'ly think you was somethin' he seen in a nightmare maybe. And he ain't goin' to laugh so easy in the mornin', neither," I says. "So why don't you go on home?"

"Nix," he says to me. "Skiddoo," he says, "twenty-three for you," and he tosses his cane up into the vestibule of the coach and clam'ers

on up after it like a cat. So that's the way Pearl du Monville come to go to St. Louis with the ball club.

I seen 'em first at breakfast the next day, settin' opposite each other; the midget playin' "Turkey in the Straw" on a harmonium and Magrew starin' at his eggs and bacon like they was a uncooked bird with its feathers still on.

"Remember where you found this?" I says, jerkin' my thumb at the midget. "Or maybe you think they come with breakfast on these trains," I says, bein' a good hand at turnin' a sharp remark in them days.

The midget puts down the harmonium and turns on me. "Sneeze," he says; "your brains is dusty." Then he snaps a couple drops of water at me from a tumbler. "Drown," he says, tryin' to make his voice deep.

Now, both them cracks is Civil War cracks, but you'd of thought they was brand-new and the funniest than any crack Magrew'd ever heard in his whole life. He started hoopin' and hollerin', and the midget started hoopin' and hollerin', so I walked on away and set down with Bugs Courtney and Hank Metters, payin' no attention to this weak-minded Damon and Phidias acrost the aisle.

Well, sir, the first game with St. Louis was rained out, and there we was facin' a double-header next day. Like maybe I told you, we lose the last three double-headers we play, makin' maybe twenty-five errors in the six games, which is all right for the intimates of a school for the blind, but is disgraceful for the world's champions. It was too wet to go to the zoo, and Magrew wouldn't let us go to the movies, 'cause they flickered so bad in them days. So we just set around, stewin' and frettin'.

One of the newspaper boys come over to take a pitture of Billy Klinger and Whitey Cott shakin' hands—this reporter'd heard about the fight—and whilst they was standin' there, toe to toe, shakin' hands, Billy give a back lunge and a jerk, and throwed Whitey over his shoulder into a corner of the room, like a sack a salt. Whitey come back at him with a chair, and Bethlehem broke loose in that there room. The camera was tromped to pieces like a berry basket. When we finely got 'em pulled apart, I heard a laugh, and there was Magrew and the midget standin' in the door and givin' us the iron eye.

"Wrasslers," says Magrew, cold-like, "that's what I got for a ball club,

290

Mr. du Monville, wrasslers—and not very good wrasslers at that, you ast me."

"A man can't be good at everythin'," says Pearl, "but he oughta be good at somethin'."

This sets Magrew guffawin' again, and away they go, the midget taggin' along by his side like a hound dog and handin' him a fast line of so-called comic cracks.

When we went out to face that battlin' St. Louis club in a double-header the next afternoon, the boys was jumpy as tin toys with keys in their back. We lose the first game, 7 to 2, and are trailin', 4 to 0, when the second game ain't but ten minutes old. Magrew set there like a stone statue, speakin' to nobody. Then, in their half a the fourth, somebody singled to center and knocked in two more runs for St. Louis.

That made Magrew squawk. "I wisht one thing," he says. "I wisht I was manager of a old ladies' sewin' circus 'stead of a ball club."

"You are, Junior, you are," says a familyer and disagreeable voice.

It was that Pearl du Monville again, poppin' up outa nowheres, swingin' his bamboo cane and smokin' a cigar that's three sizes too big for his face. By this time we'd finely got the other side out, and Hank Metters slithered a bat acrost the ground, and the midget had to jump to keep both his ankles from bein' broke.

I thought Magrew'd bust a blood vessel. "You hurt Pearl and I'll break your neck!" he yelled.

Hank muttered somethin' and went on up to the plate and struck out.

We managed to get a couple runs acrost in our half a the sixth, but they come back with three more in their half a the seventh, and this was too much for Magrew.

"Come on, Pearl," he says. "We're gettin' outa here."

"Where you think you're goin'?" I ast him.

"To the lawyer's again," he says cryptly.

"I didn't know you'd been to the lawyer's once, yet," I says.

"Which that goes to show how much you don't know," he says.

With that, they was gone, and I didn't see 'em the rest of the day, nor know what they was up to, which was a God's blessin'. We lose

the nightcap, 9 to 3, and that puts us into second place plenty, and as low in our mind as a ball club can get.

The next day was a horrible day, like anybody that lived through it can tell you. Practice was just over and the St. Louis club was takin' the field, when I hears this strange sound from the stands. It sounds like the nervous whickerin' a horse gives when he smells somethin' funny on the wind. It was the fans ketchin' sight of Pearl du Monville, like you have prob'ly guessed. The midget had popped up onto the field all dressed up in a minacher club uniform, sox, cap, little letters sewed onto his chest, and all. He was swingin' a kid's bat and the only thing kept him from lookin' like a real ballplayer seen through the wrong end of a microscope was this cigar he was smokin'.

Bugs Courtney reached over and jerked it outa his mouth and throwed it away. "You're wearin' that suit on the playin' field," he says to him, severe as a judge. "You go insultin' it and I'll take you out to the zoo and feed you to the bears."

Pearl just blowed some smoke at him which he still has in his mouth.

Whilst Whitey was foulin' off four or five prior to strikin' out, I went on over to Magrew. "If I was as comic as you," I says, "I'd laugh myself to death," I says. "Is that any way to treat the uniform, makin' a mockery out of it?"

"It might surprise you to know I ain't makin' no mockery outa the uniform," says Magrew. "Pearl du Monville here has been made a bone-of-fida member of this so-called ball club. I fixed it up with the front office by long-distance phone."

"Yeh?" I says. "I can just hear Mr. Dillworth or Bart Jenkins agreein' to hire a midget for the ball club. I can just hear 'em." Mr. Dillworth was the owner of the club and Bart Jenkins was the secretary, and they never stood for no monkey business. "May I be so bold as to inquire," I says, "just what you told 'em?"

"I told 'em," he says, "I wanted to sign up a guy they ain't no pitcher in the league can strike him out."

"Uh-huh," I says, "and did you tell 'em what size of a man he is?"

"Never mind about that," he says. "I got papers on me, made out legal and proper, constitutin' one Pearl du Monville a bone-of-fida member of this former ball club. Maybe that'll shame them big babies

292

into gettin' in there and swingin', knowin' I can replace any one of 'em with a midget, if I have a mind to. A St. Louis lawyer I seen twice tells me it's all legal and proper."

"A St. Louis lawyer would," I says, "seein' nothin' could make him happier than havin' you makin' a mockery outa this one-time baseball outfit," I says.

Well, sir, it'll all be there in the papers of thirty, thirty-one year ago, and you could look it up. The game went along without no scorin' for seven innings, and since they ain't nothin' much to watch but guys poppin' up or strikin' out, the fans pay most of their attention to the goin's-on of Pearl du Monville. He's out there in front a the dugout, turnin' handsprings, balancin' his bat on his chin, walkin' a imaginary line, and so on. The fans clapped and laughed at him, and he ate it up.

So it went up to the last a the eighth, nothin' to nothin', not more'n seven, eight hits all told, and no errors on neither side. Our pitcher gets the first two men out easy in the eighth. Then up come a fella name of Porter or Billings, or some such name, and he lammed one up against the tobacco sign for three bases. The next guy up slapped the first ball out into left for a base hit, and in come the fella from third for the only run of the ball game so far. The crowd yelled, the look a death come onto Magrew's face again, and even the midget quit his tomfoolin'. Their next man fouled out back a third, and we come up for our last bats like a bunch a schoolgirls steppin' into a pool of cold water. I was lower in my mind than I'd been since the day in nineteen-four when Chesbro throwed the wild pitch in the ninth inning with a man on third and lost the pennant for the Highlanders. I knowed something just as bad was goin' to happen, which shows I'm a clair-voyun, or was then.

When Gordy Mills hit out to second, I just closed my eyes. I opened 'em up again to see Dutch Muller standin' on second, dustin' off his pants, him havin' got his first hit in maybe twenty times to the plate. Next up was Harry Loesing, battin' for our pitcher, and he got a base on balls, walkin' on a fourth one you could 'a' combed your hair with.

Then up come Whitey Cott, our lead-off man. He crotches down in what was prob'ly the most fearsome stanch in organized ball, but

all he can do is pop out to short. That brung up Billy Klinger, with two down and a man on first and second. Billy took a cut at one you could 'a' knocked a plug hat offa this here Carnera with it, but then he gets sense enough to wait 'em out, and finely he walks, too, fillin' the bases.

Yes, sir, there you are; the tyin' run on third and the winnin' run on second, first a the ninth, two men down, and Hank Metters comin' to the bat. Hank was built like a Pope-Hartford and he couldn't run no faster'n President Taft, but he had five home runs to his credit for the season, and that wasn't bad in them days. Hank was still hittin' better'n anybody else on the ball club, and it was mighty heartenin', seein' him stridin' up towards the plate. But he never got there.

"Wait a minute!" yells Magrew, jumpin' to his feet. "I'm sendin' in a pinch hitter!" he yells.

You could 'a' heard a bomb drop. When a ball-club manager says he's sendin' in a pinch hitter for the best batter on the club, you know and I know and everybody knows he's lost his holt.

"They're goin' to be sendin' the funny wagon for you, if you don't watch out," I says, grabbin' a holt of his arm.

But he pulled away and ran out towards the plate, yellin', "Du Monville battin' for Metters!"

All the fellas begun squawlin' at once, except Hank, and he just stood there starin' at Magrew like he'd gone crazy and was claimin' to be Ty Cobb's grandma or somethin'. Their pitcher stood out there with his hands on his hips and a disagreeable look on his face, and the plate umpire told Magrew to go on and get a batter up. Magrew told him again Du Monville was battin' for Metters, and the St. Louis manager finely got the idea. It brung him outa his dugout, howlin' and bawlin' like he'd lost a female dog and her seven pups.

Magrew pushed the midget towards the plate and he says to him, he says, "Just stand up there and hold that bat on your shoulder. They ain't a man in the world can throw three strikes in there 'fore he throws four balls!" he says.

"I get it, Junior!" says the midget. "He'll walk me and force in the tyin' run!" And he starts on up to the plate as cocky as if he was Willie Keeler.

294

"I don't need to tell you Bethlehem broke loose on that there ball field. The fans got onto their hind legs, yellin' and whistlin', and everybody on the field begun wavin' their arms and hollerin' and shovin'. The plate umpire stalked over to Magrew like a traffic cop, waggin' his jaw and pointin' his finger, and the St. Louis manager kept yellin' like his house was on fire. When Pearl got up to the plate and stood there, the pitcher slammed his glove down onto the ground and started stompin' on it, and they ain't nobody can blame him. He's just walked two normal-sized human bein's, and now here's a guy up to the plate they ain't more'n twenty inches between his knees and his shoulders.

The plate umpire called in the field umpire, and they talked a while, like a couple doctors seein' the bucolic plague or somethin' for the first time. Then the plate umpire come over to Magrew with his arms folded acrost his chest, and he told him to go on and get a batter up, or he'd forfeit the game to St. Louis. He pulled out his watch, but somebody batted it outa his hand in the scufflin', and I thought there'd be a free-for-all, with everybody yellin' and shovin' except Pearl du Monville, who stood up at the plate with his little bat on his shoulder, not movin' a muscle.

Then Magrew played his ace. I seen him pull some papers outa his pocket and show 'em to the plate umpire. The umpire begun lookin' at 'em like they was bills for somethin' he not only never bought it, he never even heard of it. The other umpire studied 'em like they was a death warren, and all this time the St. Louis manager and the fans and the players is yellin' and hollerin'.

Well, sir, they fought him bein' a midget, and they fought about him usin' a kid's bat, and they fought about where'd he been all season. They was eight or nine rule books brung out and everybody was thumbin' through 'em, tryin' to find out what it says about midgets, but it don't say nothin' about midgets, 'cause this was somethin' never'd come up in the history of the game before, and nobody'd ever dreamed about it, even when they has nightmares. Maybe you can't send no midgets in to bat nowadays, 'cause the old game's changed a lot, mostly for the worst, but you could then, it turned out.

The plate umpire finely decided the contrack papers was all legal and proper, like Magrew said, so he waved the St. Louis players back

to their places and he pointed his finger at their manager and told him to quit hollerin' and get on back in the dugout. The manager says the game is percedin' under protest, and the umpire bawls, "Play ball!" over 'n' above the yellin' and booin', him havin' a voice like a hog-caller.

The St. Louis pitcher picked up his glove and beat at it with his fist six or eight times, and then got set on the mound and studied the situation. The fans realized he was really goin' to pitch to the midget, and they went crazy, hoopin' and hollerin' louder'n ever, and throwin' pop bottles and hats and cushions down onto the field. It took five, ten minutes to get the fans quieted down again, whilst our fellas that was on base set down on the bags and waited. And Pearl du Monville kept standin' up there with the bat on his shoulder, like he'd been told to.

So the pitcher starts studyin' the setup again, and you got to admit it was the strangest setup in a ball game since the players cut off their beards and begun wearin' gloves. I wisht I could call the pitcher's name—it wasn't old Barney Pelty nor Nig Jack Powell nor Harry Howell. He was a big right-hander, but I can't call his name. You could look it up. Even in a crotchin' position, the ketcher towers over the midget like the Washington Monument.

The plate umpire tries standin' on his tip-toes, then he tries crotchin' down, and he finely gets hisself into a stanch nobody'd ever seen on a ball field before, kinda squattin' down on his hanches.

Well, the pitcher is sore as a old buggy horse in fly time. He slams in the first pitch, hard and wild, and maybe two foot higher 'n the midget's head.

"Ball one!" hollers the umpire over 'n' above the racket, 'cause everybody is yellin' worsten ever.

The ketcher goes on out towards the mound and talks to the pitcher and hands him the ball. This time the big right-hander tries a under-shoot, and it comes in a little closer, maybe no higher'n a foot, foot and a half above Pearl's head. It would 'a' been a strike with a human bein' in there, but the umpire's got to call it, and he does.

"Ball two!" he bellers.

The ketcher walks on out to the mound again, and the whole infield

296

comes over and gives advice to the pitcher about what they'd do in a case like this, with two balls and no strikes on a batter that oughta be in a bottle of alcohol 'stead of up there at the plate in a big-league game between the teams that is fightin' for first place.

For the third pitch, the pitcher stands there flat-footed and tosses up the ball like he's playin' ketch with a little girl.

Pearl stands there motionless as a hitchin' post, and the ball comes in big and slow and high—high for Pearl, that is, it bein' about on a level with his eyes, or a little higher'n a grown man's knees.

They ain't nothin' else for the umpire to do, so he calls, "Ball three!"

Everybody is onto their feet, hoopin' and hollerin', as the pitcher sets to throw ball four. The St. Louis manager is makin' signs and faces like he was a contorturer, and the infield is givin' the pitcher some more advice about what to do this time. Our boys who was on base stick right onto the bag, runnin' no risk of bein' nipped for the last out.

Well, the pitcher decides to give him a toss again, seein' he come closer with that than with a fast ball. They ain't nobody ever seen a slower ball throwed. It come in big as a balloon and slower'n any ball ever throwed before in the major leagues. It come right in over the plate in front of Pearl's chest, lookin' prob'ly big as a full moon to Pearl. They ain't never been a minute like the minute that followed since the United States was founded by the Pilgrim grandfathers.

Pearl du Monville took a cut at that ball, and he hit it! Magrew give a groan like a poleaxed steer as the ball rolls out in front a the plate into fair territory.

"Fair ball" yells the umpire, and the midget starts runnin' for first, still carryin' that little bat, and makin' maybe ninety foot an hour. Bethlehem breaks loose on that ball field and in them stands. They ain't never been nothin' like it since creation was begun.

The ball's rollin' slow, on down towards third, goin' maybe eight, ten foot. The infield comes in fast and our boys break from their bases like hares in a brush fire. Everybody is standin' up, yellin' and hollerin', and Magrew is tearin' his hair outa his head, and the midget is scamperin' for first with all the speed of one of them little dashhounds carryin' a satchel in his mouth.

The ketcher gets to the ball first, but he boots it on out past the pitcher's box, the pitcher fallin' on his face tryin' to stop it, the shortstop sprawlin' after it full length and zaggin' it on over towards the second baseman, whilst Muller is scorin' with the tyin' run and Loesing is roundin' third with the winnin' run. Ty Cobb could 'a' made a three-bagger outa that bunt, with everybody fallin' over theirself tryin' to pick the ball up. But Pearl is still maybe fifteen, twenty feet from the bag, toddlin' like a baby and yeepin' like a trapped rabbit, when the second baseman finely gets a holt of that ball and slams it over to first. The first baseman ketches it and stomps on the bag, the base umpire waves Pearl out, and there goes your old ball game, the craziest ball game ever played in the history of the organized world.

Their players start runnin' in, and then I see Magrew. He starts after Pearl, runnin' faster'n any man ever run before. Pearl sees him comin' and runs behind the base umpire's legs and gets a holt onto 'em. Magrew comes up, pantin' and roarin', and him and the midget plays ring-around-a-rosy with the umpire, who keeps shovin' at Magrew with one hand and tryin' to slap the midget loose from his legs with the other.

Finely Magrew ketches the midget, who is still yeepin' like a stuck sheep. He gets holt of that little guy by both his ankles and starts whirlin' him round and round his head like Magrew was a hammer thrower and Pearl was the hammer. Nobody can stop him without gettin' their head knocked off, so everybody just stands there and yells. Then Magrew lets the midget fly. He flies on out towards second, high and fast, like a human home run, headed for the soap sign in center field.

Their shortstop tries to get to him, but he can't make it, and I knowed the little fella was goin' to bust to pieces like a dollar watch on a asphalt street when he hit the ground. But it so happens their center fielder is just crossin' second, and he starts runnin' back, tryin' to get under the midget, who had took to spiralin' like a football 'stead of turnin' head over foot, which give him more speed and more distance.

I know you never seen a midget ketched, and you prob'ly never even seen one throwed. To ketch a midget that's been throwed by a heavy-muscled man and is flyin' through the air, you got to run under him and with him and pull your hands and arms back and down when

you ketch him, to break the compact of his body, or you'll bust him in two like a matchstick. I seen Bill Lange and Willie Keeler and Tris Speaker make some wonderful ketches in my day, but I never seen nothin' like that center fielder. He goes back and back and still further back and he pulls that midget down outa the air like he was liftin' a sleepin' baby from a cradle. They wasn't a bruise onto him, only his face was the color of cat's meat and he ain't got no air in his chest. In his excitement, the base umpire, who was runnin' back with the center fielder when he ketched Pearl, yells, "Out!" and that give hysteries to the Bethlehem which was ragin' like Niagry on that ball field.

Everybody was hoopin' and hollerin' and yellin' and runnin', with the fans swarmin' onto the field, and the cops tryin' to keep order, and some guys laughin' and some of the women fans cryin', and six or eight of us holdin' onto Magrew to keep him from gettin' at that midget and finishin' him off. Some of the fans picks up the St. Louis pitcher and the center fielder, and starts carryin' 'em around on their shoulders, and they was the craziest goin's-on knowed to the history of organized ball on this side of the 'Lantic Ocean.

I seen Pearl du Monville strugglin' in the arms of a lady fan with ample bosom, who was laughin' and cryin' at the same time, and him beatin' at her with his little fists and bawlin' and yellin'. He clawed his way loose finely and disappeared in the forest of legs which made that ball field look like it was Coney Island on a hot summer's day.

That was the last I ever seen of Pearl du Monville. I never seen hide nor hair of him from that day to this, and neither did nobody else. He just vanished into the thin of the air, as the fella says. He was ketched for the final out of the ball game and that was the end of our losin' streak, like I'm goin' to tell you.

That night we piled onto a train for Chicago, but we wasn't snarlin' and snappin' any more. No, sir, the ice was finely broke and a new spirit come into that ball club. The old zip come back with the disappearance of Pearl du Monville out back a second base. We got to laughin' and talkin' and kiddin' together, and 'fore long Magrew was laughin' with us. He got a human look onto his pan again, and he quit whinin' and complainin' and wishtin' he was in heaven with the angels.

Well, sir, we wiped up that Chicago series, winnin' all four games,

and makin' seventeen hits in one of 'em. Funny thing was, St. Louis was so shook up by that last game with us, they never did hit their stride again. Their center fielder took to misjudgin' everything that come his way, and the rest a the fellas followed suit, the way a club'll do when one guy blows up.

'Fore we left Chicago, I and some of the fellas went out and bought a pair of them little baby shoes, which we had 'em golded over and give 'em to Magrew for a souvenir, and he took it all in good spirit. Whitey Cott and Billy Klinger made up and was fast friends again, and we hit our home lot like a ton of dynamite and they was nothin' could stop us from then on.

I don't recollect things as clear as I did thirty, forty year ago. I can't read no fine print no more, and the only person I got to check with on the golden days of the national pastime, as the fella says, is my friend, old Milt Kline, over in Springfield, and his mind ain't as strong as it once was.

He gets Rube Waddell mixed up with Rube Marquard, for one thing, and anybody does that oughta be put away where he won't bother nobody. So I can't tell you the exact margin we win the pennant by. Maybe it was two and a half games, or maybe it was three and a half. But it'll all be there in the newspapers and record books of thirty, thirty-one year ago and, like I was sayin', you could look it up.

From Veeck—as in Wreck

BY BILL VEECK WITH ED LINN

IN 1951, IN A MOMENT OF MADNESS, I BE-came owner and operator of a collection of old rags and tags known to baseball historians as the St. Louis Browns.

The Browns, according to reputable anthropologists, rank in the annals of baseball a step or two ahead of Cro-Magnon man. One thing should be made clear. A typical *Brownie* was more than four feet tall. Except, of course, for Eddie Gaedel, who was three feet seven and weighed 65 pounds. Eddie gave the Browns their only distinction. He was, by golly, the best darn midget who ever played big-league ball. He was also the only one.

Eddie came to us in a moment of desperation. Not his desperation, ours. After a month or so in St. Louis, we were looking around desperately for a way to draw a few people into the ball park, it being perfectly clear by that time that the ball club wasn't going to do it unaided. The best bet seemed to be to call upon the resources of our radio sponsors, Falstaff Brewery. For although Falstaff only broadcast our games locally, they had distributors and dealers all over the state.

It happened that 1951 was the fiftieth anniversary of the American League, an event the league was exploiting with its usual burst of inspiration by sewing special emblems on the uniforms of all the play-ers. It seemed to me that a birthday party was clearly called for. It seemed to me, further, that if I could throw a party to celebrate the birthdays of both the American League and Falstaff Brewery, the spon-sors would be getting a nice little tie-in and we would have their distributors and dealers hustling tickets for us all over the state. Nobody at Falstaff's seemed to know exactly when their birthday was, but that was no great problem. If we couldn't prove it fell on the day we chose, neither could anyone prove that it didn't. The day we chose was a Sunday doubleheader against the last-place Detroit Tigers, a struggle which did not threaten to set the pulses of the city beating madly.

Rudie Schaffer, the Browns' business manager, and I met with the Falstaff people—Mr. Griesedieck, Sr., the head of the company, Bud and Joe Griesedieck and their various department heads—to romance our project. "In addition to the regular party, the acts and so on," I told Bud, "I'll do something for you that I have never done before. Something so original and spectacular that it will get you national publicity."

Naturally, they pressed me for details. Naturally, I had to tell them that much as I hated to hold out on them, my idea was so explosive I could not afford to take the slightest chance of a leak.

The Falstaff people, romantics all, went for it. They were so anxious to find out what I was going to do that they could hardly bear to wait out the two weeks. I was rather anxious to find out what I was going to do, too. The real reason I had not been willing to let them in on my top-secret plan was that I didn't have any plan.

What can I do, I asked myself, that is so spectacular that *no one* will be able to say he had seen it before? The answer was perfectly obvious: I would send a midget up to bat.

Actually, the idea of using a midget had been kicking around in my head all my life. I have frequently been accused of stealing the idea from a James Thurber short story, "You Could Look It Up." Sheer libel. I didn't steal the idea from Thurber, I stole it from John J. McGraw.

McGraw had been a great friend of my father's in the days when McGraw was managing the New York Giants and my daddy was president of the Chicago Cubs. Once or twice every season he would come to the house, and one of my greatest thrills would be to sit quietly at the table after dinner and listen to them tell their lies. McGraw had a little hunchback he kept around the club as a sort of good-luck charm. His name, if I remember, was Eddie Morrow. Morrow wasn't a midget, you understand, he was a sort of gnome. By the time McGraw got to the stub of his last cigar, he would always swear to my father that one day before he retired he was going to send his gnome up to bat.

All kids are tickled by the incongruous. The picture of McGraw's gnome coming to bat had made such a vivid impression on me that it was there, ready for the plucking, when I needed it.

I put in a call to Marty Caine, the booking agent from whom I had

302

hired all my acts when I was operating in Cleveland, and asked him to find me a midget who was somewhat athletic and game for anything. "And Marty," I said, "I want this to be a secret."

I never told Marty what I wanted him for. Only five other people knew. Mary Frances, my wife; Rudie Schaffer; Bob Fishel, our publicity man; Bill Durney, our traveling secretary; and, of course, Zack Taylor, our manager.

Marty Caine found Eddie Gaedel in Chicago and sent him down to be looked over. He was a nice little guy, in his mid-twenties. Like all midgets, he had sad little eyes, and like all midgets, he had a squeaky little voice that sounded as if it were on the wrong speed of a record player.

"Eddie," I said, "how would you like to be a big-league ballplayer?"

When he first heard what I wanted him to do, he was a little dubious. I had to give him a sales pitch. I said, "Eddie, you'll be the only midget in the history of the game. You'll be appearing before thousands of people. Your name will go into the record books for all time. You'll be famous, Eddie," I said. "Eddie," I said, "you'll be immortal."

Well, Eddie Gaedel had more than a little ham in him. The more I talked, the braver he became. By the time I was finished, little Eddie was ready to charge through a machine-gun nest to get to the plate.

I asked him how much he knew about baseball. "Well," he said, "I know you're supposed to hit the white ball with the bat. And then you run somewhere."

Obviously, he was well schooled in the fundamentals. "I'll show you what I want you to do," I told him.

I picked up a little toy bat and crouched over as far as I could, my front elbow resting on my front knee. The rules of the game say that the strike zone is beween the batter's armpits and the top of his knees "when he assumes his natural stance." Since Gaedel would bat only once in his life, whatever stance he took was, by definition, his natural one.

When Eddie went into that crouch, his strike zone was just about visible to the naked eye. I picked up a ruler and measured it for posterity. It was 1½ inches. Marvelous.

Eddie practiced that crouch for a while, up and down, up and down,

while I cheered him on lustily from the sidelines. After a while, he began to test the heft of the bat and glare out toward an imaginary pitcher. He sprang out of his crouch and took an awkward, lunging swing.

"No, no," I said. "You just stay in that crouch. All you have to do is stand there and take four balls. Then you'll trot down to first base and we'll send someone in to run for you."

His face collapsed. You could see his visions of glory leaking out of him. All at once, I remembered that the twist in the James Thurber story was that the midget got ambitious, swung at the 3—0 pitch and got thrown out at first base because it took him an hour and a half to run down the baseline.

"Eddie," I said gently, "I'm going to be up on the roof with a high-powered rifle watching every move you make. If you so much as look as if you're going to swing, I'm going to shoot you dead."

Eddie went back to Chicago with instructions to return on Saturday, August 18, the day before the game. In the meantime, there were details to be attended to. First of all, there was the question of a uniform. No problem. Bill DeWitt, Jr., the seven-year-old son of our vice-president, had a little Brown's uniform hanging in the locker room. Rudie stole it and sent it out to get the number ⅛ sewed on the back. Scorecards are traditionally printed up on the morning of the game, so listing him would be no problem at all.

Just for the heck of it, I took out a $1,000,000 insurance policy to protect us in case of sudden death, sudden growth or any other pernicious act of nature. Somehow no opportunity to tell anybody about that policy ever came up, no great loss since the whole thing cost me about a buck and a half.

We were hiring Eddie for one day at $100, the minimum AGVA scale for a midget act. Still, if he was going to play in an official game he had to be signed to a standard player's contract, with a salary set on an annual basis and a guaranteed 30-day payment upon termination. That was no real problem, either. We computed the salary on the basis of $100 a game and typed in an additional clause in which Eddie agreed to waive the 30-day notice.

I must admit that by the time Eddie came back to St. Louis we were

playing the cloak-and-dagger stuff a bit strong. Eddie went directly to a hotel suite we had hired for him about ten blocks from the park. Instead of bringing the contract to his room, Bob Fishel set up a meeting on a street corner a block or two from the hotel. Bob drove up in his old Packard and Eddie slid into the front seat, scribbled his signature on two contracts and jumped back out. One of the contracts was mailed to league headquarters on Saturday night, which meant that it would not be delivered until Monday morning. The other contract was given to Zack Taylor, in case our promising rookie was challenged by the umpires. The morning of the game, I wired headquarters that we were putting player Edward Gaedel on our active list.

On Sunday morning, we smuggled Eddie up to the office for further instruction on the fine art of crouching. That was a little dangerous. I have always taken the doors off my office and encouraged people to walk right in to see me. We posted a lookout and from time to time either Mary Frances or Bob or Rudie would have to hustle Eddie out to the farm-system offices in the back. Always they'd come back with the same story. As soon as Eddie got out of my sight he'd turn tiger and start swinging his little bat. "He's going to foul it up," they all told me. "If you saw him back there you'd know he's going to swing."

"Don't worry," I'd tell them, worrying furiously. "I've got the situation well in hand."

Don't worry. . . . Just as I was leaving the office to circulate among the customers as they arrived at the park, Eddie asked me, "Bill . . . ? How tall was Wee Willie Keeler?"

Oh, boy. . . .

"Eddie," I said, "I've got your life insured for a million dollars. I've got a gun stashed up on the roof. But don't you let any of that bother you. You just crouch over like you've been doing and take four pitches, huh?"

As I was going out the door, I turned back one final time. "Wee Willie Keeler," I told him, "was six feet five."

◆

Falstaff came through nobly. We had a paid attendance of better than 18,000, the biggest crowd to see the Browns at home in four years. Since our customers were also our guests for the Falstaff birthday party,

we presented everybody with a can of beer, a slice of birthday cake and a box of ice cream as they entered the park. I also gave out one of Falstaff's own promotional gimmicks, salt-and-pepper shakers in the shape of a Falstaff bottle. The tie-in there was that we were giving the fans *midget* beer bottles as souvenirs of the day, a subtlety which managed to elude everybody completely.

The most surprising thing to me, as I moved through the crowd during the first game, was that nobody seemed to have paid the slightest attention to the rather unique scorecard listing:

1/8 GAEDEL

Harry Mitauer of the *Globe-Democrat* did ask Bob Fishel about it up in the press box, but Roberto was able to shunt the question aside. (The next day, we had a hundred or so requests from collectors, so I suppose there are quite a few of the Gaedel scorecards still in existence around the country.)

Every baseball crowd, like every theater audience, has its own distinctive attitude and atmosphere. You can usually tell as they are coming into the park whether it is going to be a happy, responsive crowd or a dead and sullen one. With the Birthday Party and the gifts and the busfuls of people from the outlying towns, the crowd arrived in a gay and festive mood. Not even the loss of the first game could dampen their spirit.

We went all out in our between-games birthday celebration. We had a parade of old-fashioned cars circling the field. We had two men and two women, dressed in gay-nineties costumes, pedaling around the park on a bicycle-built-for-four. Troubadours roamed through the stands to entertain the customers. Our own band, featuring Satchel Paige on the drums, performed at home plate. Satch, who is good enough to be a professional, stopped the show cold.

In our version of a three-ring circus, we had something going on at every base—a hand-balancing act at first base, a trampoline act on second and a team of jugglers at third. Max Patkin, our rubber-boned clown, pulled a woman out of the grandstand and did a wild jitterbug dance with her on the pitcher's mound.

Eddie Gaedel had remained up in the office during the game, under the care of big Bill Durney. Between games, Durney was to bring him down under the stands, in full uniform, and put him into a huge 7-foot birthday cake we had stashed away under the ramp. There was a hollowed-out section in the middle of the cake, complete with a board slab for Eddie to sit on. For we had a walk-on role written in for Eddie during the celebration; we were really getting our $100 worth out of him. As a matter of fact, the cake cost us a darn sight more than Eddie did.

As I hustled down the ramp, I could hear the crowd roaring at Patkin. Eddie could hear it too. And apparently the tremendous roar, magnified underground, frightened him. "Gee," I could hear him saying, "I don't feel so good." And then, after a second or two, "I don't think I'm going to do it."

Now, Bill Durney is six feet four and in those days he weighed 250 pounds. "Listen, Eddie," he said. "There are eighteen thousand people in this park and there's one I know I can lick. You. Dead or alive, you're going in there."

I arrived on the scene just as Bill was lifting him up to stuff him inside. Eddie was holding his bat in one hand and, at that stage of the proceedings, he was wearing little slippers turned up at the end like elf's shoes. Well, it is difficult enough, I suppose, for anybody to look calm and confident while he is being hung out like laundry. Nor do I imagine that anybody has ever managed to look like a raging tiger in elf's shoes. Taking all that into consideration, you could still see that Eddie was scared. He wanted out, "Bill," he said piteously, as he dangled there, "these shoes hurt my feet. I don't think I'll be able to go on."

We weren't about to let him duck out this late in the game. Durney dropped him in the cake, sat him down and covered the top over with tissue paper.

Up on the roof behind home plate we had a special box with a connecting bar and restaurant for the care and feeding of visiting dignitaries. By the time I got up there to join Bud Griesedieck and the rest of the Falstaff executive force, the cake had already been rolled out onto the infield grass. Along with the cake came Sir John Falstaff or, at any rate, a hefty actor dressed in Elizabethan clothes. *There* was a touch to warm the cockles and hops of the Falstaff crowd.

307

"Watch this," I chuckled.

Our announcer, Bernie Ebert, boomed, "Ladies and gentlemen, as a special birthday present to manager Zack Taylor, the management is presenting him with a brand-new Brownie."

Sir John tapped the cake with his gleaming cutlass and, right on cue, out through the paper popped Eddie Gaedel.

There was a smattering of applause from the stands and a light ripple of laughter.

In the Falstaff box, there was nothing but stunned silence.

"Holy smokes," Bud said, "this is what your big thing is? A little midget jumps out of a cake and he's wearing a baseball uniform and he's a bat boy or something?"

"Don't you understand?" I said. "He's a real live Brownie."

"You put funny shoes on a midget and he's a real live Brownie and that's going to get us national coverage?"

Karl Vollmer, their advertising manager, was plainly disgusted. "Aw, this is lousy, Bill," he said. "Even the cake gimmick, you've used that before in Milwaukee and Cleveland. You haven't given us anything new at all."

I begged them not to be too unhappy. "Maybe it isn't the best gag in the world," I said, "but the rest of the show was good and everybody seems happy. It will be all right."

They were determined to be unhappy, though. The gloom in that box was so thick that our Falstaff could have come up and carved it into loaves with his cutlass. (That didn't seem like a very good idea at the moment, however, because Vollmer looked as if he was just about ready to grab the cutlass and cut my throat.) "This is the explosive thing you couldn't tell us about," Vollmer muttered. "A midget jumps out of a cake and, what do you know, he's a real live Brownie."

I did my best to look ashamed of myself.

In the second game, we started Frank Saucier in place of our regular center fielder, Jim Delsing. This is the only part of the gag I've ever felt bad about. Saucier was a great kid whom I had personally talked back into the game when I bought the Browns. Everything went wrong for Frank, and all he has to show for his great promise is that he was the only guy a midget ever batted for.

308

For as we came up for our half of the first inning, Eddie Gaedel emerged from the dugout waving three little bats. "For the Browns," said Bernie Ebert over the loudspeaker system, "number one-eighth, Eddie Gaedel, batting for Saucier."

Suddenly, the whole park came alive. Suddenly, my honored guests sat upright in their seats. Suddenly, the sun was shining. Eddie Hurley, the umpire behind the plate, took one look at Gaedel and started toward our bench. "Hey," he shouted out to Taylor, "what's going on here?"

Zack came out with a sheaf of papers. He showed Hurley Gaedel's contract. He showed him the telegram to headquarters, duly promulgated with a time stamp. He even showed him a copy of our active list to prove that we did have room to add another player.

Hurley returned to home plate, shooed away the photographers who had rushed out to take Eddie's picture and motioned the midget into the batter's box. The place went wild. Bobby Cain, the Detroit pitcher, and Bob Swift, their catcher, had been standing by peacefully for about 15 minutes, thinking unsolemn thoughts about that jerk Veeck and his gags. I will never forget the look of utter disbelief that came over Cain's face as he finally realized that this was for real.

Bob Swift rose to the occasion like a real trooper. If I had set out to use the opposing catcher to help build up the tension, I could not have improved one whit upon his performance. Bob, bless his heart, did just what I was hoping he would do. He went out to the mound to discuss the intricacies of pitching to a midget with Cain. And when he came back, he did something I had never even dreamed of. To complete the sheer incongruity of the scene—and make the newspaper pictures of the event more memorable—he got down on both knees to offer his pitcher a target.

By now, the whole park was rocking, and nowhere were there seven more delirious people than my guests in the rooftop box. Veeck the jerk had become Willie the wizard. The only unhappy person in that box was me, good old Willie the wizard. Gaedel, little ham that he was, had not gone into the crouch I had spent so many hours teaching him. He was standing straight up, his little bat held high, his feet spraddled wide in a fair approximation of Joe DiMaggio's classic style. While the Falstaff people were whacking me on the back and letting

309

their joy flow unrestrained, I was thinking: *I should have brought that gun up here. I'll kill him if he swings. I'll kill him, I'll kill him.*

Fortunately, Cain started out by really trying to pitch to him. The first two deliveries came whizzing past Eddie's head before he had time to swing. By the third pitch, Cain was laughing so hard that he could barely throw. Ball three and ball four came floating up about three feet over Eddie's head.

Eddie trotted down to first base to the happy tune of snapping cameras. He waited for the runner, one foot holding to the bag like a pro, and he patted Delsing on the butt in good professional exhortation before he surrendered the base. He shook hands with our first-base coach and he waved to the cheering throng.

The St. Louis dugout was behind third base, which meant that Eddie had to cut completely across the infield. If it had been difficult to get him into the cake earlier, I was worried for a while that I would have to send Bill Durney out there again to carry him off the field. Eddie, after all, was a performer. In his small, unspectacular way he was a part of show business. He had dreamed all his life of his moment in the spotlight and now that it had come to him, he was not about to bow his head and leave quietly. He crossed that field one step at a time, stopping in between to wave his hat or bow from the waist or just to raise an acknowledging hand to the plaudits of the crowd. When he disappeared, at last, into the dugout he was the happiest little man you have ever seen.

If the thing had been done right, Delsing, running for Gaedel, would have scored and we would have won the game, 1—0. I was willing to settle for less than that. I was willing to win by one run, regardless of the final score, as long as that one run represented Edie Gaedel. As it was, there being a limit to the amount of help you can expect from either the St. Louis Browns or fortune, Delsing got as far as third base with only one out and was then left stranded. We lost the game, 6—2.

Nothing remained but to wait for the expected blasts from league headquarters and, more particularly, from the deacons of the press, those old-timers who look upon baseball not as a game or a business but as a solemn ritual, almost a holy calling.

The press, for the most part, took the sane attitude that Gaedel had

310

provided a bright moment in what could easily have been a deadly dull doubleheader between a seventh- and an eighth-place ball club. Vincent X. Flaherty of Los Angeles pretty much summed up the general reaction when he wrote: "I do not advocate baseball burlesque. Such practices do not redound to the better interests of the game—but I claim it was the funniest thing that has happened to baseball in years."

It's fine to be appreciated for a day; I recommend it highly, for the soul. It's better for the box office, though, to be attacked for a full week. I was counting on the deacons to turn Gaedel into a full week's story by attacking me for spitting in their cathedral. They didn't let me down, although I did feel the words "cheap and tawdry" and "travesty" and "mockery" were badly overworked. The spirit was willing, but I'm afraid the rhetoric was weak.

Dan Daniel, a well-known high priest from New York, wondered what "Ban Johnson and John J. McGraw are saying about it up there in Baseball's Valhalla," a good example of Dan's lean and graceful style. Non-baseball fans should understand that baseball men do not go to heaven or hell when they die; they go to Valhalla where they sit around a hot stove and talk over the good old days with Odin, Thor and the rest of that crowd. (I am assuming that the baseball people haven't driven the old Norse gods out to the suburbs. You know what guys like Johnson and McGraw do to real-estate values.)

To Joe Williams, Daniel's colleague on the New York *World-Telegram,* I was "that fellow Veeck out in St. Louis."

"It didn't matter that this made a mockery of the sport or that it exploited a freak of biology in a shameful, disgraceful way," Williams wrote. " . . . What he calls showmanship can more often be accurately identified as vulgarity."

I have never objected to being called vulgar. The word, as I never tire of pointing out to my tireless critics, comes from the Latin *vulgaris,* which means—students?—"the common people." (If you don't believe it, Joe, you could look it up.) I am so darn vulgar that I will probably never get into Valhalla, which is a shame because I would love to be able to let McGraw know how he helped that little boy who used to listen to him, enraptured, over the dinner table. From what I can remember of McGraw, he would roar with delight.

What that fellow Williams in New York didn't seem to realize—or

311

did he?—was that it was he who was gratuitously and publicly calling Eddie Gaedel a freak. Eddie was a professional midget. He made his living by displaying himself, the only way we permit a midget to earn a living in our enlightened society. In more barbaric times, they were able to achieve a certain stature as court jesters. My use of him—*vulgaris* that I am—was the biggest thing that ever happened to him. In the week that followed, I got him bookings that earned him something between $5,000 and $10,000. I kept getting him bookings here and there for the rest of his life. Eddie hungered for another chance at the spotlight. Whenever he came to a town where I was operating he would phone and say, "OK, Boss, I'm ready."

I did use him for a couple of my gags. One of the last times was at Comiskey Park in Chicago, about a year before his death. Eddie and three other midgets, all dressed in regimental Martian clothing (gold helmets and shoes, coveralls, oxygen tanks), somehow dropped out of the heavens in a helicopter and landed directly behind second base. Quickly capturing our tiny second-base combination, Nellie Fox and Luis Aparicio, they made them honorary Martians and informed them—over the remarkably handy public-address system—that they had come down to aid them in their battle against the giant earthlings.

It was during this historic meeting that Eddie Gaedel uttered those immortal words, "I don't want to be taken to your leader. I've already met him."

The battle with league headquarters had begun before Eddie stepped into the batter's box. Will Harridge, the league president—for reasons best known to himself—had gone to his office that Sunday and had seen the report come over the Western Union teletype that I was trying to send a midget up to bat. While Hurley was still looking over the papers, our switchboard operator, Ada Ireland, sent word to me that Harridge was on the phone threatening to blow a fuse unless someone in authority came out to talk to him. I sent back word that we had all disappeared from the face of the earth.

A few minutes later, I was told that Will was trying to get me on the office teletype, which is in direct communication with headquarters. I told them to turn off the machine.

The next day, Harridge issued an executive order barring Gaedel

312

from baseball. A new rule was promptly passed making it mandatory that all player contracts be filed with and *approved* by the president.

Naturally, I was bewildered and alarmed and shocked. I was a few other things too: "I'm puzzled, baffled and grieved by Mr. Harridge's ruling," I announced. "Why, we're paying a lot of guys on the Brown's roster good money to get on base and even though they don't do it, nobody sympathizes with us. But when this little guy goes up to the plate and draws a walk on his only time at bat, they call it "conduct detrimental to baseball."

If baseball wanted to discriminate against the little people, I said, why didn't we have the courage to be honest about it, write a minimum height into the rules and submit ourselves to the terrible wrath of all right-thinking Americans? "I think," I said, "that further clarification is called for. Should the height of a player be three feet six inches, four feet six inches, six feet six inches, or nine feet six inches?" Now that midgets had been so arbitrarily barred, I asked, were we to assume that giants were also barred? I made dark references to the stature of Phil Rizzuto, who is not much over five feet tall, and I implied very strongly that I was going to demand an official ruling on whether he was a short ballplayer or a tall midget.

I hammered away at the phrase "little people," which had a solid political currency in those days. I had given Eddie Gaedel a speech on that theme too. "Everybody talks about protecting the little man these days," he was supposed to say, "and now that someone has finally taken a direct step to help the plight of the little man in baseball, Harridge has stepped in and ruined my career."

Political connotations, unfortunately, were lost on Eddie. When the time came for him to deliver his statement, he blew it. "Now that someone has finally taken a direct step to help us short guys," he said, "Harridge is ruining my baseball career." Ah well, you can't win them all.

In the end I had to agree, reluctantly, to bow to superior authority. "As much as it grieves me," I said, "I will have to go along with this odd ruling." I thought that was rather big of me, especially since I had only hired Gaedel for one day.

Something else happened, though, that I was not disposed to be so

amiable about. The good deacons of the press had been wailing that unless Harridge acted immediately, the name of Eddie Gaedel would desecrate the record books for all time. Harridge dutifully decreed that Gaedel's appearance be stricken from all official records. This I wouldn't stand for. I had promised Eddie that he would live forever in the record books, which are cast in bronze, carved in marble and encased in cement. Immortality I had promised him, and immortality he would have. I reminded Harridge that Gaedel had a legal contract and had been permitted to bat in an official game presided over by the league's own umpires. If Gaedel hadn't batted, I pointed out, it would also mean that Bobby Cain hadn't thrown the pitches and that Swift hadn't caught them. It would mean that Delsing had come in to run for no one, and that Saucier had been deprived of a time at bat. It would mean, in short, that the continuity of baseball was no longer intact, and the integrity of its records had been compromised. If Desecration was the game they wanted to play, then I held a pretty strong hand myself.

Eddie crept back into the record books and remains there today. When he died, he got a front-page obituary in *The New York Times,* a recognition normally accorded only to statesmen, generals and Nobel Prize winners.

I did not recognize at the time that Gaedel's moment was my moment too. I knew it was a good gag. I knew it would delight the fans and outrage the stuffed shirts. I knew, in other words, that it would be a lot of fun. It never entered my mind, however, that it would be the single act with which I would become permanently identified. Even today, I cannot talk to anybody from St. Louis without being told that they were there the day the midget came to bat. If everybody was there who says he was there, we would have had a tidy gathering of 280,000.

I have done a few other things in baseball, you know. I've won pennants and finished dead last; I've set attendance records and been close to bankruptcy. At the age of fifteen, I was taking care of Ladies' Day passes at Wrigley Field. I owned my first ball club when I was twenty-eight. I have operated five clubs—three in the major leagues and two in the minors—and in three of the towns I won pennants and broke attendance records. Two of the three teams to beat the

314

Yankees since I came to the American League in 1946 were my teams, the 1948 Cleveland Indians and the 1959 Chicago White Sox. The only other team, the 1954 Indians, was made up for the most part of my old players.

But no one has to tell me that if I returned to baseball tomorrow, won ten straight pennants and left all the old attendance records moldering in the dust, I would still be remembered, in the end, as the man who sent a midget up to bat. It is not the identification I would have chosen for myself when I came into baseball. My ambitions were grander than that. And yet I cannot deny that it is an accurate one. I have always found humor in the incongruous, I have always tried to entertain. And I have always found a stuffed shirt the most irresistible of all targets.

I'm Bill Veeck, the guy who sent a midget up to bat?

Fair enough.

Eddie Gaedel

GAEDEL, EDWARD CARL
B. June 8, 1925, Chicago, Ill.   D. June 18, 1961, Chicago Ill.

Year	Team	Games	BA	SA	AB	H	2B	3B	HR	HR%	R	RBI	BB	SO	SB	Pinch Hit AB	H	PO	A	E	DP	TC/G	FA	G by Pos
1951	STL A	1	-	-	0	0	0	0	0	-	0	0	1	0	0	0	0	0	0	0	0	0.0	-	

My Kingdom for Jones

BY WILBUR SCHRAMM

THE FIRST DAY JONES PLAYED THIRD BASE for Brooklyn was like the day Galileo turned his telescope on the planets or Columbus sailed back to Spain. First, people said it couldn't be true; then they said things will never be the same.

Timothy McGuire, of the Brooklyn *Eagle,* told me how he felt the first time he saw Jones. He said that if a bird had stepped out of a cuckoo clock that day and asked him what time it was, he wouldn't have been surprised enough to blink an Irish eye. And still he knew that the whole future of baseball hung that day by a cotton thread.

Don't ask Judge Kenesaw Mountain Landis about this. He has never yet admitted publicly that Jones ever played for Brooklyn. He has good reason not to. But ask an old-time sports writer. Ask Tim McGuire.

It happened so long ago it was even before Mr. Roosevelt became President. It was a lazy Georgia spring afternoon, the first time McGuire and I saw Jones. There was a light-footed little breeze and just enough haze to keep the sun from burning. The air was full of fresh-cut grass and wistaria and fruit blossoms and the ping of baseballs on well-oiled mitts. Everyone in Georgia knows that the only sensible thing to do on an afternoon like that is sleep. If you can't do that, if you are a baseball writer down from New York to cover Brooklyn's spring-training camp, you can stretch out on the grass and raise yourself every hour or so on one elbow to steal a glance at fielding practice. That was what we were doing—meanwhile amusing ourselves halfheartedly with a game involving small cubes and numbers—when we first saw Jones.

The Times wasn't there. Even in those days they were keeping their sports staff at home to study for "Information Please." But four of us were down from the New York papers—the *World*, the *Herald*, Tim and I. I can even remember what we were talking about.

I was asking the *World*, "How do they look to you?"

"Pitchers and no punch," the *World* said. "No big bats. No great fielders. No Honus Wagner. No Hal Chase. No Ty Cobb."

"No Tinker to Evers to Chance," said the *Herald*. "Seven come to Susy," he added soothingly, blowing on his hands.

"What's your angle today?" the *World* asked Tim.

Tim doesn't remember exactly how he answered that. To the best of my knowledge, he merely said, "Ulk." It occurred to me that the Brooklyn *Eagle* was usually more eloquent than that, but the Southern weather must have slowed up my reaction.

The *World* said, "What?"

"There's a sorsh," Tim said in a weak, strangled sort of voice—"a horse . . . on third . . . base."

"Why don't they chase it off?" said the *Herald* impatiently. "Your dice."

"They don't . . . want to," Tim said in that funny voice.

I glanced up at Tim then. Now Tim, as you probably remember, was built from the same blueprints as a truck, with a magnificent red nose for a headlight. But when I looked at him, all the color was draining out of that nose slowly, from top to bottom, like turning off a gas mantle. I should estimate Tim was, at the moment, the whitest McGuire in four generations.

Then I looked over my shoulder to see where Tim was staring. He was the only one of us facing the ball diamond. I looked for some time. Then I tapped the *World* on the back.

"Pardon me," I asked politely, "do you notice anything unusual?"

"If you refer to my luck," said the *World*, "it's the same pitiful kind I've had since Christmas."

"Look at the infield," I suggested.

"Hey," said the *Herald*, "if you don't want the dice, give them to me."

"I know this can't be true," mused the *World*, "but I could swear I see a horse on third base."

The *Herald* climbed to his feet with some effort. He was built in the days when there was no shortage of materials.

"If the only way to get you guys to put your minds on this game is to chase that horse off the field," he said testily, "I'll do it myself."

318

He started toward the infield, rubbed his eyes and fainted dead away.

"I had the queerest dream," he said, when we revived him. "I dreamed there was a horse playing third base. My God!" he shouted, glancing toward the diamond. "I'm still asleep!"

That is, word for word, what happened the first day Jones played third base for Brooklyn. Ask McGuire.

♦

When we felt able, we hunted up the Brooklyn manager, who was a chunky, red-haired individual with a whisper like a foghorn. A foghorn with a Brooklyn accent. His name was Pop O'Donnell.

"I see you've noticed," Pop boomed defensively.

"What do you mean," the *Herald* said severely, "by not notifying us you had a horse playing third base?"

"I didn't guess you'd believe it," Pop said.

Pop was still a little bewildered himself. He said the horse had wandered on the field that morning during practice. Someone tried to chase it off by hitting a baseball toward it. The horse calmly opened its mouth and caught the ball. Nothing could be neater.

While they were still marveling over that, the horse galloped thirty yards and took a ball almost out of the hands of an outfielder who was poised for the catch. They said Willie Keeler couldn't have done it better. So they spent an hour hitting fungo flies—or, as some wit called them, horse flies—to the horse. Short ones, long ones, high ones, grass cutters, line drives—it made no difference; the animal covered Dixie like the dew.

They tried the horse at second and short, but he was a little slow on the pivot when compared with men like Napoleon Lajoie. Then they tried him at third base, and knew that was the right, the inevitable place. He was a great wall of China. He was a flash of brown lightning. In fact, he covered half the shortstop's territory and two thirds of left field, and even came behind the plate to help the catcher with foul tips. The catcher got pretty sore about it. He said that anybody who was going to steal his easy put-outs would have to wear an umpire's uniform like the other thieves.

"Can he hit?" asked the *World*.

319

"See for yourself," Pop O'Donnell invited.

The Superbas—they hadn't begun calling them the Dodgers yet—were just starting batting practice. Nap Rucker was tossing them in with that beautiful smooth motion of his, and the horse was at bat. He met the first ball on the nose and smashed it into left field. He laid down a bunt that waddled like a turtle along the base line. He sizzled a liner over second like a clothesline.

"What a story!" said the *World*.

"I wonder—" said the *Herald*—"I wonder how good it is."

We stared at him.

"I wouldn't say it is quite as good as the sinking of the *Maine,* if you mean that," said Tim.

"I wonder how many people are going to believe it," said the *Herald*.

"I'll race you to the phone," Tim said.

Tim won. He admits he had a long start. Twenty minutes later he came back, walking slowly.

"I wish to announce," he said, "that I have been insulted by my editor and am no longer connected with the Brooklyn *Eagle*. If I can prove that I am sober tomorrow, they may hire me back," he added.

"You see what I mean," said the *Herald*.

We all filed telegraph stories about the horse. We swore that every word was true. We said it was a turning point in baseball. Two of us mentioned Columbus; and one, Galileo. In return, we got advice.

♦

THESE TROUBLED TIMES, NEWSPAPERS NO SPACE FOR FICTION, EXPENSE AC-COUNT NO PROVISION DRUNKEN LEVITY, the *Herald*'s wire read. The *World* read, ACCURACY, ACCURACY, ACCURACY, followed by three exclamation points, and signed "Joseph Pulitzer." "CHARGING YOUR TELEGRAM RE BROOKLYN HORSE TO YOUR SALARY, my wire said. THAT'S A HORSE ON YOU!

♦

Have you ever thought what you would do with a purple cow if you had one? I know. You would paint it over. We had a horse that could play third base, and all we could do was sit in the middle of Georgia and cuss our editors. I blame the editors. It is their fault that for the last thirty years you have had to go to smoking rooms or Pullman cars to hear about Jones.

320

But I don't entirely blame them either. My first question would have been: How on earth can a horse possibly bat and throw? That's what the editors wondered. It's hard to explain. It's something you have to see to believe—like dogfish and political conventions.

And I've got to admit that the next morning we sat around and asked one another whether we really had seen a horse playing third base. Pop O'Donnell confessed that when he woke up he said to himself, *It must be shrimp that makes me dream about horses.* Then all of us went down to the park, not really knowing whether we would see a horse there or not.

We asked Pop was he going to use the horse in games.

"I don't know," he thundered musingly. "I wonder. There are many angles. I don't know," he said, pulling at his chin.

That afternoon the Cubs, the world champs, came for an exhibition game. A chap from Pennsylvania—I forget his name—played third base for Brooklyn, and the horse grazed quietly beside the dugout. Going into the eighth, the Cubs were ahead, 2-0, and Three-Finger Brown was tying Brooklyn in knots. A curve would come over, then a fast one inside, and then the drop, and the Superbas would beat the air or hit puny little rollers to the infield which Tinker or Evers would grab up and toss like a beanbag to Frank Chance. It was sickening. But in the eighth, Maloney got on base on an error, and Jordan walked. Then Lumley went down swinging, and Lewis watched three perfect ones sail past him. The horse still was grazing over by the Brooklyn dugout.

"Put in the horse!" Frank Chance yelled. The Cubs laughed themselves sick.

Pop O'Donnell looked at Chance, and then at the horse, and back at Chance, as though he had make up his mind about something. "Go in there son, and get a hit," he said. "Watch out for the curve." "Coive," Pop said.

The horse picked up a bat and cantered out to the plate.

"Pinch-hitting for Batch," announced the umpire dreamily, "this horse." A second later he shook himself violently. "What am I saying?" he shouted.

On the Cubs' bench, every jaw had dropped somewhere around the

owner's waist. Chance jumped to his feet, his face muscles worked like a coffee grinder, but nothing came out. It was the only time in baseball history, so far as I can find out, that Framk Chance was ever without words.

When he finally pulled himself together he argued, with a good deal of punctuation, that there was no rule saying you could play a horse in the big leagues. Pop roared quietly that there was no rule saying you couldn't, either. They stood there nose to nose, Pop firing methodically like a cannon, and Chance cracking like a machine gun. Chance gave up too easily. He was probably a little stunned. He said that he was used to seeing queer things in Brooklyn, anyway. Pop O'Donnell just smiled grimly.

Well, that was Jones's first game for Brooklyn. It could have been a reel out of a movie. There was that great infield—Steinfeldt, Tinker, Evers and Chance—so precise, so much a machine, that any ball hit on the ground was like an apple into a sorter. The infield was so famous that not many people remember Sheckard and Slagle and Schulte in the outfield, but the teams of that day knew them. Behind the plate was Johnny Kling, who could rifle a ball to second like an 88-mm. cannon. And on the mound stood Three-Finger Brown, whose drop faded away as though someone were pulling it back with a string.

Brown took a long time getting ready. His hand shook a little, and the first one he threw was ten feet over Kling's head into the grandstand. Maloney and Jordan advanced to second and third. Brown threw the next one in the dirt. Then he calmed down, grooved one, and whistled a curve in around the withers.

"The glue works for you, Dobbin!" yelled Chance, feeling more like himself. Pop O'Donnell was mopping his forehead.

The next pitch came in fast, over the outside corner. The horse was waiting. He leaned into it. The ball whined all the way to the fence. Ted Williams was the only player I ever saw hit one like it. When Slagle finally got to the ball, the two runners had scored and the horse was on third. Brown's next pitch got away from Kling a few yards, and the horse stole home in a cloud of dust, all four feet flying. He got up, dusted himself off, looked at Chance and gave a horselaugh.

If this sounds queer, remember that queerer things happen in Brooklyn every day.

322

"How do we write this one up?" asked the *Herald*. "We can't put just 'a horse' in the box score."

That was then the horse got his name. We named him Jones, after Jones, the caretaker who had left the gate open so he could wander onto the field. We wrote about "Horse" Jones.

Next day we all chuckled at a banner headline in one of the Metropolitan papers. It read: Jones Puts New Kick In Brooklyn.

♦

Look in the old box scores. Jones got two hits off Rube Waddell, of Philadelphia, and three off Cy Young, of Boston. He pounded Eddie Plank and Iron Man McGinnity and Wild Bill Donovan. He robbed Honus Wagner of a hit that would have been a double against any other third baseman in the league. On the base paths he was a bullet.

Our papers began to wire us, WHERE DOES JONES COME FROM? SEND BACKGROUND, HUMAN INTEREST, INTERVIEW. That was a harder assignment than New York knew. We decided by a gentleman's agreement that Jones must have come from Kentucky and got his first experience in a Blue Grass league. That sounded reasonable enough. We said he was long-faced, long-legged, dark, a vegetarian and a non-smoker. That was true. We said he was a horse for work, and ate like a horse. That was self-evident. Interviewing was a little harder.

Poor Pop O'Donnell for ten years had wanted a third baseman who could hit hard enough to dent a cream puff. Now that he had one he wasn't quite sure what to do with it. Purple-cow trouble. "Poiple," Pop would have said.

One of his first worries was paying for Jones. A strapping big farmer appeared at the clubhouse, saying he wanted either his horse or fifty thousand dollars.

Pop excused himself, checked the team's bank balance, then came back.

"What color is your horse?" he asked.

The farmer thought a minute. "Dapple gray," he said.

"Good afternoon, my man," Pop boomed unctuously, holding open the door. "That's a horse of another color." Jones was brown.

There were some audience incidents too. Jonathan Daniels, of Raleigh, North Carolina, told me that as a small boy that season he saw a whole row of elderly ladies bustle into the box seats, take one

look toward third base, look questioningly at one another, twitter about the sun being hot, and walk out. Georgia police records show that at least five citizens, cold sober, came to the ball park and were afraid to drive their own cars home. The American medical journals of that year discovered a new psychoneurosis which they said was doubtless caused by a feeling of insecurity resulting from the replacement of the horse by the horseless carriage. It usually took the form of hallucination—the sensation of seeing a horse sitting on a baseball player's bench. Perhaps that was the reason a famous pitcher, who shall here go nameless, came to town with his team, took one incredulous look at Brooklyn fielding practice, and went to his manager, offering to pay a fine.

But the real trouble was over whether horses should be allowed to play baseball. After the first shock, teams were generally amused at the idea of playing against a horse. But after Jones had batted their star pitchers out of the box, they said the Humane Society ought to protect the poor Brooklyn horse.

The storm that brewed in the South that spring was like nothing except the storm that gathered in 1860. Every hotel that housed baseball players housed a potential civil war. The better orators argued that the right to play baseball should not be separated from the right to vote or the responsibility of fighting for one's country. The more practical ones said a few more horses like Jones and they wouldn't have any jobs left. Still others said that this was probably just another bureaucratic trick on the part of the Administration.

Even the Brooklyn players protested. A committee of them came to see old Pop O'Donnell. They said wasn't baseball a game for human beings? Pop said he had always had doubts as to whether some major league players were human or not. They said touché, and this is all right so long as it is a one-horse business, so to speak. But if it goes on, before long won't a man have to grow two more legs and a tail before he can get in? They asked Pop how he would like to manage the Brooklyn Percherons, instead of the Brooklyn Superbas? They said, what would happen to baseball if it became a game for animals—say giraffes on one team, trained seals on a second and monkeys on a third? They pointed out that monkeys had already got a foot in the door by being used to dodge baseballs in carnivals. How would Pop

324

like to manage a team of monkeys called the Brooklyn Dodgers, they asked.

Pop said heaven help anyone who has to manage a team called the Brooklyn Dodgers. Then he pointed out that Brooklyn hadn't lost an exhibition game, and that the horse was leading the league in batting with a solid .516. He asked whether they would rather have a World Series or a two-legged third baseman. They went on muttering.

But his chief worry was Jones himself.

"That horse hasn't got his mind on the game," he told us one night on the hotel veranda.

"Ah, Pop, it's just horseplay," said the *World,* winking.

"Nope, he hasn't got his heart in it," said Pop, his voice echoing lightly off the distant mountains. "He comes just in time for practice and runs the minute it's over. There's something on that horse's mind."

We laughed, but had to admit that Jones was about the saddest horse we had ever seen. His eyes were great brown pools of liquid sorrow. His ears drooped. And still he hit well over .500 and covered third base like a rug.

One day he missed the game entirely. It was the day the Giants were in town, and fifteen thousand people were there to watch Jones bat against the great Matty. Brooklyn lost the game, and Pop O'Donnell almost lost his hair at the hands of the disappointed crowd.

"Who would have thought," Pop mused, in the clubhouse after the game, "that that (here some words are omitted) horse would turn out to be a prima donna? It's all right for a major league ballplayer to act like a horse, but that horse is trying to act like a major league ballplayer."

It was almost by accident that Tim and I found out what was really bothering Jones. We followed him one day when he left the ball park. We followed him nearly two miles to a race track.

Jones stood beside the fence a long time, turning his head to watch the thoroughbreds gallop by on exercise runs and time trials. Then a little stable boy opened the gate for him.

"Po' ol' hoss," the boy said. "Yo' wants a little runnin'?"

"Happens every day," a groom explained to us. "This horse wanders up here from God knows where, and acts like he wants to run, and some boy rides him a while, bareback pretending he's a race horse."

325

Jones was like a different horse out there on the track; not drooping any more—ears up, eyes bright, tail like a plume. It was pitiful how much he wanted to look like a race horse.

"That horse," Tim asked the groom,"is he any good for racing?"

"Not here, anyway," the groom said. "Might win a county-fair race or two."

He asked us whether we had any idea who owned the horse.

"Sir," said Tim, like Edwin M. Stanton, "that horse belongs to the ages."

"Well, mister," said the groom, "the ages had better get some different shoes on that horse. Why, you could hold a baseball in those shoes he has there."

"It's very clear," I said as we walked back, "what we have here is a badly frustrated horse."

"It's clear as beer," Tim said sadly.

That afternoon Jones hit a home run and absent-mindedly trotted around the bases. As soon as the game was over, he disappeared in the direction of the race track. Tim looked at me and shook his head. Pop O'Donnell held his chin in his hands.

"I'll be boiled in oil," he said. "Berled in erl," he said.

Nothing cheered up poor Pop until someone came in with a story about the absentee owner of a big-league baseball club who had inherited the club along with the family fortune. This individual had just fired the manager of his baseball farm system, because the farms had not turned out horses like Jones. "What are farms for if they don't raise horses?" the absentee owner had asked indignantly.

◆

Jones was becoming a national problem second only to the Panama Canal and considerably more important than whether Mr. Taft got to be President.

There were rumors that the Highlanders—people were just beginning to call them the Yankees—would withdraw and form a new league if Jones was allowed to play. It was reported that a team of kangaroos from Australia was on its was to play a series of exhibition games in America, and President Ban Johnson, of the American League, was quoted as saying that he would never have kangaroos in the American

League because they were too likely to jump their contracts. There was talk of a constitutional amendment concerning horses in baseball.

The thing that impressed me, down there in the South, was that all this was putting the cart before the horse, so to speak. Jones simply didn't want to play baseball. He wanted to be a race horse. I don't know why life is that way.

Jones made an unassisted triple play, and Ty Cobb accused Brooklyn of furnishing fire ladders to its infielders. He said that no third baseman could have caught the drive that started the play. At the end of the training season, Jones was batting .538 and fielding .997, had stolen twenty bases and hit seven home runs. He was the greatest third baseman in the history of baseball, and didn't want to be!

Joseph Pulitzer, William Randolph Hearst, Arthur Brisbane and the rest of the big shots got together and decided that if anyone didn't know by this time that Jones was a horse, the newspapers wouldn't tell him. He could find it out.

Folks seemed to find it out. People began gathering from all parts of the country to see Brooklyn open against the Giants—Matty against Jones. Even a tribe of Sioux Indians camped beside the Gowanus and had war dances on Flatbush Avenue, waiting for the park to open. And Pop O'Donnell kept his squad in the South as long as he could, laying plans to arrive in Brooklyn only on the morning of the opening game.

The wire said that night that 200,000 people had come to Brooklyn for the game, and 190,000 of them were in an ugly mood over the report that the league might not let Jones play. The governor of New York sent two regiments of the national guard. The Giants were said to be caucusing to decide whether they would play against Jones.

By game time, people were packed for six blocks, fighting to get into the park. The Sioux sent a young buck after their tomahawks, just in case. Telephone poles a quarter of a mile from the field were selling for a hundred dollars. Every baseball writer in the country was in the Brooklyn press box; the other teams played before club reporters and society editors. Just before game time I managed to push into Pop O'Donnell's little office with the presidents of the two major leagues, the mayor of New York, a half dozen other reporters, and a delegation from the Giants.

"There's just one thing we want to know," the spokesman for the Giants was asking Pop. "Are you going to play Jones?"

"Gentlemen," said Pop in that soft-spoken firm way of his that rattled the window blinds, "our duty is to give the public what it wants. And the public wants Jones."

Like an echo, a chant began to rise from the bleachers, "We want Jones!"

"There is one other little thing," said Pop. "Jones has disappeared."

There were about ten seconds of the awful silence that comes when your nerves are paralyzed, but your mind keeps on thrashing.

"He got out of his boxcar somewhere between Georgia and Brooklyn," Pop said. "We don't know where. We're looking."

A Western Union boy dashed in. "Hold on!" said Pop. "This may be news!"

He tore the envelope with a shaky hand. The message was from Norfolk, Virginia. HAVE FOUND ELEPHANT THAT CAN BALANCE MEDICINE BALL ON TRUNK, it read. WILL HE DO? If Pop had said what he said then into a telephone, it would have burned out all the insulators in New York.

Down at the field, the President of the United States himself was poised to throw out the first ball. "Is this Jones?" he asked. He was a little nearsighted.

"This is the mayor of New York," Pop said patiently. "Jones is gone. Run away."

The President's biographers disagree as to whether he said at that moment, "Oh, well, who would stay in Brooklyn if he could run?" or "I sympathize with you for having to change horses in midstream."

That was the saddest game ever covered by the entire press corps of the nation. Brooklyn was all thumbs in the field, all windmills at bat. There was no Jones to whistle hits into the outfield and make sensational stops at third. By the sixth inning, when they had to call the game with the score 18-1, the field was ankle deep in pop bottles and the Sioux were waving their tomahawks and singing the scalp song.

You know the rest of the story. Brooklyn didn't win a game until the third week of the season, and no team ever tried a horse again,

except a few dark horses every season. Pittsburgh, I believe, tried trained seals in the outfield. They were deadly at catching the ball, but couldn't cover enough ground. San Francisco has an entire team of Seals, but I have never seen them play. Boston tried an octopus at second base, but had to give him up. What happened to two rookies who disappeared trying to steal second base against Boston that spring is another subject baseball doesn't talk about.

There has been considerable speculation as to what happened to Jones. Most of us believed the report that the Brooklyn players had unfastened the latch on the door of his boxcar, until Pop O'Donnell's *Confidential Memoirs* came out, admitting that he himself had taken the hinges off the door because he couldn't face the blame for making baseball a game for horses. But I have been a little confused since Tim McGuire came to me once and said he might as well confess. He couldn't stand to think of that horse standing wistfully beside the track, waiting for someone to let him pretend he was a race horse. That haunted Tim. When he went down to the boxcar he found the door unlatched and the hinges off, so he gave the door a little push outward. He judged it was the will of the majority.

And that is why baseball is played by men today instead of by horses. But don't think that the shadow of Jones doesn't still lie heavy on the game. Have you ever noticed how retiring and silent and hangdog major league ballplyers are, how they cringe before the umpire? They never know when another Jones may break away from a beer wagon or a circus or a plow, wander through an unlocked gate, and begin batting .538 to their .290. The worry is terrible. You can see it in the crowds too. That is why Brooklyn fans are so aloof and disinterested, why they never raise their voices above a whisper at Ebbets Field. They know perfectly well that this is only minor league ball they are seeing, that horses could play it twice as well if they had a chance.

That is the secret we sports writers have kept all these years; that is why we have never written about Jones. And the Brooklyn fans still try to keep it a secret, but every once in a while the sorrow eats like lye into one of them until he can hold it back no longer, and then he sobs quietly and says, "Dem bums, if dey only had a little horse sense!"

329

"I don't know much about this guy as a hitter. Let's see what it says on his bubblegum card."

♦

These selections are from a 1950s syndicated comic strip by Ray Gotto called "Cotton Woods." Gotto was also a popular daily sports cartoonist and the creater of another baseball strip called "Ozark Ike." While "Cotton Woods" is admittedly not the most hilarious entry in this book, it is noteworthy as one of the few baseball strips that successfully made it to the comics pages. It's a good-natured story, with an authentic baseball feel, plenty of old-fashioned heroics, very well drawn. Being really funny would have made it perfect.

No matter how diligently umpires practice their unpopular art, everyone picks on them—lyricists and cartoonists, even clergymen and their own children. No wonder they're abused; they're supposed to be impartial, and yet the camera catches an umpire reaching out to shake a player's hand! The player was Willie Mays, who had just hit his 535th home run, the most ever for a righthanded batter, and the gladhanding umpire, Chris Pelekoudas, turned himself in to the National League president. He was forgiven.

Let's Get the Umpire's Goat

BY NORA BAYES AND JACK NORWORTH

Young Jimmy Croker was clerk for a broker.
  To be a good clerk was his aim:
When the ball season started then Jim was light hearted,
  For baseball was Jim's middle name.
To his boss he would say: My poor aunt died to-day.
  So his boss said: For heaven's sake go!
Then he'd hike to the bleachers with six other screechers,
  And yell if the game was too slow:
                  Chorus.
  Let's get the umpire's goat, goat, goat, goat.
  Let's make him go up in the air:
  We'll yell: Oh, you robber! go somewhere and die,
  Back to the bush, you've got mud in your eye!
  Oh, what an awful decision! Why don't you put spectacles on?
  Let's holler like sin, and then our side will win
  When the umpire's nanny is gone.

Jimmy kept wishin', in fact his ambition
  Was nat'ral for one of his age:
He wanted to be like Mike Donlin, you see,
  And play ball or else go on the stage.
He knew each player's name and kept tab on the game,
  And could tell you how pennants are won.
But each bleacherite fan was with Jim to a man
  When his home team just needed a run.

334.

The Umpire

BY MILTON BRACKER

The umpire is a lonely man
Whose calls are known to every fan
Yet none will call him Dick or Dan
  In all the season's games.

They'll never call him Al or Ed
Or Bill or Phil or Frank or Fred
Or Jim or Tim or Tom or Ted—
  They'll simply call him names.

◆

◆

NANCY   Ernie Bushmiller

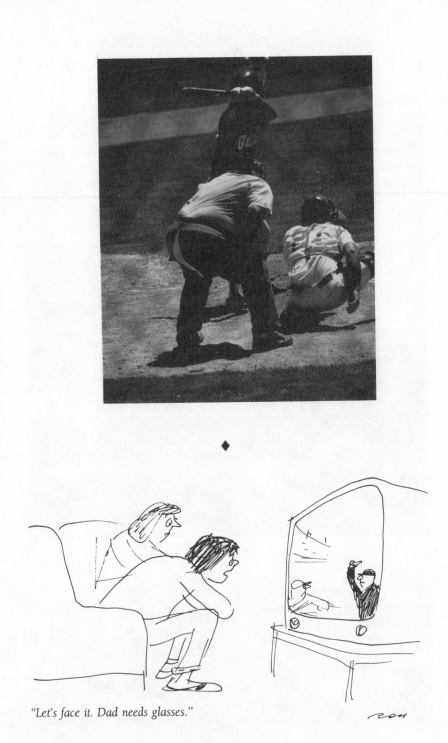

"Let's face it. Dad needs glasses."

"Thou hast eyes to see, and see not!"

"I thought *there* was something funny going on here this afternoon."

338

"It was the greatest moment of my career—standing there with the boos of seventy-two thousand fans thundering down on me."

Charles Schulz, who almost certainly has turned out more baseball cartoons than anyone else, needs no introduction. But the man who gave birth to "Peanuts" does provide a nostalgic introduction to a brilliant Murderers' Row of cartoons celebrating kids on the baseball diamond.

From Peanuts Jubilee

BY CHARLES SCHULZ

THERE ARE CERTAIN SEASONS IN OUR LIVES that each of us can recall, and there are others that disappear from our memories like the melting snow. When I was fourteen, I had a summer that I shall always remember. We had organized our own neighborhood baseball team, but we never played on a strict schedule, for we didn't know when we could find another team to play. I lived about a block from a grade school called Maddocks in St. Paul where there was a rather large crushed-rock playground, which did have two baseball backstops, but no fences. A hard-hit ground ball could elude the second baseman or shortstop and very easily roll into the outfield so fast that none of the outfielders would be able to stop it, and it would be quite possible for a fast runner to beat it out for a home run. This field also could make sliding into second base reasonably painful if you were not careful. Fortunately, it was smooth enough so ground balls hit to the infielders did not take too many bad bounces.

A man named Harry (I never knew his last name) was the playground director that summer. He saw our interest in playing baseball and came up with the idea that we should organize four teams and have a summer league. This was the most exciting news that had come to any of us in a long time. There were two games each Tuesday and Thursday and I could hardly wait for them to begin. One game was to start at nine between two of the teams, and the other game was to start at ten-thirty between the other two teams. I was always at the field at seven-thirty

340

with all of my equipment, waiting for something to happen. Our team came in first place that year, probably because we practiced more than the other teams, and one day I actually pitched a no-hit, no-run game. It was a great summer and I wish that there were some way I could let that man, whom we knew only as Harry, know how much I appreciated it.

We knew little about Harry because boys that age are never quite that interested in people older than they. At my mother's suggestion, all the boys on our team chipped in and bought him a cake one day to demonstrate our appreciation for what he had done for us. He was a gentle man, probably not more than twenty-three or twenty-four, and I doubt if he was married. This was probably only a temporary job for him during times when it was difficult to find work, but he did his job well and he gave all of us a happy summer.

♦

PEANUTS   Charles Schulz

PEANUTS   Charles Schulz

PEANUTS Charles Schulz

NANCY Ernie Bushmiller

CALVIN AND HOBBES Bill Watterson

342

Small Fry

BY WILLIAM STEIG

Sandlot baseball

Circus catch

"Here it is. Take a good look at it."

Three easy outs

Relief pitcher warming up

Rookie

Butterfingers

"I was traded for three packs of baseball cards."

Jules Feiffer

ELEVEN
YEARS
OLD AND
I'M
NEVER
PICKED
FOR THE
TEAM.

LOOK AT
THOSE
OTHERS.
THEY
ALWAYS
PLAY.

BATTING THE
BALL . . .
CATCHING IT.

RUNNING . . .
LAUGHING . . .

OTHERWISE
I MIGHT
NOT HAVE
NOTICED.

IT'S VERY
LUCKY THEY
WON'T LET
ME PLAY.

THE WAY THEY
GATHER
TOGETHER.
THE WAY THEY
CHOOSE
UP SIDES.

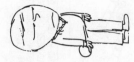

THERE'S
SOMETHING
BASICALLY
WRONG
THERE.

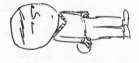

SOMETHING
BAD.
SOMETHING
UNHEALTHY.

● 345

It was probably Yogi Berra who first noticed that intellectuals, many of them, love baseball, and love to show off that love.
Phillip Roth, a most serious author, focused on baseball in a work modestly titled The Great American Novel. *If you use a little imagination in reading the Henry Morgan radio script, you might be able to hear his clipped, ultracultured, snobby tone, narrating an opera with baseball overtones.*

From <u>The Great American Novel</u>

BY PHILIP ROTH

NE SUNNY SATURDAY MORNING EARLY IN August, the Ruppert Mundys boarded a bus belonging to the mental institution and journeyed from their hotel in downtown Asylum out into the green Ohio countryside to the world-famous hospital for the insane, there to play yet another "away" game—a three-inning exhibition match against a team composed entirely of patients. The August visit to the hospital by a P. League team in town for a series against the Keepers was an annual event of great moment at the institution, and one that was believed to be of considerable therapeutic value to the inmates, particularly the sports-minded among them. Not only was it their chance to make contact, if only for an hour or so, with the real world they had left behind, but it was believed that even so brief a visit by famous big league ballplayers went a long way to assuage the awful sense such people have that they are odious and contemptible to the rest of humankind. Of course the P. League players (who like all ballplayers despised any exhibition games during the course of the regular season) happened to find playing against the Lunatics, as they called them, a most odious business indeed; but as the General simply would not hear of abandoning a practice that brought public attention to the humane and compassionate side of a league that many still associated with violence and scandal, the tradition was maintained year

after year, much to the delight of the insane, and the disgust of the ballplayers themselves.

The chief psychiatrist at the hospital was a Dr. Traum, a heavyset gentleman with a dark chin beard, and a pronounced European accent. Until his arrival in America in the thirties, he had never even heard of baseball, but in that Asylum was the site of a major league ball park, as well as a psychiatric hospital, it was not long before the doctor became something of a student of the game. After all, one whose professional life involved ruminating upon the extremes of human behavior, had certainly to sit up and take notice when a local fan decided to make his home atop a flagpole until the Keepers snapped a losing streak, or when an Asylum man beat his wife to death with a hammer for calling the Keepers "bums" just like himself. If the doctor did not, strictly speaking, become an ardent Keeper fan, he did make it his business to read thoroughly in the literature of the national pastime, with the result that over the years more than one P. League manager had to compliment the bearded Berliner on his use of the hit-and-run, and the uncanny ability he displayed at stealing signals during their annual exhibition game.

Despite the managerial skill that Dr. Traum had developed over the years through his studies, his team proved no match for the Mundys that morning. By August of 1943, the Mundys weren't about to sit back and take it on the chin from a German-born baseball manager and a team of madmen; they had been defeated and disgraced and disgraced and defeated up and down the league since the season had begun back in April, and it was as though on the morning they got out to the insane asylum grounds, all the wrath that had been seething in them for months now burst forth, and nothing, but nothing, could have prevented them from grinding the Lunatics into dust once the possibility for victory presented itself. Suddenly, those '43 flops started looking and sounding like the scrappy, hustling, undefeatable Ruppert teams of Luke Gofannon's day—and this despite the fact that it took nearly an hour to complete a single inning, what with numerous delays and interruptions caused by the Lunatics' style of play. Hardly a moment passed that something did not occur to offend the professional dignity of a big leaguer, and yet, through it all, the Mundys on both

348

offense and defense managed to seize hold of every Lunatic mistake and convert it to their advantage. Admittedly, the big right-hander who started for the institution team was fast and savvy enough to hold the Mundy power in check, but playing just the sort of heads-up, razzle-dazzle baseball that used to characterize the Mundy teams of yore, they were able in their first at bat to put together a scratch hit by Astarte, a bunt by Nickname, a base on balls to Big John, and two Lunatic errors, to score three runs—their biggest inning of the year, and the first Mundy runs to cross the plate in sixty consecutive innings, which was not a record only because they had gone sixty-seven innings without scoring earlier in the season.

When Roland Agni, of all people, took a called third strike to end their half of the inning, the Mundys rushed off the bench like a team that smelled World Series loot. "We was due!" yelped Nickname, taking the peg from Hothead and sweeping his glove over the bag—"Nobody gonna stop us now, babe! We was due! We was *overdue!*" Then he winged the ball over to where Deacon Demeter stood on the mound, grinning. "Three big ones for you, Deke!" Old Deacon, the fifty-year-old iron-man starter of the Mundy staff, already a twenty-game loser with two months of the season still to go, shot a string of tobacco juice over his left shoulder to ward off evil spirits, stroked the rabbit's foot that hung on a chain around his neck, closed his eyes to mumble something ending with "Amen," and then stepped up on the rubber to face the first patient. Deacon was a preacher back home, as gentle and kindly a man as you would ever want to bring your problems to, but up on the hill he was all competitor, and had been for thirty years now. "When the game begins," he used to say back in his heyday, "charity ends." And so it was that when he saw the first Lunatic batter digging in as though he owned the batter's box, the Deke decided to take Hothead's advice and stick the first pitch in his ear, just to show the little nut who was boss. The Deacon had taken enough insults that year for a fifty-year-old man of the cloth!

Not only did the Deke's pitch cause the batter to go flying back from the plate to save his skin, but next thing everyone knew the lead-off man was running for the big brick building with the iron bars on its windows. Two of his teammates caught him down the right-field

line and with the help of the Lunatic bullpen staff managed to drag him back to home plate. But once there they couldn't get him to take hold of the bat; every time they put it into his hands, he let it fall through to the ground. By the time the game was resumed, with a 1 and 0 count on a new lead-off hitter, one not quite so cocky as the fellow who'd stepped up to bat some ten minutes earlier, there was no doubt in anyone's mind that the Deke was in charge. As it turned out, twice in the inning Mike Rama had to go sailing up into the wall to haul in a long line drive, but as the wall was padded, Mike came away unscathed, and the Deacon was back on the bench with his three-run lead intact.

"We're on our way!" cried Nickname. "We are on our God damn way!"

Hothead too was dancing with excitement; cupping his hands to his mouth, he shouted across to the opposition, "Just watch you bastards go to pieces now!"

And so they did. The Deke's pitching and Mike's fielding seemed to have shaken the confidence of the big Lunatic right-hander whose fastball had reined in the Mundys in the first. To the chagrin of his teammates, he simply would not begin to pitch in the second until the umpire stopped staring at him.

"Oh, come on," said the Lunatic catcher, "he's not staring at *you*. Throw the ball."

"I tell you, he's right behind you and he is too staring. Look you, I see you there behind that mask. What is it you want from me? What is it you think you're looking at, anyway?"

The male nurse, in white half-sleeve shirt and white trousers, who was acting as the plate umpire, called out to the mound, "Play ball now. Enough of that."

"Not until you come out from there."

"Oh, pitch, for Christ sake," said the catcher.

"Not until that person stops staring."

Here Dr. Traum came off the Lunatic bench and started for the field, while down in the Lunatic bullpen a left-hander got up and began to throw. Out on the mound, with his hands clasped behind his back and rocking gently to and fro on his spikes, the doctor conferred with

350

the pitcher. Formal European that he was, he wore, along with his regulation baseball shoes, a dark three-piece business suit, a stiff collar, and a tie.

"What do you think the ol' doc's tellin' that boy?" Bud Parusha asked Jolly Cholly.

"Oh, the usual," the old-timer said. "He's just calmin' him down. He's just askin' if he got any good duck shootin' last season."

It was five full minutes before the conference between the doctor and the pitcher came to an end with the doctor asking the pitcher to hand over the ball. When the pitcher vehemently refused, it was necessary for the doctor to snatch the ball out of his hand; but when he motioned down to the bullpen for the left-hander, the pitcher suddenly reached out and snatched the ball back. Here the doctor turned back to the bullpen and this time motioned for the left-hander *and* a right-hander. Out of the bullpen came two men dressed like the plate umpire in white half-sleeve shirts and white trousers. While they took the long walk to the mound, the doctor made several unsuccessful attempts to talk the pitcher into relinquishing the ball. Finally the two men arrived on the mound and before the pitcher knew what had happened, they had unfurled a straitjacket and wrapped it around him.

"Guess he wanted to stay in," said Jolly Cholly, as the pitcher kicked out at the doctor with his feet.

The hundred Lunatic fans who had gathered to watch the game from the benches back of the foul screen behind home plate, and who looked in their street clothes as sane as any baseball crowd, rose to applaud the pitcher as he left the field, but when he opened his mouth to acknowledge the ovation, the two men assisting him in his departure slipped a gag over his mouth.

Next the shortstop began to act up. In the first inning it was he who had gotten the Lunatics out of trouble with a diving stab of a Bud Parusha liner and a quick underhand toss that had doubled Wayne Heket off third. But now in the top of the second, though he continued to gobble up everything hit to the left of the diamond, as soon as he got his hands on the ball he proceeded to stuff it into his back pocket. Then, assuming a posture of utter nonchalance, he would start whistling between his teeth and scratching himself, as though waiting for the

351

action to *begin*. In that it was already very much underway, the rest of the Lunatic infield would begin screaming at him to take the ball out of his pocket and make the throw to first. "What?" he responded, with an innocent smile. "The ball!" they cried. "Yes, what about it?" "Throw it!" "But I don't have it." "You *do!*" they would scream, converging upon him from all points of the infield, "You do too!" "Hey, leave me alone," the shortstop cried, as they grabbed and pulled at his trousers. "Hey, cut that out—get your hands *out* of there!" And when at last the ball was extracted from where he himself had secreted it, no one could have been more surprised. "Hey, the *ball*. Now who put that there? Well, what's everybody looking at *me* for? Look, this must be some guy's idea of a joke . . . Well, Christ, I didn't do it."

Once the Mundys caught on, they were quick to capitalize on this unexpected weakness in the Lunatic defense, pushing two more runs across in the second on two consecutive ground balls to short—both beaten out for hits while the shortstop grappled with the other infielders—a sacrifice by Mike Rama, and a fly to short center that was caught by the fielder who then just stood there holding it in his glove, while Hothead, who was the runner on second, tagged up and hobbled to third, and then, wooden leg and all, broke for home, where he scored with a head-first slide, the only kind he could negotiate. As it turned out, the slide wasn't even necessary, for the center-fielder was standing in the precise spot where he had made the catch—and the ball was still in his glove.

With the bases cleared, Dr. Traum asked for time and walked out to center. He put a hand on the shoulder of the mute and motionless fielder and talked to him in a quiet voice. He talked to him steadily for fifteen minutes, their faces only inches apart. Then he stepped aside, and the center-fielder took the ball from the pocket of his glove and threw a perfect strike to the catcher, on his knees at the plate some two hundred feet away.

"Wow," said Bud Parusha, with ungrudging admiration, "now, that fella has a arm on him."

"Hothead," said Cholly, mildly chiding the catcher, "he woulda had you by a country mile, you know, if only he'd a throwed it."

But Hot, riding high, hollered out, "Woulda don't count, Charles— it's dudda what counts, and I dud it!"

Meanwhile Kid Heket, who before this morning had not been awake for two consecutive innings in over a month, continued to stand with one foot up on the bench, his elbow on his knee and his chin cupped contemplatively in his palm. He had been studying the opposition like this since the game had gotten underway. "You know somethin'," he said, gesturing toward the field, "those fellas ain't thinkin'. No sir, they just ain't usin' their heads."

"We got 'em on the run, Wayne!" cried Nickname. "They don't know *what* hit 'em! Damn, ain't nobody gonna stop us from here on out!"

Deacon was hit hard in the last of the second, but fortunately for the Mundys, in the first two instances the batsman refused to relinquish the bat and move off home plate, and so each was thrown out on what would have been a base hit, right-fielder Parusha to first-baseman Baal; and the last hitter, who drove a tremendous line drive up the alley in left center, ran directly from home to third and was tagged out sitting on the bag with what he took to be a triple, and what would have been one too, had he only run around the bases and gotten to third in the prescribed way.

The quarrel between the Lunatic catcher and the relief pitcher began over what to throw Big John Baal, the lead-off hitter in the top of the third.

"Uh-uh," said the Lunatic pitcher, shaking off the first signal given by his catcher, while in the box, Big John took special pleasure in swishing the bat around menacingly.

"Nope," said the pitcher to the second signal.

His response to the third was an emphatic, "N-O!"

And to the fourth, he said, stamping one foot, "Definitely *not!*"

When he shook off a fifth signal as well, with a caustic, "Are you kidding? Throw him that and it's bye-bye ballgame," the catcher yanked off his mask and cried:

"And I suppose that's what I want, according to you! To lose! To go down in defeat! Oh, sure," the catcher whined, "what I'm doing, you see, is deliberately telling you to throw him the wrong pitch so I can have the wonderful pleasure of being on the losing team again. Oh brother!" His sarcasm spent, he donned his mask, knelt down behind the plate, and tried yet once more.

This time the pitcher had to cross his arms over his chest and look to the heavens for solace. "God give me strength," he sighed.

"In other words," the catcher screamed, "I'm wrong *again*. But then in your eyes I'm *always* wrong. Well, isn't that true? Admit it! Whatever signal I give is *bound* to be wrong. Why? Because *I'm* giving it! I'm daring to give *you* a signal! I'm daring to tell *you* how to pitch! I could kneel here signaling for the rest of my days, and you'd just stand there shaking them off and asking God to give you strength, *because I'm so wrong and so stupid and so hopeless and would rather lose than win!*"

When the relief pitcher, a rather self-possessed fellow from the look of it, though perhaps a touch perverse in his own way, refused to argue, the Lunatic catcher once again assumed his squat behind the plate, and proceeded to offer a seventh signal, an eighth, a ninth, a tenth, each and every one of which the pitcher rejected with a mild, if unmistakably disdainful, remark.

On the sixteenth signal, the pitcher just had to laugh. "Well, that one really takes the cake, doesn't it? That really took brains. Come over here a minute," he said to his infielders. "All right," he called back down to the catcher, "go ahead, show them your new brainstorm." To the four players up on the mound with him, the pitcher whispered, "Catch this," and pointed to the signal that the catcher, in his mortification, was continuing to flash from between his legs.

"Hey," said the Lunatic third-baseman, "that ain't even a finger, is it?"

"No," said the pitcher, "as a matter of fact, it isn't."

"I mean, it ain't got no nail on it, does it?"

"Indeed it has not."

"Why, I'll be darned," said the shortstop, "it's, it's his thingamajig."

"Precisely," said the pitcher.

"But what the hell is that supposed to mean?" asked the first-baseman.

The pitcher had to smile again. "What do you think? Hey, Doc," he called to the Lunatic bench, "I'm afraid my battery-mate has misunderstood what's meant by an exhibition game. He's flashing me the signal to meet him later in the shower, if you know what I mean."

The catcher was in tears now. "He made me do it," he said, covering himself with his big glove, and in his shame, dropping all the way to his knees, "everything else I showed him wasn't *good* enough for him— no, he teases me, he taunts me—"

By now the two "coaches" (as they were euphemistically called), who had removed the starting pitcher from the game, descended upon the catcher. With the aid of a fielder's glove, one of them gingerly lifted the catcher's member and placed it back inside his uniform before the opposing players could see what the signal had been, while the other relieved him of his catching equipment. "He provoked me," the catcher said, "he always provokes me—"

The Lunatic fans were on their feet again, applauding, when their catcher was led away from the plate and up to the big brick building, along the path taken earlier by the starting pitcher. "—He won't let me alone, ever. I don't want to do it. I never wanted to do it. I *wouldn't* do it. But then he starts up teasing me and taunting me—"

The Mundys were able to come up with a final run in the top of the third, once they discovered that the second-string Lunatic catcher, for all that he sounded like the real thing—"Chuck to me, babe, no hitter in here, babe—" was a little leery of fielding a bunt dropped out in front of home plate, fearful apparently of what he would find beneath the ball upon picking it up.

When Deacon started out to the mound to pitch the last of the three innings, there wasn't a Mundy who took the field with him, sleepy old Kid Heket included, who didn't realize that the Deke had a shutout working. If he could set the Lunatics down without a run, he could become the first Mundy pitcher to hurl a scoreless game all year, in or out of league competition. Hoping neither to jinx him or unnerve him, the players went through the infield warm-up deliberately keeping the chatter to a minimum, as though in fact it was just another day they were going down to defeat. Nonetheless, the Deke was already streaming perspiration when the first Lunatic stepped into the box. He rubbed the rabbit's foot, said his prayer, took a swallow of air big enough to fill a gallon jug, and on four straight pitches, walked the center-fielder, who earlier in the game hadn't bothered to return the ball to the infield after catching a fly ball, and now, at the plate, hadn't

355

moved the bat off his shoulder. When he was lifted for a pinch-runner (lifted by the "coaches") the appreciative fans gave him a nice round of applause. "That's lookin' 'em over!" they shouted, as he was carried from the field still in the batting posture, "that's waitin' 'em out! Good eye in there, fella!"

As soon as the pinch-runner took over at first, it became apparent that Dr. Traum had decided to do what he could to save face by spoiling the Deacon's shutout. Five runs down in the last inning and still playing to win, you don't start stealing bases—but that was precisely what this pinch-runner had in mind. And with what daring! First, with an astonishing burst of speed he rushed fifteen feet down the basepath—but then, practically on all fours, he was scrambling back. "No! No!" he cried, as he dove for the bag with his outstretched hand, "I won't! Never mind! Forget it!" But no sooner had he gotten back up on his feet and dusted himself off, than he was running again. "Why not!" he cried, "what the hell!" But having broken fifteen, *twenty,* feet down the basepath, he would come to an abrupt stop, smite himself on his forehead, and charge wildly back to first, crying, "Am I crazy? Am I out of my *mind?*"

In this way did he travel back and forth along the basepath some half-dozen times, before Deacon finally threw the first pitch to the plate. Given all there was to distract him, the pitch was of course a ball, low and in the dirt, but Hothead, having a great day, blocked it beautifully with his wooden leg.

Cholly, managing the club that morning while Mister Fairsmith rested back in Asylum—of the aged Mundy manager's spiritual crisis, more anon—Cholly motioned for Chico to get up and throw a warm-up pitch in the bullpen (one was enough—one was too many, in fact, as far as Chico was concerned) and meanwhile took a stroll out to the hill.

"Startin' to get to you, are they?" asked Cholly.

"It's that goofball on first that's doin' it."

Cholly looked over to where the runner, with time out, was standing up on first engaged in a heated controversy with himself.

"Hell," said Cholly, in his soft and reassuring way, "these boys have been tryin' to rattle us with that there bush league crap all mornin',

Deke. I told you fellers comin' out in the bus, you just got to pay no attention to their monkeyshines, because that is their strategy from A to Z. To make you lose your concentration. Otherwise we would be rollin' over them worse than we is. But Deke, you tell me now, if you have had it, if you want for me to bring the Mexican in—"

"With six runs in my hip pocket? And a shutout goin'?"

"Well, I wasn't myself goin' to mention that last that you said."

"Cholly, you and me been in this here game since back in the days they was rubbin' us down with Vaseline and Tabasco sauce. Ain't that right?"

"I know, I know."

"Well," said the Deke, shooting a stream of tobacco juice over his shoulder, "aint a bunch of screwballs gonna get my goat. Tell Chico to sit down."

Sure enough, the Deacon, old war-horse that he was, got the next two hitters out on long drives to left. "Oh my God!" cried the base runner, each time the Ghost went climbing up the padded wall to snare the ball. "Imagine if I'd broken for second! Imagine what would have happened then! Oh, that'll teach me to take those crazy leads! But then if you don't get a jump on the pitcher, where are you as a pinch-runner? That's the whole idea of a pinch-runner—to break with the pitch, to break *before* the pitch, to score that shutout-breaking run! That's what I'm in here for, that's my entire purpose. The whole thing is on *my* shoulders—so then what am I doing *not* taking a good long lead? But just then, if I'd broken for second, I'd have been doubled off first! For the last out! But then suppose he hadn't made the catch? Suppose he'd dropped it. Then where would I be? Forced out at second! *Out*—and all because I was too cowardly. But then what's the sense of taking an unnecessary risk? What virtue is there in being foolhardy? None! But then what about playing it too safe?"

On the bench, Jolly Cholly winced when he saw that the batter stepping into the box was the opposing team's shortstop. "Uh-oh," he said, "that's the feller what's cost 'em most of the runs to begin with. I'm afraid he is goin' to be lookin' to right his wrongs—and at the expense of Deacon's shutout. Dang!"

From bearing down so hard, the Deacon's uniform showed vast dark

357

continents of perspiration both front and back. There was no doubt that his strength was all but gone, for he was relying now solely on his "junk," that floating stuff that in times gone by used to cause the hitters nearly to break their back swinging at the air. Twice now those flutter balls of his had damn near been driven out of the institution and Jolly Cholly had all he could do not to cover his eyes with his hand when he saw the Deke release yet another fat pitch in the direction of home plate.

Apparently it was just to the Lunatic shortstop's liking too. He swung from the heels, and with a whoop of joy, was away from the plate and streaking down the basepath. "Run!" he shouted to the fellow on first.

But the pinch-runner was standing up on the bag, scanning the horizon for the ball.

"Two outs!" cried the Lunatic shortstop. "Run, you idiot!"

"But—where is it?" asked the pinch-runner.

The Mundy infielders were looking skywards themselves, wondering where in hell that ball had been hit to.

"Where *is* it!" screamed the pinch-runner, as the shortstop came charging right up to his face. "I'm not running till I know where the *ball* is!"

"I'm coming into first, you," warned the shortstop.

"But you can't overtake another runner! That's against the law! That's *out!*"

"Then *move!*" screamed the shortstop into the fellow's ear.

"Oh, this *is* crazy. This is exactly what I *didn't* want to do!" But what choice did he have? If he stood his ground, and the shortstop kept coming, that would be the ballgame. It would be all over because he who had been put into the game to run, had simply refused to. Oh, what torment that fellow knew as he rounded the bases with the shortstop right on his tail. "I'm running full speed—and I don't even know where the ball is! I'm running like a chicken with his head cut off! I'm running like a madman, which is just what I don't want to do! Or be! I don't know where I'm going, I don't know what I'm doing, I haven't the foggiest idea of what's happening—and I'm running!"

When, finally, he crossed the plate, he was in such a state, that he fell to his hands and knees, and sobbing with relief, began to kiss the

358

ground. "I'm home! Thank God! I'm safe! I made it! I scored! Oh thank God, thank God!"

And now the shortstop was rounding third—he took a quick glance back over his shoulder to see if he could go all the way, and just kept on coming. "Now where's *he* lookin'?" asked Cholly. "What in hell does he see that I can't? Or that Mike don't either?" For out in left, Mike Rama was walking round and round, searching in the grass as though for a dime that might have dropped out of his pocket.

The shortstop was only a few feet from scoring the second run of the inning when Dr. Traum, who all this while had been walking from the Lunatic bench, interposed himself along the foul line between the runner and home plate.

"Doc," screamed the runner, "You're in the way!"

"That's enough now," said Dr. Traum, and he motioned for him to stop in his tracks.

"But I'm only inches from pay dirt! Step aside, Doc—let me score!"

"You just stay vere you are, please."

"*Why?*"

"You know vy. Stay right vere you are now. And giff me the ball."

"What ball?" asked the shortstop.

"You know vat ball."

"Well, I surely don't have any ball. I'm the *hitter*. I'm about *to score*."

"You are not about to score. You are about to giff me the ball. Come now. Enough foolishness. Giff over the ball."

"But, Doc, I haven't got it. I'm on the offense. It's the *defense* that has the ball—that's the whole idea of the game. No criticism intended, but if you weren't a foreigner, you'd probably understand that better."

"Haf it your vay," said Dr. Traum, and he waved to the bullpen for his two coaches.

"But, Doc," said the shortstop, backpedaling now up the third-base line, "*they're* the ones in the field. *They're* the ones with the gloves— why don't you ask them for the ball? Why me? I'm an innocent base runner, who happens to be rounding third on his way home." But here he saw the coaches coming after him and he turned and broke across the diamond for the big brick building on the hill.

It was only a matter of minutes before one of the coaches returned

359

with the ball and carried it out to where the Mundy infield was now gathered on the mound.

The deacon turned it over in his hand and said, "Yep, that's it, all right. Ain't it, Hot?"

The Mundy catcher nodded. "How in hell did *he* get it?"

"A hopeless kleptomaniac, that's how," answered the coach. "He'd steal the bases if they weren't tied down. Here," he said, handing the Deacon a white hand towel bearing the Mundy laundrymark, and the pencil that Jolly Cholly wore behind his ear when he was acting as their manager. "Found this on him too. Looks like he got it when he stumbled into your bench for that pop-up in the first."

◆

PHILOSOPHER'S HOLIDAY
WITTGENSTEIN AT THE WORLD SERIES

360

Baseball as Aida

FROM "THE HENRY MORGAN SHOW"

MORGAN: Speaking of baseball, as we were a couple of hours ago—and this is true as you'll know if you read the papers—the New York Yankees Baseball Club has announced that it will sponsor a symphony program over the radio this year. It's true. It's a fine idea, and I wish them well. But where it will lead to is anybody's guess. My own guess is that someday soon you'll tune in the Metropolitan Opera and hear something like this:

[Crowd Noises, Fading Out]

ANNOUNCER: (WITH A STUFFY ACCENT) Good evening, opera fans. This is Milton J. Morgan bringing you an evening of opera through the courtesy of the Blue Sox, the baseball team that gives you ten innings for the price of nine. *[Laughter]* There's a double header tonight at the Opera House, and a twin bill offers *Aida* and *Il Trovatore*. The bleachers are filled to overflowing, and it looks like a big night for Verdi. (IN A NEW YORK ACCENT) Git your scorecard here! You can't tell who's singing without a scorecard! *[Laughter]*

[Music]

ANNOUNCER: Now let's look over the lineup for this evening. For *Aida*, the battery is Lefty Bernardo Greene conducting, and Slats Osavitsky prompting. In the role of Aida, I think Lippy Roscarini plans to start Babe Pinnelo, promising young rookie from Milan. *[Laughter]* Radamais will be Trout Bendetta. Yes, I can hear him. He's warming up back there now.

[Opera Singing, Moaning Heard in Background]

ANNOUNCER: I don't think he can go the distance so early in the season.

[Laughter] Lippy will probably use him for just the first two acts and then send him to the showers.

361

VENDOR: Peanuts! Popcorn! Diamonds, emeralds, rubies!

ANNOUNCER: And here is the first pitch . . .

[Music, Full Orchestra, Turns into Carnival Tune]

ANNOUNCER: While we're waiting, I'll give you a little background on the opera *Aida*. Aida is a lady shortstop from Ethiopia [*Laughter*], and she's been farmed out to Egypt. There she meets Radamais, a pitcher on the Egyptian team. She tries to get Radamais to throw the next game with Ethiopia. He finally consents. But while they're discussing it, who should pop out from behind the door but Happy Chandler.

[Crowd Noises]

ANNOUNCER: Oh yes, I see that now Lefty Bernardo Greene is walking out to the podium swinging three batons. [*Laughter*] Last season, you know, in Boston, he stepped right in and carried on after Butch Kusakoff was popped by a pop bottle at the pop concert. [*Laughter*] Now Lefty throws away two of the batons. He's limbering up, goes into his stretch, reels back, and here it comes . . .

[Drum Rolls and Silly Music]

ANNOUNCER: Bravo. Now the orchestra is spread out in the infield as the boys are about to leave for Egypt. Riccora sings "Ritorna Vincitor," "Bring Back the Pennant." [*Laughter*] Senoir Gullermo has had a touch of indigestion, and Lippy Roscarini has sent in a pinch tenor. Lefty Greene has caught the signal. He's winding up, and as we go into the last half of the third act. . . .

[Music]

ANNOUNCER: This broadcast of the Metropolitan Opera was brought to you with the compliments of the Blue Sox baseball team and its manager, Larry McFillo. Tune in next week when the Blue Sox will present two operas, *Lucia de l'Amamore*, by Joseph DiMaggio [*Laughter*], and *The Red Barber of Seville*.

[Music and Applause]

362

"Honus Wagner had a lifetime batting average of .329 and wrote 'Lohengrin.' Ask me another."

◆

Ball players speak in their own special voices, ranging from the virtually unlettered to the relatively intellectual. Ring Lardner captured the voice of a brash young pitcher in his classic You Know Me Al, *a novella (excerpted here) in the form of letters from the fictional Jack Keefe to his buddy Al. Lardner later collaborated with a popular cartoonist of the 1920s, Dick Dorgan, a skilled draftsman, on a "You Know Me Al" comic strip. Lardner, you may have noticed, plays every position on these pages: He pops up (not in the baseball sense) as reporter, short-story writer, novelist, lyricist and comic-stripper. He also plays muse, his Keefe letters inspiring Peter De Vries, the bard of Westport, Connecticut, to produce "You Know Me Alice," letters from a Little League manager.*

Half a century after Jack Keefe pitched, George Plimpton, the erudite editor of The Paris Review, *took the mound, facing a group of major-league All-Stars, the fodder for a magazine article that turned into the book* Out of My League, *the first of Plimpton's Walter Mittyish excursions into the competitive athletic world. (He also boxed, golfed and played quarterback, against pros.) In Plimpton's baseball adventure, he made a point of detailing his last-minute difficulties in finding a suitable glove, a point parodied, among others, in Roger Angell's "Over My Head," an account of a pitcher who turns editor for a day. The sainted Angell usually takes baseball very, very seriously.*

Inevitably, of course, ball players began writing in their own voices. Jim Brosnan, a righthanded pitcher, pioneered the practice wonderfully in two books, The Long Season *(excerpted here) and* Pennant Race, *and Jim Bouton (same initials, same position, no relation) did it a decade later in* Ball Four. *(Why are Keefe, Plimpton, Brosnan and Bouton all pitchers? is a question for psychologists, or catchers, to decide.) Brosnan, as the first to invite readers into the clubhouse, caused some controversy; Bouton, more candid and more scatological, caused considerably more. Brosnan, incidentally, wrote his books himself, without a collaborator or a ghost writer; Bouton had help from a newspaperman named Leonard Shecter. But since* Ball Four, *Bouton has written often and well without the aid of a certified writer, or a certifiable one.*

From You Know Me Al

A Busher's Letters

BY RING LARDNER

New York, New York, September 16.

FRIEND AL: I OPENED THE SERIOUS HERE and beat them easy but I know you must of saw about it in the Chi papers. At that they don't give me no fair show in the Chi papers. One of the boys brought one here and I seen in it where I was lucky to win that game in Cleveland. If I knowed which one of them reporters wrote that I would punch his jaw.

Al I told you Boston was some town but this is the real one. I never seen nothing like it and I been going some since we got here. I walked down Broadway the Main Street last night and I run into a couple of the ball players and they took me to what they call the Garden but it ain't like the gardens at home because this one is indoors. We sat down to a table and had several drinks. Pretty soon one of the boys asked me if I was broke and I says No, why? He says You better get some lubricateing oil and loosen up. I don't know what he meant but pretty soon when we had had a lot of drinks the waiter brings a check and hands it to me. It was for one dollar. I says Oh I ain't paying for all of them. The waiter says This is just for that last drink.

I thought the other boys would make a holler but they didn't say nothing. So I give him a dollar bill and even then he didn't act satisfied so I asked him what he was waiting for and he said Oh nothing, kind of sassy. I was going to bust him but the boys give me the sign to shut up and not to say nothing. I excused myself pretty soon because I wanted to get some air. I give my check for my hat to a boy and he brought my hat and I started going and he says Haven't you forgot something? I guess he must of thought I was wearing a overcoat.

Then I went down the Main Street again and some man stopped me and asked me did I want to go to the show. He said he had a ticket. I asked him what show and he said the Follies. I never heard of it but I told him I would go if he had a ticket to spare. He says I will spare

you this one for three dollars. I says You must take me for some boob. He says No I wouldn't insult no boob. So I walked on but if he had of insulted me I would of busted him.

I went back to the hotel then and run into Kid Gleason. He asked me to take a walk with him so out I go again. We went to the corner and he bought me a beer. He don't drink nothing but pop himself. The two drinks was only ten cents so I says This is the place for me. He says Where have you been? and I told him about paying one dollar for three drinks. He says I see I will have to take charge of you. Don't go round with them ball players no more. When you want to go out and see the sights come to me and I will stear you. So to-night he is going to stear me. I will write to you from Philadelphia.

Your pal,
Jack.

Philadelphia, Pa., September 19.

Friend Al: They won't be no game here to-day because it is raining. We all been loafing round the hotel all day and I am glad of it because I got all tired out over in New York City. I and Kid Gleason went round together the last couple of nights over there and he wouldn't let me spend no money. I seen a lot of girls that I would of liked to of got acquainted with but he wouldn't even let me answer them when they spoke to me. We run in to a couple of peaches last night and they had us spotted too. One of them says I'll bet you're a couple of ball players. But Kid says You lose your bet. I am a bellhop and the big rube with me is nothing but a pitcher.

One of them says What are you trying to do kid somebody? He says Go home and get some soap and remove your disguise from your face. I didn't think he ought to talk like that to them and I called him about it and said maybe they was lonesome and it wouldn't hurt none if we treated them to a soda or something. But he says Lonesome. If I don't get you away from here they will steal everything you got. They won't even leave you your fast ball. So we left them and he took me to a picture show. It was some California pictures and they made me think of Hazel so when I got back to the hotel I sent her three postcards.

Gleason made me go to my room at ten o'clock both nights but I was pretty tired anyway because he had walked me all over town. I guess we must of saw twenty shows. He says I would take you to the grand opera only it would be throwing money away because we can hear Ed Walsh for nothing. Walsh has got some voice Al a loud high tenor.

To-morrow is Sunday and we have a double header Monday on account of the rain to-day. I thought sure I would get another chance to beat the Athaletics and I asked Callahan if he was going to pitch me here but he said he thought he would save me to work against Johnson in Washington. So you see Al he must figure I am about the best he has got. I'll beat him Al if they get a couple of runs behind me.

Yours truly,

Jack.

P.S. They was a letter here from Violet and it pretty near made me feel like crying. I wish they was two of me so both them girls could be happy.

Washington, D.C., September 22.

Dear Old Al: Well Al here I am in the capital of the old United States. We got in last night and I been walking round town all morning. But I didn't tire myself out because I am going to pitch against Johnson this afternoon.

This is the prettiest town I ever seen but I believe they is more colored people here than they is in Evansville or Chi. I seen the White House and the Monumunt. They say that Bill Sullivan and Gabby St. once catched a baseball that was threw off of the top of the Monumunt but I bet they couldn't catch it if I throwed it.

I was in to breakfast this morning with Gleason and Bodie and Weaver and Fournier. Gleason says I'm surprised that you ain't sick in bed to-day. I says Why?

He says Most of our pitchers gets sick when Cal tells them they are going to work against Johnson. He says Here's these other fellows all feeling pretty sick this morning and they ain't even pitchers. All they have to do is hit against him but it looks like as if Cal would have to send substitutes in for them. Bodie is complaining of a sore arm which

367

he must of strained drawing to two card flushes. Fournier and Weaver have strained their legs doing the tango dance. Nothing could cure them except to hear that big Walter had got throwed out of his machine and wouldn't be able to pitch against us in this serious.

I says I feel O. K. and I ain't afraid to pitch against Johnson and I ain't afraid to hit against him neither. Then Weaver says Have you ever saw him work? Yes, I says, I seen him in Chi. Then Weaver says Well if I have saw him work and ain't afraid to hit against him I'll bet you would go down to Wall Street and holler Hurrah for Roosevelt. I says No I wouldn't do that but I ain't afraid of no pitcher and what is more if you get me a couple of runs I'll beat him. Then Fournier says Oh we will get you a couple of runs all right. He says That's just as easy as catching whales with a angle-worm.

Well Al I must close and go in and get some lunch. My arm feels great and they will have to go some to beat me Johnson or no Johnson.

Your pal,
Jack.

Washington, D. C., September 22.

Friend Al: Well I guess you know by this time that they didn't get no two runs for me, only one, but I beat him just the same. I beat him one to nothing and Callahan was so pleased that he give me a ticket to the theater. I just got back from there and it is pretty late and I already have wrote you one letter to-day but I am going to sit up and tell you about it.

It was cloudy before the game started and when I was warming up I made the remark to Callahan that the dark day ought to make my speed good. He says Yes and of course it will handicap Johnson.

While Washington was takeing their practice their two coachers Schaefer and Altrock got out on the infield and cut up and I pretty near busted laughing at them. They certainly is funny Al. Callahan asked me what was I laughing at and I told him and he says That's the first time I ever seen a pitcher laugh when he was going to work against Johnson. He says Griffith is a pretty good fellow to give us something to laugh at before he shoots that guy at us.

368

I warmed up good and told Schalk not to ask me for my spitter much because my fast one looked faster than I ever seen it. He says it won't make much difference what you pitch to-day. I says Oh, yes, it will because Callahan thinks enough of me to work me against Johnson and I want to show him he didn't make no mistake. Then Gleason says No he didn't make no mistake. Wasteing Cicotte or Scotty would of been a mistake in this game.

Well, Johnson whiffs Weaver and Chase and makes Lord pop out in the first inning. I walked their first guy but I didn't give Milan nothing to bunt and finally he flied out. And then I whiffed the next two. On the bench Callahan says That's the way, boy. Keep that up and we got a chance.

Johnson had fanned four of us when I come up with two out in the third inning and he whiffed me to. I fouled one though that if I had ever got a good hold of I would of knocked out of the park. In the first seven innings we didn't have a hit off of him. They had got five or six lucky ones off of me and I had walked two or three, but I cut loose with all I had when they was men on and they couldn't do nothing with me. The only reason I walked so many was because my fast one was jumping so. Honest Al it was so fast that Evans the umpire couldn't see it half the time and he called a lot of balls that was right over the heart.

Well I come up in the eighth with two out and the score still nothing and nothing. I had whiffed the second time as well as the first but it was account of Evans missing one on me. The eighth started with Shanks muffing a fly ball off of Bodie. It was way out by the fence so he got two bases on it and he went to third while they was throwing Berger out. Then Schalk whiffed.

Callahan says Go up and try to meet one Jack. It might as well be you as anybody else. But your old pal didn't whiff this time Al. He gets two strikes on me with fast ones and then I passed up two bad ones. I took my healthy at the next one and slapped it over first base. I guess I could of made two bases on it but I didn't want to tire myself out. Anyway Bodie scored and I had them beat. And my hit was the only one we got off of him so I guess he is a pretty good pitcher after all Al.

They filled up the bases on me with one out in the ninth but it was

369

pretty dark then and I made McBride and their catcher look like suckers with my speed.

I felt so good after the game that I drunk one of them pink cocktails. I don't know what their name is. And then I sent a postcard to poor little Violet. I don't care nothing about her but it don't hurt me none to try and cheer her up once in a while. We leave here Thursday night for home and they had ought to be two or three letters there for me from Hazel because I haven't heard from her lately. She must of lost my road addresses.

Your pal,
Jack.

P. S. I forgot to tell you what Callahan said after the game. He said I was a real pitcher now and he is going to use me in the city serious. If he does Al we will beat them Cubs sure.

Chicago, Illinois, September 27.

Friend Al: They wasn't no letter here at all from Hazel and I guess she must of been sick. Or maybe she didn't think it was worth while writeing as long as she is comeing next week.

I want to ask you to do me a favor Al and that is to see if you can find me a house down there. I will want to move in with Mrs. Keefe, don't that sound funny Al? sometime in the week of October twelfth. Old man Cutting's house or that yellow house across from you would be O. K. I would rather have the yellow one so as to be near you. Find out how much rent they want Al and if it is not no more than twelve dollars a month get it for me. We will buy our furniture here in Chi when Hazel comes.

We have a couple of days off now Al and then we play St. Louis two games here. Then Detroit comes to finish the season the third and fourth of October.

Your pal,
Jack.

370

Dear Old Al: Thanks Al for getting the house. The one-year lease is O.K. You and Bertha and me and Hazel can have all sorts of good times together. I guess the walk needs repairs but I can fix that up when I come. We can stay at the hotel when we first get there.

I wish you could of came up for the city serious Al but anyway I want you and Bertha to be sure and come up for our wedding. I will let you know the date as soon as Hazel gets here.

The serious starts Tuesday and this town is wild over it. The Cubs finished second in their league and we was fifth in ours but that don't scare me none. We would of finished right on top if I had of been here all season.

Callahan pitched one of the bushers against Detroit this afternoon and they beat him bad. Callahan is saveing up Scott and Allen and Russell and Cicotte and I for the big show. Walsh isn't in no shape and neither is Benz. It looks like I would have a good deal to do because most of them others can't work no more than once in four days and Allen ain't no good at all.

We have a day to rest after to-morrow's game with the Tigers and then we go at them Cubs.

Your pal,
Jack.

P. S. I have got it figured that Hazel is fixing to surprise me by dropping in on me because I haven't heard nothing yet.

Friend Al: Well Al you know by this time that they beat me to-day and tied up the serious. But I have still got plenty of time Al and I will get them before it is over. My arm wasn't feeling good Al and my fast ball didn't hop like it had ought to. But it was the rotten support I got that beat me. That lucky stiff Zimmerman was the only guy that got a real hit off of me and he must of shut his eyes and throwed his bat because the ball he hit was a foot over his head. And if they hadn't been makeing all them errors behind me they wouldn't of been nobody on bases when Zimmerman got that lucky scratch. The serious now

371

stands one and one Al and it is a cinch we will beat them even if they are a bunch of lucky stiffs. They has been great big crowds at both games and it looks like as if we should ought to get over eight hundred dollars a peace if we win and we will win sure because I will beat them three straight if necessary.

But Al I have got bigger news than that for you and I am the happyest man in the world. I told you I had not heard from Hazel for a long time. To-night when I got back to my room they was a letter waiting for me from her.

Al she is married. Maybe you don't know why that makes me happy but I will tell you. She is married to Kid Levy the middle weight. I guess my thirty dollars is gone because in her letter she called me a cheap skate and she inclosed one one-cent stamp and two twos and said she was paying me for the glass of beer I once bought her. I bought her more than that Al but I won't make no holler. She all so said not for me to never come near her or her husband would bust my jaw. I ain't afraid of him or no one else Al but they ain't no danger of me ever bothering them. She was no good and I was sorry the minute I agreed to marry her.

But I was going to tell you why I am happy or maybe you can guess. Now I can make Violet my wife and she's got Hazel beat forty ways. She ain't nowheres near as big as Hazel but she's classier Al and she will make me a good wife. She ain't never asked me for no money.

I wrote her a letter the minute I got the good news and told her to come on over here at once at my expense. We will be married right after the serious is over and I want you and Bertha to be sure and stand up with us. I will wire you at my own expence the exact date.

It all seems like a dream now about Violet and I haveing our mis-understanding Al and I don't see how I ever could of accused her of sending me that postcard. You and Bertha will be just as crazy about her as I am when you see her Al. Just think Al I will be married inside of a week and to the only girl I ever could of been happy with instead of the woman I never really cared for except as a passing fancy. My happyness would be complete Al if I had not of let that woman steal thirty dollars off of me.

Your happy pal,
Jack.

P. S. Hazel probibly would of insisted on us takeing a trip to Niagara falls or somewheres but I know Violet will be perfectly satisfied if I take her right down to Bedford. Oh you little yellow house.

Chicago, Illinois, October 9.

Friend Al: Well Al we have got them beat three games to one now and will wind up the serious to-morrow sure. Callahan sent me in to save poor Allen yesterday and I stopped them dead. But I don't care now Al. I have lost all interest in the game and I don't care if Callahan pitches me to-morrow or not. My heart is just about broke Al and I wouldn't be able to do myself justice feeling the way I do.

I have lost Violet Al and just when I was figureing on being the happyest man in the world. We will get the big money but it won't do me no good. They can keep my share because I won't have no little girl to spend it on.

Her answer to my letter was waiting for me at home to-night. She is engaged to be married to Joe Hill the big lefthander Jennings got from Providence. Honest Al I don't see how he gets by. He ain't got no more curve ball than a rabbit and his fast one floats up there like a big balloon. He beat us the last game of the regular season here but it was because Callahan had a lot of bushers in the game.

I wish I had knew then that he was stealing my girl and I would of made Callahan pitch me against him. And when he come up to bat I would of beaned him. But I don't suppose you could hurt him by hitting him in the head. The big stiff. Their wedding ain't going to come off till next summer and by that time he will be pitching in the Southwestern Texas League for about fifty dollars a month.

Violet wrote that she wished me all the luck and happyness in the world but it is too late for me to be happy Al and I don't care what kind of luck I have now.

Al you will have to get rid of that lease for me. Fix it up the best way you can. Tell the old man I have changed my plans. I don't know just yet what I will do but maybe I will go to Australia with Mike Donlin's team. If I do I won't care if the boat goes down or not. I don't believe I will even come back to Bedford this winter. It would drive

373

me wild to go past that little house every day and think how happy I might of been.

Maybe I will pitch to-morrow Al and if I do the serious will be over to-morrow night. I can beat them Cubs if I get any kind of decent support. But I don't care now Al.

Yours truly,
Jack.

Chicago, Illinois, October 12.

Al: Your letter received. If the old man won't call it off I guess I will have to try and rent the house to some one else. Do you know of any couple that wants one Al? It looks like I would have to come down there myself and fix things up someway. He is just mean enough to stick me with the house on my hands when I won't have no use for it.

They beat us the day before yesterday as you probably know and it rained yesterday and to-day. The papers says it will be all O. K. to-morrow and Callahan tells me I am going to work. The Cub pitchers was all shot to peaces and the bad weather is just nuts for them because it will give Cheney a good rest. But I will beat him Al if they don't kick it away behind me.

I must close because I promised Allen the little lefthander that I would come over to his flat and play cards a while to-night and I must wash up and change my collar. Allen's wife's sister is visiting them again and I would give anything not to have to go over there. I am through with girls and don't want nothing to do with them.

I guess it is maybe a good thing it rained to-day because I dreamt about Violet last night and went out and got a couple of high balls before breakfast this morning. I hadn't never drank nothing before breakfast before and it made me kind of sick. But I am all O.K. now.

Your pal,
Jack.

Chicago, Illinois, October 13.

Dear Old Al: The serious is all over Al. We are the champions and I done it. I may be home the day after to-morrow or I may not come for a couple of days. I want to see Comiskey before I leave and fix up about my contract for next year. I won't sign for no less than five thousand and if he hands me a contract for less than that I will leave the White Sox flat on their back. I have got over fourteen hundred dollars now Al with the city serious money which was $814.30 and I don't have to worry.

Them reporters will have to give me a square deal this time Al. I had everything and the Cubs done well to score a run. I whiffed Zimmerman three times. Some of the boys say he ain't no hitter but he is a hitter and a good one Al only he could not touch the stuff I got. The umps give them their run because in the fourth inning I had Leach flatfooted off of second base and Weaver tagged him O. K. but the umps wouldn't call it. Then Schulte the lucky stiff happened to get a hold of one and pulled it past first base. I guess Chase must of been asleep. Anyway they scored but I don't care because we piled up six runs on Cheney and I drove in one of them myself with one of the prettiest singles you ever see. It was a spitter and I hit it like a shot. If I had hit it square it would of went out of the park.

Comiskey ought to feel pretty good about me winning and I guess he will give me a contract for anything I want. He will have to or I will go to the Federal League.

We are all invited to a show to-night and I am going with Allen and his wife and her sister Florence. She is O. K. Al and I guess she thinks the same about me. She must because she was out to the game to-day and seen me hand it to them. She maybe ain't as pretty as Violet and Hazel but as they say beauty isn't only so deep.

Well Al tell the boys I will be with them soon. I have gave up the idea of going to Australia because I would have to buy a evening fulldress suit and they tell me they cost pretty near fifty dollars.

Your truly,
Jack.

375

Friend Al: Never mind about that lease. I want the house after all Al and I have got the surprise of your life for you.

When I come home to Bedford I will bring my wife with me. I and Florence fixed things all up after the show last night and we are going to be married to-morrow morning. I am a busy man to-day Al because I have got to get the license and look round for furniture. And I have also got to buy some new cloths but they are haveing a sale on Cottage Grove Avenue at Clark's store and I know one of the clerks there.

I am the happyest man in the world Al. You and Bertha and I and Florence will have all kinds of good times together this winter because I know Bertha and Florence will like each other. Florence looks something like Bertha at that. I am glad I didn't get tied up with Violet or Hazel even if they was a little bit prettier than Florence.

Florence knows a lot about baseball for a girl and you would be surprised to hear her talk. She says I am the best pitcher in the league and she has saw them all. She all so says I am the best looking ball player she ever seen but you know how girls will kid a guy Al. You will like her O. K. I fell for her the first time I seen her.

Your old pal,
Jack.

"I think you just missed something. The ball went up in the air and somebody caught it and the crowd's yelling like mad."

You Know Me Alice

*(Some Correspondence We Might
Have If Ring Lardner Were Alive Today)*

BY PETER DE VRIES

Westport, Conn., May 2.

DEAR ALICE: WELL HON HERE I AM MANaging a little league team in Westport. The job at the Bridgeport Brass is all set and we can get personaly welded as soon as your mother's hip mends and you can get out here. Meanwhile I'm living in a rooming house near the New Haven R.R. tracks here riding the train to work so I'm what you could call a commuter only going the other way, not one them Madison Ave. birds carrying one them lether reticules into the Big Town and back every day. So hence the postmark which must of gave you quite a turn.

Managing a ball team ain't what it use to be in the old days and may still be out there in Keokuk. Time was when all you had to know about your material was wether they could do something with a bat besides supply a little extra ventilation on hot days or pull down a fast clothesliner off second. Now you have to worry about tension spans and what they call stribling rivalry and one thing another—in other words why they might not be performing up to snuff on the above. The last mentioned is when you have two brothers on the same team as I happen to of drew. Their mother told me they have these feelings of mutual hostility due to a family situation which she will go into with me in more detail later if they is any danger of our not copping the penant and that it was her experience that the best way out of a jam was substitute situations. So I says how would it be if I always had one them warming the bench to go in for the other if needs be and she siezed my hand and kissed it and then went and hid in the car she had brung them in, a blue Jag convertible which the family have been driving with the top up I understand because they are in mourning.

Well kid they being the first arrivals for the opening practise I got a bat and started hitting them some fungos. The mother sat shivering

in the Jag watching the proseedings through the windshield. This is what she seen.

The one kid whose name is Martin had this idea that somebody had ast him to impersonate a croquet wicket in creative play because every time I hit him a grounder he would have his feet planted the exact distance apart at just the right time for the ball to pass through without no hindranse. After about five or six of these flawless imitations the mother came over to shed some light on it. He has this will to fail she said and went back to shiver in the Jag some more. I thanked her for this piece of info to help me in forming my first team and turned to look for the brother.

This kid is a compulsory eater they call them. He was nowheres to be seen at first then I made out a speck against the refreshment stand which at this field is about 500 yards from our diamond, one of 3, no doubt telling the woman on hot dogs there to keep 'em coming. The mother started up the Jag and drove over to get him hollering out the window at me He fears competition and seeks escape in food as she went by. When the car was gone I yelled to the other kid What's your brother's name? and he yelled back Stringfellow and I had the case diagnozed.

By now the mothers were arriving in droves with their hopefuls by auto (nobody walks in Westport unless an ump gives them a base on balls) most of the mothers and an occasional father staying to have a word with me and there being enough kids to keep theirselves busy for a while on their own I went over to the bleachers where I set up a small office to hear out the parents lining up with dossiers on the prospective athaletes.

I'll give you my starting lineup next time preferring to use the rest of this sheet to remind you that letter writing ain't my fort and that I wisht you was here in person holding it with me. You know me Alice.

Yours sincerely, Ed.

Dear Alice: Well hon I'm writing this in the shop where I got a little lunch time left over on top of a crate.

Well Alice my starting lineup on the first game was as follows. In left, center and right I got three oral types which is fine for talking it up around the outfield. On first a kid who has a thing about sliding. I let him bat just before my two best hitters so in case he gets on third he'll have the highest possible chance to coalchute it home looking dramatic and important like his mother says he needs to while he spanks the dust off hisself to gain confidence. Martin is on second. I can't do nothing with his brother while he is on the pickalily and if he muffed one might head strait for the refreshment stand to seek consolation there and never be seen again. I can't take the responsibility. Shortstop and third I have very little to go on as they are underpriviledged kids from the r.r. tracks nobody ever gives no thought to, just good ball players in the hot spots though I am told one of them might be out stealing something more serious than second if they wasn't second to steal with the girls looking on. The catcher is a swell natured kid whose as broad as he's long and can stop any reasonable pitch because of the sheer bulk there is to get past. You can always use an obesity case behind the plate.

Now on this level hon which is the beginners from 8 on up your ever-perennial problem is pitching. Few have the experience or control at that age. In making up my notes on my squad a woman named Mrs. Niswonger said to me in a interview I granted her conserning her son Artie who wanted to pitch Nicknames are very revealing don't you know and they call Artie the Strike Out King. Well I learned through some side investigation that they call him that when he is at bat, when he is on the mound he is known as the Sultan of Swat due to how good he can make even a kronic whiffer look. I ast her didn't she think in that case we had ought to start somebody else in the box and she says What and deel him a blow to his eggo from which he might never recover? In this part the country where they know more about those things you put players in where they're weak so as to bolster their confidense and make athaletes out of them. The only other pitcher I had was no better than Niswonger anyway so I started Niswonger.

381

So that was the opening roster for our first game. It was with the Bluejays. We're the Robins so you can see we have a bird moteef this yr. The plate ump was the guidance counselor for one of the schools so hence he knew most of the kids' potenshul already and how to sound off the calls wether loud or easy on their nerves and etc. A local dentist umped bases for us.

Niswonger wasn't no worse than the Bluejays' pitcher. He walked the first eight of our batters giving us five runs and three men on base with none away. The suspense was unbearable—when would he put one over? In the consulting room (formerly known as the bleachers) the mothers were yacking it up amongst theirselves, trading slants on their sons and occasinally shouting That's looking 'em over! and It only takes one! and so on from lists that they carried with suitable things to holler. At this point the kid with the thing about sliding was on third and with ball four called on the batter he came home—another forced run. As he strolls home his mother jumps to her feet in the stands and yells Slide! He does. He takes a running start and then dropping down on one side just as pretty as you'd want shoots across the plate like a torpedo nearly spiking the guidance counselor who got his feet out of the way just in time.

Suddenly the pitcher got his range and retired three of us in a row and in the bottom of the inning Niswonger promply oblidged the opposition by starting up the Big Parade around the bags again. He walked seven in a row and then finally got one over that the Bluejay at bat sent into left field for a homer and a two run lead for the enemy.

At this junkture I debated yanking Niswonger. But sensing what was in the wind Mrs. Niswonger hightailed it over to our dugout hauling the plate ump with her—this guidance counselor. He sketched in the basic factors in the bind we were in. The kid's father couldn't get past the Biltmore Men's Bar unless hogtied and dragged past and then only with the reminder that they was still the bar car to sit in and overshoot his station by a couple stops landing him closer to Wallingford than Westport and this together with the threat of iminent divorce it led to give the kid such a feeling of uncertainty that if I pulled him at this crisis I and I alone would have to answer for the consequences. He wouldn't—the ump that is. He seemed to know what he was talking

382

about. He got his P.H.D. at the U. of Pennsylvania with a thesis on sulking which he is the leading authority on so I let things ride. All this while the base ump was handing out spice drops to the infield from a good supply he had on him. As a town dentist he can't see why all the to do about a few cavities.

Suffise it to say Niswonger worked his way out of the hole and we tied the score and then they was a sudden shower which the way they performed I says they should ought to all go take anyways includeing the mothers. One woman listening to me dish it out in that vain said You must get a grate deal of compensation out of bossing a bunch of kids around and I says to her Lady nobody offered me a nickle to do this and I would not except it if they did. I couldn't button my lip but went on to say that I liked working with boys if only I could get rid of the full cooperation of the parents espesially the women. Then the kid with the will to fail's mother got into the act to my surprise. She was eavesdropping on the rhubarb from the Jag where she suddenly must of got her courage up because she says Evadently you are equally good at pushing ladies around and do we deserve to sirvive as a race and I says If you weren't all ladies I would give you my opinion of you in two words, blather skites. Then she says My husband will wish to see you tomorrow or so and I says Send him around, haveing visions of being strode up to by this guy in one them gaberdeen suits Alice and being slapped across the chops with one them lether handbags that they carry. Which would at least bring the rhubarb up to the man to man level where it belongs. All this while we were getting no dryer accept for the woman snug in the Jag. I was between her and the first woman with two out in the top of the third and the score tied eight all and a man on second. Then the first woman says You certainly seem to have a lot of hidden hostilities and I says What's hidden about them? and she didn't have no comeback. I may of been a little sharp but my job is hard enough with a lot of bystanders going off ½ cocked about how it should ought to be done.

Well with the rain showing no signs of letting up they was nothing to do but call the game a tie to be played off later though who picked up the marbles on the rhubarb I will leave you to be the judge. You know me Alice. I don't want nobody sticking their $0.02 into my affairs

383

though I am perfectly willing to listen to any reasonable offer of advice even in this matriarky I think they call this type of culture.

I agree with you about the amount of furniture we should start off with though why it should all be bird's eye maple I fail to see. I have always kind of had this feeling of mutual hostility toward bird's eye maple. More of this later.

Yours, Ed.

Westport, Conn., july 2.

Dear Alice: It's grate news your mother's hip is better and well enough for you to practically garantee you'll be here in a week. All as I can say is I'll be glad when we can get settled. But I wisht you could of been here with me last night. As you know we finally had this playoff of that tie game with the Bluejays which was also a game breaking a tie with them for fourth place and brother! I never see such excitement. It was the most satisfying evening of my life sports-wise.

To begin with they was no mothers around. They all went to the Mental Health Ball which is more important this year than ever before they tell me because of the whopping amount that has to be raised. Malajustments are on the increase in all these communities where they take such an interest in their children's minds and organize their play and all for some strange reason another. The guidance counselor was chairman of the affair so he wasn't on hand neither. The dentist umped both plate and bases, doing so from the pitcher's box.

While he may be a firstrate dentist he could use a good eye doctor hisself judging from some them calls Alice. The kid with the thing about sliding has got another thing about ducking pitches. It's the same thing really the way they explain it. He has the same chance to drop beautifully putting on the same kind of show stirring up dust which he spanks off his uniform like one who has just escaped sudden death to bolster his eggo. They was a fast ball heading straight for his coco but even as he made for terra firma the ump yelled Steerike! pointing a thumb over his shoulder in the general direction of Cos Cob to say he was out. Well Alice it is the first time I ever see a man called out

on two strikes but the ump's memory was as stubborn as it was wobbly and he stood on his right not to have to reverse a decision if he didn't feel like it. I for my part told the kids to show some sportsmanship and stow the repertee such as Get a tin cup with some pencils in it! and etc. But that ain't how we made Little League history that night. I'm coming to that now.

Emotions by this junkture were raw. Both sides had suffered equally from the ½ baked umping so never mind that but by the last inning as a result and with no mothers to guide them they were playing like fiends. Since we were the home team this time we had last licks. Not that we ever got them—and thereby hangs the tale.

Midway through their licks the Bluejays put in a pinch hitter with two on and two away and the score tied five all. Here the Bluejay runner on first started yelling to the batter Put one through second where you like to Jack! He couldn't catch a cold in an icebox in Alaska! Meaning rightly enough Martin our croquet wicket. But by now Martin had had it. His dandruff was up like nothing I ever see. Thank God his mother wasn't around to badger me with no substitute situations, just let him stay there and take it. When our catcher threw a bad return to Niswonger who was pitching it went over Niswonger's head toward Martin and this time he managed to get hold of it. Well taunts the wit on first what happened? This says Martin and threw the ball at him like a rock. He caught it making sure to keep his foot on the bag so as not to be called out and shot it right back just as hard as *he* could. This time it went as usual through Martin's legs and the other kid says You'd make a grate football player—a center. That did it. Martin ran over and let him have it with both fists.

Well hon don't ask me to describe in detail what happened because I couldn't. In a second the whole infield was a malay I couldn't begin to give a blow by blow account of and blow by blow it would have to be because this wasn't just no ordinary rhubarb. This was It. Neither I or the other manager interfered. It did our hearts too good to see it. It thrilled us. Something went up my spine like band music good and loud at the sight of those boys out there mixing it up. Being boys at last. I never see a group so integrated. You couldn't tell whose arms and legs belonged to who they was such a solid tangle of them whaling

the tar out of one another. The ump didn't interfere neither having even less objection to loose teeth than to cavities. He stood smiling by along with us managers.

I'd say we beat the Bluejays that night though I'd have no way of proving it accept by a count of shiners and bloody noses. By the time we did pull the last ones apart figuring we had had our hearts done enough good and got our charges tidied up a little it was too dark to resoom. The other manager and I chipped in to buy them all pop at the refreshment stand where they all rushed pellmell like one happy family now.

Well so ends one Little League season for one manager. Probably his last judging from what the mothers said when they heard what happened. But it's just as well they bad me a fond ado before the official farewell because the boys chipped in and bought me a beautiful silver money clip with my inishles on it whereas if the mothers had of still had a hand in the proseedings you and I might now be libel to own one them pieces of dead wood that look so charming on tables that ain't got no shape neither and how would you fit that in with bird's eye maple Alice? But it has been a mighty educational experience for this gink. I picked up some pretty good pointers on raising kids so come on out here and let's get started on that family. Boys that is. We'll add the girls later for you if needs be. Financially speaking-wise I know what a full house means these days but I'm game. You know me Alice.

Love, Ed.

◆

BIG-LEAGUE POTABLE LINEUP

First base—Sherry Robertson   Outfield—Half Pint Rye
Second base—Mickey Finn   Outfield—Tinsley Ginn
Shortstop—Bobby Wine   Catcher—Josh Gibson
Third base—Billy Lush   Pitcher—Wedo Martini
Outfield—Brandy Davis   Pedro Borbon

Over My Head

BY ROGER ANGELL

MY AGENT, MORRIE, CAME TO SEE ME IN the locker room after a night game in May. I was surprised to see him; he hadn't done any business for me all season. Last year, it was different. After I'd hung up that good E.R.A., third best in the league, and pitched five shutout relief innings in the Series, I was a hot item, and Morrie was busy for me all the time. I did TV plugs for Gillette blades and Camels, spoke on juvenile delinquency at a Father-Son dinner of the McKeesport P.T.A., had a guest shot on "Omnibus," and all that stuff. I made a bundle. Then, this spring, I was a holdout for five weeks, because the management sent me a contract that must have been meant for some kid signed out of the Little Leagues, so I never did get trained right. I had a sore arm all through April. Then I got racked up in Kansas City and again in Cleveland on the same Western swing, and I was finished as a celebrity. They made me second long man in the bull pen—the victim they bring in when the club is five runs down in the third inning and your infielders are stopping easy grounders with their chests. I'd got so I was picking up the paper every morning expecting to read I'd been traded to the Phillies. So why would Morrie want to see me?

"Hi ya, Buzz," Morrie said. "How's the arm?"

"It fell off last week," I said. "I'm having it embalmed."

"How'd you like to make a wad of cash?" he asked.

"Doing what—selling birdseed door to door?"

"No, Buzz. It's a special deal, something brand-new. There's a thousand clams in it for you. Listen, you ever read that magazine *Sports Illusory?*"

"Are you *kidding?*"

"I know what you mean," Morrie said. "Let me put it another way. Did you read that book by that writer who pitched against an all-star big-league team in an exhibition game? George Plimpton his name is.

387

You know—he'd never pitched since school, and he wanted to see what it would feel like out there and then write about it all. He wrote it first for some sports magazine—they put up the money for the ballplayers—and then he turned it into this book. It's called 'Out of My League.' "

"I heard about it." I said, "but I haven't read the book yet. But I've told everybody I'd like it for my birthday. Marianne Moore gave it a terrific review in the *Trib*." I was getting interested.

"Good," Morrie said. "Well, *Sports Illusory* wants you to do the same thing, almost. They want you to spend a day working on the staff of a magazine, just like a big-time writer or editor. Then they want you to write a piece about it for them. Get the idea? It's a hell of a human-interest story, backing up their big theme that ballplayers are fine, normal people, interested in the arts and all, just like other average Joes. They'll pay a G note for the job. How does it hit you?"

"Well . . . " I said. I tried to sound dubious, but the truth is my heart was racing with excitement. It was crazy and it would take nerve, but what big-leaguer could turn down a chance like this? Like every red-blooded American ballplayer, I've always wanted to be a writer. I've read every word Ernest Hemingway has written for *Life*. Ever since my sand-lot days, I have stayed up late Sunday nights to watch Bennett Cerf on "What's My Line?" And other ballplayers have made it in the world of letters, haven't they? Whenever we play Cincinnati in spring exhibition games, I get a kick just being on the same field with Jim Brosnan, the author of "The Long Season." I've even copied some of his mannerisms on the mound—the way he mutters those lines from Eliot and Pound when he's glaring down at the batters. "What's the magazine I'd be working for?" I managed to ask.

"It's the best, Buzz," he said. "The *Dijon Review*."

"Wow!" I murmured. This *was* the big league! The *Dijon Review*— the most intellectual, the most shrill, the most unforgiving of the little reviews! I could feel the sweat beginning to trickle down my wrists, and I knew I'd lose my nerve if I thought about it a minute longer. "O.K.," I said, looking up at Morrie and trying to manage a smile. "I'll do it."

◆

The day set for my adventure was a Monday in June, an open date on the team's schedule, and the intervening weeks flew by all too fast for my heightened state of nerves. More than once, I picked up the telephone to call Morrie and tell him I had thought better of the whole foolhardy scheme, but some curious sense of pride always made me put it down again. After all, I'd remind myself, I was introspective, well read, full of normal literary ambitions. Even if I got my ears knocked off, it would be something to tell my grandchildren about— the day I matched my taste against the best aesthetes of my time. I found it hard to concentrate on my work; sitting in the bull pen during a Sunday doubleheader, I would lose track of the score. The roar of the crowd and the harsh cries of the peanut venders would fade from my ears, replaced in my mind by the crisp crackle of manuscripts, the sibilant crawl of blue pencils across paper, and the civilized murmur of apothegms and witty, barbed rejoinders. My sleep became irregular, and on the road I fell into the habit of arising during the small hours to copy out passages from Cyril Connolly's "The Unquiet Grave" on the backs of hotel menus. Once, in New York, I slipped out of my room at five in the morning and walked through the dawn-swept streets and found myself at last standing in front of the West Side brownstone that houses the editorial offices of the *Dijon Review*. "In there," I whispered to myself, eying the temple, "just a few days from now . . ." Inside my pockets, my typing fingers were tapping out unconscious arpeggios.

In the last few days, the realities of plans and training helped to steady me. Morrie and I had a final conference with the editor of *Sports Illusory*, who feigned indifference toward my coming ordeal. Just before I left, however, the expression on his tanned athlete's face softened, and he said, "I can't help admitting I'm going to envy you in there, Buzz. You know, just before I go to sleep at night, I always have this same crazy thought. I find myself reading and then *rejecting* this long, long poem by Randall Jarrell!"

I went to J. Press, the literary costumers, and had myself outfitted— charcoal flannel trousers, linen hopsack jacket, black knit tie. I bought a pair of plain white sneakers at Feron's, and then, as an act of pure braggadocio, completed the outfit with the purchase of a green tweed

cap, belted in back, at Paul Stuart. One day, when I arrived thus attired at the ballpark, Clancy, the manager, stopped me with a puzzled look on his big face. "You got a shoulder kink, Buzz?" he asked. "You're walking kinda crooked. Maybe you need an hour in the whirlpool bath, hunh?"

I blushed and straightened up, assuring him I was all right. But I knew what had happened. My old Tom Wolfe crouch, the one I affected so assiduously in my youth, had come back upon me. A good omen indeed!

Friday night before my Monday, Buck Willis, my roomie, and I drove up to Yaddo. It was after ten when we arrived, however, and a surly gatekeeper barred our way. "All the typewriters is locked up for the night," he muttered. "All the writers, too. Besides, I can't go around letting just any old hack in here." Disappointed, we saved something from the journey by circling through Bread Loaf, where a kindly lady who teaches Middle English at Mount Holyoke allowed me to loosen up on her big Remington. I worked out for an hour, testing old muscles. My motion was good, but I wasn't hitting the space bar with the old confidence.

I was ready when Monday morning came. I arose feeling refreshed, aware of a faint tremor in the backs of my knees, but grateful, on the whole, that *der Tag* had arrived. Then, as I stood in front of my mirror, making last adjustments to my uniform, my heart gave a great thump of dismay. I had no Fowler! It was a shocking oversight on my part. I could not turn up at the *Dijon Review* and confess to such an omission, and I was only too aware that no editor willingly lends his Fowler, even to an officemate who is trying to break out of a slump. That is one of the oldest superstitions in the game. I made a frantic, ridiculous search of my room, but I knew only too well where my own Fowler was—among my broken toys and rusted electric trains in the back attic of my parents' house in Des Moines. I grabbed the telephone and called Lefty Kolb, our team's affable knuckleballer. "Listen, Lefty," I said, spilling out the words in my haste, "have you got an old Fowler you could lend me for the day?"

"A what?" he said sleepily.

"A Fowler's 'Modern English Usage.' Any edition will do, but I've got to have it right away."

390

"Gee, no, Buzz," he said. "I happen to know, because I was looking for mine only last week. I'm sorry as hell."

I thanked him, hung up, and hurried out to see if I could buy the volume. But no bookstores were open at that early hour. I had to settle for a Little Golden Dictionary, purchased from a drugstore. I carried it under my arm all day, hoping my temporary colleagues would accept it as a personal literary eccentricity.

◆

"Editors' entrance?" I inquired, standing outside an open door in the dim third-floor corridor. I could feel my heart thumping under my button-down shirt.

"It's the only door we got," said the young man sitting inside, not lifting his eyes from his *Daily News.*

I entered, removed my cap, and extended my hand. "Ty Cobb," I said, employing the amusing sobriquet we had agreed upon at *Sports Illusory.* "I'm sort of working here today."

"I heard," the man said, giving me a soft, dry handshake. "I'm Eric." He had a shock of very blond hair that hung down over his eyes, and I noticed that he wore purple socks and a pair of cracked patent-leather pumps.

The room was littered with newspapers, disorderly piles of letters— bills, by the look of them—and empty cardboard containers of coffee. There was a standing screen to my left, and from behind this I heard the low hum of voices and the clink of teacups in the next room. These scholarly sights and sounds unmanned me for a moment. "Look," I said to Eric. "Can I warm with you for a few minutes? Before I go in there?"

"O.K.," he said indifferently. "But I'm just the office boy around here."

We warmed for ten minutes, tossing aphorisms and capping easy quotations. I began to feel better, and I ventured a pitch I had used with some success in college. "Isn't it curious," I said, "that neither Cowley nor Trilling has observed that the watery images in the final sentences of both 'A Farewell to Arms' and 'Tender Is the Night' are direct, if unconscious, inheritors of a lineage tracing back to the closing passages of 'Moby Dick,' in which the Pequod slips beneath those

391

tiresomely symbolic waves? It's a curious lacuna in our critical thesaurus."

The effect of this upon Eric was unexpected. He straightened up and glared at me angrily. "Watch that stuff," he said bitterly. "No rhetorical questions without you give me a warning, see? Watch that showboating, bo."

"Oh, sure," I said, abashed. "Sure, sure, sure. I'm sorry. Anything you say."

I was now ready; the hour had come. Eric led me into the back room, and I introduced myself awkwardly. I recognized most of the faces, of course; as a boy, I had pasted their likenesses, clipped from Sunday book-review sections, inside my locker door. Blevins Carroll, the editor, was seated at a high old-fashioned roll-top desk, his great forehead gleaming palely above a green eyeshade. Morgan MacPhee and Hastings Latrobe, the devastating pair recently purchased from *Partisan Review* in exchange for five British critics and an undisclosed amount of cash, were bent over the morning *Times,* working the cross-word puzzle together. A fourth figure was stretched out on an old cot against one wall, his head buried in his arms. From time to time, he groaned. Too much *espresso* the night before, I guessed privately. The first three acknowledged my presence with curt nods. I was aware of a professionalism, a true, burning intolerance, in this room, and I knew happily that I would not encounter any false bonhomie here today. These men were admitting me to their company as an equal, with all the cynical hostility of the élite.

Thus encouraged, I began to take careful note of details—material to flesh out my narrative for *Sports Illusory*. I perceived that although Blevins Carroll talked out of the right side of his mouth, he wrote with his left hand, a tremendous defensive advantage in an editor who is also a novelist. (Most editors are right-handed.) Like all true intellectuals, these men smoked cigarettes. There were open packs all over the room, in pockets and on desks, within reach of limber, preoccupied fingers. Intellectuals light their cigarettes with matches, never lighters, striking flame with a single, deft inward motion, and usually throwing the used match stubs on the floor. I noted that the members of the staff usually addressed each other by their first names, only rarely

392

employing such alternatives as "old chap" or "fella." This fact, in turn, led me to a further discovery: many critics have first names that are more customarily surnames—Blevins, Morgan, Hastings, and so forth. This gives them a superiority in bylines almost from birth.

"Well, we might as well get to it," Carroll said at last. He leaned forward and tossed me a thick, untidy sheaf of manuscript. "Anything here we should use?" he asked.

I licked my lips. I was aware that the three were watching me closely. I looked down at the manuscript. It had been scrawled, apparently with a blunt pencil, on flimsy sheets of pink paper. It was in a language I didn't recognize, but the varying length of the lines made me guess it was a piece of free verse. "Hmm," I said, stalling. "Well . . . Well, it isn't typewritten."

The three men looked at each other in surprise, exchanging smiles of apparent relief. "Yes," Latrobe said eagerly, "and we don't accept untyped submissions."

"I never thought of that!" MacPhee said.

"And he didn't enclose any return postage," Carroll added. He took the manuscript from me and dropped it in a wastebasket. "Nice work, Mr. Cobb," he said, looking at me with new respect.

Alas, it was not to remain as easy as that. Overconfident, working too fast, I soon found myself making the simplest anti-intellectual blunders. I voted against a film review, a reëvaluation of Bugs Bunny as the American *Übermensch,* on the ground that it was frivolous. Carroll snatched it back angrily, stating that it would probably be the lead article in their next issue. "Don't you know Warner Brothers cartoons are way, way in, man?" he said. Then I voted *for* an essay on the pre-pubertal years of Samuel Beckett, which struck me as fresh and amusing. "Pap!" Carroll snorted. *"Kitschy-*koo," Latrobe muttered. The figure on the couch shuddered at my obtuseness. A terrible exhaustion flowed over me. I was in deep waters, far over my head.

At this juncture, Eric's face appeared around the side of the screen. "Omnescu is here for his interview," he announced.

For a moment, my nerve failed me utterly. Tired, flustered, my ill-conditioned critical reflexes already screaming in protest, I was now to face the most feared literary slugger of our time. Omnescu, the free-

393

swinging Rumanian avant-gardist, author of three volumes of *haiku* written in classical Etruscan, was about to take part in one of the *Dijon Review*'s famed interviews-in-depth, and *I* was expected to lead our team's assault. "No, no!" I cried weakly. "It's too much to ask. I can't go on. These bone chips in my writing hand . . ."

"Courage, Cobb," Latrobe whispered in my ear. "We'll be here behind you, fielding the answers. Just lay your searching questions down the middle."

Well, I tried. I'll say that for myself in retrospect. When the great man had been ushered in and seated in a broken armchair, I cleared my throat and forced myself to look at his fearsome visage rising above his filthy turtleneck sweater and huge shoulders like an angry winter moon over a range of mountains. His cold zircon eyes, which I had seen heretofore only from a seat in the back rows of the Y.M.H.A. Poetry Center auditorium, now fixed themselves on me with horrid anticipation. I thought confusedly of my success with the foreign manuscript, and stammered out, "Mr. Omnescu, do you, uh, write with a p-pencil?"

To my astonishment, he popped a soft answer straight back to my teammates. "Hah!" he said. "Axcellant qvastion. Axcellant! Until last year, Omnescu writes always with pancil. But last January, with Guggenheim money, Omnescu buys electric typewriter. Results: electric!" And for the next ten mintues he chatted warmly about his rapport with a writing device so happily symbolic of our depersonalized milieu, while the editors scribbled busily and gratefully in their notebooks.

Unfortunately, I was now so emboldened that I decided on another change-up pitch. It was to be my last effort of the day. "Sir," I said, "have you read and been influenced by Yogi Berra's autobiography?"

His face turned red, then purple. "Yoga!" he exploded. "You ask me—Omnescu—about yoga? That qvackery? You waste my time with meesticism, with Indian gymnastics, with something for screenwriters on nut diets? Omnescu will put you straight on yoga, you meeserable counter-intellactual." Spluttering, jabbering incoherently, lapsing frequently into his native tongue, he launched on a monologue so verbose and so rambling that long before he had finished, Carroll and MacPhee and Latrobe had dropped their pencils out of sheer ennui.

"That'll be all," Carroll said to me crisply. He beckoned to Eric to take my place in the circle of chairs. I had been relieved again. I was washed up in this league.

Weeping, I dropped my little Golden Dictionary and stumbled out and down the stairs toward the street. I had forgotten my tweed cap, but I knew I would never need it again. Dejected, sore of head and spirit, I trudged slowly toward the subway. Then, just before I reached the corner, my glance fell upon two ragged urchins in my path. They were bent over, unaware of me, writing busily with chalk on the pavement. Their scrawled words stretched the entire width of the sidewalk, from curb to building front.

"Hey, Jim-mee!" one of them yelled. "Watch me, Jim-mee! Watch me write. I'm William Faulkner, Jim-mee! I'm Faulkner writing!"

"Go-wann!" the other called back, scribbling excitedly. "Lookit me, Billy. Watch *me* write! *I'm* Van Wyck Brooks!"

Touched, deeply moved by these innocent gamins, I blew my nose and began to cheer up. "The game will go on," I whispered to myself. "Even without me, it will go on. The great American pastime will never die."

NEW INDUCTEES

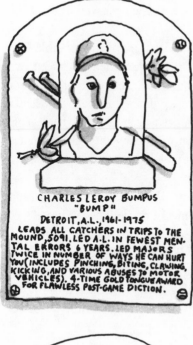

CHARLES LEROY BUMPUS
"BUMP"
DETROIT, A.L., 1961-1975
LEADS ALL CATCHERS IN TRIPS TO THE
MOUND, 5091. LED A.L. IN FEWEST MEN-
TAL ERRORS 6 YEARS. LED MAJORS
TWICE IN NUMBER OF WAYS HE CAN HURT
YOU (INCLUDES PINCHING, BITING, CLAWING,
KICKING, AND VARIOUS ABUSES TO MOTOR
VEHICLES). 4-TIME GOLD TONGUE AWARD
FOR FLAWLESS POST-GAME DICTION.

DARRYL HUTCHINS STILLPASS
"THE GUY"
CHICAGO, N.L., 1965-1969
HOLDS MANY N.L. RECORDS, AMONG
THEM: OUT-OF-PLAY BALLS TOSSED TO
SCREAMING FANS, 3012; DOUBLE-PUMPS
ON THROWS FROM RIGHT FIELD, 1619;
UNNECESSARY SLIDES, 3006. PIONEERED
USE OF AIR BAG TO REDUCE RISK
OF INJURY IN OUTFIELD COLLISIONS.

LAWRENCE MUTZ FOYLE
"MOP"
CINCINNATI, N.L. 1963-1978
LED N.L. IN BOO-INCURRING PICK OFF
ATTEMPTS 4 YEARS; FIRST MODERN
LEFT-HAND "SHORT MAN" TO LOWER
PANT LEG BELOW CALF. N.L. CAREER LEADER
IN SIGNS SHAKEN OFF, 6327. HOLDS
WORLD SERIES RECORD FOR MOST
APPEARANCES WITHOUT USING
RESIN BAG, 17.

BENJAMIN TODD BARNES
"B.T."
BALTIMORE, A.L., 1957-1974
ALL-TIME MAJOR-LEAGUE LEADER
IN MOST ROUTINE POP-UPS TURNED
INTO ADVENTURES, 2781. FIRST A.L.
PLAYER TO ADJUST CAP PRIOR TO
BATTING. LED LEAGUE TWICE IN
FALSE STARTS TO FIRST BASE AFTER
ASSUMING BALL FOUR. MOST
AMUSING A.L. PLAYER IN 1970.

CRAWFORD

From The Long Season

BY JIM BROSNAN

March 9, 1960—St. Petersburg, Fla.

SOLLY HEMUS [MANAGER OF THE ST. LOUIS Cardinals] called a meeting for the last workout before the start of the exhibition season. "We're going to use the same signs in these games as we will all year. So let's pay attention." He turned to Johnny Keane. "John?"

Keane jumped onto a bat trunk waving his ever-present fungo stick for quiet. Broglio murmured to me, "I think he sleeps with that god-damn bat."

"These are the signs we're gonna give from third base. Solly will be on the bench." Keane waved his bat, relegating Hemus forever to the dugout. "You pitchers get together with the catchers later and work out your own signs. These are for the hitters, and we don't want anybody missing signs, 'cause it just messes up everybody, including the guy who messes it up. Now, then, we're gonna have an Indicator, signs for bunting, taking, and hit-and-run. We're gonna have a take-off sign, and a sign for the squeeze play.

"The most important sign is the Indicator. When I rub my hand over the Cardinal on my shirt, that means a sign is on. You see me rub the bird and you watch my right hand . . . right hand only. Forget I got a left hand. With my right hand I'm gonna touch some part of my uniform or body. One touch . . . it might be my cap, or neck, or pants, or arm sleeve . . . one touch, and you're taking. Two touches and you're bunting; three touches, hit-and-run . . . on that pitch, 'cause the runner is going. Those are the three signs you gotta look for when you go up to hit.

"Now, when you're at the plate, look down at me on every pitch. Maybe I don't wanna give you a sign, but I may be pulling at my pants leg, or rubbing my ear, or tugging at my cap, anyway. They will be looking at me, too, trying to steal the signs, so I'll be trying to confuse them by doing the same things when I'm *not* giving a sign as I do when

397

I am. Get me? *Only* when you see me hit that bird do you know something's on. And when I give you the Indicator, count the number of touches that follows. Maybe I'll give you more than three signs! Maybe I'll give you four or five! I'm just doing that as a decoy, in case they start to pick something up, or we suspect they might. It only means something if I use one, two, or three touches after the Indicator."

Keane had the earnest manner of a second lieutenant outlining the intricacies of an espionage detail. All major league clubs use Indicators, decoys, and signs for everything but nose-blowing. The passion for disguising these signs defies reason, although it does give the players on the bench something to do. (The manager will say, "Try to get their signs, boys.") Yet, 90 per cent of the time, the situation determines the strategy, and an experienced player knows who will bunt or when the batter is taking. Even more predictable are the steal and the hit-and-run, since there are only a few men on each club that can do either one. What's more incongruous, although mathematical progression makes it improbable, I've seen the same sign used by two different clubs in the same game!

"The steal sign," Keane went on, "will be given to the runner only after the batter gets the *Take*. We don't want you hitting when that runner is trying to steal. If we did we'd give the hit-and-run. The steal sign is either hand gripping the opposite elbow. It's a figure 4, and that's *for* stealing." He grinned. Nobody seemed to get it. "Let's not be missing the steal sign. You don't have to go on that particular pitch, if you don't get a good jump on the pitch. If you slip in starting, or don't think you can make it, stay on first. The only time you *have* to go is the hit-and-run, 'cause that hitter is swinging at the ball no matter where it is. If you don't go, you penalize the batter for no good reason. We're gonna run a lot this year 'cause we got a running club . . . that right, Solly?"

Hemus nodded. "Whatever John says you can consider it came from me."

"Now, there's the squeeze. We have just one squeeze play. Suicide! You gotta bunt the ball! So you gotta know the play's on, and we gotta know you know it. So with a man on third base I rub across the bird, and touch my pants leg. One touch after the Indicator! You're bunting.

398

You answer me, telling me you got the sign, by showing me the palm of your hand. Don't wave your hand at me. Pick up some dirt, look the other way, and rub the back of your hand across your back pocket. Then I see your palm and I know you got the squeeze.

"Now, I yell to the runner on third, 'Make the ball go through!' and that's the sign to him that he's going in on the next pitch. Got that, you runners? If the batter answers the sign by showing you the palm of his hand you still gotta wait for me to say, 'Make the ball go through!' "

Keane cupped his hands at his mouth as he described what he would do during a squeeze play. His fungo bat slipped to the floor, its clatter echoing in the tense silence. The squeeze play commands breathless attention from ballplayers. Actually, major league clubs don't use it but twenty times a year, and it works only half the time, but the great importance of the squeeze is vividly impressed on the mind because of the depth of managerial despair at its failure. "That'll cost you fifty bucks, Brosnan! For Christ's sake, all you gotta do is bunt the ball!"

Coach Ray Katt whispered to Julio Gotay, the nineteen-year-old Puerto Rican phenom who was to open the exhibition season at short-stop. Julio's command of English was giving him a stomach-ache—his vocabulary was not equal to ordering a decent meal—and Katt was translating Keane's instructions.

"Do you understand, Julio?" asked Keane.

Gotay shook his head.

"Well," Keane frowned, "we'll go over them again tomorrow."

"There's no hot water."

400.

From Ball Four

BY JIM BOUTON

March 12, 1968

I OVERHEARD LOU PINIELLA HAVING A heated discussion with [Seattle manager] Joe Schultz and, nosy as I am, I asked him what it was about. Piniella said that a couple of players had heard Joe tell a sportswriter yesterday that if Piniella couldn't throw any better than he was throwing he wouldn't make the club. Lou said his arm had bothered him last year and he just wanted to nurse it this spring. I can understand why he was upset. He's only been here two weeks and that's not enough time to get your arm ready or for them to decide that someone could make the club or not make it. It's ridiculous particularly since Lou hit .300 last year with a Triple-A club and he was one of their $175,000 draftees. Sounds like somebody up there wants to unload Lou Piniella.

Either that, or Joe Schultz is pushing the panic button. It's a managerial disease Johnny Keane fell victim to when he managed the Yankees. John was a good, decent man, and no doubt there was lots of pressure on him. He seemed to feel that each day was the most important day of the season and it started right with the opening game of spring training. John always seemed willing to sacrifice a season to win a game. And this caused a lot of long-range problems. Guys played when they were hurt and then were out longer than they would have been if they hadn't been pushed back too soon. Mantle used to love to tell about his conversations with Keane. He said they'd go like this:

"How do your legs feel today, Mick?"

"Not too good."

"Yes, but how do they feel?"

"It hurts when I run, the right one especially. I can't stride on it or anything."

"Well, do you think you can play?"

"I don't know. I *guess* I can play. Yeah, hell, what the hell. Sure I can play."

"Good. Great. We need you out there. Unless you're hurt—unless it really hurts you. I don't want you to play if you're hurt."

"No, it's okay. I hurt, but it's okay. I'll watch it."

"Good, good. We sure need you."

After a while we used to joke in the outfield. I'd go over to Mick and say, "Mick, how does your leg feel?"

"Well, it's severed at the knee."

"Yes, but does it hurt?"

"No, I Scotch-taped it back into place."

"And how's your back?"

"My back is broken in seven places."

"Can you swing the bat?"

"Yeah, I can swing. If I can find some more Scotch tape."

"Great. Well, get in there then. We need you."

August 11

I'm still trying to decide why I haven't been in more ballgames in crucial situations and all I can do is agree with Hovley that it's because they think I'm weird and throw a weird pitch. I need a new image. What I ought to do is take up chewing tobacco and let the dark brown run down the front of my uniform and walk up and down the dugout with a slight, brave limp and tape on my wrist and say things like, "goddammit" and "shit" and "let's get these guys." Then, instead of being weird, I'd be rough and tough.

I think I'd do it, except I can't stand the thought of all that brown down the front of my uniform.

"Talk about making obscene gestures towards the fans!"

◆

Note to the Young

BY MILTON BRACKER

No blot and no onus
Attend a big bonus
  So what if your bonus be whopping?
It still won't embarrass
Mays, Mantle or Maris
  And Mom will adore it for shopping.

Once, when Babe Ruth was reminded that he was being paid more money than the President of the United States, the Babe said, "Why not? I had a better year than he did." Now even players coming off bad years get paid more than the President, a fact of life lamented by columnist Tony Kornheiser of the Washington Post *and by cartoonist Charles Addams.*

Occasionally, however, baseball offers bargains—theoretically, players become available for a dollar apiece—and Marvin Kitman, who writes a television column for Newsday, *once tried to turn this theory into reality. Several years later, as the item about Bo Jackson indicates, life imitated Kitman's art.*

Paaay Ball!
And Not Necessarily Well

BY TONY KORNHEISER

EVERY DAY, AFTER I TAKE MY CHILDREN to school, I grab my baseball glove and a hard rubber ball, and go out in the alley behind my house, and start throwing curves and sliders against the garage door. My plan is to get ready by April 1, then offer my services to major league baseball. I figure if I can put together a couple of 4-9 seasons, then two years from now, when I'm Nolan Ryan's age, I can earn $2.2 million. Matt "I Was 8-18, And Those Zany Boston Red Sox Think I'm Sandy Koufax" Young makes that. Why can't I?

Can you believe these baseball contracts?

Can you imagine the kind of bets Pete Rose would be able to make it he were still playing?

Of course Jim Palmer is trying to make a comeback. Underpants ads are fine, but the Yankees are paying Tim Leary $2 million for going 9-19. (You can't tell me whoever offered that contract wasn't on LSD.) The teeth-gnashing about George Steinbrenner wanting to get back

404

into day-to-day baseball misses the point. He doesn't want to run the Yankees, he wants to play for them.

Take Roger Clemens's contract.

(I will. Please. Oh, pretty please with a cherry on top.)

Clemens, last seen modeling straitjackets for an upcoming issue of Psychiatric Monthly, will get paid more than $5.3 million a year by the Sawx. I appreciate that such numbers are hard for the average working stiff to comprehend; as Everett Dirksen once said about government spending, "Five million here, five million there, and pretty soon you're talking about real money." So to bring it down to an understandable level, assuming Clemens gets his average number of starts—34—that means he'll earn slightly more than $158,000 each time he goes to the mound in 1995. If Clemens lasts nine innings, it works out to about $1,000 per pitch. (If Terry Cooney's umping, it's $7,500 per pitch.) I'm slaving away here at less than a buck a word. Where did I go wrong?

Twenty years ago the grandiose salary to shoot at was $100,000. The batboys make that now. Sure, there's been inflation. In 1971, a nice pair of shoes cost $25. Now they're $100. Cars have rocketed up higher still. A nice car in 1971 went for $6,500. The basic 1991 Beemer runs $40,000. But baseball's top salary has gone up 50 times what it was. How can a father in good conscience tell his kid to put down that bat and ball, and come in and do his French homework? Did I miss something? Are translators at the U.N. signing multiyear, million-dollar deals?

As I write this, and be advised the toteboard is changing every hour, there are 37 baseball players—most of them on the Red Sox—making more than $3 million a year. (While you're eating Tuna Helper, right?) Not that $3 million is such a big deal. Bobby Bonilla shook his head at $3.75 million a year over four like it smelled bad. But it's not the superstars' salaries that are the true outrages. Someone named Jim Gott, who purportedly pitches for the Dodgers, is getting $1.75 million. A Mr. Ken Caminiti of Houston got a $425,000 raise for hitting .242 with four homers and 51 RBI. This is in American money, ladies and gentlemen.

Not that long ago you'd walk into a GM after hitting .242 with four

homers and 51 ribbies and you'd take a huge pay cut—and be happy you weren't shot. Nobody gets cut anymore. Roto League nightmare Lloyd McClendon just got a $50,000 raise for batting .164 last year. He should have held out for triple that. Jeff Ballard went 2-11, and got a $170,000 raise. Imagine what he could've gotten if he'd won three games.

The money is so large, so amazing, that we need a new statistical category to put it in perspective. Some years ago my colleague Tom Boswell came up with Total Average (T.A.), which quantifies all offensive production into one tangible figure. I propose adding salary plus endorsements and autograph income, then subtracting alimony, fees to divorce lawyers (you know who) and mistress upkeep (you know who too) for (T.I.) Total Income.

Day after day higher baseball salaries come whizzing by. Glenn Davis, who hasn't seen one pitch in the American League, just signed a one-year deal with the Orioles for $3.275 million, which is essentially just a good-faith gesture, a door prize, since the Orioles will now begin trying to sign Davis to a multiyear pact. Some of the cash-poorer clubs cannot hope to keep up with the cost of labor. Any day now I expect the Seattle Mariners to announce an austerity move where they'll scale back to a two-man outfield.

What can we conclude from these astronomical salaries?

1) This recession can't be that bad.

2) Owners are stupid. (Minnesota handed a potential windfall of $11 million over the next three years to Jack Morris, who'll be 36 in May, and is 21-32 his last two seasons. What's this, thanks for the memories? Who's the underwriter, Bob Hope?)

3) Boy, was Willie Mays born way too early.

You have to understand that once you hit the big money—after three or four seasons batting .245—you'll continue to make the big money for years and years. Every year, whether you need it or not, another $2 million falls out of the sky and lands on your lawn. Better than Skylab, huh?

You like expensive cars? You want five Rolls-Royces? That still leaves you with $1 million. Even if you buy five new Rolls-Royces every year, the trade-in on the old ones is $750,000. How many CDs can you

406

buy? With the money you have, M.C. Hammer will come to your house and sing live. What's expensive enough for these zillionaires? A Van Gogh? ("Hey bubba, I want the one with the two ears. This guy's on the DL.") Is the next generation of fine art collections coming from the Milwaukee Brewers?

◆

Lefty Duke Signs for a van Gogh Painting

Hard-hitting outfielder K.T. (Lefty) Duke signed a four-year contract with the Baltimore Orioles for which he will receive van Gogh's painting "The Crooked Road."

This contract exceeds that of Bananas Rohak, who signed yesterday for three years. Rohak will receive an early-nineteenth-century Regency desk. If he hits over .290, he will get the matching chair.

Duke hit .287 last season. Van Gogh painted "The Crooked Road" in 1834, and was unable to sell it in his lifetime. It was most recently owned by a private collector in Caracas.

407

"The game's gotten too damn big-business, if you ask me."

My Son the Outfielder, and My Major Leaguer, Dick Stuart

BY MARVIN KITMAN

TREAD IN THE PAPER SEVERAL WEEKS AGO that a baseball player named Dick Stuart had been given his outright release by the New York Mets. As a free agent, the story explained, the first baseman was now able to make his own deals. Theoretically, anybody could hire a free agent by buying his contract for one dollar. I suddenly realized that an ordinary fan like me could become the first person on his block to own a private major-league ballplayer.

But I wasn't going to spend money to keep Stuart on the bench in front of my house in Leonia, New Jersey, as a mere status symbol. He would play ball every day with my son, the utility outfielder.

Stuart seemed an ideal tutor for my eight-year-old boy because I wanted somebody who wasn't perfect. A young ballplayer can be ruined psychologically by having to measure up to a perfectionist. To err is human, and Stuart's performance in the field proved that he was a regular fellow. His ability to turn a routine ground ball into a sports thrill had earned him the honorary title "Dr. Strangeglove." He liked working with kids, judging by the way he had fielded questions from boys on his *Stump Stuart* pregame TV show.

I was in the market for a major-leaguer because of what happened this spring in my son's first season of organized ball. His lifetime baseball record with the Petite Cleaners of the Leonia Skeeter League is not impressive. But scouting reports on my boy were encouraging. The only thing wrong with him, according to neighborhood bird dogs, is his father.

The boner I pulled as manager of his career was believing those psychological articles about the dangers of pushing your boy to star in the Little Leagues to gratify your own sick needs. When we talked about this in the hot-stove league last winter, the Petite Cleaners fathers

409

agreed it was best to let the kids learn the game at their own speed. But on opening day, I discovered I was the only enlightened father who hadn't been taking his boy behind the ranch house at night to teach him everything he knew. Well, I would show them how a father *really* can encourage his boy to become a star.

The ex-Met slugger leads the league in self-confidence, so I wrote to him in his own language. "Congratulations," began my letter to Stuart at his home in Greenwich, Connecticut, where he was awaiting job offers. "I've decided to pick up your contract for 1967." To prove it was a firm offer, I enclosed my personal check for one dollar.

"Your duties will be to teach my boy the fundamentals of the game." I wrote, "especially fielding. With a man of your stature tutoring him I see no reason why he can't be ready for the majors within 12 years. None of the Little Leagues in New Jersey offer instruction in basic economics for young ballplayers, so this is an area where my son really can benefit from your wisdom. He endorsed Petite Cleaners by wearing the company's shirt all season without collecting a penny."

I closed by assuring my new ballplayer that I hoped to sit down with him as soon as possible to talk salary for 1967. "I'm sure we'll be able to work out a fair price for your services," I wrote, "based on the fact that you are currently unemployed. P.S. What size Petite Cleaners shirt will you need?"

Several days later I wrote him a second letter. "I hope your silence doesn't mean you're planning to be a holdout for 1967. Let's stop this haggling and come to terms. Incidentally, my son says that since I'm buying ballplayers, he would prefer Willie Mays."

A few days after that, the phone rang at my house. "It's somebody named Dick Stuart," my wife called out.

"I was out of town and just got your letter," Dick Stuart said. "How much money are you talking about for 1967?"

"Mr. Stuart, I've always been one of your great admirers," I said. "I'm the former president of the Dick Stuart Fan Club of Leonia. I resigned in protest when the club voted to change its name to the Ed Kranepool Fan Club after the Mets released you—"

My ballplayer interrupted, "How much money did you have in mind?"

"I've analyzed your career," I said, stalling while I figured how to

410

explain to my wife that I had bought a major leaguer for the house when we didn't have a maid. "Branch Rickey said a winning player has to be hungry. By working for me, you could work yourself into proper financial condition."

Again Stuart asked about money.

"You only hit .218 for the Mets before they dropped you," I said.

"Do you realize I made $40,000 last season?" he asked. "And that a lot of clubs are still after me?"

Obviously Stuart, the master bargainer, was escalating his salary demands by mentioning offers he was getting to jump to Japanese baseball. "Don't think you're the only player who could help my boy," I said, as cold as any major-league magnate dealing with a hireling. "Dee Fondy and Wayne Terwilliger are also free agents."

"Why don't you teach the kid how to play ball yourself?" Stuart suggested.

"And have the kid hate me because I pushed him into baseball?" I asked. "I did show him how to take a cut at the ball before one game. He struck out every time. But that was just his way of rebelling against his father."

"Nobody can teach your boy how to play," Stuart said.

"Are you trying to tell me my son is hopeless?"

"I mean all you can do is *show* kids the fundamentals of the game. Not even Ted Williams could *teach* an eight-year-old. A kid has to mature first."

To break the impasse, I made a concrete offer. "I'm sure your account would prefer a deferred-payment deal. I'll give you fifty percent of the bonus the kid gets when he signs with a major-league club, plus the Cadillac."

Stuart shrewdly avoided saying no—and he left the door open by telling me to get in touch as soon as I figured out what I could pay him next year.

One solution to the high cost of owning a private major leaguer was to lease him to other fathers who wanted their sons to sit at the feet of a master. I had two days of Stuart's time booked for 1967 when I read that my ballplayer had been lured away by a cartel of West Coast oil and real-estate tycoons called the Los Angeles Dodgers.

411

Connie Mack once said, "You can't win them all." But I wasn't discouraged. I had a hunch Stuart might soon be a free agent again, and my strategy now was to play a waiting game. I wrote Stuart a letter congratulating him on his new job with the Dodgers. "Just a reminder that my offer still holds for next season. Spring training begins on April 1 at Sylvan Park in Leonia. I don't want to influence your decision, but Sylvan Park has a short left-field wall."

◆

In March 1991, when the Kansas City Royals placed the injured Bo Jackson on waivers, he was claimed for the standard $1.00 fee by the Live Oaks (Florida) Gray Ghosts, a Little League team. Jackson did not report to the Gray Ghosts.

◆

"It's our new incentive system."

412

"Sometimes we sell them, lady, but only to other teams."

In the 1980s, before he became the deputy commissioner of baseball, Steve Greenberg was a players' agent. One day, he told his father, Hank Greenberg, Hall of Famer and former part owner of the Cleveland Indians and the Chicago White Sox, about a young player he was representing in salary negotiations.

"What should I ask for?" Steve said.

"What'd he hit last year?" Hank asked.

"Two thirty-eight," Steve said.

"Ask for a uniform," Hank said.

Steve shook his head.

"Dad," he said, "you just don't understand the game anymore."

◆

"Here comes his trainer, the manager, his agent, his lawyer, and his mother to the mound."

"How does it feel when I swat one over the fence? Well, I guess it gives me a feeling of satisfaction to think I am able to justify the front office's investment in my contract."

Credits

Every effort has been made to trace copyright, but if any omissions have been made, please notify the publisher. We gratefully acknowledge permission from the following:

A.P./Wide World Photos. "A man named Mays," reprinted by permission of A.P./Wide World Photos.

The Bettmann Archive. The photo of "Japanese umpires" is from UPI/Hall of Fame Photos. It is reprinted with permission from UPI and The Bettmann Archive.

Georges Borchardt Agency. "McDuff on the Mound" appeared in *The Iowa Review*, Vol. 2, No. 4, Fall 1971. Reprinted by permission of Georges Borchardt, Inc., for the author. Copyright © 1971 by Robert Coover.

Jim Bouton. Excerpts from *Ball Four* by Jim Bouton. Copyright © 1989 by Jim Bouton. Forward, by Jim Bouton to *The Baseball Fan's Guide to Spring Training*. Copyright © 1989 by Jim Bouton.

Jimmy Breslin. "Just Like the WPA" from *Can't Anybody Here Play This Game?*, 1963, Viking Press. Copyright © 1963, Jimmy Breslin. Reprinted by permission.

William C. Brown Publishers. "In the Owner's Box" by Steve Lehman. From Vol. 10, No. 3, of *The Minneapolis Review of Baseball* (now *Elysian Fields Quarterly: The Baseball Review*). Copyright © 1991 Brown and Benchmark, 25 Kessel Court, Madison, Wisconsin 53711, 608-277-7345.

Cartoonists & Writers Syndicate. "Flubs & Fluffs" by Jerry Robinson. Copyright © 1991 by Cartoonists & Writers Syndicate. Reprinted by permission.

Avery Corman. Excerpt from *Oh, God!* By permission of the author.

Creators Syndicate, Inc. "B.C." cartoons by Johnny Hart are reprinted by permission of Johnny Hart and Creators Syndicate, Inc.; © 1991 Creators Syndicate, Inc.

417

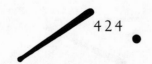